Publications of the John Gower Society

II

JOHN GOWER'S POETIC

THE SEARCH FOR A NEW ARION

Publications of the John Gower Society

General editors   R. F. Yeager and A. J. Minnis

ISSN 0954-2817

I

A Concordance to
John Gower's Confessio Amantis
edited by J. D. Pickles and J. L. Dawson

PR
1987
,Y43
1990

JOHN GOWER'S POETIC
THE SEARCH FOR A NEW ARION

R. F. Yeager

WITHDRAWN

D. S. BREWER

HIEBERT LIBRARY 6 3154
Fresno Pacific College - M.B. Seminary
Fresno, CA 93702

© R. F. Yeager 1990

All Rights Reserved. Except as permitted under current legislation no part of this
work may be photocopied, stored in a retrieval system, published, performed in
public, adapted, broadcast, transmitted, recorded or reproduced in any form or
by any means, without the prior permission of the copyright owner.

First published 1990 by D. S. Brewer, Cambridge

D. S. Brewer is an imprint of Boydell & Brewer Ltd
PO Box 9, Woodbridge, Suffolk IP12 3DF
and of Boydell & Brewer Inc.
PO Box 41026, Rochester, NY 14604, USA

ISBN 0 85991 280 9

British Library Cataloguing in Publication Data
Yeager, Robert F.
    John Gower's Poetic : the search for a new Arion. — (Publications of the
John Gower Society, ISSN 0954 – 2817 ; V2).
    1. Poetry in English. Gower, John, 1330? – 1408
    I. Title   II. Series
    821'.1
    ISBN 0-85991-280-9

Library of Congress Cataloging-in-publication Data applied for

This publication is printed on acid-free paper

Printed in Great Britain by
St Edmundsbury Press, Bury St Edmunds, Suffolk

CONTENTS

ABBREVIATIONS

GOWER'S WORKS

CA	*Confessio Amantis*
CB	*Cinkante Ballades*
CTr	*Cronica Tripertita*
MO	*Mirour de l'Omme*
Tr	*Traitié*
VC	*Vox Clamantis*

CHAUCER'S WORKS

CT	*Canterbury Tales*
BD	*Book of the Duchess*
HF	*Hous of Fame*
LGW	*Legend of Good Women*

JOURNALS AND SERIES

DAI	*Dissertation Abstracts International*
EETS o.s.	Early English Text Society, Original Series
EETS e.s.	Early English Text Society, Extra Series
EETS, SS	Early English Text Society, Supplementary Series
JEGP	*Journal of English and Germnanic Philology*
PG	*Patrologia Graeco*, ed. J.-P. Migne
PL	*Patrologia Latina*, ed. J.-P. Migne
PMLA	*Publications of the Modern Language Association*
RES	*Review of English Studies*

DICTIONARIES AND OTHER REFERENCE WORKS

MED	*Middle English Dictionary*, ed. Hans Kung, et al.
OED	*Oxford English Dictionary*, ed. James H. A. Murray, et al.

ACKNOWLEDGEMENTS

This book has taken a very long time to complete, and has changed shape often. In its course, I have acquired a substantial debt to a host of benefactors — too many to acknowledge appropriately here. Some, upon whose ideas I have presumed to build, I have tried to identify in the footnotes as my arguments proceed. Others, whose advice or criticism was no less essential but harder to tag with a note number, will no doubt recognize themselves — their insights and learning — enlightening many places throughout these pages. But to Stephen A. Barney, Morton W. Bloomfield, Marie Borroff, V. A. Kolve, John H. Fisher, A. J. Minnis, and Fred C. Robinson, all of whom read assorted drafts and pointed the way, I owe a special gratitude — as much for their generous patience as for their invariably sound and useful advice. To the Andrew W. Mellon Foundation I am doubly indebted, once for support as a Faculty Fellow at Harvard University during 1982-83, and once as a Fellow (1986-87) at the National Humanities Center where, amidst those gracious surroundings and warm collegiality, much of the final version of this book was completed. In different forms, some portions of these chapters have appeared in the following journals, and should be acknowledged: *South Atlantic Review*, *Res Publica Litterarum*, *Studies in Philology*, *Chaucer Review* and *Studies in the Age of Chaucer*. And finally I am grateful to Robin Ledbetter Hinson, research assistant *extraordinaire*, whose devotion to 'getting it right' often redefined the call of duty (and got the proofreading done); as well as to my wife, Leda Neale, who once asked not to be mentioned here, but *mea culpa* — she was, and is, an inspiration. Thanks.

CHAPTER I: STYLISTICS

I

More than twenty years ago, John H. Fisher began his important study of the life and poetry of John Gower by remarking, 'It has been the fate of John Gower to appear to succeeding ages almost constantly in the company of Geoffrey Chaucer.' As Fisher noted, Gower traditionally has come off the worse for it, but there are good reasons for thinking of the two poets together. 'They were acquainted, they acknowledged one another in their writings, they reacted against the same social and spiritual shortcomings, and they wrote lyric, didactic, and narrative works with similar themes and forms. Comparison is inevitable.'[1]

And, he might have added, useful as well. Even those many readers who have found Chaucer the ideal stick with which to beat the slow mule Gower have judged the process helpful: It taught them to value Chaucer more highly, is the usual assessment. In such studies, the method is to begin with Gower, illustrate a point or two and then proceed to prove that Chaucer handled the same problem with superior aplomb. This has been the model since John Leland's *Commentarii de scriptoribus Britannicis*, ca. 1545.

But those are of course books about Chaucer; and this one, like John Fisher's, is about Gower. Thus, while I shall begin my discussion of Gower's poetic style with Chaucer (thereby bowing to tradition), I shall not complete the hoary pattern (albeit in reverse) by finding Chaucer less 'good' than he. Chaucer is, after all, Chaucer, and John Gower 'only' himself. That is precisely the point of the ensuing pages — to unravel a little more of who that 'himself' might be, by inquiring after Gower's theory of poetry.

I want to start with what often seem to many of us who are not poets the 'least' things about the art. These I term 'metrics' and 'stylistics,' for lack of a better way to gather up for discussion the appearance of the words on the page, their form, their arrangement, their sound when pronounced, individually and together, and certain ambiguities of meaning related to these which I have found in Gower's work.

I begin with these because such matters concerned both Gower and Chaucer a good deal. In this they seem to be like each other, and unlike their contemporaries and immediate forebears. Chaucer has left us direct testimony of his attitude in several places. One comes at the end of *Troilus and Criseyde*, when the author sends up a prayer for the proper treatment of his poem:

---

[1] John H. Fisher, *John Gower: Moral Philosopher and Friend of Chaucer* (New York, 1964) 1.

And for ther is so gret diversitee
In Englissh and in writyng of oure tonge,
So pray I god that non myswryte the,
Ne the mysmetre for defaute of tonge.
And red wherso thow be, or elles songe,
That thow be understonde, God I biseche!   (V, 1793-98)[2]

What worries Chaucer here is what probably worries most poets — that his
poem 'be understonde.' Writing when, where and in the language he did,
however, gave Chaucer more than common cause to fear the worst.[3] Although
French was no longer the only polite tongue at court, it was yet somewhat daring
to attempt the sort of poem *Troilus* is in English in the mid-1380s, when we think
Chaucer was at work on it. Social barriers aside, there were also the two
problems Chaucer recognizes in these lines: the 'gret diversitee in Englissh,' the
result of the beginning of the Great Vowel Shift, of multiple dialects (for which,
in the *Reeve's Tale*, Chaucer shows he had a sharp ear), and 'myswriting' — by
which Chaucer doubtless meant miscopying of his text by careless scribes. Of his
frustrating experience with Adam, 'His Owne Scriveyn,' whose 'negligence and
rape' cost him much labor to 'correcte and eek to rubbe and scrape,' Chaucer has
of course left us a well known record.[4]

Moving and wry as Chaucer may be on these matters, however, it was Gower
who in the end seems to have been the more actively involved to ensure the
accuracy of the copies of his poems. Unlike his friend and fellow poet, Gower has
left us no direct statement of his attitude toward either form of 'myswriting.' Yet
there is testimony to be found in his manuscripts. In four copies of the *Vox
Clamantis* and two of the *Confessio* (MSS Fairfax and Stafford, the earliest and in
certain ways the best we have), variations appear which are most easily explained
as authorial. They include the insertion of new leaves in place of older ones cut
away, and revised passages written over erased text. This, and other physical
properties of the manuscripts (armorial insignia, elaborate decoration), have
brought one recent reader to conclude that 'These alterations can only have been
made under carefully prepared instructions which are . . . most easily attributed
to the poet.'[5]

Such supervision of the copying of his own manuscripts by a late medieval
writer is most unusual. For all Chaucer's poetic recognition of the problem of
accurate texts, we have no evidence that he committed much time to the
production of his books.[6] While we know now that most of the manuscripts once

[2] All quotations from Chaucer are taken from *The Riverside Chaucer*, ed. L. D. Benson, 3rd
edn. (Boston, 1987).
[3] See further my discussion, 'O Moral Gower:' Chaucer's Dedication of *Troilus and
Criseyde*,' *Chaucer Review*, 19 (1984) 87-99.
[4] See 'Chaucer's Wordes unto Adam, His Owne Scriveyn,' Benson, *Riverside*, p. 650.
[5] Peter Nicholson, 'Gower's Revisions in the *Confessio Amantis*,' *Chaucer Review*, 19 (1984)
136.
[6] This of course may not be Chaucer's fault, since no manuscripts of his work survive
which could have been copied during his lifetime.

attributed to Gower's 'personal' scriptorium at St. Mary Overeys priory, where he lived for many years, are in fact copies made by professional scribes in London copy-shops after his death, we nonetheless have in Gower a rather unique phenomenon — a late medieval poet who busied himself with page editing.[7] Indeed, to find another English writer who took the same trouble we must go as far into the future as Ben Jonson, in the early seventeenth century.

Linking Jonson and Gower in this manner is illuminating in other ways as well. Jonson thought enough of the language of the *Confessio Amantis* (whatever his opinion of it as poetry — it would have been interesting to overhear Jonson talk about it with Shakespeare, when the latter was adapting *Pericles* from Book VIII) to make it the most frequent source of examples in his *English Grammar*.[8] And well he might: For we can give Gower credit for the unusual consistencies of language in the majority of his manuscripts. We can say (as has indeed been said) that Gower carefully pursued a stable spelling system and a uniform grammar, sought to sort out with a sense of etymology words of Anglo-Saxon and French origin, and somehow insisted that the forms he chose appear from under the pens of most of the scribes who worked on his copying.[9]

This is a true Jonsonian sensibility — rigorous, exacting, meticulous to the point of direct involvement with the inky process Chaucer described, to 'correcte and eek to rubbe and scrape.' It is also an aspect of Gower we have dwelt on little in modern times, largely, I suspect, because our great interest in Chaucer has drawn us quite understandably to follow the leads he gave us, to investigate 'moral' Gower's philosophies, and 'incestuous' Gower's natural law, while leaving aside 'linguistic' Gower with his (much less exciting) vernacular experiments. We need other voices to remind us sometimes of other views, speaking from an age closer to Gower's own. Jonson is one; John Leland is another. 'Gower we hold up', Leland wrote about 1545,

---

[7] On Gower's recourse to professional copy-shops, see A. I. Doyle and Malcolm B. Parkes, 'The Production of Copies of the *Canterbury Tales* and the *Confessio Amantis* in the Early Fifteenth Century,' in *Medieval Scribes, Manuscripts and Libraries: Essays Presented to N. R. Ker*, edd. Malcolm B. Parkes and Andrew G. Watson (London, 1978) 163-210; and also Doyle, 'English Books in and out of Court from Edward III to Henry VII,' in *English Court Culture in the Later Middle Ages*, edd. V. J. Scattergood and J. W. Sherbourne (London, 1983) 163-82. R. Vance Ramsey, 'Paleography and Scribes of Shared Training,' *Studies in the Age of Chaucer*, (1986), especially 123-27, presents a valuable, if somewhat different, view.
[8] See *The English Grammar of Ben Jonson*, ed. A. V. Waite (New York, 1909) 112-45, passim.
[9] The details of Gower's language have been looked at extensively, beginning with G. C. Macaulay, Gower's best editor. See *The Complete Works of John Gower*, 4 vols. (Oxford, 1899-1902) II, xcii-cxx. See also K. Fahrenberg, 'Zur Sprache der *Confessio Amantis*,' *Archiv*, 8 (1892), 389-412; Morton Easton, *Readings in Gower*, Publications of the University of Pennsylvania Series in Philology, Literature and Archaeology, (Philadelphia, 1895); and J. C. Horton-Burch, 'Notes on the Language of Gower,' *English Studies*, 1 (1934), 209-15. An important recent contribution is that of Michael L. Samuels and Jeremy J. Smith, 'The Language of Gower,' *Neuphilologische Mitteilungen*, 82 (1981), 295-304.

. . . as the first refiner of our native language. For before that time the
English language lay uncultivated and nearly wholly raw. Nor was there
anyone who could write, in the vernacular, works suitable for a
discriminating reader. Thus the value of [Gower's] works lies in their
careful cultivation, that, the rude weeds stamped out, instead of thistles
arise the pliant violet and purple narcisssus.[10]

In Leland's assessment we hear the luxuriant tones of the Renaissance, and
commendations which very likely would have confounded Gower before they
pleased him. Not for Gower, a plainer stylist by far than Leland, had the 'pliant
violet and purple narcissus' such attractive charm. But for the gist of what Leland
is saying, his central insight that the heart of Gower's enterprise is a hope for a
poetic language — clear, consistent, reliable and enabling — there is quite strong
evidence indeed. It is in Gower's manuscripts — those he had contact with; in the
way he brought about their making.

Knowing that Gower devoted the effort he did to polish his words and control
the quality of their reproduction raises an obvious question: Why did he do this,
since the practice was not common? One answer seems implicit in what has been
said already. Anyone deeply concerned about language, we might think, will
strive to establish and maintain firm standards for its use. But apparently this
notion did not occur to as many in the Middle Ages as it does now. The monk
Orm had it, in his curious way, and Gower; beyond them, however, not even
Chaucer gives solid proof of its having exercised him past the composition of a
prayer and a semi-umbrageous attack on Adam Scriveyn. No, the more attention
we pay to Gower's energetic pursuit of textual consistency, the more it seems to
require other than a general explanation. It is something he was doing alone —
more importantly, something he must have *felt* alone doing, as far as we know
(since the *Ormulum*'s example would scarcely have offered encouragement, even
in the extraordinary unlikelihood that Gower had seen it). And for this reason
Gower's fastidious treatment of his manuscripts becomes an interesting poetic
decision.

Perhaps we can better understand how this might be if we recall the position
occupied by Gower and Chaucer in their time. Each of them was, in his own
way, remaking the face of English poetry. Or more accurately, poetry written in
England: because the *Mirour de l'Omme*, the two ballade sequences (*Cinkante
Ballades* and *Traitié*) and the *Vox Clamantis* were all experiments in setting
standards for English letters, even though they were composed in French and

---

[10] '. . . ut inter nobiles Anglos, quidem illos, suae aetatis facile antesignanus fuerit.
Coluit forum patrias leges, lucri causa; praeter caetera tamen humaniores literas: multum
in poesi sudavit. Hoc eius testantur carmina, quae multa latine scripsit . . . & ostendamus
illum omnium fuisse primum patriae linguae expolitorem. Nam ante ejus aetatem
Anglica lingua inculta, & fere tota rudis jacebat. Nec erat qui opus aliquod, vernaculo
idiomate, eleganti lectore dignum scriberet. Itaque operae pretium esse duxit, diligentem
adhibere cul turam, ut sic extirpatis tandem rudibus herbis, pro carduo paliuro, mollis
viola purpureus surgeret narcissus.' John Leland, *Commentarii de scriptoribus Britannicis*, ed.
A. Hall, (Oxford, 1709) 414-15.

Latin, and are now seldom read. These poems, and possibly Chaucer's lost French lyrics, claimed new territory. They showed Englishmen capable of writing complex verse, intellectually and aesthetically challenging verse — or so it must have seemed to Gower and Chaucer, and their cluster of readers. John Burrow has eloquently recaptured for us what doubtless was their outlook when the two poets began to write:

> Most of the 'lost literature of medieval England,' after all, was lost as much to Chaucer and Gower as it is to us; and much of what we do know (Anglo-Saxon poetry for example) they did not. Collections such as the Auchinleck MS., despite their great bulk, offered little work of sufficient distinction to command the respect of sophisticated London readers. If that was their native heritage (and where else are we to look for it?), then it was a poor thing — poorer by far than the inheritance of later English poets, and poorer even than that of some of their own English contemporaries.[11]

It matters little that the non-English, supposedly early pieces can be improved upon: Gower and Chaucer did so themselves, in their own vernacular, with the *Confessio*, the *Troilus*, the *Canterbury Tales*. The salient point is that *every* poem of Gower's pen and Chaucer's had successively — until the next one came along to raise the ante — little competition for the best poetry produced in England in the memories of its audience. As another critic has remarked, when Chaucer and Gower were born, 'the tradition of verbal art had been debased, and poets were often too easily satisfied.'[12] When they died, it was a different country altogether.

II

The revolution Gower and Chaucer brought about resulted as much from the *kind*, as from the quality, of what they wrote. That is because their verse — in French and Latin, as well as in English — depended upon well-governed metrical patterns, rhyming patterns, or both, for major effects. In a way, this is to say no more than that it was poetry; but I put it like this because it is necessary, as a step toward making my larger point, to emphasize the contrast between what Gower and Chaucer *did* know of their native tradition, and what they themselves chose to do.

That these two writers were alive to indigenous poetry, as well as to what they found in books, is of course not in doubt. A good deal of scholarship, and

---

[11] John A. Burrow, *Ricardian Poetry: Chaucer, Gower, Langland and the Gawain Poet* (New Haven, 1971) 23.
[12] E. V. Gordon, *Pearl* (Oxford, 1953) xxxvii.

scholarly speculation, has been amassed to argue they each read this or that.[13] The best (because the *only*) evidence, however, is in their poems; and this makes plain two things. With the *material* of their countrymen, Chaucer and Gower held no quarrel. They both could recognize a useful story, whether it came from an English dinner companion or a French manuscript. But the *style* of contemporary English verse was quite clearly a problem for them. Consider what was available: lyrics, some charming, satiric, salacious, but hardly the stuff poetic ambition builds on; alliterative long-line, powerful enough in Langland's hands, subtle and capacious in *Gawain* and *Pearl*, but again, by the 1350's — as one long-line poet himself remarked — the 'makeres' too often were hacks, 'That never wroghte thurgh witt three wordes togedire;'[14] and finally the tail-rhyme romances which, with their many calls to 'Listeth, lordes!,' confirm the suspicion that some of their auditors gave over to sleep.

Insubstantiality, metrical anarchy, tedium.[15] Why join such company? Particularly if one were highly literate and had travelled, either actually or through books, to the continent, where subtle, consistent metrics were not a lost art and where rhyme was used copiously, imaginatively, and well? How could Gower, after Virgil and Machaut, or Chaucer after Dante, not wish to emulate their polish and control?

Chaucer and Gower each gave clear — and characteristic — answers to these questions. Chaucer's are of course the better known. The Parson's stern refusal to 'geeste "rum, ram, ruf" by lettre' (*CT* X, 43) is now read most often as Chaucer's own dismissal of alliterative verse, just as the *Tale of Sir Thopas* is seen

---

[13] On Gower's English reading see Sigmund Eisner, *A Tale of Wonder: A Source Study of the Wife of Bath's Tale* (Wexford, 1957) 7, 9, 14, 50, 57, 62-72, 141; Laura Hibbard Loomis, *Medieval Romance in England: A Study of the Sources and Analogues of the Non-Cyclic Metrical Romances, New edn. with Supplementary Bibliographical Index (1929-1959)* (New York, 1963) 24, 63, 165, 168, 192, 202, 231; and Judith Davis Shaw, '*Confessio Amantis*: Gower's Art in Transforming His Sources into Exempla of the Seven Deadly Sins,' Ph. D. dissertation, University of Pennsylvania, 1977. Chaucer's reading has received much attention. A helpful review is that of J. Burke Severs, 'The Tales of Romance,' in *A Companion to Chaucer Studies*, ed. Beryl Rowland (London, 1968) 229-46. A recent addition to the subject is Alexander Weiss, *Chaucer's Native Heritage* (New York, Berne, Frankfurt a. M., 1985).

[14] *A Good Short Debate between Winner and Waster: An Alliterative Poem on Social and Economic Problems in England in the Year 1352, With Modern English Rendering*, ed. Sir Israel Gollancz (1921; rep. Cambridge, 1974) l. 25.

[15] Two recent studies by Hoyt N. Duggan seek to reverse the standing view of the metrical chaos of the alliterative romances. See his 'The Shape of the B-Verse in Middle English Alliterative Poetry,' *Speculum*, 6 (1986), 564-92; and 'Alliterative Patterning as a Basis for Emendation in Middle English Alliterative Poetry,' *Studies in the Age of Chaucer*, (1986), 73-105. See also the sensitive defense of alliterative style by Marie Borroff, *Sir Gawain and the Green Knight: A Stylistical and Metrical Study* (New Haven, 1962), 70-73; and 'The Style' in Larry D. Benson's *Art and Tradition in Sir Gawain and the Green Knight* (New Brunswick, N.J., 1965) 110-66. Borroff and Benson, however, are discussing achievements in the very best alliterative poem. *Gawain* is scarcely representative of the tradition which Chaucer and Gower would have known.

as a thorough (if rollicking) demolition of tail-rhyme romance style. On the other hand, his response to the native lyric tradition is more complex, since Chaucer wrote songs himself. Some hint is given by the subject matter, tone and imagery of these songs, all of which bespeak a cosmopolitan, not an insular, sensibility. But finally, I think, it is his formal antecedents that most give him away. Chaucer's lyrics are all French dances — rondels, virelays, ballades. He did not come to write them by recalling snatches of 'Maiden in the More Lay' or 'Sumer Is Icumen In,' despite the legitimate high value we (or Chaucer) might have placed on them as English poems. And that form itself should be the clue betraying Chaucer's roots is appropriate, too: because the true challenge of the kind of lyric Chaucer wrote is, after all, formal. It is *difficult* to control the meter tightly and supply the often-intricate rhymes on call. No poetry in the English tradition which Chaucer could have known, lyrics included, presented those problems. That he consistently chose to respond to them, rather than to peculiarly native ones — even used his short poems as laboratories to experiment with new stanzas, like terza rima, borrowed from abroad and demanding yet greater control — strongly suggests an established aesthetic preference.[16] In the end, then, Chaucer rejected the model of his country's lyrics, along with the rest of its poetic tradition that he knew, in favor of a stricter metrics born in Italy and France.[17]

It is typical that, to discover Chaucer's attitude toward poetry he saw about him in England, we must resort to inferential arguments like these. Chaucer seldom voices an opinion straight out; it is part of his stance as an ironist. John Gower, on the other hand, usually speaks his mind without delay and in plain terms. Certainly he seems to be doing so, about books and poetry, at the beginning of the *Confessio Amantis*.

> Of hem that writen ous tofore
> The bokes duelle, and we therfore
> Ben tawht of that was write tho:
> Forthi good is that we also
> In oure tyme among ous hiere
> Do wryte of newe som matiere,
> Essampled of these olde wyse
> So that it myhte in such a wyse,
> Whan we ben dede and elleswhere,

[16] Chaucer tried out terza rima in 'A Complaint to His Lady.'
[17] Weiss, *Chaucer's Native Heritage*, has recently argued Chaucer's debt to the English lyric in glowing terms: '. . . he was in no small measure indebted to these predecessors for providing models that paved the way for his own triumph in bringing this tradition to its greatest pitch of perfection' (p. 169). I have no quarrel with this conclusion; my point is that Chaucer found the tradition wanting and sought more challenging models elsewhere.

Beleve to the worldes eere
In tyme comende after this.[18]   (CA Pro., 1-11)

This is very direct language, surely. Gower reminds us of our debt to ancient authors, to their books as the sole conduits of past wisdom; and he prods us to leave a similar legacy to coming generations by writing such works ourselves. The passage accomplishes several things at once. It gives, first, a rationale for Gower's own book, which we have before us. (For we assume the narrative voice here to be his, *in propria persona*, although we are not told so.) Now we know why he wrote it. We know, too, that it will pass on wisdom in some way resembling what we find in venerable tomes — so we can begin to predict its contents. And we are told that the process of handing on this sort of wisdom is 'good.' Thus, less directly, the lines suggest as well that the poet holds at least two broad assumptions about the world, and the individual's place within it: that civilization means intellectual *communitas* of the highest order; that each man bears responsibility for its maintenance across time. (Since both ideas preface major themes of Gower's, we shall examine their development closely in subsequent chapters.)

The passage is not simply about books, however; it is also about poetry, as we discover when we read the next fourteen lines. Here Gower reveals that since a work 'al of wisdom . . . / . . . dulleth oft a mannes wit,' his will be 'a bok betwen the tweie,/ Somwhat of lust, somwhat of lore.' Moreover, he will write it 'for Engelondes sake,' because 'few men endite/ in oure englissh' (CA Pro., 12-24).

This description, of what he calls the 'middel weie' of writing, may be Gower's best known statement.[19] It is quoted frequently because it offers us a look at a fourteenth-century poet making a decision about style. Such open windows are unusual in the circumspect Age of Chaucer; we tend to rush toward them often when we find them, and stand before them long. But this one does deserve careful scrutiny, on its own terms, for what it has to show us about John Gower.

In the first place it demonstrates that, not only was Gower aware of his audience, but he also had expectations for them. He knew what would keep them attentive (good stories) and what wouldn't (being forced to read wisdom 'aldai') — and he wanted their wit sharp for the duration. 'Wit' is probably a significant word here, for it tells us that despite the strategic necessity of 'lust,' it is not the center of the *Confessio Amantis*. 'Lore' is, which to apprehend requires a mind both refreshed and engaged. These are perhaps obvious points, but helpful, in that we sometimes seem to forget Gower knew things like this. All his apparent bluntness aside, he like Chaucer was a poetic strategist. Gower could (and did) use the *way* he wrote to manipulate us, too.

[18] All quotations from the poetry of Gower are taken from *The Complete Works*, ed. Macaulay.
[19] See CA Pro., 17 ff. The fullest modern inquiry into Gower's intention is by Goetz Schmitz, *'The middel weie:' Stil- und Aufbauformen in John Gowers Confessio Amantis* (Bonn, 1974).

But more specific concerns are expressed in the passage, having to do with poetry and language. Gower says that he will write in English, for his country's sake, because 'fewe men' do so. A number of conclusions probably ought to be drawn from this. On one plane there is what more we learn of Gower as strategic stylist, thinking again of his audience, of who they were and how best to compose a poem to reach them, adopting his mother tongue after careful consideration. The picture is of a deliberative man of letters, one for whom every matter of language — even the choice *of* language — had weight. And this line of argument brings us to another plane.

Perhaps because we have so much of his extant poetry in Latin and Anglo-Norman, it is easier to see Gower's decision to write his last major poem in English as the conscious choice it was — easier, that is, than to visualize Chaucer at the same moment of selection. But we know both men were multi-lingual, and alive at a time when English was neither the obvious nor even the sensible medium for a 'career' poet to adopt. Strong arguments could be raised against it: serious work should be done in Latin; French was the language of court and the courtly; the vocabulary was inadequate for all but the coarsest sentiments; and we have noted already what the tradition looked like which, by writing in English, one would join.

Described like this, the risks inherent in becoming an 'English' poet seem insurmountable. Nobody would do it, who could do something else. And perhaps Gower thought precisely this way for most of his early career, as he forged ahead in French and Latin. He may even have argued about it with Chaucer, who apparently hedged his bets but little, if at all. Yet Chaucer, and Gower eventually, do write in English — and given the circumstances, we have some reason to ask why.

Not surprisingly, Chaucer's cogitations remain obscure. Like a secretive geometer he gives us the product without the proof. Here at the beginning of the *Confessio*, however, Gower lets us know *his* motives: He writes 'in oure englissh . . . for Engelondes sake,' and be cause it is used by so few. These are both interesting grounds, and prompt further reflection.

Immediately striking is an obvious patriotism. It is *oure* English, and we must treat it well for the sake of the nation. These are scarcely ideas original to Gower (although, as a moralist in the *speculum regis* tradition, they have been close to his themes for some time), but neither are they fourteenth-century commonplaces. Where did he get such notions? we might well ask. An elaborate, thoroughly justifiable answer can, I know, be prepared from contemporary history: They were a natural outgrowth of the Hundred Years War; they were fanned by shifting commercial relationships with Low Country weavers both in England and overseas; they became inevitable after King John forced his nobility to choose between holdings in England or Normandy in the thirteenth century; you can find them in the anonymous political songs and ballads for years.[20]

---

[20] The bibliography on these issues is extensive, but good general studies are still Oliver H. Richardson's *The National Movement in the Reign of Henry III and Its Culmination in the Barons' War* (New York, 1897) 75 ff. and F. M. Powicke's *The Loss of Normandy, 1189-1204* (Manchester, 1913) 411-49, and his *The Thirteenth Century*, 2nd edn. (Oxford, 1962). On

Nonetheless, while not wishing to discount any of this, I'd like to think that the *immediate* source of Gower's special brand of patriotism is suggested by the passage just examined, the very first lines of the *Confessio*.

The 'bokes' Gower calls our attention to there are, as we have seen, those 'of hem that writen ous tofore.' That leaves an uncomfortable lot of room for speculation, were we to try to guess which ones he meant — if indeed he had in mind to refer here to anything more precise than the generic category, 'old books by wise ancestors.' But let us suppose that Gower *did* mean something particular. We can whittle down the possibilities if we consider what we know of his sources. Gower was a wide reader, as has been frequently shown, with debts visible in his poetry from Virgil to Augustine to Dante to French romances; but given that here he is thinking about books containing 'wisdom,' it is probably safe to reduce the field to religious works, and works of classical authors.

We can narrow our focus more sharply still by reading a bit further in the Prologue. Gower speaks again of old books, noting that 'be daies olde' the books were 'levere' ['better'], and that then 'Wrytinge was beloved evere/ Of hem that weren vertuous' (*CA* Pro., 36-39). The purpose of these works was 'to magnifie/ The worthi princes that tho were' — to record the '*pris* of hem that weren goode' (*CA* Pro., 42, 44 ff.) — and also to condemn

> . . . tho that deden thanne amis
> Thurgh tirannie and crualte,
> Right as thei stoden in degre,
> So was the wrytinge of here werk.   (*CA* Pro., 48-51)

As the next four lines in sequence tell us ('clerk,' below, rhymes with 'werk,' above), it is among this company of books and writers that Gower places the *Confessio* and himself:

> Thus I, which am a burel clerk,
> Purpose forto wryte a bok
> After the world that whilom tok
> Long tyme in olde daies passed.   (*CA* Pro., 52-55)

While there is nothing which makes it impossible to understand Gower to mean the writings of the Church Fathers here — their pages praise occasional 'worthi princes' and certainly condemn often enough the tyrannical, the cruel, and the generally wrong-doing — he probably intended something else. For one thing his use of the word *pris* (I have italicized it in the quotation above), a

---

the Flemings see especially J. F. Bense, *Anglo-Dutch Relations from the Earliest Times to the Death of William the Third* (London Oxford University Press, 1925) 32-95. For popular poetic expression, see Thomas Wright, *Political Poems and Songs*, Rolls Series, 14 (London, 1859).

chivalric term borrowed from romances, to describe the kind of 'goode' he finds 'ensampled' in the ancient heroes he has in mind flatly undercuts whatever resonance that latter word carries of the exemplum tradition whence it comes.[21] And for another, the whole set of terms and propositions Gower develops here — princes, tyrants, a period and a civilization in which 'wrytinge was beloved evere' — resounds more of the classical as it would have appeared to Gower, idealized through literature, than it does of the religious that he knew so well.

Finally, however, our best clue to what Gower may have meant is the *Confessio Amantis* itself, the book he attached to this prologue and which he says will follow in the steps of the 'olde bokes' he has been imagining. True, the *Confessio* uses as a framework the model of Christian confession, and its lessons (to say nothing of its ultimate purposes) are Christian throughout. Yet as has been pointed out (and as we shall examine further in a subsequent chapter) confession is but *one* of the framing devices of this complex poem. Two others, both secular, are the dream-vision and the tradition of the *speculum regis*.[22] Moreover, if we calculate the sources of the individual tales narrated by Genius, we find the majority overwhelmingly to be secular, and especially classical, works.

If this line of reasoning holds, and Gower is casting back to the classics to establish contextual precedent for the *Confessio*, then his patriotic resolve to write a poem 'for Engelondes sake' in 'oure englissh' also had classical roots for him. Both notions — of the poet's duty to the state, and of the poet as guardian of the common treasure of language — were primary themes of the great Augustans Ovid (much of whose work Gower apparently had by heart) and Virgil, whom he read and admired.[23] For Gower to be seeking actively to set the *Confessio Amantis*

---

[21] 'Ensample' carried strong overtones of the exemplum tradition. See the discussions of J. A. Mosher, *The Exemplum in the Early Religious and Didactic Literature of England* (New York, 1911), pp. 1-20; J. T. Welter, *L'Exemplum dans la littérature religieuse et didactique du Moyen Âge* (Paris, 1927) pp. 65-108; and G. R. Owst, *Literature and the Pulpit in Medieval England: A Neglected Chapter in the History of English Letters and the English People*, 2nd rev. edn. (Oxford, 1966), pp. 149-209. A stimulating recent assessment is by Charles A. J. Runacres, 'Art and Ethics in the *Exempla* of *Confessio Amantis*, in *Gower's Confessio Amantis: Responses and Reassessments*, ed. A. J. Minnis (Woodbridge, 1983) 106-34.

[22] On Gower and the confessional style, see John J. McNally, 'The Penitential and Courtly Traditions in Gower's *Confessio Amantis*, in *Studies in Medieval Culture*, ed. John R. Sommerfeldt (Kalamazoo, 1964) 74-94, and Gerald Kinneavy, 'Gower's *Confessio Amantis* and the Penitentials,' *Chaucer Review*, 19 (1984), 144-61; on dream-vision, see Constance Hieatt, *The Realism of Dream-Vision: The Poetic Exploitation of the Dream-Vision in Chaucer and His Contemporaries* (The Hague, 1967) 47-49; on the *speculum regis* tradition, see George R. Coffman, 'John Gower in His Most Significant Role,' in *Elizabethan Studies and Other Essays in Honor of George F. Reynolds, University of Colorado Studies*, Series B, II, (Boulder, 1945) 52-61; Russell A. Peck, *Kingship and Common Profit in Gower's Confessio Amantis* (Carbondale and Edwardsville, 1978) 139-59; and also Patricia J. Eberle's unpublished 'Vision and Design in John Gower's *Confessio Amantis*,' Ph.D. dissertation, Harvard University, 1977. Other models have also been proposed by Alastair J. Minnis, 'Moral Gower and Medieval Literary Theory,' in Minnis, *Responses and Reassessments*, pp. 50-78.

[23] Toward 'the recapturing of "classical" epic style in the vernacular,' Charles Muscatine has pointed out, '. . . Chaucer seems to have lent himself for perhaps a decade in the 1370s and '80s.' See *Poetry and Crisis in the Age of Chaucer* (Notre Dame and London,

among such company is at first arresting, especially if we are accustomed to think of his poem as either a dream-vision or an exploration of the Seven Sins. Yet in so doing Gower may merely be following the precedent set at the close of the *Troilus* by Chaucer, when he addressed his completed poem:

> Go, litel bok, go, litel myn tragedye,
> Ther God thi makere yet, er that he dye,
> So sende myght to make in som comedye!
> But litel book, no makyng thow n'envie,
> But subgit be to alle poesye;
> And kis the steppes where as thow seest pace
> Virgile, Ovide, Omer, Lucan, and Stace.   (*TC* V, 1786-92)

Interestingly, Chaucer here calls his poem both a 'bok' and a 'tragedye' — and implies that, if he live long enough, he will write a 'comedye.' Presumably this will be a 'bok' as well. Then it, like the 'tragedye' of *Troilus* already finished, will take its place (humble but deserving) beside the great books — the great 'poesye' — of the major poets of antiquity. 'Bok' is thus a word which Chaucer employed to mean 'poem,' at least sometimes — unlike, say, 'tretys,' which he never did.[24]

Another interesting feature of this passage is its placement. The lines immediately precede Chaucer's stanza on 'myswryting' and the diversity of English which we examined a few pages ago (*TC* V, 1793-98). Apparently to Chaucer the future reputation of his English poem, the works of the classical poets, and the state of his native language were connected. Attention paid to one brought to mind the next, and then the next, as if they all were aspects together of a single enterprise.

So, several elements of Gower's Prologue are present in the concluding lines of *Troilus*. Not all, to be sure: Nothing here about writing 'for Engelondes sake,' for one. But then at the end of *Troilus* Chaucer wants us to turn our thoughts away from earthly kingdoms toward a higher sphere. Nonetheless, I suggest that Chaucer's hopes to join, via his 'litel bok,' the tiny band of Virgil, Ovid, Homer,

---

1972) 119. Richard L. Hoffman summarizes scholarly opinion in his chapter 'The Influence of the Classics on Chaucer,' in *Companion to Chaucer Studies*, ed. Beryl Rowland (Toronto, New York and London, 1968) 162-75. A valuable overview of Gower's Latin reading is the 'Introduction' to Eric W. Stockton's *The Major Latin Works of John Gower* (Seattle, 1962) 3-46. This may be supplemented by Dorothy Speed, 'Gower's Narrative Technique as Revealed by His Adaptation of Source Material in the *Confessio Amantis*,' unpublished Ph.D. dissertation, University of London, 1970.

[24] On Chaucer and 'the book,' see Donald R. Howard, *The Idea of the Canterbury Tales* (Berkeley and Los Angeles, 1976) 56 ff., and the interesting recent study of Jesse M. Gellrich, *The Idea of the Book in the Middle Ages: Language Theory, Mythology, and Fiction* (Ithaca and London, 1985) 240 ff. For Chaucer's use of 'tretys,' see James A. Work, 'Chaucer's Sermon and Retractions,' *Modern Language Notes* 47 (1932) 257-60; John W. Clark, ' "This Litel Tretys" Again,' *Chaucer Review* 6 (1971) 152-56; and Paul Strohm, 'Some Generic Distinctions in the *Canterbury Tales*,' *Modern Philology* 68 (1971) 321-28.

Lucan and Statius can teach us how Gower hoped his Prologue, and his poem, would be interpreted.

Of course Gower knew Chaucer's stanzas well. Since only a short space later (*TC* V, 1856) Chaucer dedicated *Troilus* to Gower and to the 'philosophical Strode,' his 'moral' friend could scarcely have missed this passage. But probably Gower didn't have to read these lines to be familiar with Chaucer's ideas about English poems and the classics. They would have come to him in a less formal way — from Chaucer himself, in conversations the two poets shared at the time. The mid-1380s, when the *Troilus* was finished and the *Confessio Amantis* just begun, were undoubtedly the closest years spent by Gower and Chaucer. (If a quarrel occurred, as used to be supposed, it happened later, in the nineties.)[25] Words about poetry must have passed between them, as well as powers of attorney; indeed, we can assume they concurred on a number of significant issues.[26] About the meaning of 'bok,' for example I doubt we would be much in the wrong to agree with John Burrow, that 'bok' had a 'neo-classical' ring for Chaucer, and for Gower as well.[27] Certainly such a resonance is appropriate in the passages from *Troilus* and the *Confessio* we have been looking at above. Or, on another point: Chaucer's 'neo-classicism' (to expand upon Burrow's term) very likely provides a gloss to the 'fewe men' Gower speaks of in his Prologue — those whom he felt were using their native language significantly, to 'endite' (*CA* Pro., 22) for the honor of their nation and the glory of English. 'Fewe' here is, I suspect, a euphemism. 'Two' (and only two) is the number meant.

And so at last we can begin to close the circle. Like Chaucer, Gower decided to write in English, even as he rejected as crude and moribund its native poetic traditions. For both poets, the decision to do so is traceable to a humanism they shared in various measure — an early (or 'neo' classicism fostered by reading of antique books.[28] What authoritative support they may have needed to elect their own language — Gower, at least, assuredly required *some* — they collected initially from Augustan notions of the poet's duty to native tongue and soil, and next — in Chaucer's case directly — among the pages of Italians who shared these interests.[29] Their study of the classics doubtless had a second consequence, too: It could only have made them aware of metrics in a *theoretical* way, a different

---

[25] The notion that Gower and Chaucer fell out began with Tyrwhitt; see Fisher's summary, *John Gower*, p. 27 ff.

[26] Chaucer gave his power of attorney to Gower and Richard Forester when he went to Italy in 1378. See Martin M. Crow and Clair C. Olson, eds., *Chaucer Life-Records* (London, 1966) 12 note 5, 54, 60; and Fisher, *John Gower*, p. 61.

[27] Burrow, *Ricardian Poetry*, pp. 59-60.

[28] Howard's is a helpful description of late 14th-century English humanism; see *Idea*, pp. 40, 66-67.

[29] The point has been made well for both Chaucer and Gower by D. W. Robertson, Jr., who remarks on Petrarch's 'extravagant defense of things Italian in general and of Italian letters in particular,' especially in the dispute with Jean de Hesdin; see his *A Preface to Chaucer: Studies in Medieval Perspectives* (Princeton, 1962) 277. For Augustan expressions of national pride and connections with individual poetic reputation see *Aeneid* VI, and *Metamorphoses* I, 199-205; XVI, 871-79. I have in mind here not the recent ironic readings given these passages, but rather that Chaucer and Gower would have understood them

manner of knowing about patterns of stress and rhythm than what was current in England, in France, or yet in the rhetoric books. Mastering 'Virgile, Ovide, Omer, Lucan and Stace' — even if 'Omer' seems a bit of a boast — establishes a *feel* for meters regularly kept. More important still, such reading inculcates a sense of how highly 'numbers' had been valued, by the antique writers whose works Chaucer and Gower so admired, as parts essential to a serious poetic enterprise.

And it was finally for this reason that Gower took such care to proofread his manuscripts, I think. For a poetry built around metrical consistency demands assiduous reproduction, lest its effects be forfeit. Ben Jonson understood this well; and once again bearing his example in mind may help us, when we try to imagine the choices Gower made designing and polishing his poems.[30] Because, clearly, there were many decisions: only a little reflection should tell us this.

III

Among the multiple ironies of our culture is our willingness to accept the regular and the consistent as normative (hence, 'uninteresting'), while we expend much energy to explain (and so 'normalize' what we perceive to be irregular.[31] This is probably the appropriate response to most cases (the sun rising daily is 'dull;' the day it fails to rise will see nothing but hypotheses!), but not for all. In an asylum, for example, sane behavior is in a certain sense abnormal, yet it is not what we choose to examine.[32] Thus a different though related irony attends upon our

seriously and taken them as a kind of charge. Brooks Otis strikes the tone I mean, in his reconstruction of Virgil's thought; see his introduction to *The Aeneid*, tr. Frank O. Copley, 2nd edn. (Indianapolis, 1979) x-xxiv. Chaucer's classical and Italian reading was detected early: Leland remarked upon it in the *Commentarii*, p. 421.

[30] Wesley Trimpi offers a lucid description of Jonson's exactitude and stylistic concerns; see his *Ben Jonson's Poems: A Study of the Plain Style* (Stanford, Ca., 1962), pp. 3-59.

[31] I follow M. H. Abrams lead in tracing the equation of consistency and the uninteresting to what he has called the Romantics' 'expressive theory of art,' in which 'the artist himself becomes the major element generating both the artistic product and the criteria by which it is to be judged,' and for which spontaneity is the highest criterion of poetry. See *The Mirror and the Lamp: Romantic Theory and the Critical Tradition* (London, 1953), esp. pp. 22, 24, 48-50, 138-84; and further James Engell, who has recently traced the progress of the idea through the eighteenth century in *The Creative Imagination: Enlightenment to Romanticism* (Cambridge, Ma., 1981), pp. 3-10, and pp. 331 ff. for Coleridge's belief that 'the poet had to link together ideas, images, and feelings in a lively, unexpected way.'

[32] The psychoanalyst R. D. Laing describes the case of a young female patient in a German hospital who walked constantly up and down, clutching a piece of bread in one hand. The attending psychiatrist diagnosed her as schizophrenic after he could not stop her walking except by force (this caused weeping) and could not get her to release the bread except by prying her hand open. When stuck with a needle in the forehead by the doctor, she gave no sign of pain, and did not answer when addressed. Laing asks the question: In any other environment but a hospital, whose behavior would seem the more deviant, the girl's or the doctor's? See *The Politics of Experience* (New York, 1967) 73.

belief that, on one hand, the world is a chaotic place, unpredictable, a 'jungle' without purpose or law; and that, on the other, all things accord to a larger, often invisible but ultimately 'just' system or plan. (It matters not a jot if by this 'plan' we prefer to speak of God or ecology: my point is simply that we hold these beliefs, that they are on the surface contradictory, and that they conflict with our beliefs about other things — like the place and value of regularity, in life or verse — as well.)[33]

In avoiding these pitfalls the medievals were somewhat more successful than our own time has been, perhaps. Christianity at least institutionalized for them the means to see through a world violent, mutable and — for those reasons — uncertain and threatening, to a purposive hand beneath.[34] Not that all found lasting reassurance in the message of the Church.[35] Even Chaucer, who was plainly a religious man, shows in his work as great a measure of hopefulness that his beliefs are correct as he gives us evidence of that devotion itself. Donald R. Howard has written — convincingly, I think — that for this the majority of us approve of Chaucer, find him *simpatico* in the ironies he seems to have perceived, and then either embraced or struggled with.[36]

[33] As far as I am aware, Hume is the first since ancient times to recognize this paradox, in his consideration 'Of Miracles' in *An Enquiry Concerning Human Understanding*: 'The maxim, by which we commonly conduct ourselves in our reasonings, is, that the objects, of which we have no experience, resemble those, of which we have; and that where there is an opposition of arguments, we ought to give the preference to such as are founded on the greatest number of past observations. But though, in proceeding by this rule, we readily reject any fact which is unusual and incredible in an ordinary degree; yet in advancing farther, the mind observes not always the same rule; but when anything is affirmed utterly absurd and miraculous, it rather the more readily admits of such a fact, upon account of that very circumstance, which ought to destroy all its authority.' (I quote from the edition of Eric Steinberg, *David Hume: An Enquiry Concerning Human Understanding; A Letter from a Gentleman to His Friend in Edinburgh* [Indianapolis, 1977], p. 78.) Hume attributes this behavior to human nature — but the fact of his notice dates the phenomenon, and marks it a modern sea-change. (After having written this and the following note, I came upon the work of Benedicta Ward, *Miracles and the Medieval Mind: Theory, Record and Event, 1000-1215* [Philadelphia, 1982]. I was pleased to see my assumptions corroborated in her first two chapters, at least for the early period she covers.)

[34] The point was made by John of Jandun (d. 1328), whose opinion (on the independent existence of accidents) it is helpful to compare with Hume's view of miracles, above: 'We gain merit from that which we believe and cannot demonstrate. There is no natural principal by which [to] resolve the matter, but only a supernatural and miraculous one. Aristotle and the Commentator, speaking naturally, did not see this, since they had to see philosophically, by means of sensible things.' *Questions on De caelo*, I, 29; quoted from Stuart MacClintock, *Perversity and Error Studies on the 'Averroist' John of Jandun* (Bloomington, IN, 1950) 89. Ockham makes similar arguments; see *Quaestiones in lib. I. Physicorum*, Q. 136, and *Quodlibeta*, I, Q. i.

[35] I am not speaking here of heresy, of course, but of a Christian skepticism ultimately able to resolve itself within the Church. For the outlines of such a skepticism, see Mary E. Thomas, *Medieval Skepticism and Chaucer* (New York, 1950); and Sheila Delany, *Chaucer's House of Fame: The Poetics of Skeptical Fideism* (Chicago and London, 1972), chapter 2.

[36] Howard, *Idea*, pp. 117-25.

Not so John Gower. While the world he shared with Chaucer had, in the opinions of both men, 'grown upside-down,' Gower's response to his times precludes our finding in his work any reflection of the cultural ironies which attract us to Chaucer.[37] Chaucer, whose work has been described in paradoxical terms ('unfinished but complete,' to quote Howard), engages our attention because his authorial presence is that of a mind seemingly 'in process' of making itself up.[38] Like his own Alisoun of Bath, Chaucer appears to know 'muchel of wandrynge by the weye,' with all of the changes of direction that implies. Gower in contrast seems steadfast, a maker — and an executor — of firm plans. The images we bring to mind most often — of an Ellesmere Chaucer as pilgrim, horsed and mobile, on the road, and of Gower as a stationary confessant before the catechizing Genius — confirm this, even as they reveal how we respond to the theories of poetry which underlie and shape their poems.

What blurs matters for us as far as Gower is concerned is the contradictory way we view regularity. Preferring its opposite as more interesting (even as we try to reduce disarray to rule, *pace* attempts to reorder the *Canterbury Tales*), we forget that consistency prolonged over time is itself 'irregular.'[39] It is not natural. It seldom 'springs up' uncultivated, to flourish like the dunghill rose of the proverb — especially not in the kind of world which we, the medievals and ourselves, have agreed to find chaotic. Indeed, in such a *situs* we perhaps ought to treat *any* regularity, if strictly maintained, as good evidence of purpose — one possible reply to the challenge of discord. It is not, in any case, the status quo.

My argument, then, is that both Chaucer and Gower understood the world as many do today, as a tumultuous place full of irony and contradiction. Necessarily they developed responses to what they saw around them, and these responses were very different. Chaucer's, because his irony compares closely with modern disengagement, has seemed for long the more consciously determined of the two. Chaucer, we believe, possessed a poetic theory. He *thought out* an approach to poetry. Gower, so the story goes, produced an *oeuvre* which, like Topsy in the novel, 'jes' grew.'

But let us consider this notion in light of some facts for a moment. Many years ago Jakob Schipper commended Gower for his uniform meter, noting that he avoided the 'principal licenses of Middle English poetry.'[40] Subsequently G. C. Macaulay interpreted this remark to mean three things: that Gower almost never dropped an unaccented first syllable (as Chaucer often did, e.g., 'Whan that

---

[37] See Muscatine, *Poetry and Crisis*, pp. 111-1 for a pellucid description of Chaucer's ironic stance. Gower's response is vehement engagement, of which no better statement exists than the opening Book of the *Vox Clamantis*, sometimes called the 'Visio.' See Macaulay, *Works*, IV, 20-81.

[38] Howard, *Idea*, p. 1.

[39] The controversy over the 'real' order of the *Canterbury Tales* has been extensive. See the summary of opinion by Charles D. Owen in Rowland, *Companion*, pp. 192-207, and also Larry D. Benson, 'The Order of *The Canterbury Tales*,' *Studies in the Age of Chaucer*, (1981) 77-120. The question continues to spark argument, however: see Derek Pearsall, ed., *The Canterbury Tales* (London, 1985) 14-23.

[40] Jakob Schipper, *Englische Metrik, in historischer und systematischer Entwicklung dargestellt*, 2 vols. (Bonn, 1881) I, 279.

Aprill with his shoures soote'); seldom included extrametrical syllables in his lines; and only rarely 'displaced the natural accent' of good English speech.[41] Moreover, what holds for the English poetry is true as well for the French and Latin. Of the 28,000 lines in the *Mirour de l'Omme*, for example, the indefatigable Macaulay counted 'not more than about a score [which] even suggest the idea of metrical incorrectness.'[42]

What are we to make of these facts? A single irregular line every 1400, in Anglo-Norman and with no concessions made in the count for what might have been scribal error, is straight shooting indeed. It is hard to imagine it — or the consistent metrics of the *Confessio Amantis* either, for that matter — as a random event. So to begin with, these discoveries ought to convince us of Gower's commitment to metrical 'correctness': Clearly he valued it highly enough to have labored to produce it in different languages, throughout his career.

But these details may tell us more than this. They suggest as well that regular metrics are not just a part, but actually help comprise the core, of Gower's thoughts about style. We can test this notion by taking up three cases. The most elaborate of these I shall discuss last. The second relates to the remarks of Schipper and Macaulay, noted above. The first concerns a curious habit of Gower's, with the placement of the conjunctions 'and' and 'but.' In the following two examples, I give the surrounding context to illuminate the unusual word-order:

> Fulofte hir wordes sche reherceth,
> Er sche his slepi Eres perceth;
> With mochel wo *bot* ate laste
> His slombrende yhen he upcaste
> And seide hir that it schal be do.   (*CA* IV, 3029-33)

or:

> And thus acorded hom sche wente.
> Into the chambre *and* whan sche cam,
> Hire housebonde anon sche nam
> In bothe hire Armes and him kiste . . ..   (*CA* VII, 1936-39)

---

[41] Macaulay, *Works*, II, cxx-cxxi. Macaulay's comments are virtually a translation of Schipper: 'In . . . *Confessio Amantis* . . . findet sich keine einzige der bisher betrachteten nationalen Licenzen, weder Fehlen der ersten Senkung, noch doppelter Auftakt, noch auch Silbenverschliefungen oder Umstellungen des Taktes, ebenso wenig naturlich Fehlen einer Senkung im Innern des Verses, so dass die Verszeile nur selten eine kraftigere Casur aufweist, stets streng jambischen Rhythmus und durchgangig 8 oder 9 Silben hat . . . .' *Englische Metrik*, I, 279.

[42] Macaulay, *Works*, I, xliv. He lists 'the lines in question;' there are 21.

To my knowledge, Gower is the only Ricardian poet to adopt this particular license toward conjunctions.[43] Perhaps for good reason: it is not a very happy innovation, because it requires us to reverse the word-order to make syntactical sense of the line (i.e., 'Bot ate laste with mochel wo,' '*And* whan sche cam into the chambre'). We can see easily one problem Gower is trying to solve. In the first example he wants a rhyme for 'upcaste,' probably, and in the second a mate for 'nam.' Now, it seems possible that Gower's extensive *Latinitas* furnished him a precedent for his English usage here; and there may have been other factors too, such as the iambic/trochaic preference of his ear, which I shall take up in a moment. But these, in any event, would be exterior causes, serving only to account for the *shape* given an idea. It is the idea itself which should interest us — which draws the question, 'Why did these inversions occur in Gower's poetry especially?'

Let us look at our second case, before trying to answer this directly. Macaulay (and Schipper too, for all practical purposes) notes that Gower produced uniform lines, neither lacking a half-foot nor swollen with hypermetrical syllables; and that he rarely disturbed the 'natural accent' of good English speech while doing it. These are interesting claims, the more so because they are not wholly congruent. 'Good English speech' has a proclivity to turn out in iambs (or trochees, the reverse foot), but it is of course not metrically *regular*. Any extended statement includes inconsistencies — stressed syllables separated by too many or too few light ones to permit easy classification. So what Macaulay has pointed up is evidence of his poet's stylistic priorities. In the *Confessio Amantis* Gower did not reproduce 'good English speech' (or 'good conversational Anglo-Norman' in the *Mirour de l'Omme*) as he heard it around him, in court or on the street, with all of its irregularities. Rather, he chose to *approximate* the spoken language, to create the impression of live speech. He achieved this the way all poets do: by selectively adapting its cadences and for the most part its vocabulary, pruning away what wouldn't scan (or didn't rhyme) to fit limitations he himself imposed on his verse.

Macaulay's observation is a good one, then, but it can be refined. Like Chaucer, Gower did place a high priority on making a poetry of 'natural' English — but it was not his chief concern. Nor was it as important to him as to Chaucer that verse seem 'spoken'. As Ian Robinson has shown us, Chaucer often incorporated an idiomatic but metrically irregular expression into his work.[44] Not so John Gower. It would seem that when conflicts of meter and idiom occurred, Gower's poetic directed that the latter be sacrificed to preserve the strict regularity of the former.

This understanding of Gower's consistent metrics opens a number of doors. It helps us to explain, for example, the unusual treatment of conjunctions described above as a kind of case in point. Variable placement of 'bot' and 'and' increases

---

[43] This treatment of conjunctions has been remarked by Haruo Iwasaki, 'A Peculiar Feature in the Word-Order of Gower's *Confessio Amantis*,' *Studies in English Literature* (English Literature Society of Japan), 14 (1969) 205-20.

[44] Ian Robinson, *Chaucer's Prosody: A Study of the Middle English Verse Tradition* (Cambridge, 1971) 1-18.

the number of available ways to write a regular line. Such flexibility would have been important to Gower if regular metrics were a high priority for him. Looked at this way, it makes sense too that only Gower, and none of his contemporaries, should have employed this option. His work shows the greatest regularity of any in his time. The puzzle seems to fall neatly together if, in short, regularity of meter was at the heart of Gower's theory of technical style.

But, it can be objected, is this the *only* way to describe what we see? May it not have been, as the charge traditionally is levelled, that Gower had no standards at all, no theory, but just scratched down whatever language *some*thing — call it his muse — educed? By now, obviously, it should surprise no one if I say I don't think so — but, before going on to explore other 'doors' which I believe are opened by recognizing Gower's commitment to regular meter, we ought to assay the hypothesis one time more, and take up our third and final test case.

In the past much has been written of Chaucer's so-called 'good English ear.'[45] No one, to my knowledge, has studied whether Gower was equally gifted, but certain evidence — at least confirming its 'Englishness' — is not far to seek. Much can be learned about it by a look at the French poetry.

Despite his facility with other languages, it is clear that, regarding meter at least, Gower was an Englishman writing other tongues, rather than the 'compleat trilingual.' Thus, while the verse of the *Mirour de l'Omme* is syllabic, in the French manner, with no strong caesura at mid-line reminiscent of Old English meter, and nearly entirely regular, it nonetheless maintains a sort of English rhythm. In explanation, Macaulay seems to be correct when he posits that 'the verse is in a certain sense accentual as well as syllabic, the writer imposing upon himself generally the rule of the alternate beat of accents and seldom allowing absolutely weak syllables to stand in the even places of the verse.'[46] The example Macaulay offers — comparing a couplet from the *Mirour* (ll. 11404-05) with its source (Hélinant de Froidmont's *Vers de la Mort* ll. XV,11-12) illustrates his point:

> Hélinant: Tex me couve dessous ses dras,
>   Qui cuide estre tous fors et sains.[47]
>
> Gower: Car tiel me couve soubz ses dras,
>   Q'assetz quide estre fortz et seins.

The 'Englishness' of this, the drift toward medial caesura and iambic stress, is characteristic of the verse in the *Mirour* generally.

---

[45] The relevant early study is Dorothy Everett's 'Chaucer's "Good Ear",' *RES*, 23 (1947), 201-08; rep. in Everett, *Essays on Middle English Literature*, ed. Patricia Kean (London, 1955) 139-48. Paull F. Baum, *Chaucer's Verse* (Durham, N.C., 1961) 80-107, extends her discussion.
[46] Macaulay, *Works*, I, xlv.
[47] Ibid., xlvi.

And Gower's ear seems English in other ways as well. There are in the *Mirour* and the *Confessio* lines which echo each other closely, sometimes in sense, sometimes in vocabulary also, as do these:

> Thanne is he wys after the hond   (*CA* IV, 893)
>
> Lors est il sage apres la mein   (*MO*, 5436)

or:

> Of Armes and of brigantaille   (*CA* Pro., 213)
>
> Ou d'armes ou du brigantaille   (*MO*, 18675)

Juxtaposed like this, such pairs add a new but reinforcing dimension to the argument, notably advanced by John Fisher, that Gower's thought was singularly homogeneous.[48] Like the examples from the *Mirour* and the *Vers de la Mort*, they reveal a linguistic convergence in Gower's work, extant alongside those metaphoric and philosophical unities which Fisher culled for special study. (Indeed, because the formulative, or generative, power of language is basic, it might be argued that examples like these make Fisher's point at greater depth.) But more importantly for present purposes, they also suggest an inclination of Gower's ear toward the natural cadences of his native speech. Even when he was writing in Anglo-Norman, it would seem, Gower 'heard' an English music. Doubtless, for some of its medieval readership the French of the *Mirour* recalled, like that of Chaucer's Prioress, Stratford-atte-Bowe and not Paris.

So Gower probably thought 'in English': or, if not in the language itself, then certainly in the iambic/trochaic patterns dominating its speech rhythms. But our real question is speculative, and carries us beyond the mere fact. What we want to know about are the consequences. Did having an 'English' ear make writing metrically uniform verses, page after page, any easier for Gower? So easy (to put it more precisely) that they could be turned out as if from an assembly line, without care or decision, to fill hundreds of vellum sheets in three languages? On the face of it, it seems too much to suppose. Gower's 'good English ear,' helpful as it undoubtedly must have been, scarcely suffices to explain the metrical regularity of his work. A theory alone can do that — one which Gower developed and carried out, for himself and on his own.

Here of course it would be ideal to cite several early readers who recognized regular metrics as Gower's hallmark among his peers. This would help because, having pursued Gower's metrical theory thus far, one wonders whether his contemporaries noticed it, and how it affected them, if they did. Sadly (but not surprisingly), this evidence has disappeared, if ever it existed — for medieval and Renaissance commentators seem to have taken Gower's metrics for granted, preferring to speak (when they speak) about his contributions to the vocabulary.

---

[48] Fisher, *John Gower*, p. 135 'The most striking characteristic of Gower's literary production is its single-mindedness . . . . In a very real sense, Gower's three major poems are one continuous work.'

Occasional scraps turn up nonetheless, tantalizing because they *might* convey the wished-for metrical acuity, if only we could read them properly. Holinshed, for example, in 1577, amidst the familiar enconmia about leaving the vernacular 'rich and plentifull in wordes,' commends Gower (and Chaucer also) for making English 'so proper and apt to expresse that which the mind conceyued as any other usuall language.'[49] Curiosity aside about the nature of a 'usuall' language, it would be good to know what linguistic propriety and aptness meant, for Holinshed? Did his sense include metrical correctness? Probably not, but it is hard to say. Of the intent of George Ashby, who a century earlier (ca. 1470) praised the 'fresshe, douce englisshe and *formacion/ Of newe balades*' of Gower and Chaucer, we can be more certain. 'Formacion,' suggestive at first of technical sagacity, loses most of its critical teeth when Ashby extends the compliment to Lydgate in the same two lines.[50]

Not until Tyrwhitt in 1775 do we find appreciation for regular metrics in Middle English poetry, and then it is about Chaucer, not Gower, that Tyrwhitt speaks. But Tyrwhitt, too, puzzled over what the words of early writers meant regarding prosody, and his conclusions, interesting in themselves, are helpful to make a point. Chaucer's contemporaries, he observed,

> . . . and they who lived nearest to his time, universally extoll him as the 'chief Poete of Britaine,' 'the flour of Poetes,' etc., titles, which must be supposed to implie their admiration of his metrical skill, as well as of his other poetical talents; but the later critics, though they leave him in possession of the same sounding titles, are almost unanimously agreed, that he was either totally ignorant or negligent of metrical rules, and that his verses (if they may be so called) are frequently deficient, by a syllable or two, of their just measure.[51]

Subsequently, Tyrwhitt sets out to 'restore' Chaucer to his 'original' regular meters by adding and subtracting syllables as needed. The result, as Ian Robinson has called it, a 'De dum de dum de dum de dum de dum (de)' Chaucer, has been with us until very recent times.[52]

But of course Tyrwhitt's is not a medieval voice, or even a Renaissance one. The dearth of similar criticism from centuries preceding the Enlightenment

[49] Raphael Holinshed, *The Chronicles of England, Scotlande, and Irelande . . . Faithfully gathered and compiled by Raphael Holinshed* (London, 1577) 1163. The relevant passage is reprinted in Carolyn F. E. Spurgeon, *Five Hundred Years of Chaucer Criticism and Allusion, 1357-1900*, 3 vols. (New York, 1960) I, 114-15.
[50] George Ashby, *Active Policy of a Prince*, prologue; reprinted in Spurgeon, *Criticism and Allusion*, I, 54.
[51] Thomas Tyrwhitt, *The Poetical Works of Geoffrey Chaucer with An Essay on His Language and Versification and an Introductory Discourse* (London, 1775; rep. London, 1871) xvii.
[52] Robinson, *Chaucer's Prosody*, p. 5.

shows us that. And his subject was Chaucer, not Gower at all. Nevertheless, Tyrwhitt is useful because he helps us to see Gower as we seldom imagine him — as an experimental poet, working out principles of his own devising. In many ways, Gower's idea of the well-made poem was a metrically regular one. In this at least it resembled Tyrwhitt's more closely than it did Chaucer's. Or perhaps I should say, that of our most recent Chaucer, as he appears to be emerging now from the blur of editorial practices like Tyrwhitt's, replete with emendations.[53] This Chaucer seems but loosely bound by metrical strictness and rather intrigued by irregular lines. It is at once a modern, and a more medieval portrait than Tyrwhitt's — and doubtless truer. It stands Chaucer (in this one sense at least) square alongside Langland, Lydgate, Hoccleve and all the rest who must have considered variable metrics an option completely open to them as writers. And it attunes Chaucer, too, with the 'critics' of his age: none of whom record notice of his metrics, good or bad, amidst their praises for the 'douce language' of his verse. Metrics, as we speak of them, and as Tyrwhitt did, were simply not a significant theoretical issue for English poets during the late Middle Ages, I suspect.[54]

Except, that is, for John Gower; who, in order to compose his thousands of regular lines, must have taken metrics very seriously indeed. This makes him experimental, albeit in an unusual way. At a time wide-open to metrical variation, Gower chose to test the effects of consistency. He standardized when standard metrics were neither required, nor even considered interesting by those who wrote, or wrote about, poetry. It is thus scarcely surprising that his regularity failed to provoke coeval comment. His experimentalism was at one with the Zeitgeist of the age. Moreover, Gower himself may not have thought of his work as revolutionary. Very likely he just imagined it to be *his* voice, different from others but not necessarily *better* — not, that is, in the way Tyrwhitt meant better when he 'corrected' Chaucer. But for us, looking backward and reversing

---

[53] I have in mind approaches such as Pearsall's, in his edition of the *Tales*, p. 1 ff., and his 'Texts, Textual Criticism, and Fifteenth Century Manuscript Production,' in *Fifteenth-Century Studies: Recent Essays*, ed. Robert F. Yeager (Hamden, CT, 1984) 121-36.
[54] Lydgate, seeking Chaucer's ghostly help while composing his *Troy Book*, does remark (Book II, 4701-06):

> To god I pray that he his soule haue
> After whos help of nede I most crave
> And seke his boke [*Troilus*] that is left be hynde
> Som goodly worde ther in for to fynde
> To sette amonge the crokid lynys rude
> Whiche I do write as by similitude.

See the edition of Henry Bergen, *Lydgate's Troy Book*, 4 vols., E.E.T.S., E.S. 97, 103, 106, 126 (London, 1906, 1908, 1910, 1935), I, 229. One might take Lydgate's 'crokid lynys' several ways here, even to imply a critique of his own ragged meters compared with Chaucer's smooth product. On the other hand, since he hopes to find in *Troilus* 'Som goodly *worde*' (and not, say, 'measure'), it is probably best to assume that Lydgate meant no technical assessment, but only one more general compliment to his 'master,' made at his own expense.

Tyrwhitt's critical glass, the picture of Gower as singular experimentalist in an experimental age should be instructive. The process adds trenchancy to a remark of Donald Davie's, several years old now, that Gower was in certain ways an English Augustan, at work before his time.[55]

Of course, not all of Gower's 'experiments' were successful. To write the kind of lengthy poem Gower favored using strictly regular meter is parlous work, if one has fears of an audience dozing off, or clapping shut the book in boredom. Undeniably, Gower churned out his share of numbing passages. Like the following, this is plain, serviceable verse of the near-'de dum de dum de dum (ho hum)' variety:

> Whan themperour it herde sein,
> And knew the falshed of the vice,
> He seide he wolde do justice;
> And ferst he let the Prestes take,
> And for thei scholde it noght forsake,
> He put hem into questioun;
> Bot thei of the suggestioun
> Ne couthen noght a word refuse,
> Bot for thei wolde hemself excuse,
> The blame upon the Duck thei leide.   (*CA* I, 1008-17)

Nothing *really* exceptionable here, certainly; the meter is kept well and the story progresses cleanly and economically. Nothing is wasted. But nothing impresses, either; so that, all of Gower's Prologue arguments to the contrary, at last this sort of writing, when prolonged, must blunt rather than hone the attention. It is a lesson Gower learned less well than did the true Augustan, Pope — and to his detriment.

Yet in contrast to such joyless passages there are others, fortunately numerous, in which Gower's metrical judiciousness is apparent. The following is a good example:

> Phebus, which makth the daies lihte,
> A love he hadde, which tho hihte
> Cornide, whom aboven alle
> He pleseth: bot what schal befalle

---

[55] Davie attempts to isolate what he calls 'chaste diction' in English poetry; Gower, he says, plays a kind of Johnson to Chaucer's Pope. See his *Purity of Diction in English Verse* (London, 1967) 31-33. C. S. Lewis came close to making a similar point with the remark that Gower 'stands almost alone in the centuries before our Augustans in being a poet perfectly well bred.' See *The Allegory of Love: A Study in Medieval Tradition* (London, 1936) 201.

> Of love ther is noman knoweth,
> Bot as fortune hire happes throweth.
> So it befell upon a chaunce,
> A yong kniht tok hire acqueintance
> And hadde of hire al that he wolde:
> Bot a fals bridd, which sche hath holde
> And kept in chambre of pure yowthe,
> Discoevereth all that evere he cowthe.   (*CA* III, 783-94)

With a single inversion of iamb to trochee ('Phebus . . .') excepted, these lines
are perfectly regular. Nonetheless, they do not bore us, for reasons which are
instructive. Here a careful use of enjambment, caesura and narrative pacing
combine to enliven the passage and generate interest. The result approximates
closely the movement and tenor of informal, but cultured, conversation. It is the
'good English speech' identified by Macaulay, adapted to Gower's requirements
for regularized verse. Here he has merged his two aims successfully.

IV

We can see that Gower creates more sophisticated imitations of speech if we
broaden our discussion from metrics to 'stylistics,' defined as we did at the
beginning of this chapter. The *Confessio Amantis* is a dialogue between two figures
of very different purposes and temperaments. In that sense it is dramatic — a
point Gower sought to underscore by creating two voices, one for Genius, the
somewhat pedantic priest of Venus, another for the love-sick Amans. These
voices Gower develops over the full expanse of his poem, establishing the
individual qualities of each character's way of talking by accretion. At times, the
progress seems almost sculpturally slow; and it is, in a certain sense, a luxurious
strategy. Nonetheless, by controlling how quickly his audience became aware of
his major speakers' separate voices, Gower gained several advantages. One is
that, by the conclusion of the *Confessio*, we have come to recognize the 'sounds' of
Genius and of Amans in a relatively natural way. We know them as we do the
timbres and expressions of friends: not precisely (if we had to give, say, the police
a description) but still thoroughly enough, so that only a few words over the
telephone reveal their identities. In a poem fundamentally dependent on what we
might call concentric verisimilitudes, this aura of 'realism' provided by the chief
voices is significant, if not essential, to the success of the *Confessio Amantis*. But by
the same token, because the effect is cumulative, it is difficult of demonstration,
except through lengthy quotation. The following exchange, however, is
illustrative:

> Confessor.   And in this wise now a day
>   In loves court a man mai hiere

> Fulofte pleigne of this matiere,
> That many envious tale is stered,
> Wher that it mai noght ben ansuered;
> Bot yit fulofte it is belived,
> And many a worthi love is grieved
> Thurgh bacbitinge of fals Envie.
>   If thou have mad such janglerie
> In Loves court, mi sone, er this,
> Schrif thee therof.

Amans.   Mi fader, yis;
> Bot wite ye how? noght openly,
> Bot otherwhile, prively,
> Whan I my diere ladi mete,
> And thenke how that I am noght mete
> Unto hire hihe worthinesse,
> And ek I se the besinesse
> Of all this yonge lusty route,
> Whiche alday pressen hire aboute,
> And ech of hem his time awaiteth,
> And ech of hem his tale affaiteth
> Al to deceive an innocent,
> Which woll noght ben of here assent . . .

(CA II, 444-66)

The first voice belongs to Genius. By careful modulation of the pace of Genius's sentences, Gower is able to give him the serious, contemplative tone which is his throughout the *Confessio*. The priest's is a periodic style, of Ciceronian paragraphs measured and composed. It builds in wheels around balances, point and counterpoint, thesis and antithesis. Genius is the master of the well-placed 'bot' upon which, as in the lines quoted above, the thought simultaneously turns.

In contrast here is the Lover's plaintive breathlessness — an effect achieved in part through the division of Amans's lines into short segments by strong central caesurae in close juxtaposition with tumbling, almost run-away periods. These capture the Lover's swelling emotion as appropriately as the priest's talk vouchsafes his disengagement. Of course, Amans is not always in the same efferent state in all parts of the poem — but our search is for signatures here, and the Lover's agitation commonly marks off his discourse from his confessor's. Moreover, in the example above, the initial signal of difference is both represented and bolstered by repeated verbal patterns. These accord each speaker's voice and his emotional state — a rhetorical technique Gower uses often. Thus, if an unruffled Genius expends four lines to complete a figure of thought ('*That many* envious tale is stered . . . *And many* a worthi love is grieved'), the increasingly heated Amans allows but two ('And ech of hem his time awaiteth,/ And ech of hem his tale affaiteth'). The lines illustrate, too, the speakers' dissimilar thoughts on conjunctions. For Genius, an 'and' or a 'bot' is a fulcrum, a pivot; while for Amans such words, like staples or glue, most often couple ideas of mere tangential association.

The passage is a controlled performance, again typical of Gower's regularizing. His range extends to other effects as well, all involving a judicious fitting of technique to thought. There is, for example, real 'water music' in a line like 'In Temse whan it was flowende' (*CA* Pro., 39); and when Amans, allowed to touch his lady's hand, describes his elation:

> The Ro, which renneth on the Mor,
> Is thanne noght so lyht as I   (*CA* IV, 2786-87)

one senses that not only is the simile apt but the evocative metrics — fleeting like both hart and heart — are precise also. These instances can be bettered by others whose length makes full quotation difficult. Again, Gower achieves some of his finest effects by disciplined accretion, one small suggestion building judiciously upon another and the next over many lines.

Medea's restoration of Eson's lost youth in Book V of the *Confessio* presents a good case in point. The motion of the poetry follows the action described. With the old man asleep before her, Medea applies her charms:

> Tho lay ther certein wode cleft,
> Of which the pieces now and eft
> Sche made hem in the pettes wete,
> And put hem in the fyri hete,
> And tok the brond with al the blase,
> And thries sche began to rase
> Aboute Eson, ther as he slepte;
> And eft with water, which sche kepte,
> Sche made a cercle about him thries,
> And eft with fyr of sulphre twyes:
> Ful many an other thing sche dede,
> Which is noght writen in this stede.
> Bot tho sche ran so up and doun,
> Sche made many a wonder soun,
> Somtime lich unto the cock,
> Somtime unto the Laverock,
> Somtime kacleth as a Hen,
> Somtime spekth as don the men:
> And riht so as hir jargoun strangeth,
> In sondri wise hir forme changeth,
> Sche semeth faire and no womman . . .   (*CA* V, 4085-105)

The Protean energy of Medea's sorcery is helpfully reinforced by the metrics here. Like Medea herself, the lines reshape themselves rapidly, building from the deliberate circling about the drugged Eson to the swift shape-shifting emphasized by the repetition of 'Somtime.' It is a passage over which Gower demonstrates a full control.

But, someone might query, how consistent was he? Is this passage just a lucky hit? Let us look at quite a different example, from Book IV of the *Confessio*. The subject is the Cave of Sleep, inhabited by the god Morpheus.

> Under an hell ther is a Cave,
> Which of the Sonne mai nought have,
> So that noman mai knowe ariht
> The point betwen the dai and nyht:
> Ther is no fyr, ther is no sparke,
> Ther is no dore, which mai charke,
> Wherof an yhe scholde unschette,
> So that inward ther is no lette.
> And forto speke of that withoute,
> Ther stant no gret Tree nyh aboute
> Wher on ther myhte crowe or pie
> Alihte, forto clepe or crie:
> Ther is no cok to crowe day,
> Ne beste non which noise may
> The hell, bot al aboute round
> Ther is growened upon the ground
> Popi, which berth the sed of slep,
> With othre herbes such an hep.
> A stille water for the nones
> Rennende upon the smale stones,
> Which hihte of Lethes the rivere,
> Under that hell in such manere
> Ther is, which yifth gret appetit
> To slepe.
>   (*CA* IV, 2991-3014)

The description of Morpheus's Cave accepts the same challenges as do the lines portraying Medea's magic. They set a tone, then hold and build it over an extended moment; they employ meter to pace, and thereby enhance, explicit figuration. Yet the effects of these passages are as different as the subjects they describe. As the first passage seems to accelerate with Medea's every ritual, whirling with her finally, chirping and cackling, so in the second passage when Gower turns to Morpheus's slumbrous realm we feel a slow, clogged weight beset the pace as, aptly, the meter brakes the narrative motion as a blow is diffused among pillows. If we are forced to race with Medea, we here experience the drowsiness of Morpheus as Lethe's 'stille water . . . rennende upon the smale stones' carries us 'to slepe.' Stylistically, these descriptions of Medea's magic and Morpheus's cave are good examples of what Gower could bring off by paying close attention to language choice and pace.

The same passages may also serve to open other matters of sound play which, along with the movement of the the verse, help to illustrate Gower's poetic style. For his 'good ear' was tuned to apprehend and develop subtleties such as onomatopoeia:

> Somtime lich unto the cock,
> Somtime unto the Laverock,
> Somtime kacleth as a Hen,
> Somtime speketh as don the men . . .

Here the repetition of 't,' 'k' and 'l' in the first two lines sets up a pattern of sound aptly preparatory for 'kacleth,' the striking word of the series. This deliberate development amplifies and enriches the onomatopoeic effect. When the crucial 'kacleth' finally falls, it does so not into a vacuum but into a context like an echo chamber, already iterant with similar sounds. Nor is this an idle gesture, devoid of design. 'Kacleth' functions catalytically, both connecting the group of lines, and drawing them sharply to a point. For the next line creates an instructive disjunction. Suddenly the avian *bruit* is poised against its opposite human speech, the way of noisemaking 'as don the men.' It is a contrast Gower furthers through his choice of rhyme ('Hen/men'). And this in turn recalls for us that *logos* was God's gift to man alone. Like rationality and laughter, language was, properly imagined, a guidepost for the peregrine soul.[56] In this passage, then, Gower's controlled technique permits him to harness sound and sense to raise — and answer *in parvo* — a major issue confronting both his faith and his final poem.

Nor is this an isolated example. Gower works with the same acuity throughout the *Confessio Amantis*. In the foregoing description of the Cave of Morpheus we find another example:

> Ther is growenede upon the ground
> Popi, which berth the sed of slep,
> With othre herbes such an hep.
> A stille water for the nones
> Rennende upon the smale stones,
> Which hihte of Lethes the rivere,

---

[56] The *locus classicus* for medieval notions of man as a rational, risible animal is Aristotle's *De partibus animalium*, III, 10. The question of whether laughter was essential to human nature was much discussed; see E. R. Curtius, *European Literature and the Latin Middle Ages*, trans. Willard R. Trask (New York, 1953), pp. 420-24 and V. A. Kolve, *The Play Called Corpus Christi* (Stanford, CA, 1966), pp. 124-44. Language use for Augustine was problematic, because it came as a consequence of the fall; nonetheless, it was intrinsic to human nature as we know it. See the discussion of Robert J. O'Connell, *St. Augustine's Early Theory of Man, A.D. 386-91* (Cambridge, MA, 1968), pp. 162-65. Aquinas took a similar position; see Joseph LeGrand, *L'Universe et l'homme dans la philosophie du Seint Thomas*, 2 vols. (Paris, 1946), II, 228-32.

> Under that hell in such manere
> Ther is . . .

Here the combination of the 'h,' 'th,' and 's' sounds join with nasals and liquids ('n,' 'l,' 'r') to accommodate both the 'hep' of 'Popi' and the trickle and drip of the water over the gravel bed of Lethe. It is a deft performance, and characteristic of Gower's mature style.

V

One further example of Gower's careful manipulation of sound will help confirm what has gone before, and lead on as well to other issues. A line such as 'The grete, gastli serpent glyde' (*CA* V, 5026) conveys something of the motion of the serpent through the accents and caesura; yet there is about it as well the artful approximation of a reptilian hiss ('*gastli serpent*') and dry scrape of scale in the repeating, gutteral 'gr/gas/gly.' The words play on several sounds at once, and consequently reinforce the image formed by the meaning.

A line like this can teach us much about Gower's style, not only via his control over movement but also through the alliteration. As the example suggests, Gower approached this as judiciously as he did the subtleties of metrics. Indeed, in his handling of alliteration, and the attendant techniques of assonance and consonance, Gower was the equal of Chaucer, whose writing not infrequently contains lines such as these from the *General Prologue*:

> This worthy man ful wel his wit bisette
> Ther wiste no wight that he was in dette   (*Gen. Pro.* 279-80)

A great deal is at work stylistically here, in brief space. Chaucer links his couplet not only by means of the concluding rhyme, but also with the alliteration of 'w' across the two lines ('*worthy/wel/wiste/wight/was*') and with assonance: the repeated [ɛ]'s ('w*e*l/bis*e*tte/d*e*tte') and [I]'s ('w*i*t/w*i*ste/w*i*ght').[57] Consonance — what Percy Adams has called 'the repetition of the sound of a final consonant or consonant cluster in stressed syllables near enough to each other for the echo to affect the ear' — is also in play in this pair, creating configurations of 'wi*t*/wigh*t*' and 'bise*tte*/de*tte*.'[58]

Gower's phonal repetitions cover this full range, albeit while striking us differently than Chaucer's do. One essential reason is the even number of stresses in Gower's octosyllabic lines, in contrast to the five feet of Chaucer's customary

---

[57] See further Percy G. Adams's discussion, 'The Tradition that Dryden Was Given,' in *Graces of Harmony: Alliteration, Assonance, and Consonance in Eighteenth-Century British Poetry* (Athens, GA, 1977), especially 36-38.
[58] Ibid., p. 15.

pentameters. Now, a good deal of just praise has been heaped on Chaucer over the years for anchoring English poetry in the five-beat iambic line, even as (less justly, I think) Gower's briefer measures have provoked other assessments, ranging from disinterest to scorn.[59] But, if the portrait I have been painting of Gower's poetic is a true likeness, it would be reasonable — even consistent — to suppose that Gower elected octosyllabics after due evaluation of the alternatives.[60] Certainly by the time Gower started on the *Confessio* Chaucer had shown him in the *Troilus* what iambic pentameter could do.[61] And Gower too wrote in other measures. Amans's so-called 'Supplication' to Venus (*CA* VIII, 2217-2300) is iambic pentameter, as is Gower's other English poem, 'To King Henry the Fourth, In Praise of Peace.' What did Gower achieve with the four-beat line which might provide a clue about why he chose it for the *Confessio*?

One sort of evidence, perhaps, is the way he developed patterns of alliteration. In the *Confessio Amantis* we find three basic alliterative schema: AABB ('Ther *mai* no *m*annes *t*unge *t*elle,' *CA* VII, 5080); ABAB ('A *m*an, which *w*olde *m*ake him *w*ys,' *CA* VII, 2452); and ABBA ('Wher *m*any a *w*onder *w*oful *m*one,' *CA* IV, 834).[62] What is most interesting about these patterns is the way they take advantage of the pairings possible in the four-beat line to forge connections of sound and sense to justify their presence.

In the AABB type, the sentences are divided by the alliteration into rough units, one primarily involved with the subject, the other with the predicate:

[59] Shakespeare, possibly, set the tone for the future with his wicked parody of Gower's meters in the choruses of *Pericles*. For the Moderns, James Russell Lowell has few rivals for low opinion of Gower's octosyllabics (as well for vascular prose. A sample: 'As you slip to and fro on the frozen levels of [Gower's] verse, which give no foothold to the mind, as your nervous ear awaits the inevitable recurrence of his rhyme, regularly pertinacious as the tick of an eight-day clock and reminding you of Wordsworth's "Once more the ass did lengthen out/ The hard, dry, seesaw of his horrible bray," you learn to dread, almost to respect, the powers of this indefatigable man.' *My Study Windows* (Boston and New York, 1871) 259.

[60] One reason might have been the relative conservatism of the choice. While iambic pentameter is Chaucer's own creature, four-stress lines were familiar as the regular form for metrical romances, in French and English; see Jakob Schipper, *A History of English Versification* (Oxford, 1910) 183 ff. And it is undoubtedly worth noting that Gower was used to tetrameter of a certain kind from the *Mirour de l'Omme*.

[61] We can date the *Troilus* about 1385 and the beginning of the *Confessio* somewhat after — although, of course, neither date is a firm one; see Fisher's approximate chronology in *John Gower*, p. x.

[62] Paul Höfer, who first suggested Gower might have had some interest in this kind of effect, lists 316 examples of some 13 types of pattern; see his *Alliteration bei Gower* (Leipzig, 1890) 26 ff. However, many of Höfer's patterns are fallacious (he contends 'wh' alliterates with 'w' for example), and some (his A/AAA, AAA/AAA, and AA/AB) appear only once in all the *Confessio*. Macaulay (*Works*, II, cxxvii) observes in passing the similarity of some of Gower's alliterative combinations ('lusty lif,' 'sword or spere,' etc.) to some of 'the new artistic style of poetry.' His understatement supplies a healthy antidote to Höfer's enthusiasm.

The *freisshe floures sprede* and *springe*   (*CA* VII, 808)

In isolation, such a device seems of slight significance, but the technique has greater effect when read aloud, as Gower must have had some expectation his poem would be. Balanced alliteration points the lines up for the audience, guiding them toward the important comparisons in the sentence, keeping the comprehension level higher over time.

On the other hand, a crossed pattern implies antithesis. Most examples which alliterate ABAB are on the model of 'And *now* I *singe*, and *now* I *sike*' (*CA* IV, 1179), where the phonal repetition emphasizes the contrast of 'singe' and 'sike.' Some ABAB lines have a 'folksy' ring ('Or *be* him *lief* or *be* him *loth*,' *CA* II, 999) which exposes Gower's willingness to reach into the popular tradition for effect. Here their form kept them memorable — the same reason, in other words, that Gower uses them himself. But most he struck fresh to suit his context: 'Til *what* be *sleighte*, and *what* be *strengthe*' (*CA* V, 7583).

The third pattern, ABBA, affects meaning differently. Often when he employed it Gower seems to have had in mind tightly-bound opposites identifiable as single units: 'In *hevene*, in *Erthe*, and *eke* in *helle*' (*CA* V, 1633); 'But *Oule* on *Stock* and *Stock* on *Oule*' (*CA* III, 585); 'With *many* a *lord* and *Lady mo*' (*CA* III, 1496). However, a few examples appear to have been crafted to connect elements of an idea in the center of a line, thus focussing attention on them and rendering them more impressive: 'I *can* the *women wel excuse*' (*CA* VII, 4269); 'Bot *such* a *grace God* hire *sente*' (*CA* VIII, 1428).

All of these pairs work more readily in even-footed lines than in odd — and four beats are perhaps the best number in which to register such duple effects. Whether Gower saw the possibilities before or after he began writing octosyllabics we cannot say, of course; but as his frequent employment of these alliterative figures shows, he clearly knew how to exploit them.

Not all alliterating lines in the *Confessio Amantis* fit one of these patterns, however. There are other cases, like the following:

> And *with* his *wordes* slyhe and queinte
> The /*wh*/iche he co/*w*/the *wisly* peinte . . .   (*CA* II, 2853-54)

Here the repetition of 'w' in primary stressed syllables ('*with/wordes/wisly*') does not form a consistent pattern, but it is ear-catching, particularly since it is echoed by similar sounds in '/*wh*/iche' and 'co/*w*/the.' The jointure of the couplet is furthered, too, by the assonant [I]'s in 'with,' 'slyhe,' 'whiche,' and 'wisly.' A happy mellifluity results — but it would be difficult to argue, I think, for a deeper purpose.

Often, however, Gower appears to be up to more than sonancy when he applies alliterative techniques, even when he does so extraschematically. He can for example turn a kind of trope upon opposites, using alliteration to bind words with important, and contradictory, meanings. When in Book I (1581-82) Gower writes:

> And thus this yonge *l*usty kniht
> Unto this olde *l*othly wiht

we feel that the contrast initiated by 'yonge' and 'olde' is continued and reinforced by the sound-play of 'lusty/lothly.' Since the affective power of the 'Tale of Florent,' from which these lines are drawn, hinges on the creation in the audience of a certain horror at the fate of a vigorous, handsome youth being forced into marriage with a shrivelled 'wolesak' of a woman, the alliterative jointure here underscores the tale's central fiction. In another context, lines like:

> The *w*yn /wh/ich he was *w*ont to drinke
> He tok thanne of the /w/elles brinke . . . (*CA* I, 2979)

emphasize through the sound-play a contrast integral to the moral interpretation of the story: in this case, the fall of King Nebuchhadnezzar. Quite obviously, the 'wine' that the mad king, transformed for his sin of vain-glory into a bull, obtains from the well is of humbler order than that 'which he was wont to drinke.' The figurative description is far more telling than a direct statement (such as, 'the king now drinks water') might be. Its irony devolves from the resonant progression of 'wine/wont/welle,' with some additional support from the assonant vowels in 'wont' and 'tok.'

What examples like these tell us, perhaps, is never to underestimate the possiblity of careful thought behind any of Gower's lines. Even when they fit no neat pattern, they often seem crafted to focus the sum of their elements, including alliteration, toward making a larger point. Moreover, small effects like these would be less telling stretched over longer lines. 'Out of pattern' too, then, Gower can be seen to work the potential of the octosyllabic line.

Nor did Gower confine his experiments with sound only to pairs of lines. He makes use of the same techniques to unify blocks of many lines running. Two passages may illustrate what I mean. In the first:

> A king mai spille, a king mai save,
> A king mai make of lord a knave,
> And of a knave a lord also
> The power of a king stant so;
> That he the lawes overpasseth
> What he wol make lasse, he lasseth,
> What he wol make more, he moreth. (*CA* VII, 1835-41)

the alliteration of 'k,' 's,' 'm,' and 'l' is supported by the underlying 'w''s ('power/lawes/wol/wol') and 'wh's ('what/what'), and by the assonant vowels [a] ('save/make/knave/stant/lawes/ . . . passeth/make/lasse/lasseth/make) and types of [o] ('lord/power, also/so/over . . . /wol/wol/more/moreth'). This interweaving of sounds helps to emphasize the point of the passage — that a king's puissance is inseparable from everything within his reach. Here the sonant involution carries out a larger narrative purpose.

Even more striking, perhaps, is this example:

> The wordes maken frende of fo
> And fo of frende, and pes of werre,
> And werre of pes, and out of herre
> The word the worldes cause entriketh
> And reconcileth who on him liketh.   (*CA* VII, 1574-78)

As in the case above, these lines exhibit a tight technical control which brings about a complex counterpoint of sound and sense at once pleasing and purposive. Gower's ostensible subject is the persuasive talents of Ulysses, but his true concern is much more ambitious: the power of words themselves — especially that of *the* Word, the God-uttered Logos — to affect all creation. As Patrick J. Gallacher has shown, for Gower, whose faith in his art as an instrument of change was as great as that of the early Spenser, such a theme has great importance, whenever it appears in his work.[63] In the context of Book VII, however, where Gower expresses himself directly on the qualities proper to a king, the passage is the more suggestive; for here, speaking through the mouth of Genius, Gower hoped to present to his sovereign a kind of blueprint for the good king. The passage above is excerpted from a longer one found in the subsection on 'Rhetoric' (*CA* VII, 1507-1640). Nearly three-quarters of these lines (87 of 133) are concerned specifically with 'the word' and seem designed to convince partly through the repetition of sound. 'Word' and 'wordes' occur 24 times in 87 lines, beginning less frequently and building toward a kind of crescendo. In the last 14 lines of the section 'word' appears eight times. Within such a strategy, the techniques of disciplined alliteration and assonance (e.g., 'fo/fo/word/worldes/ who') play important parts.

VI

And so we have in Gower's treatments of sound-play several good indications of how his poetry was built. What we may call the aural 'color,' or tone, of Gower's English work is supported in significant measure by elements common to the indigenous tradition, and which he he adapted to compliment a lengthy, short-lined poem. To a lesser but still significant degree, such sonant echoes push along

---

[63] Patrick J. Gallacher, *Love, the Word, and Mercury: A Reading of John Gower's Confessio Amantis* (Albuquerque, NM, 1975) 1-25.

the sense. Nevertheless, we would be mistaken to think of Gower as too much an alliterative poet. For stylistic precept and inspiration he turned, like Chaucer, to classical poets, to the *Roman de la Rose*, and to the lyrics of Deschamps and Machaut. Given these models, it is no surprise to find rhyme a *primus inter pares* alongside other phonal repetitions in Gower's vernacular poetry. We need to look now more closely at what Gower did with rhyme.

As a general rule, Gower wrote masculine rhymes and concluded lines regularly on stressed syllables. In his French poetry, this is less often the case than in his English work. There are many feminine rhymes in the *Mirour*, as one might expect; and they echo both each other and masculine rhymes too, as in the following:

> Tant perservoit le deble a gré
> Sa jofne file en son degré
> Et tant luy fist plesant desport,
> Dont il fuist tant enamouré,
> Que sur sa file ad engendré
> Un fils, que l'en appella Mort.   (*MO*, 217-22)

Moreover, Gower's rhymes are almost always 'true.' Usually they repeat a single syllable (i.e., 'preie/weie,' 'pacience/defence') although sometimes two syllables rhyme ('kinges/thinges') when the context and meter require it. Perhaps his 'fanciest' rhyme is of the 'thus/Phorceus' (*CA* I, 389-90) sort; he has nothing to equal the complex and startling music Chaucer achieved when he rhymed several syllables: 'annueleer/many a yeer' (*CYT*, VIII, 1011-12); 'Morpheus/ moo fees thus' (*BD* 265-66). On the whole, Gower's rhyming is conservative, even if it includes occasional moments of surprise.

Yet to describe Gower's rhymes in this way is not to dismiss them as easily achieved. Again, we ought to see in the unbroken regularity of his English rhymes evidence of deliberate and judicious choice. Clear, true and strong rhyme defines his style, and it represents one thoughtful response to a shifting English language just as, in its different way, Chaucer's does. Perhaps we can get a sharpened sense of this by taking a close look at a single example. *Rime riche*, as Gower handles it, makes a good case in point.

Rime riche is, as the critical handbooks tell us, the jointure at verse-end of words which sound the same. These may be homonyms, the same word used as a rhyme for itself, or different grammatical forms of the same word, as in the following:

> When every bird has chose his *make*
> And thenkth his merthes for to *make*.   (*CA* I, 101)

Like Chaucer, Gower employed *rime riche* often. The technique was highly praised, particularly in France, and it seems likely that Gower fastened onto it early in his career, when he was writing primarily in French. *Rime riche* turns up in the *Mirour*, for example, about once every hundred lines.[64] Since several of these same rhyming pairs recur, minimally Anglicised, in the late verse, it looks as if Gower learned his craft in French and borrowed from himself.[65] But whenever he started, and under whatever influence, clearly Gower liked *rime riche* for the patterns it could create. Its aesthetics must have pleased him, its potential for elegant, aural interlace. At the end of Book III (2750-61), for example, Genius and Amans share the following exchange:

> Mi sone, er we departe atwinne,
> I schal behinde nothing *leve*.
>   Mi goode fader, *be your leve*,
> Than axeth forth what so you list,
> For I have in you such a trist,
> As ye that be my Soule *hele*,
> That ye fro me wol nothing *hele*,
> For I schal telle you the trowthe.
>   Mi Sone, art thou coupable of Slowthe
> In eny point which to him *longeth*?
>   Mi fader, of tho pointz me *longeth*
> To wite pleinly what they meene.

The jointure of speeches here using *rime riche* — Genius first to Amans, then Amans again to Genius — is pretty work, and in the French poetic manner quite fancy. 'Hele/hele' at about mid-point in Amans's reply is a nice addition, too. Of course, this sort of jingling is hardly profound work. Yet there is good reason for us to take notice of it. It offers us something we overlook too often when we conjure up 'moral Gower': a glimpse of him having a bit of fun in verse.

But — gracenote appeal aside — Gower had uses for *rime riche* beyond mere ornament. His development of the form is quite sophisticated, evolving in several directions at once. At the center, however, is the challenge of the octosyllabic couplet itself. All choices, we know, have consequences. Because it is a simple, repetitive structure, the couplet — especially the shorter couplet — is a demanding form. Great skill is needed to keep a long poem written in couplets from sing-song monotony. Chaucer and Gower both faced this problem when they settled on couplets for the *Canterbury Tales* and the *Confessio Amantis*. Among Chaucer's solutions was the casting of some of his tales in other patterns — rhyme royal, tail-rhyme, 'Monk's stanza,' even prose. Chaucer could do this

[64] The statistic is Masayoshi Ito's; see 'Gower's Use of Rime Riche in the *Confessio Amantis*, as Compared with His Practice in the *Mirour de l'Omme* and with the Case of Chaucer,' *Studies in English Literature* (English Literature Society of Japan), 46 (1969), 29-44.
[65] *Rimes Riches* common to the *Mirour* and the *Confessio* are (in order of frequency) commune/commune (*MO*, communer), 5; mesure/mesure, 4; preie/preie (*MO*, proie), 3; point/point (*MO*, poignt), 2; pleigne/ pleigne, 2; peine/peine, 2; note/note, 2; glose/glose, 1; blame/blame, 1. The figures are Ito's, 'Rime Riche,' p. 32.

with a certain fictive justification, since in theory the tales are told by different narrators, each of whom would have had a separate voice. But this course was not open to Gower, or at least not so easily, in a poem with essentially a single narrator. (When he had the chance — in Amans's 'Supplication' to Venus in Book VIII — Gower adopted Chaucer's program and used iambic pentameter rhyme royal stanzas.) And Gower was working with a line a foot shorter than Chaucer's. What to do?

Gower's answer, like Chaucer's, was 'several things,' and we have looked at one or two of them already. The passages above, describing Medea's sorcery and Morpheus's cave, show how Gower sometimes chose to treat the problem. There, as we saw, he varied the rhythm, the meter and caesurae, and irregularly alternated end-stopped and enjambed lines. These methods overrule the line-ends, and hence mask the repeating rhyme.

But again — there is a cost. To have variation you must retain a sense of the norm. We know this from the sonata, for example, where a recurrent motif unifies what are often quite dissimilar movements, thereby providing the thin line between our pleasure and shapelessness. Gower's second strategy to subvert monotony in his couplets must have been analogously designed. He emphasizes the structure itself at intervals, returning to it forcefully, just as a musician reestablishes a melodic line. For this, *rime riche* is a splendid vehicle. The identical rhyme recalls the couplet form and, amid the variety, keeps us mindful of the poem's dominant 'tune.'

But in the *Confessio Amantis* especially, Gower also used *rime riche* in two additional ways — and they, in terms of his poetic, are perhaps more important. To see these we must pursue two apparently separate, but ultimately relatable, tracks. The first requires us to consider again how 'good English speech' works in the *Confessio*. For the second — the larger in scope — we must scrutinize the ironic potential of *rime riche*, as Gower exploited it in both his English and French poems.

A careful tabulation of the appearances of *rime riche* in the *Confessio Amantis* turns up a curious fact: Gower includes it more frequently in the conversations between Amans and Genius than he does in narrative situations.[66] What should we make of this? One conclusion, certainly, is that Gower deemed these speeches the most in need of embellishment. Stories on their own (he may have supposed), if they were good ones, offered sufficient material to keep his audiences attentive. Yet in many ways the exchanges between Genius and Amans are the most attractive parts of the *Confessio*. It is interesting, even charming, to watch the two of them grow into characters increasingly subtle and complex. Presumably Gower labored hard to create this unfolding; so that, logically, we might guess other factors molded his thinking, as well.

Primary among these is a dilemma of credibility generic to all art, including dramatic poems like the *Confessio Amantis*. One aspect of the problem is essentially technical. By what means does the artist persuade us to enter into a fiction far enough that we suspend our disbelief in its reality? The question has immediate

66 Ibid., p. 33.

relevance because 'real' dialogue isn't metrical; it does not conclude, as in the *Confessio*, in perfect rhyme every four beats. So, for his audience to accept as 'true' his proffered fiction ('good English speech,' as overheard from the mouths of 'good English speakers' — Amans, and Genius by proxy), Gower had to find a means to persuade us not to remark the obvious. But for a poet of Gower's learning, the issue would have had a complicated theoretical aspect as well. It surely raised the specter of an old debate about the proper way to regard poetic fictions, begun in the *Gorgias* and carried on into the Middle Ages by men whose works Gower knew: Aristotle, Cicero, Horace, Augustine.[67] How did one evaluate the illusionism art requires, especially in a universe controlled by a deity whose nature was Truth? Augustine's answer (Plato's exile of poets from the Republic notwithstanding) was to draw a fine distinction between the nature and purposes of fiction making. Art, *ipso facto* pretense, is most 'true' in its own terms when it deceives us fully. We acknowledge this when we praise one work for being 'like life,' and condemn another because it 'seems false.'[68] On the other hand, duplicity for its own sake, or for gain, was reprehensible.[69] Enlisted as a means to teach a moral lesson, therefore, the artist's deception could have significant worth.

Both Gower and Chaucer show themselves at home with this tradition, to different degrees. Chaucer seems the more comfortable, creating narratorial personae and poking fun at them right up to the end. Ultimately, however, he steps away from his masks and recalls us abruptly to Truth in the highest sense, at the conclusion of the *Troilus* and with the Parson's exhortation and the Retraction in the *Canterbury Tales*. But Gower, while he too develops Amans in the *Confessio* to stand in for himself, betrays his lack of confidence in the method from the outset. One function of his Prologue is, in fact, to warn the reader of the fictiveness of what his verses will recount; that is one effect of the authorial talk we find there about selecting a level of style. Likewise, in the Latin marginalia (*CA* I, 60), Gower provides a running commentary to gloss, from a seat of vision quite outside the poem, the value of the poetry as Truth. Here he tells us baldly that the narrator's 'I' is a calculated manufacture ('fingens se auctor esse Amantem') — and thus that the events of the *Confessio* did not take place.

In effect, then, Gower gives us Troilus's view from the eighth sphere (or Chaucer's from the Retraction) continually throughout his poem. He builds it in, so that — in good Augustinian fashion — his deception will be revealed to serve Truth. Yet Augustine's dicta are paradoxical masters. Good art involves

---

[67] See *Gorgias*, fragment 23; Aristotle, *De partibus animalium*, I, 5.645A, *Poetics*, IV, 1448B (Aristotle's remarks have to do with interpreting representations, in which category he includes animals as creations of an 'artistic spirit' — views which probably influenced Augustine); Cicero, *De inventione*, I, 27 and (in the medieval view, at least) *Rhetorica ad Herennium*, I, 13; Horace, *De arte poetica*, 151, 333-46; Augustine, see below, n. 68. The topic is explored in some depth by Edgar De Bruyne, *Études d'esthétique médiévale*, 3 vols. (Brussells, 1946), II, and more recently by Wesley Trimpi, 'The Ancient Hypothesis of Fiction: An Essay on the Origins of Literary Theory,' *Traditio* 27 (1971), 1-78.

[68] Augustine, *De ordine*, II, 40; *Soliloquies*, II, 17.

[69] Augustine, *Soliloquies*, II, 10, 15-17.

deception both complete as well as transparent. To solve this dilemma Gower
turned, as he usually did, to possibilities inherent in his language.

This is what Gower seeks to accomplish, in part through the use of *rime riche*. A
hint of what he is about is given by the vocabulary he chose for these rhymes. For
here we find a second curious fact: In the *Confessio rimes riches* are generally built of
word-pairs of native origin. Their elements have Old English, not French,
roots.[70] Looking closer, we discover that these very often take the form of the
following:

> And sche the king with wordes *wise*
> Knelende thonketh *in this wise*. (*CA* I, 3345-46)

Professor B. J. Whiting, who spent much time counting and classifying *bijoux* like
this in Chaucer's writing and in Gower's, called such phrases as *in this wise*
'colloquial devices.'[71] It is a helpful nomenclature, because expressive: Whiting's
term captures the prosaism of the language — both its 'Englishness' and its
'filler' quality — while, at the same time, suggesting that it might become a
'device' for making art. Familiar figures of speech like 'in this wise,' 'by your
leve,' 'as I rede,' which often turn up in Gower's *rimes riches*, serve three purposes
in the *Confessio Amantis*. Often they announce the advent of a new speaker — a
valuable technique in a long poem designed to be read aloud. ('In this wise' has
that function in the lines above: 'Sche' is the Bachilier's Daughter.) More
importantly (though just as clearly) they heighten the conversational flavor of the
poetry, urging us to forget that it *is* poetry, by bringing into it the sorts of
parentheses and qualifications with which average Englishmen commonly pace
their discourse. Such figures contribute directly to that sense of verisimilitude
required of dramatic poems.

But a third thing happens when, as Gower does, a poet joins 'colloquial
devices' with other lines, in *rime riche* couplets. Then a kind of hybrid language is
formed which sounds, at one and the same time, both like talking and like music:

> Bot for men sein, and soth it is,
> That who that al of wisdom writ
> It dulleth ofte a mannes wit
> To him that schal it aldai *rede*,
> For thilke cause, if that ye *rede*,
> I wol go the middel weie . . . (*CA* Pro., 12-17)

The example shows the technique at its simplest. Gower, in his authorial voice,
addresses us much as if he were standing before us, telling us that — if *we* choose

[70] See Ito, 'Rime Riche,' p. 30.
[71] Bartlett Jere Whiting, *Chaucer's Use of Proverbs*, Harvard Studies in Comparative
Literature, 11 (Cambridge, 1934).

('rede') — his poem will not only be of 'loore,' but will have as well some 'game' for us to 'rede' about. Of course, there is some deception here. When we have these lines (or the author) before us, the rest of the *Confessio* sprawls out, quite finished, ahead. The fact is that, truly, we do not have a choice. By opening the book, or taking a seat in the audience, we have already made a tacit commitment to hear the narrative out. Gower has gathered us successfully into the fictive universe of his poem, where both the 'voices' and the 'choices' seem legitimate.

Except that the *rime riche* keeps reminding us, like a kind of signpost, of our position *vis-à-vis* reality: that this is a poem, that we are engaged in an act of reading, or hearing, *about* events, not living them ourselves. The touch is light, but efficient. The single note restores an essential equilibrium. For, if Gower the 'speaker' ought to sound like anyone with whom we might have conversation, yet so is he also Gower the poet — and he must sound like *that*, as well.

Partly through the use of *rime riche*, then, Gower forged a recognizeable poetic idiom, one simultaneously 'natural' and (because melodic) artful too. This double vision, of the poem as experience and as artifact, is essential to Gower's larger purposes in the *Confessio*. It contributes directly to that 'middel weie' he identifies in the Prologue as his stylistic goal, and for which he strove throughout.

Another, more didactic use Gower had for *rime riche* he evolved from the abeyant contrast of elements in the rhymes themselves. Here a potential for irony exists which Gower frequently exploited, both in the *Confessio* and in the *Mirour de l'Omme*.

> For al such time of love is lore,
> And lich unto the *bitterswete*;
> For thogh it thenke a man ferst *swete*,
> He schal wel fielen ate *laste*
> That it is sour and may noght *laste*. (*CA* VIII, 190-94)

These are two neat tropes, at once pleasing to the ear and pointedly didactic. The whole passage from which the lines above are excerpted contains Genius's admonition to Amans to avoid the illusory pleasures of lust and embrace instead the just and satisfying joys of marriage. The *rimes riches* underscore this point, first and most obviously in the yoking of 'bitterswete' and '[ferst] swete,' where lurks the implicit irony of satisfaction's inevitable decline; then, more subtly, with the bringing together of '[ate] laste' (noun) with '[may noght] laste' (verb). The grammatical differences bear noting here. If 'ate laste' expresses finality, an achieved state, proof against mutability, so the idea of 'may noght laste,' caught by the motile verb, signifies the opposite. And if we recall that some among Gower's audience might have heard in 'ate laste' an echo, as of some distant bell, of that great and coming finality — the Judgment at the end of time — the irony grows apace.[72] As does, of course, our sense of what Genius knows and can tell us about the wages of fleshly love.

---

[72] See *MED*, s.v. 'laste,' adj., 7(b), in the phrase 'ate laste,' defined as 'At the end of

VII

Gower's handling of *rime riche*, then, can be both subtle and highly suggestive.
Clearly he thought the technique more than just a little fun with the way words
sound. In his poetic, *rime riche* offered a means to reinforce the special lesson of a
passage, even to advance the larger issues of a lengthy poem. The *Mirour de
l'Omme* includes a good illustration:

> Au jour present, car de saint Piere
> Om monte et prent la digneté,
> Le dyademe et la *chymere*,
> Mais ja n'en font plus que *chymere*
> Au remenant la dueté.   (*MO*, 18812-16)

Here the *rime riche* directs our attention to a play on sound *and* sense. Gower's
'joke' is rather learned, but probably not so recondite that the *Mirour*'s clerical
readers missed its nasty barb. The subject here is the Antipope, Clement VIII,
reigning in Avignon at the time of Gower's writing. In the verses preceding these
lines, Gower compares Clement to the Antichrist (ll. 18793 ff.), to the scribes and
Pharisees who blasphemously preached from the seat of Moses (ll. 18805 ff.),
and, in the line immediately following those quoted, to a 'monstre . . . due . . .
quelque gendre.' The *rime riche* 'chymere/chymere' is thus also a pun — on
'chimere,' a bishop's hat, and 'chimaera,' the lion-headed, goat-bodied, serpent-
tailed beast from Greek myth, slain by Bellerophon. Gower's complex framing is
characteristic. The succeeding idea of a 'monstre' judiciously underscores the
point; and so does the trajectory of metaphor as we follow it throughout the
passage. The images form an arc, descending from the potent evil of Antichrist to
scrabbling scribes and Pharisees to, finally, the French pope arrayed as fraud's
icon, a brute whose limbs themselves are not its own, but only a collocation of
thefts.
    Puns are not always related to *rime riche*, of course — not in the rhetoric books,
and not in Gower's practice. Yet (some might say, unfortunately) Gower punned
often; and often enough the ironic effect of his *rime riche* couplets depends, as in

---

one's life, at one's death; at the end of the world.' Examples of this usage include John of
Trevisa and *Castle of Love*, ca. 1390. The *OED*, s.v. 'last,' adj., 2, gives a similar reading:
'Belonging to the end or final stage, especially belonging to the end of life or the end of the
world.' But even more interesting may be another possible connotation of the word. *OED*,
s.v. 'last,' sb. 3 and *MED*, s.v. 'last,' n. 3 devolve from OE 'læst' and ON/OI 'lostr'/
'löstr' meaning (in the *MED* definition) 'a) a moral defect, a vice, a sin; b) quality of
sinfulness, wickedness, guilt; c) grounds for blame, fault, discredit.' Citations showing
this usage include *Cursor Mundi*, *Patience*, *Cleanness*, *Brut*, *Sir Ferumbras*. None of these are
courtly works, and indeed they show provincial dialect features in which ON derivatives
figure more prominently than in London speech. But Gower might have played on this
meaning too; and if so, the final couplet would carry a double pun, including the meaning
'He shall feel that sin, once committed, is sour and its sweetness will not stay.'

the example above, on an intricate paranomasia. I say 'unfortunately,' because
our limited modern view of puns as 'the lowest form of humor' makes a short
digression necessary here, to sharpen our awareness of Gower's praxis. Few of
his puns are, or were meant to be, funny. Rather, he was following what for him
was the classical rhetorical tradition, where puns — and rhymes too — were
anatomized as kinds of verbal ornament.[73] In the Latin poetry (which of course
he never rhymed), Gower made grammatical puns primarily:

> Sic differt *Clemens* nunc a *clemente* vocatus,
> Errat et Acephalo nomine nomen habens.   (*VC* III, 955-56)

The subject of the attack is again Pope Clement. Two puns are actually
functioning here. The more obvious is a play on Clement's name (from Latin
'clemens,' 'kind' or 'merciful'). Given his behavior as pope, Gower points out,
Clement really ought not to keep his name 'Acephalo' — that is, 'without a
head,' or a prefix. Clearly the reader is intended to add the prefix himself,
making Clement no longer 'clemens' but '*in*clemens' ('harsh,' 'unmerciful'). As
it happens, this pun has a history which Gower possibly knew.[74] His original
touch here is to combine this pun with 'acephalus,' which meant both 'headless'
and also 'heretic.'[75] The economy of the pun makes it powerful: With two strokes
Gower has reduced Pope Clement to (In)clement and heretic. Save Milton, no
other English poet exerted such control over Latin satiric punning.

In English, it is unnecessary to go beyond the first hundred lines of the
Prologue to the *Confessio Amantis* to learn what Gower can do with a 'simple' pun:

> What wysman that it underfongeth,
> He schal drawe into remembrance
> The fortune of this worldes chance,
> The which noman in his persone
> Mai know, bot the god *al one*.   (*CA* Pro., 68-72)

---

[73] That is, the tradition which included Geoffrey of Vinsauf and the *Rhetorica ad
Herennium*, which Gower would have thought the work of Cicero. R. B. Daniels, 'Rhetoric
in Gower's "To King Henry IV, In Praise of Peace",' *Studies in Philology*, 32 (1935) 6273,
claims that Gower knew and used Geoffrey's *Poetria Nova*. James Murphy, 'John Gower's
Confessio Amantis and the First Discussion of Rhetoric in the English Language,'
Philological Quarterly, 41 (1962) 401-11, traces Gower's rhetoric to Brunetto Latini.
Whatever Gower's precise sources, it is certain that such books formed part of his
training.
[74] Geoffrey of Vinsauf plays upon 'Innocent' and 'nocent' to describe Pope Innocent III;
see his 'Dedication' to the *Poetria Nova* in Edmond Faral, *Les Artes poétiques du XIIe et du
XIIIe siècle: Recherches et documents sur la technique littéraire du moyen âge* (Paris, 1962), p. 97.
[75] *A Latin Dictionary*, ed. Charlton T. Lewis and Charles Short (Oxford, 1879), s.v.
'acephalus,' with examples.

'One,' from Old English 'an,' carries the two meanings 'single' and 'solitary,' 'alone.'[76] Thus, while the primary contextual sense of the line is 'God alone knows the fate of the world,' there is also a strongly doctrinal overtone: 'the one, true, *single* God' who includes three persons simultaneously within His unity. The diaeresis facilitating the pun is particularly well placed: Gower's specific aim in the rest of the passage is to hold man's meagre knowledge up against the deep wisdom of God — a wisdom rooted in, and exemplified by, the triune mystery of 'three in one.'

Gower's puns, then, can be knotty things. Invariably they are learned, didactic and, for the most part, heavily ironic. This is particularly the case when he joins them to *rime riche* couplets. I want to consider two further examples, from the *Confessio Amantis*, to illustrate his range. Describing the avaricious clergy as corrupt shepherds who ravage their own flocks, Gower remarks:

> The scharpe pricke in stede of salve
> Thei usen now, wherof the *hele*
> Thei hurte of that they scholden *hele*.   (*CA* Pro., 396-98)

The primary meaning of the lines is 'Wicked priests destroy the (spiritual) health ('hele') of those whom they should cure ('hele'). However, 'hele' may also mean 'heel' (OE 'haela'), and this thickens the reading considerably.[77] The image of the greedy priests using a 'scharpe pricke' to wound the heel of those they ought to serve recalls one of the best-known Biblical admonitions, God's words to the serpent in Genesis 3:15:

> I will put enmities between thee and the woman, and thy seed and her
> seed: she shall crush thy head, and thou shalt lie in wait for her heel.[78]

Commentators sometimes linked this passage with Gen. 49:17: 'Let Dan be a snake, a serpent in the path, that biteth the horse's heels that his rider may fall backward.' Gower's pun thus operates within a congeries of Biblical allusion. The 'scharpe pricke' becomes the shadow of the serpent's fang, and the priests the serpent. The fate of the Danites is probably telling, too. They turned away from God, to worship idols (Judges 30-31). Later, in Book V of the *Confessio*, Gower, following Augustine, defined avarice as a form of idolatry — suggesting a

---

[76] We see in Gower's usage the etymology of our modern 'alone,' which represents the combination of the adverb 'al' ('wholly') and 'on'/'oon'/'one' in order to emphasize unity either temporary or continuous. The collocation appears in the thirteenth century and was common in Gower's time (*MED*, s.v. 'on,' pn., 3[b]). Chaucer, in *Boece* III, met. 6, 23, employs 'allone' in this manner. See also *Troilus and Criseyde*, V, 1863-65.

[77] Gower's orthographic practice is to employ 'hiel(le)' throughout, to render OE '-ae;' but 'hele' appears in Chaucer (e.g., *HF* 2154; *LGW* 863), and regardless of how Gower himself heard the word, he could have counted on his audience hearing a pun.

[78] This and other translations of the Bible are from the Douai-Rheims version.

reticulation here for him of these scriptural passages and covetous clergy.[79] Thus
Gower has made his point artfully, using *rime riche* and a sophisticated pun.
Another example, somewhat more extended, of Gower's interplay of puns and
rime riche is apparent in the following:

> And thus cam ferst to mannes Ere
> The feith of Crist and alle *goode*
> Thurgh hem that thanne weren *goode*
> And sobre and chaste and large and wyse.
> Bot now men sein is otherwise,
> Simon the cause hath undertake,
> The worldes swerd on honde is take;
> And that is wonder natheles,
> Whan Crist him self hath bode pes
> And set it in his testament,
> And now that holy cherche is went,
> Oft that here lawe positif
> Hath set to make were and strif
> *For worldes good*, which may noght laste.　　(*CA* Pro., 236-49)

Ecclesia, Gower asserts, has been corrupted by simoniacs who wage war for lucre.
These hypocrites have turned the church from the best interests of the world
('good,' in the moral sense) to its 'goods,' while cynically mouthing the gospel
('good news') of Christ. The *rime riche* 'goode/goode' thus focuses attention on
'worldes good,' in effect preparing an ironic context for the rhetorical question it
poses: What *is* the good of the world, and for man? Gower thus exacts a
meditated vengeance here. His pun, so carefully furthered by the preceding *rime
riche*, repays the church in kind for its hypocrisy — with 'double talk' of his own.

And so we come to the point of a chapter like this — which is, really, to be able to
return to the beginning with a richer idea of what was said there. John Fisher,
whose words got us started, has found a 'most impressive feature' of Gower's to
be 'the unity and coherence of [his] world-view and the success with which he
managed to infuse into a heterogeneous mass of conventional material a personal

---

[79] For the idolatry of the Danites, see Judges 18:29-31, and III Kings 12:29-30.
Augustine, in *De magistro* IX.26, takes the position that any substituted thing, including
words for the Divine Word, constitutes an idol. Dante echoes this in his punishment of the
usurers in *Inferno* XVII, 54-57:
> . . . ma io m'accorsi
> Che dal collo a ciascun pendea una tasca
> Ch'avea certo colore e certo segno,
> E quindi par che'l loro occhio si pasca.
The 'tasca,' each with its own emblem, was all the usurers cared for in life; it was then, as
now in hell, the idol on which they placed their hopes. Theirs is a fitting punishment.
Gower's treatment of the avaricious parallels Dante's.

vision capable still of commanding our respect.'[80] I have claimed that Gower's poetic was an encompassing one, as meticulously responsive to the 'least' details of verse as to the 'large.' This is the way, I believe, he shaped a 'personal vision' from the 'heterogeneous mass.' For my argument is that Gower did not himself distinguish between 'large' and 'least,' 'poetry' from 'mere metrics' or 'rhetoric' (or moral philosophy) when he wrote. He was aware — as I hope even these few pages show — of the holistic nature of the literary enterprise, of how in the end the measure of the world's great effects is the sum of many small gestures done well.

---

[80] Fisher, *John Gower,* p. 203.

CHAPTER II: GOWER'S LINES

I

With the argument I have been making so far, I have tried to demonstrate how seriously Gower took matters of language, from scribal miswriting to the effective use of meter, rhyme, and word-play. The poetic limned in these pages is thus a man's portrait of sorts; and, if it is an accurate description, it should suggest to us a Gower more ambitious than we customarily see him, more meditative about the elements of *poesis*, more deliberative and artful about the choices of the writer's craft.

By 'ambitious' here I mean two closely related things. Individual aspiration, Gower's hope to acquire renown through authorship, is one, of course. Probably his great attention paid to small matters indicates that. But also inherent in Gower's approach to style is an ambitious expectation for the reading and/or listening skills of his audience. As we have seen, some of the effects Gower worked for require care and a degree of learning to appreciate. His contemplated readership is not quite Milton's high-toned 'fit . . . though few' — yet neither should we think he conceived the voice and techniques of the 'middel weie' to suit exclusively the middle-brow.

Certainly Gower was not unique in imagining, and writing for, an audience so seasoned. Chaucer we know anticipated thoughtful responses to *Troilus* from among his public — from Gower at least, and Strode. But there are differences between Chaucer's perspective and Gower's on this point which are real, and illuminating. Whereas Chaucer could accommodate gracefully a variety of tastes and abilities, serving up what might seem 'a folye/ As of a fox, or of a cok and hen' (*CT* VII, 3438-9) to those who wanted so to take it, Gower's narrower moral tolerance required a tighter linkage of didacticism and literary effect. In this he resembles another Ricardian, William Langland, more closely than he does Chaucer — a remark made less surprising if both poets' common ties to contemporary preaching are recalled.[1] Gower parts company with Langland, however, over the issue of language, and how it should be used. This distinction has been sensed, albeit not directly addressed, before. John Burrow offers us testimony when he says a comparative look at how the two writers revised texts left him 'the impression that Langland was, in general, more concerned [than was Gower] with what he said — what he had said in the earlier version, and

45

---

[1] For a comparative assessment of the preacherly characteristics of Chaucer, Langland and Gower see G. R. Owst, *Literature and Pulpit in Medieval England: A Neglected Chapter in the History of English Letters and of the English People* (New York, 1961) 227-31.

what he wanted to say now — than with how he said it.' Burrow means that when
Langland changed a passage he was apt to write it fresh, and incorporate new
matter; but Gower's revisions were more often single alterations of a word or
words.[2]

   Burrow's observation, despite his coming to it from an unrelated perspective,
is thus of a piece with the view of the poet we have been developing in these
pages. Both this assessment, and Burrow's, depend upon our seeing Gower
choosing every word, weighing each against another, refining and revising until
he made his point. Yet this assumption has not been made universally. Over the
years some of Gower's better readers have expressed suspicion that he worked
less responsibly. Whenever he could, so the argument goes, Gower used
verbatim other poets' words without citation, clearly hopeful they would be
mistaken for his own. Indeed, for such 'schoolboy plagiarism' he has been
criticized by his major editor, G.C. Macaulay.[3]

   Plagiarism is a hard charge; but it is also a rather anachronistic — and hence
inappropriate — one to levy against most medieval poets. We have various
grounds to dismiss it. The term presupposes distinct ideas of artistic originality
and literary property unfamiliar to most medieval writers. Indeed in England (if
we can assume a coterminous appearance for the concept and the word), few
would have understood Macaulay's accusation until the early seventeenth
century.[4] Standard rhetorical training, especially for writers in Latin, was, we
know, by example and imitation; nor were words considered the private
possessions they are today. Thus when we detect in a passage written by Geoffrey
of Vinsauf half a line from Virgil's third *Eclogue*, 'Cum totum vicisse putes, *latet
anguis in herba*,' we do not need to cry 'plagiarism.'[5] The anachronism of the
charge provides a ready defense for Geoffrey's practice. It seems unlikely that he
would have considered the phrase uniquely Virgil's, or his unacknowledged use
of it a theft.

   Most medieval cases of silent quotation are, like Geoffrey's, clear cut.
Nonetheless, the question itself is not altogether open-and-shut. Some medieval
writers were obviously aware of the 'otherness' of texts; indeed, they used that
knowledge for specific literary effect. In *The Consolation of Philosophy*, for example,
Boethius borrows well-known lines from Seneca's plays, excerpting and adapting
them to fit his moral context. This he does without explanatory comment.

---

[2] Burrow, *Ricardian Poetry*, 32.

[3] Macaulay, *Works*, IV, xxxii.

[4] The word in its various forms seems to appear in English about the turn of the century.
The *OED* cites Bishop Hall (*Satires*, IV as the earliest to use 'plagiary,' ca. 1597-98; Ben
Jonson (*Poetaster*), 'plagiarist,' 1601; Bishop Montagu (*Diatribes*), 'plagiarism,' 1621.

[5] For Geoffrey's text, see Faral, *Les artes poétiques*, 205. Following the advice of the author
of the *Rhetorica ad Herennium*, Geoffrey wrote his own examples; see the discussion by
Marjorie Curry Woods, ed., *An Early Commentary on the Poetria Nova of Geoffrey of Vinsauf*
(New York, 1985) xvi, n. 9.

Boethius's purpose seems to have been to provoke an educated readership to compare the wisdom of Lady Philosophy with Seneca's Orpheus and Hercules, and in this way to expose stoic heroism as an inadequate response to adversity.[6] Another sort of example is Langland's incorporation of bits of the Bible and the psalter into *Piers Plowman*, to ballast conclusions drawn by his characters.[7] It is hard to imagine a medieval audience holding the 'authorship' of the Latin lines in doubt (or — still less perhaps — Langland wanting to keep it secret), even when a quotation slips in unheralded by a customary tag.[8] Like Boethius, Langland must have calculated the effectiveness of his device directly in terms of an intertextuality he counted on being recognized. This, too, is a far cry from thievery.

For different reasons, then, it is difficult to call the practices of Geoffrey, Boethius and Langland plagiarism. But through their different examples we may see better the real problem Macaulay raises with his concerns about unacknowledged quotation. If Geoffrey's appropriation of Virgil's half-line suggests a 'typical' medieval attitude toward texts as common property, Boethius's use of Seneca, and Langland's of the Bible, tell us something else. They offer evidence that, at least at the beginning and at the close of the Middle Ages, authorial proprietorship was recognized, and drawn upon by poets seeking particular poetic effects. One way to compass such a conclusion is to acknowledge its anachronism, set against the standard characterized by Geoffrey. And this in turn opens the floodgates. For if Langland's preacherly quoting of scripture must represent a specific kind of recognition of the 'otherness' of texts, what do we say about Dante, or Petrarch, or Boccaccio? Clearly they too were anachronistic in the proprietary way they thought about their own — and others' — writing. Nor is it difficult to add Chaucer to this list as one who shared the Italians' attitudes. Patricia Kean, for one, has found at the center of the *Hous of Fame*. 'the relation of art . . . to other works of art as the objects of imitation' and also 'the problem of Chaucer's own, personal identity as a poet — his relationship to the great past, as represented by Virgil, and also his position in a line of descent which includes the little poets of the vernacular languages.'[9] Whether or not John Gower also belongs on such a list of 'moderns' is, in part, the major question of the following

[6] The argument is well made by Seth Lerer, *Boethius and Dialogue: Literary Method in The Consolation of Philosophy* (Princeton, N.J., 1985) 237-53.

[7] On Langland's use of quotation, see John A. Alford, 'Some Unidentified Quotations in *Piers Plowman*,' *Modern Philology*, 7 (1975), 390-99, and his 'More Unidentified Quotations in *Piers Plowman*,' *Modern Philology*, 81 (1984), 278-85.

[8] That is, Langland often locates his quotations: 'And Salomon seide þe same þat Sapience made,/ *Qui parcit virge odit filium*' (B.5. 38-39). Compare this with B.9. 186-88: 'Wreke þee wið wyuyng if þow wolt ben excused:/ *Dum sis vir fortis ne des tua robora scortis*;/ *Scribitur in portis, meretrix est ianua mortis*.' Alford, 'Some Unidentified Quotations,' 393, cites Prov. 7: 26-2 as the source. References to the B-text of Langland are taken from *Will's Visions of Piers Plowman, Do Well, Do-Better and Do-Best*, ed. George Kane and E. Talbot Donaldson (London, 1975).

[9] Patricia M. Kean, *Chaucer and the Making of English Poetry*, 2 vols. (London and Boston, 1972) I, 111.

pages. Thus, anachronistic or not, we have reason to treat Macaulay's accusation seriously.

It is with the Latin poems that Macaulay is concerned. These, he discovered, Gower built by piecing work of his own together with extensive quotations from others:

> not lines or couplets only, but passages of eight, ten, or even twenty lines from the *Aurora* of Peter Riga, from the poem of Alexander Neckham *De Vita Monachorum*, from the *Speculum Stultorum*, or from the *Pantheon*, so that in many places the composition is entirely made up of such borrowed matter variously arranged and combined.[10]

Subsequent studies have pursued the question further. John H. Fisher has drawn attention to the many excerpts from Ovid Gower spliced into the *Vox Clamantis* — but he has argued strongly against considering them mere copying. Fisher observes that in Gower's poem the borrowed lines 'do not express any experience or sentiment taken from Ovid. The . . . quotations . . . come from such a variety of contexts and are so tailored to fit their positions that if the passage [in the *Vox*] has any meaning, it must be that of the immediate author.'[11] Paul Beichner, who has examined Gower's treatment of Peter Riga, reached conclusions similar to Fisher's. In Beichner's view, whether Gower

> created a mosaic from slightly changed passages separated by hundreds or thousands of lines in the *Aurora*, or whether he used a long excerpt from one place, his context is original. And the general context of the *Vox Clamantis* . . . gives originality even to passages borrowed without change by removing them from the plane of the exegete's timeless moral interpretation of Scripture to the reformer's criticism of his own day.[12]

What is clear, then, is the fact of Gower's borrowing. But remaining under a cloud is the more important issue: *Why* did Gower treat texts in this manner? For the real question Macaulay raises (and which Fisher and Beichner do not answer) concerns intent. Plagiarism, like any theft, requires deliberation: Something known to belong to another must be taken, and a deception about true ownership be carried out. Implicit in the charge too is a notion of weakness — that a plagiarist steals what eludes his own production. Thus learning what we may

---

[10] Macaulay, *Works*, IV, xxxii-xxxiii.
[11] Fisher, *John Gower*, p. 149.
[12] Paul E. Beichner, 'Gower's Use of the *Aurora* in the *Vox Clamantis*,' *Speculum*, 30 (1955), 592.

about Gower's possible purposes for borrowing is important in ways we cannot ignore. If he did so out of strength, with a full cognizance of what he was about and a purpose behind it, we reach a different assessment of him at all levels of his craft than we can if, behind his practice, there lies an insufficiency, either of inspiration or art.

Let us look now at a sample of the evidence, ll. 1501-20 from Book I of the *Vox Clamantis*. (In the following, Gower's work appears first; below each line, and indented, is his Ovidian source.)

Qui prius attulerat *verum michi semper amorem*
    nam cum praestiteris *verum mihi semper amorem* (*Ex Ponto*, 4.6.23)
Tunc *tamen aduerso tempore* cessat *amor*:
    hic *tamen adverso tempore* crevit *amor* (*Ex Ponto*, 4.6.24)
Querebam fratres tunc fidos, non tamen ipsos
    quaerebam fratres, exceptis scilicet illis (*Tristia*, 3.1.65)
Quos suus optaret non genuisse pater.
    quos suus optaret non genuisse pater (*Tristia*, 3.1.66)
Memet in insidiis semper locuturus habebam,
Verbaque sum spectans pauca locutus humum:
    verbaque sum spectans pauca locutus humum (*Fasti*, 1.148)
Tempora cum blandis absumpsi vanaque verbis,
Dum mea sors cuiquam cogerat vlla loqui.
Iram multociens frangit responsio mollis,
Dulcibus ex verbis tunc fuit ipsa salus;
Sepeque cum volui conatus verba proferre,
Torpuerat gelido lingua retenta metu.
    torpuerat galido lingua retenta metu (*Heroides*, 11.82)
Non meus vt querat noua sermo quosque fatigat,
Obstitit *auspiciis lingua* retenta *malis*;
    substitit *auspicii lingua* timore *mali* (*Heroides*, 13.86)
Sepe meam mentem volui dixisse, set hosti
Prodere me timui, linguaque tardat ibi.
Heu! *miserum tristis fortuna tenaciter vrget,*
    an *miseros tristis fortuna tenaciter urget* (*Heroides*, 3.43)
Nec venit in fatis *mollior hora* meis.
    nec venit inceptis *mollior hora* malis (*Heroides*, 3.44)
Si genus est mortis male vivere, credo quod illo
    si genus est mortis male vivere, terra moratur (*Ex Ponto*, 3.4.75)
Tempore vita mea morsque fuere pares.[13]

Clearly, much has been introduced from Ovid to bolster this passage. As Fisher and Beichner noted, however, the borrowing shows an originality worth

[13] Macaulay, *Works*, IV, 63. Ovidian quotations are taken from the Loeb Library

remarking. The Ovidian lines are drawn from four unrelated poems and, within
them, from widely disparate contexts. They have also been combined in Gower's
passage to develop a wholly new meaning. A comparison of Gower's lines with
some of the original contexts of his excerpts will show this more precisely. As
Gower composed it, the passage may be translated:

> One who before had *always borne a sincere love for me* — even his love had
> ceased *in this time of adversity*. I then made a search for *faithful brothers, not
> those whom their father wished he had never begotten*. Whenever I was on the
> point of speaking, I considered myself to be in ambush; and *looking upon
> the ground, I uttered only a few words*. When my lot forced me to say
> something to somebody, I passed the time idly with glib talk. Again and
> again a soft answer turned away wrath, and my very safety depended
> upon agreeable words to convey my inclinations, *my halting tongue grew
> numb from a chilling fear*. In order that my talk might not consist of
> complaint about recent happenings and become burdensome to people,
> *my tongue remained firmly tied because of the hostile circumstances*: I was often
> inclined to declare my mind, but I was fearful of handing myself over to
> the enemy, and then my tongue grew hesitant. Alas! *A sad fate was
> persistently dogging me in my wretchedness, and an easier hour did not enter into my
> destinies. If to live in misery is a kind of death*, I believe that at that time my
> life and death were just alike.[14]

These verses form part of a description of the poet's dream, a lightly-veiled
allegory of the Peasants' Revolt of 1381. Speaking here as if in his own person,
Gower relates in preceding lines how he hid in the woods beneath a pile of loose
grass, weeping and in fear for his life should he be discovered by the marauding
bands of rebels, which he portrays — not inappropriately — as wild beasts. In
contrast, Gower found his 'always a sincere love for me' (*verum michi semper
amorem*) in a letter addressed by Ovid to his otherwise-unidentified friend Brutus.
'In this time of adversity' (*tamen adverso tempore*), however, Brutus stands by Ovid,
as Gower's nameless comrade does not. The larger context from the *Ex Ponto* is as
follows:

> I can swear with a clear conscience that you too utter the same prayer,
> Brutus — you whom I know from indubitable proof. For although you
> have *ever granted me sincere love*, yet your love has encreased *in this time of*

---

editions of Arthur Leslie Wheeler, *Tristia and Ex Ponto* (1953); Grant Showerman, *Heroides
and Amores* (1914); and Sir James George Frazer, *Fasti* (1951).
[14] The translation is primarily that of Stockton, *Major Latin Works*, 82. I have, however,
changed some punctuation and one or two words.

adversity. One who saw your tears that matched mine would have believed that both were to suffer punishment.[15]

The difference in meaning of the lines is, if anything, increased by viewing the contexts. Comparison of the next two lines as they appear in the *Vox Clamantis* and in Ovid's *Tristia*, where Gower found them, yields the same results. The faithful 'brothers' (*querebam fratres*) for whom Gower sought, 'not those whom their father had wished he had never begotten' (*quos suus optaret non genuisse pater*), are difficult to identify in the *Vox* — though perhaps Gower intended a religious allusion.[16] No obscurity exists in Ovid's poem, however. There, the first-person narrator is Ovid's latest book, come home to Rome in search of poetical 'brothers' whose 'father' — the exiled Ovid himself — regrets writing, since they have cost him dear. The book describes a search through the library in the temple of Apollo on the Palatine:

Then with even pace up the lofty steps I was conducted to the shining temple of the unshorn god, where alternating with the columns of foreign marble stand the figures of the Belids, the barbarian father with a drawn sword, and all those things which the men of old or of modern times conceived in their learned souls are free for the inspection of those who would read. *I was seeking my brothers, save those indeed whom their father would he had never begot*, and as I sought to no purpose, from that abode the guard who presides over the holy place commanded me to depart.[17]

However he meant us to understand this passage, the meaning of the lines Gower borrowed in no way corresponds to the sense of those lines in his source. Juxtaposing the remaining borrowed verses in Gower's passage against their

[15]   te quoque idem liquido possum iuare precari,
               o mihi non dubia cognite Brute nota.
           nam cum praesteteris verum mihi semper amorem,
               hic tamen adverso tempore crevit amor.
           quique tuas pariter lacrimas nostrasque videret,
               passuros poenam crederet esse duos.
See Wheeler, *Tristia and Ex Ponto*, p. 442.

[16] Fisher has suggested that the 'fratres' here may be intended to signify 'the faithful brothers of St. Mary Overeys.' See *John Gower*, p. 148.

[17]   inde tenore pari gradibus sublima celsis
               ducor ad intonsi candida templa dei,
           signa peregrinis ubi sunt alterna columnis,
               Belides et stricto barbarus ense pater,
           quaeque viri docto veteres cepere novique
               pectore, lecturis inspicienda patent.
           quarebam fratres, exceptis scilicet illis,
               quos suus optaret non genuisse pater.
           quaerentem frustra custos e sedibus illis
               praepositus sancto iussit abire loco.

original contexts yields the same results — but the exercise is unnecessary to make the point here. Nor need we cite further composite passages to do so, though this is quite possible: approximately one third of the *Vox Clamantis* contains splicings from other sources, altered, like those just examined, very slightly and put to serve a meaning wholly new.[18] What Gower attempted with these expropriations was not, in any strict sense, plagiarism, then. But can it be said to be anything in particular?

Indeed, very likely it can. In its concentration and method Gower's quotation resembles nothing so much as the technique of cento or ('patchwork') verse, a poem comprised of lines and line-parts selected from the work of a renowned poet of an earlier time and recombined in a fresh order and to a different effect.[19] Historically, however, cento has not been thought a late medieval form. There are a number of early Greek examples, reaching back as far as Aristophanes. Lucian wrote them, and even the Byzantine empress Eudocia is reported to have composed *Homerokentrones*.[20] Among Latin writers, Virgil replaced Homer as the source for centos most often quarried. We have extant the *Medea* of Hosidius Geta from the second century A.D., employing passages from the *Aeneid* throughout, and some suggestion as well of earlier effort.[21] The Virgilian tradition lasts into the fourth century, as is represented by the *Cento Nuptialis* of Ausonius, and by the Christian centos of Anicia Faltonia Proba, Pomponius, Luxorius, and perhaps Sedulius.[22] During these years too the works of Ovid and Statius became acceptable sources. Thereafter a decline in the popularity of cento seems to have occurred. Although we may agree with F.J.E. Raby that 'the centos continued . . . to be admired and read' and that 'the Carolingians can hardly have overlooked them,' we know of no new centos being composed until the tenth century when the *Ecbasis Captivi* and one or two lesser pieces re-established medieval interest in the form.[23] Scholarly opinion commonly holds that the following three centuries produced no surviving examples, if in fact centos were written at all; the next great period of cento production appears to

Lines and translation are from Wheeler, *Tristia and Ex Ponto*, p. 104.
[18] Other significant 'cento' sections in the *Vox Clamantis* include: Book III, chap. 2 (primarily Peter Riga and Ovid); Book IV, ll. 395-486 (primarily Alexander Neckham); Book V, ll. 957-76 (primarily *Remedia Amoris*); Book VI, ll. 937-92 (primarily Peter Riga). See further Stockton, *Major Latin Works*, notes and index for additional *loci*.
[19] See *The Oxford Classical Dictionary*, ed. N.G.L. Hammond and H.H. Scullard, 2nd edn. (Oxford, 1970), s.v. 'cento.'
[20] For Aristophanes's mention of cento, see *Peace*, 1090-94. Lucian, *Convivium*, 17, tells of a 'very funny song' composed using Hesiod, Anacreon, Pindar and Homer by one 'Histiaeus the Grammarian.' For the cento of Empress Eudocia, see Eduard Stemplinger, *Das Plagiat in der griechischen Literatur* (Leipzig and Berlin, 1912) 193 ff.
[21] On Hosidius, see August Pauly and Georg Wissowa, *Real-Encyclopaedie der classischen Altertumswissenschaft, Neue Bearbeitung, unter Mitwirkung zahlreicher fachgenossen*, 2nd series, 67 vols. (Stuttgart, 1894-1972) VI, col. 1932. Petronius mentions possible early centos of, or using, Pindar, *Satyricon*, 2; the parodies of Aelius Donatus, *Vita Vergiliana*, 43, should also be compared.
[22] See Pauly-Wissowa, *Real-Encyclopaedie*, VI, cols. 1931-32.
[23] F.J.E. Raby, *A History of Secular Latin Poetry in the Middle Ages*, 2 vols., 2nd edn. (Oxford, 1957) I, 44-45.

have begun in fifteenth-century Italy, whence it spread throughout the Renaissance.[24]

The objections to Gower's embellishing the *Vox Clamantis* with cento, then, are potentially large, and we will do best to state them forthrightly. Cento appears to flourish when certain conditions are in place: available texts, a literate audience well schooled in the same works, a social aptitude and custom for close reading of poetry. These were present for Ausonius, for Proba; and for the second efflorescence of centos in Italy there was the community of humanistic writers to support and direct interest, as well as the ready availability of antique verse in manuscript and (by then) printed books. If Gower were writing cento — deliberately, and with near-classical skill — he would have been rather solitary in the poetic world of fourteenth-century London; conceivably, indeed, he stood unique amidst his times. Would it have been possible for him to discover the cento and understand its characteristics, working alone and with resources extant in England in the latter 1300s?

A variety of factors combine to suggest a positive answer. What we know of Gower's biography and cast of mind marks him a bookish man, deeply and widely read, with access to a significant collection of texts. Whether these were his own possessions, or the property of the library at St. Mary Overeys priory in Southwark where he lived for many years, or were borrowed from friends and libraries in and about London is impossible to say. The results of his extensive reading are clear nevertheless from the many sources, medieval and ancient, which lie behind his poems. In addition to Ovid, Peter Riga, Nigel Wirecker, and Alexander Neckham — names we have already mentioned — a list of others whose work influenced Gower would include Virgil, Statius, Livy, Hyginus, Lucretius, Brunetto Latini, Vincent of Beauvais, Jean de Meun, Alain de Lille, Dante, Martianus Capella, John of Garland, Nicholas Trivet, Peter Lombard, John of Salisbury, Jacobus de Voragine, and Geoffrey of Monmouth.[25] Nor

---

[24] See Max Manitius, *Geschichte der lateinischen Literatur des Mit telalters*, 3 vols. (Munich, 1911-13) I, 618; and also O. Delepierre, *Révue analytique des Ouvrages écrits en Centons, depuis les Temps anciens, jusqu'au XIXieme Siècle* (London, 1868) 107-3 and 141-47, for one or two additional anonymous centos of late Latinity and the thirteenth century. See further R. Lammachia, 'Dall'arte allusiva al centone,' *Atene e Roma*, n.s. 3 (1958), and Raby, *A History of Christian-Latin Poetry from the Beginnings to the Close of the Middle Ages*, 2nd edn. (Oxford, 1953) 138-39, who notes that 'reminiscences of Virgil, Ovid, Horace, Juvenal, Claudian, and Sallust, to say nothing of Prudentius' are to be found in the prose and poetry of Columban. On early Renaissance editions of centos, see Delepierre, *Révue analytique*, pp. 148-363, who prints a number; Sister Maria Jose Byrne, *Prolegomena to an Edition of the Works of Decimus Magnus Ausonius* (New York, 1916), 81-83; and Filipo Ermini, *Il centone di Proba e la poesia centonaria latina* (Rome, 1909), 68-70.

[25] No single study attempts to deal with all of Gower's sources. Useful, however, are discussions by Maria Wickert, *Studien zu John Gower* (Cologne, 1953), now translated by Robert J. Meindl as *Studies in John Gower* (Washington, D.C., 1981); Gallacher, *Love, the Word, and Mercury*; Peck, *Kingship and Common Profit*; and Macaulay's notes, passim. See also the 'Subject Index' to my own *John Gower Materials: A Bibliography through 1979* (New York, 1981).

should we forget Chaucer, whose reading Gower must have shared, at least vicariously, in many ways. Gower's thorough knowledge of his books can be stressed, too. Unlike many medieval writers who seem to have relied primarily upon *florilegia*, Gower gives evidence again and again of an intimate acquaintance with his manuscripts from beginning to end. From them he drew not only narrative material and rhetorical ornament, but also the learning they contained. Reading habits such as these might have brought Gower into contact with cento verse, if any were to be found in England; moreover, his customary thoroughness with texts would have been suited to absorbing, as well as practicing, the style.

Determining what examples of cento Gower could have seen in England is problematic, given the state of surviving records. Nevertheless, certain inferences may be drawn, some of them helpful. To begin with we may rule out the *Ecbasis Captivi*, an extensive beast-allegory similar in many ways to Book I of the *Vox Clamantis*. Manuscripts of the *Ecbasis* are rare (two are believed to exist today), and they appear to have circulated only in Germany.[26] With Ausonius we are on somewhat firmer ground. Manuscripts of the *Cento Nuptialis* existed in England, at Peterborough and Glastonbury at least.[27] Ausonius retained some fame in the fourteenth century as a rhetor and maker of verbal ornament, and it is logical to suppose that a man with Gower's evident taste for classical authors would have been led to read (if hardly enjoy) him, were the opportunity available. That Gower makes no mention of Ausonius is not evidence to the contrary. Like most medieval writers he seldom cites all of his sources; and even when he does the information is often too general to be clear. Probably significant, however, is his failure to follow Ausonius's expressly stated opinion that the best centos are constructed of partial lines, never of a whole line or more taken intact.[28] As the example shows above, Gower frequently incorporated lines in clusters. Of

---

[26] Both manuscripts of the *Ecbasis*, now in the Royal Library at Brussels, very likely came from the monastery of St. Eucharius in Trier, and seem to have remained close by; see Karl Strecker, ed., *Ecbasis cuiusdam Captivi per Tropologiam*, in *Scriptores rerum Germanicarum in usum Scholarum ex Monumentis Germaniae Historicis* (Hannover, 1935) viii-x.

[27] On the manuscripts of Ausonius, see Rudolf Peiper, ed., *Decimi Magni Ausonii Burdigalensis, Opuscula* (Leipzig, 1886), xviii-lviii; and Manitius, *Geschichte*, I, 307, n. 6.

[28] As Ausonius described it, cento was the fitting together of 'scattered tags . . . into a whole,' to 'harmonize different meanings, to make pieces arbitrarily connected seem naturally related, to let foreign elements show no chink of light between, to prevent the far-fetched from proclaiming the force which united them' ('. . . colligere et integrare lacerata . . . pari modo sensus diversi ut congruant, adoptiva quae sunt, ut cognate videantur, aliena ne interlucent arcessita ne vim redarguant . . .'); but he also stated pointedly, in the prefatory letter to his *Cento Nuptialis*, 'And if you will suffer me, who need instruction myself, to instruct you, I will expound what a cento is. It is a poem compactly built out of a variety of passages and different meanings, in such a way that either two half-lines are joined together to form one, or one line and the following half with another half. For to place two [whole] lines side by side is weak, and three in succession is mere trifling' ('Et si pateris, ut doceam docendus ipse, cento quid sit, absolvam. variis de locis sensibusque diversis quaedam carminis structura solidatur, in unum versum ut coeant aut caesi duo aut unus et sequens [medius] cum medio. nam duos iunctim locare ineptum est, et tres una serie merae nugae.') Text and translation from the Loeb Library edition of Hugh G. Evelyn White (Cambridge, Mass, 1951) I, 372-73.

Sedulius's supposed cento, the *De Verbi Incarnatione*, we have no report which places it within Gower's reach — although its content would seem to be potentially more to his taste. While it is possible Gower read Sedulius in some form (for his poems were often combined in manuscript with such familiar poets as Venantius Fortunatus), no proof exists to confirm or deny the supposition.[29] Nor do we know of manuscripts of Pomponius or Luxorius which Gower might have seen.

Where then might Gower have encountered cento? All factors considered, the work and reputation of Anicia Faltonia Proba offers the strongest likelihood of being Gower's source. Although Gower never refers to her, or quotes from her directly, various signs point toward his having known of her *Cento Virgilianus*. It was the most famous cento in the Middle Ages, with many manuscripts still extant. Several are of late provenance, and testify to a continuing interest in the poem.[30] And some of these manuscripts were in England in Gower's time — though whether he was aware of them we cannot say.[31]

One intriguing possibility is offered by MS Trinity College, Cambridge 0.7.7, however. This manuscript, copied in the early thirteenth century, contains a dozen pieces in addition to Proba's *Cento*. Nearly all of these — by Bernard Sylvestris, Ovid, Seneca, and Jerome — are works familiar to Gower.[32] Two pieces especially are striking the anonymous 'Letter of Alexander to Aristotle from India,' and part of the *Res Gestae Alexandri Macedonis* of Julius Valerius.

Now, Alexander stories were popular with Gower. They appear throughout his writings, in the narrative poems and the lyrics as well, perhaps because Alexander's mythical life exemplified so many of Gower's major themes of love, chivalry and kingship. In the *Confessio Amantis* they figure prominently. All of Book VII represents Aristotle's program of education for Alexander — a recitation Genius provides at the special request of Amans, whose 'herte sore longeth' (ll. 2408 ff.) to hear it.

The long central narrative of Book VI (ll. 1789-2352) also concerns Alexander. There Genius relates the apocryphal sireing of the king by the Egyptian magician Nectanabus. For this tale, Julius Valerius's *Res Gestae* served as Gower's primary source. (That there are also two others, which he used to supplement Valerius, suggests a commitment to getting details 'right' — and so his seriousness about the way the story mattered.)[33] The *Res Gestae* was a relatively popular piece in the Middle Ages, so that Gower was scarcely limited to the Trinity College

[29] Ermini, *Il centone*, lists contents of various manuscripts containing works by Sedulius, pp. 65-66; see also Pauly-Wissowa, *Real Encyclopaedia*, 2nd series, 3 (1921), cols 1025-26.
[30] Manuscripts of Proba's work are listed by Ermini, *Il centone*, pp. 63-65; several were copied in the twelfth and thirteenth centuries.
[31] Ermini, ibid., pp. 63 and 65, notes manuscripts at Peterborough and at Cambridge.
[32] MS Trin. Col. Camb. O.7. is described by M.R. James, *Western Manuscripts in the Library of Trinity College, Cambridge: A Descriptive Catalogue*, vols. (Cambridge, 1902) II, 348-50.
[33] Gower's other sources were the *Roman de toute Chevalerie* by Thomas of Kent, and the *Historia Alexandri de Preliis* by the Archpresbyter Leo; see Macaulay, *Works*, III, 519, n. to ll. 178 ff., and Peter G. Beidler, ed., *John Gower's Literary Transformations in the Confessio Amantis: Original Articles and Translations* (Washington, D.C., 1982) 119.

manuscript to read Valerius; but one correspondence between that version and
Gower's is worth noting. Valerius's account of Alexander's making, birth and
boyhood occupies only the first few pages — a fraction — of his total narrative.
MS Trinity College Cambridge 0.7.7, while now fragmentary, appears to have
contained a similar segment of the *Res Gestae* — that is, just those opening
passages describing Nectanabus's beguiling of Olympia and the birth and youth
of Alexander, culminating where Gower also finishes his tale, in the magician's
death by his son's unsuspecting hand.[34]

Coincidence of course does not constitute proof; but if Gower had known the
Trinity College manuscript, it would have provided him with precisely the part of
the *Res Gestae* on which he drew in Book VI. (In this regard it seems suggestive as
well that Gower nowhere relies on other material exclusively traceable to
Valerius in all his works.) And since Proba's *Cento Virgilianus* is also in the Trinity
manuscript, he perhaps read it there, along with Valerius and the other texts
which we know he knew.

Gower might, then, have learned the discipline of cento from Proba directly —
but most certainly he would have recognized her name, and possessed as well a
clear enough idea of her achievement for the *Cento Virgilianus* to have been his
inspiration, even if such knowledge came to him second-hand. This is because
Proba, and the making of cento, are prominently discussed by two writers well
known to Gower — Isidore of Seville and Giovanni Boccaccio.[35] Isidore speaks of
her twice, in two separate works. In his *De Viris Illustribus*, Isidore commends the
ingenuity with which Proba linked 'selections' from Virgil into centos honoring
Christ ('componens centonem de Christo, Virgilianis cooptatum versiculis').[36] A
more valuable locus occurs in the first book of the *Etymologies*, where Isidore

---

[34] MS Trin. Col. Camb. O.7. has 7 leaves in its present state, with the *Res Gestae*
beginning on fol. 76; see James, *Western Manuscripts*, II, 349-50. James's description of the
quires also indicates very little missing from the end of the manuscript (p. 349), enough
probably to complete the Nectanabus/ Alexander story, but not the entire *Res Gestae*. In
the edition of Bernard Kubler, *Res Gestae Alexandri Macedonis, Translate ex Aesopo Graeco*
(Leipzig, 1888), this story occupies the first nine pages, and could be completed in the
manuscript on another leaf or two. The remainder of the *Res Gestae*, by comparison, fills
168 pages.

[35] For Gower's reading of Isidore, see Stockton, *Major Latin Works*, pp. 420, n. 6 and 451,
n. 2. Fisher, *John Gower*, p. 93, finds a manuscript ('The Book of St. Mary Overes,' Brit.
Lib. Cot. Faustina A.viii), 'a bookbinder's compilation of various manuals and registers
once belonging to the priory' where Gower lived and worked, which mentions Isidore's
work. T.O. Wedel, *The Medieval Attitude toward Astrology, Particularly in England*, Yale
Studies in English, 60 (New Haven, 1920), p. 132, believes Gower's distinction between
astrology and astronomy at *Confessio* VII, 670, is taken from Isidore. For Gower's reading
of Boccaccio, see Macaulay, *Works*, II-III, notes, especially to Pro. 389; Dorothy A. Dilts,
'John Gower and the *Genealogia Deorum*,' *Modern Language Notes*, 57 (1942), 23-25; Charles
L. Regan, 'John Gower and the Fall of Babylon: *Confessio Amantis* Pro. 670-86,' *English
Language Notes*, 7 (1969), 85-92 (on Gower's use of the *De Casibus Illustrium Virorum*);
Fisher, *John Gower*, pp. 226-27, argues Gower's involvement with Chaucer's *Troilus and
Criseyde*, based on Boccaccio's *Filostrato*, pp. 235 ff.

[36] Isidore of Seville, *De Viris Illustribus*, cap. 18; in J.P. Migne, *Patrologiae Cursus
Completus: Series Latina* (Paris, 1844-1903) LXXIII, col. 1095.

includes cento as a verse-form practiced by skilled writers. After a succinct
description of cento as a poem from many sources, 'patched together into one
whole' ('ex multis hinc inde compositis in unum sarciunt corpus'), Isidore cites
Proba as his first example of those who turn the work of the great pagans into
songs with Christian worth.[37] This of course is Gower's enterprise too, especially
in the *Vox* and the *Confessio*.

Boccaccio devoted the ninety-fifth chapter of *De Claris Mulieribus* to Proba. He
had apparently read Isidore, and borrows from him certain biographical details.[38]
But Boccaccio's account is very full, delineating both Proba's achievement and
the technical aspects of her style. It will merit examination at some length. After
noting that Proba 'became so well informed and familiar with Virgil's poems
through continuous devotion to them that she seemed to have them always
present and in her mind,' Boccaccio continues:

> Perhaps some time when she was reading these works with more than
> careful attentiveness, the idea came to her that with them one could
> write the history of the Old and New Testaments in calm, graceful verses
> full of vigor . . . Carrying out her pious thought, she searched here and
> there through the *Bucolics*, the *Georgics*, and the *Aeneid*, sometimes taking
> entire lines from one place or another, and at times, parts of lines. She
> collected them for her purpose with such great skill, aptly placing the
> entire lines, joining the fragments, observing the metrical rules, and
> preserving the dignity of the verses, that no one except an expert could
> detect the connections . . . . This distinguished woman wanted the book
> which she had composed to be called *Cento*, and I have seen it several
> times.[39]

Several points here are worth our notice. First, there is the description of the
cento method as involving borrowed lines as well as line-fragments. This as we
have seen is characteristic of Gower's practice, although it is condemned by
Ausonius. Then too there is Boccaccio's implication that Proba's *Cento*, seen by

[37] Isidore of Seville, *Etymologiae*, Lib. I, cap. 39, 25-26; text in Migne, *PL*, LXXXII, col.
121.
[38] Boccaccio's description of Proba as 'Adelphi coniuge' derives from Isidore; see Pier
Giorgio Ricci, ed., *Giovanni Boccaccio Opere in versi*, La Letteratura Italiana, Storia e Testi,
9 (Milan and Naples, 1964), 764-66, n. 4. All quotations from Boccaccio are taken from
this edition.
[39] 'Verum, inter alia eius studia, adeo pervigili cura virgiliani carminis docta atque
familiaris effecta est, ut, fere omni opere a se confecto teste, in conspectu et memoria
semper habuisse videatur. Que dum forsan aliquando perspicaciori animadvertentia
legeret in existimationem incidit ex illis omnem Testamenti Veteris hystoriam et Novi
seriem placido atque expedito et succipleno versu posse describi . . . Operam igitur pio
conceptui prestans, nunc huc nunc illuc per buccolicum georgicumque atque eneidum
saltim discurrendo carmen, nunc hac ex parte versus integros nunc ex illa netrorum
particulae carpens, miro artificio in suum redegit propositum, adeo apte integros
collocans et fragmenta connectens, servata lege pedum et carminis dignitate, ut nisi

him 'several times,' is a book of some familiarity, at least in Italy. Boccaccio's
statement may not be true, of course; he may be attempting to lend authority to
his claims by giving an impression of substantial erudition. And it is the case as
well that books common in Italy in the fourteenth century were not always
available in such numbers in England. So a statement like Boccaccio's, about
Proba and the dissemination of her *Cento*, adds little to the argument that Gower
read Proba. Yet could Gower have read Boccaccio (as seems possible, since
Chaucer knew the *De Claribus*) and not have concluded that cento was a poetic
type admired by serious men of letters?[40] For we should observe here the tone of
reverence with which Boccaccio speaks of Proba's achievement Hers are
'graceful verses full of vigor,' the product of 'continuous devotion' to Virgil and
biblical history, turned out with 'great skill' in 'aptly placing the entire lines,
joining the fragments, observing the metrical rules, and preserving the dignity of
the verses . . . .' This is language with great appeal for a poet like Gower who, if
we have been correct thus far in our characterization, was himself committed to a
poesis of binding standards, and regular metrical rules. Boccaccio makes the
description of cento almost challenging, a note he strikes more firmly further on:

> But I ask if anything more praiseworthy has been heard than that a
> woman scanned the verses of Virgil and Homer and, taking those
> suitable to her work, put them together so marvelously. And let learned
> men consider how, in spite of their being distinguished in the profession
> of sacred letters, it would be difficult and arduous to select parts here and
> there from Holy Scripture, which is very long, and put them together in
> a series to give the life of Christ in prose or verse, as she did with the
> verses of poets who were not believers . . . But, being zealous in her
> sacred studies, she removed from her intellect the rust of sloth and
> achieved eternal fame . . . And let them realize how much difference
> there is between seeking glory with praiseworthy works and having one's
> name buried together with one's corpse, leaving this life as if he had
> never lived.[41]

Such warm treatment of the cento, and of the potential honor one might derive
by writing it, would encourage a poet to attempt the form himself, if he felt sure

experitissimus compages possit advertere . . . Voluit insuper egregia femina labore suo
compositum opus vocari *Centonam*, quod ipsi persepe vidimus.' For the Latin text, see
Ricci, *Opere*, 766. The translation is that of Guido A. Guarino, *Concerning Famous Women*
(New Brunswick, N.J., 1963) 219-20.

[40] Fisher connects the *Confessio* with the *Legend of Good Women*, based in part on
Boccaccio's *De Claris Mulieribus*; see *John Gower*, pp. 23 ff. See further Peter Godman,
'Chaucer and Boccaccio's Latin Works,' in *Chaucer and the Italian Trecento*, ed. Piero
Boitani (Cambridge, 1983) 269-95.

[41] 'Sed queso nunc: quid optabilius audisse feminam Maronis et Homeri scandentem
carmina, et apta suo operi seponentem Selecta artificioso contextu nectentem eruditissimi
prospectent viri, quibus, cum sit sacrarum literarum insignis professio, arduum est et
difficile ex amplissimo sacri voluminis gremio nunc hinc nunc inde partes elicere et ad

of the formidable resources necessary. As the only late medieval English poet known to have composed major work in three languages, one of them Latin, Gower seems as likely as any to have had this confidence, as well as the requisite ambition. In part, surely, this is due as much to the substance of Boccaccio's description as to its challenging language. For he praises Proba's matter along with her method and this, I think, would have much recommended her to Gower as a poetic model. Unlike Ausonius, whose *Cento Nuptialis* was famous because it was salacious, Proba in Boccaccio's portrait possessed a spirit kindred to Gower's own in her concern to use the classics to treat subjects in a Christian manner. To find her lauded by Boccaccio (and Isidore) too for successfully turning to hand the ancient poets for the glory of Christ would have been attractive to Gower — the more so because of the high purpose toward which her skill was directed.

Finally, we should note a technical compliment to Gower's cento in the descriptions of Isidore and Boccaccio. Their representations of Proba's style contrast sharply with the intertextual referentiality essential to reading quotations in the *Consolation of Philosophy* or *Piers Plowman*. In these works, as we have observed, quotation compels comparison between previous and present contexts. As we find either contrast or support for the ideas of the new context by juxtaposing it against the old, we understand the larger meaning of the lines at hand.

But cento, as Isidore and Boccaccio have it, discourages comparative reading of this sort. For them the meaning of a quotation in its original context is irrelevant to cento, except in one way. By remarking how widely that meaning has been altered from its first to its current context, we can judge the poet's skill who made the cento. Basically their equation is, the more arduous the borrowing task, the more praiseworthy the success. Boccaccio says as much when he marvels at Proba's ability to string together excerpts from 'the verses of poets who were not believers' to tell the life of Christ, when it would be a substantial feat just to do this using 'parts . . . from Holy Scripture, which is very long.' The sources of Boccaccio's admiration are two: that Proba was able to borrow so successfully from so compact a body of material (the Bible has more lines of value from which to choose); and that the transformation of the borrowed matter could be so great — i.e., that pagan poetry might be 'converted' to serve the ends of Christ.

The point has significance for Gower's cento, because by implication Boccaccio's view of Proba leads us directly to it, while the examples of *The Consolation of Philosophy* and *Piers Plowman* do not. For what has been tacit all along should be uttered explicitly now, that neither Boethius nor Langland wrote cento. It was useful to speak of them in connection with Gower, however, both because doing so helps provide an obscure poetic form with a definition by contraries, and also because Gower might have produced a cento closer in kind to

seriem vite Cristi passis verbis prosaque cogere, uti hec fecit ex gentilitio carmine . . . sed quantum sedula studiis sacris ab ingenio segniciei rubiginem absterxit omnem, in lumen evasit eternum . . . quantum differentie sit inter famam laudandis operibus querere, et nomen una cum cadavere sepelire et tanquam non vixerint et vita discedere!' Latin text in Ricci, *Opere*, p. 768; translation by Guarino, *Famous Women*, p. 220.

Boethius's and Langland's use of quotation had he read, instead of Proba and her commentators, the writings of Ausonius instead.

We have remarked one major difference already between Ausonius's cento and Gower's, on whether whole lines could be appropriately excerpted; yet there remains another contrariety dividing them which may be more profound. What elevates Ausonius's *Cento Nuptialis* above the level of pornography is, finally, its referentiality. We laugh instead of leer when we read it because we recognize how adeptly he has turned Virgil's noble lines — the nobler the better — to suggestive use. Most of the fun evaporates if we do not know the Virgilian context. Ausonius thus treats Virgil exactly the way Boethius does Seneca, though to the accomplishment of very different ends.

But Gower, we have seen, did not concern himself with the meanings of his borrowed lines in their first contexts. Apparently for him it was sufficient to know he had transformed them. For this reason, when we trace a fragment of the *Vox Clamantis* like 'querebam fratres' to its source in Ovid's *Tristia*, we need not puzzle long over what it meant there — a book of verse gone searching for its lost 'brothers' in a library on the Palatine — or how that odd locus might affect our reading of the *Vox*. The approach to cento is Proba's, perhaps as explicated by Boccaccio; and if we think for a moment, we can easily understand why Proba might have derived her technique. The keys are her Christianity, Virgil's paganism, and the use she had for cento — in Boccaccio's words, to 'write the history of the Old and New Testaments in calm, graceful verses full of vigor.' Here irony, of an Ausonian or even a Boethian kind, is inappropriate. What have Virgil's meanings to do with scriptural narrative? Whether Proba asked herself this question of course we cannot say, but what *is* apparent (to Boccaccio, for one) is how little we may gain from reading her *Cento Virgilianus* beside an open copy of Virgil. Her selections — lines and fragments, as Boccaccio noticed, taken 'here and there through[out] the *Bucolics*, the *Georgics*, and the *Aeneid*' — range too widely to reward close intertextual reading. Proba's was an attitude of poetic high seriousness; and this, like her eclectic choice of sources, would have held substantial appeal for Gower.

Carefully examined and weighed, then, there appears to be evidence both internal and external that the lines from the *Vox Clamantis* Macaulay thought 'plagiarised' in fact represent Gower's experiments with cento technique. What Gower borrowed he put to a purpose for which there was precedent in ancient and early medieval models, and in which there was developing interest among early humanists like Boccaccio. Rather than a plagiarist, Gower seems instead to have been something of an innovator — or an antiquary, in the Renaissance sense, a rediscoverer and conserver of classical poetic forms.

II

The probability that Gower wrote cento is telling in other ways we may explore here and in the following chapter. On one level, it suggests that the unit of first importance for Gower was not the verse-sentence but the line and its component fractions. This seems so because the technique requires a certain cast of mind and eye, both to approve and to practice it. If there is (or we can imagine) a 'cento way of thinking,' then Gower had it; and it is not a sensibility he shared in similar measure with other English poets of his time.

How variously Gower relies on this approach to language will be clearer if we look at some vernacular examples. Here is Gower, describing the multi-headed beast from the vision of St. John in *Mirour de l'Omme* 9889-97:

> *L'apocalips* q'est tout celeste
> Reconte d'un *horrible beste,*
> *Q'issoit de la* parfonde *mer*:
> *Corps leopart*, ce dist la geste,
> Mais *du leoun ot qeule* et teste,
> *Des piés fuist urce* a resembler
> *Sept chief* portoit cil adversier,
> Si ot *disz corns* pour fort hurter,
> Ove *disz couronnes du conqueste* . . .

His source is a passage from the *Somme le Roi*:

> Mais sire sains jehans on liure des reuelations quit est appelez *la pocalice/* si dist que il vit vne *beste* qui estoit *issue de la mer/* meruilleusement desguisée et trop espoentable. Car il *cors* de la *beste* estoit de *liepart. Les piez estoient dours.* Et la *quele de lyon.* Et si auoit *vii chiez et x couronnes.* Et vit monseigneur saint jehan que cette *horrible beste* quoit pouor de soi combatre aus sains et de les vaincre et *conquerre.*[42]

Gower has adapted the French of the *Somme* to his Anglo-Norman dialect, shifting the order and adding vocabulary of his own to the important words — mostly nouns and verbs — he borrows. In a strict sense, this is not cento. Gower establishes no new context for the words and phrases he takes. But the example broadly illustrates Gower's working habits, and offers insight into his theoretical assumptions about how poetry could be constructed. His is a judicious, deliberative process. Clearly he thought of words almost as plastic material, to be sized and jointed end-to-end until a line was made and then, accretionally, a poem.

---

[42] On Gower's use of the *Somme le Roi*, see R. Elfreda Fowler, *Une source française des poèmes de Gower* (Macon, 1905) 19; and J.B. Dwyer, 'Gower's *Mirour* and Its French Sources A Re-examination of Evidence,' *Studies in Philology*, 48 (1951), 482-505. Also helpful are Mosher, *Exemplum*, 124-27; and Welter, *L'Exemplum*, 207-09. Text printed by Dwyer, 'Gower's *Mirour*,' 505.

Gower's Latin techniques are worth recalling when we assess his translation
methods, too. Cento ought to make us look twice at passages like *Mirour* 5329-32:

> Ly sages dist parole voire:
> *O come amiere est la memoire*
> A l'omme pensant de la *mort*,
> Quant est enmy sa tendre gloire!'

The source is Ecclesiasticus 4:1:

> *O mors, quam amara est memoria* tua,
> *Homini* pacem habenti in substantiis suis.

To be sure, Gower's acquisition of vocabulary here is not unique. Chaucer for
one translates in a similar way, particularly in the dream-poetry — e.g., 'An
ydole of fals portraiture' (*BD* 626), cf. 'Une ydole est de fausse pourtraiture'
(Machaut's eighth Motet, 9) — and examples could be compounded.[43] But at
issue here is not whether Gower was alone in his practice. The real points to be
made are two: first that, in company or not, Gower *does* proceed in this way; and
second that in his case (unlike Chaucer's, or other Ricardian poets') there seems
to be a *pattern* of borrowing apparent, to which we can put a name and which can
help us develop a broad picture of his work. We can, for example, apply the cento
model to his handling of sources as well as language, and thereby derive a richer
context for each. Let us consider two passages from the *Confessio Amantis*. The
first is from Book VI, ll. 1957-84. Describing the magician Nectanabus's spell-
casting, Gower writes:

> And thurgh the craft of *Artemage*
> Of wex he forgeth an *ymage*.
> He loketh his *equacions*
> And ek the constellacions,
> He loketh the *conjunccions*,

[43] Barry A. Windeatt, in *Chaucer's Dream Poetry: Sources and Analogues* (Woodbridge,
Suffolk, 1982), proposes that 'Chaucer the translator is both borrowing and originating'
as he employs a 'power of co-ordinating his sources into something individual' (p. x). His
introduction discusses various cases from the dream-poems, while seeming to suggest that
Chaucer's borrowing practices are different elsewhere. On Chaucer's adoption of French
vocabulary generally, see Stephen Knight, *ryming craftily: Meaning in Chaucer's Poetry*
(Sydney, 1973) 105, 110; and Ralph W.V. Elliott, *Chaucer's English* (London, 1974) 19-2
and *passim*. Also helpful is the study of Joseph Mersand, *Chaucer's Romance Vocabulary*, 2nd
edn. (New York, rep. 1968); and see further Elliott, ' "Faire subtile wordes": An
Approach to Chaucer's Verbal Art,' *Parergon*, 13 (1975), 3-20.

He loketh the recepcions,
His *signe*, his houre, his acendent,
And drawth fortune of his assent:
The name of queene Olimpias
In thilke *ymage* write was
Amiddes in the front above . . .
And thanne ferst he hath enoignted
With sondri *herbes* that figure,
And therupon he gan *conjure*
So that thurgh his enchantement
This ladi, which was innocent
And wiste nothing of this guile,
Mette, as sche slepte thilke while,
Hou fro the hevene cam a lyht;
And as sche loketh to and fro,
Sche sih, hir thoghte, a *dragoun* tho . . .

Among Gower's several sources for these lines is the *Roman de toute Chevalerie* by
Thomas of Kent, ll. 234-48:

Li maistre prent congié, à son ostel en va;
Canque mestier li fu à cel art purçhaca
Les *herbes* acceptables [con]coilli [et] tribla,
Puis en après les jucs par son sen si medla
E puis de virgine cire une *ymage* molla;
Le non de la reïne par lettre figura,
En un lit qu[e] ot fait cele *ymage* cocha,
Environ icel lit chandeles aluma,
Del jus qu'il ot des *herbes* cel' *ymage* arusa,
Par charmes qu'il saveit souvent la *conjura*.
Qanque Nectanabus à l'*ymage* parla
La reïne en son lit par avision songa:
Vis lit fut que uns *dragons* enz la *chambre* entra,
Puis vint jusq'à son lit, en home se mua,
Après li s'cocha e estreit l'enbraça . . .[44]

The significant vocabulary here is drawn from Thomas of Kent. Moreover, a
few lines ahead of the passage quoted (i.e., ll. 215-16) we find in the *Roman* 'la
lune e les planetes es *signes* que trova,/ Par lur *equacium* largement assuma,' a
couplet which provided Gower with 'equacions' (l. 1959) and 'signe' (l. 1963). A
bit below the passage quoted (i.e., l. 275), the *Roman* has 'Par *artemage* fist tele
conjunction,' Gower's source for 'artemage' (l. 1957) and 'conjunccions' (l.

[44] Text in *Alexandre le Grand dans la littérature française du Moyen Âge*, ed. Paul Meyer, 2 vols.
(Paris, 1886) I, 205; and Beidler, *Literary Transformations*, 102, which reprints Meyer. On
the name 'Thomas' rather than 'Eustace' of Kent, see Meyer, II, 282-83.

1961).[45] But my immediate concern is less with the borrowed words (which is not
especially remarkable by contemporary standards); rather, it is with the
relationship of this to another passage, in Book VII (ll. 528-36):

> So as these olde clerkes spieke,
> And sette proprely the bounde
> After the form of *Mappemounde*,
> Thurgh which the ground be *pourparties*
> *Departed is in thre parties*,
> That is *Asie*, *Aufrique*, *Europe*,
> The whiche under the hevene cope
> Als fer as strecceth eny ground,
> Begripeth al this Erthe *round*.

Again, Gower probably drew upon the *Roman de toute Chevalerie* for these lines (ll.
33-39):

> Lisage homme a[n]cien mesurerent le *mounde*,
> Cum le firmament turn e [cum] la terre est *rounde*;
> *En treis* la *departirent* sanz compas, sanz espounde.
> L'une *partie* est *Asye*, *Affrike* le secunde;
> *Europe* est la tierz, de toz biens est fecunde.
> Doze signes ad el ciel dont clarté nus habunde . . .[46]

Nearly six hundred lines separate these two passages, which come in the
Confessio in reverse order from the way they appear in the *Roman*. Unless he used
different manuscripts of the *Roman* at different times, Gower in composing Book
VI must at first have skipped over this description of the world, for his treatment
of Nectanabus does not begin to draw on his source until about line 5 of the
Roman. Later, to produce this sketch of the globe in Book VII, he returned to the
early, unused lines of the *Roman*, splicing them in among matter otherwise taken
predominantly from Brunetto Latini's *Trésor*.[47] The treatment of language and of
sources in these examples is indicative, I believe, of Gower's 'patchwork'
strategies for turning poems out of lines. Clearly this isn't cento; but the
techniques are of a piece, both related parts of a single poetic sensibility.

[45] It is worth noting the exotic ring that these words would have had for Gower's
audience. The *MED* credits this passage as the earliest occurrence in English of
'artemage,' 'carecte,' 'conjuren,' and of 'conjunccions' (in the astrological sense),
'herbes' (in the sense of magical apparatus), 'ramp' (in the sense of 'to creep or crawl on
the ground'). Gower's usages here of 'astrelabe,' and 'image' (meaning 'a figure made for
purposes of magic or divination') are listed as second examples, behind Chaucer's. See
further Theodore H. Kaplan, 'Gower's Vocabulary,' *JEGP*, 31 (1932), 395-402.
[46] Text in Meyer, *Alexandre le Grand*, I, 197, and Beidler, *Literary Transformations*, p. 94.
[47] On Gower's use of Brunetto here, see Macaulay's notes to Book VII, *Works*, III, 521 ff.

We can see Gower working in a similar way, to build native elements into the *Confessio Amantis*, too. Initially we must look sharp, however. There is little evidence that Gower took much notice of English verse other than Chaucer's, and it would seem, at first, that nothing resembling cento turns up in his English poems. Like Chaucer, however, he had his ears open to the talk around him, and what he heard he put to work. Consider the string of proverbs uttered by Genius in Book III, 1625-40:

> Men sen alday that rape reweth;
> And who so wiked Ale breweth,
> Fulofte he mot the werse drinke;
> Betre is to flet than to sincke;
> Betre is upon the bridel shiewe
> Thanne if he felle and overthrewe,
> The hors and stikede in the myr:
> To caste water in the fyr
> Betre is than brenne up al the hous:
> The man which is malicious
> And folhastif, fulofte he faileth,
> And selden is whan love him calleth.
> Forthi betre is to soffre a throwe
> Than to be wilde and overthrowe;
> Suffrance hath evere the best
> To wissen him that secheth rest.

Speech of this kind is dramatic. It characterizes Genius by enlivening him, setting off his tone of instruction both from his own narratorial voice (where he uses proverbs infrequently), and from the voice of Amans.[48] In the narrower context of the *Confessio Amantis*, it is a solid bit of fiction-making, of effective verisimilitude. And it shows, too, how Gower could draw art from a native 'voice.' In the broader context of Gower's poetic enterprise, however, the lines represent a sophisticated handling of a 'centonic' impulse, thoughtful in its place

---

[48] B. J. Whiting has counted and averaged the frequency of proverbs in the *Confessio Amantis*; see his *Chaucer's Use of Proverbs*. In the lines of Genius's dialogue with Amans, the priest resorts to proverbs 159 times by Whiting's calculation, for an average of about two proverbs per hundred lines of his speech; in his illustrative stories, Genius's average is somewhat lower, about one per hundred lines. This has led Whiting to conclude (presumably on the basis of the averaged figures) that while 'the overwhelming majority of proverbs are uttered by Genius' (p. 152), 'we never feel . . . that Genius is being characterized in any way by this use of proverbs; he has no more individuality than a didactic manual' (p. 153). With all due respect to Whiting, I think that his concern for averaged numbers has deceived him. The *art* of creating character with verbal devices like proverbs is knowing when to cluster them and when to go lightly. To Shakespeare's awareness of this we owe Polonius, who shares a number of characteristics with Genius, including a 'proverbial' personality which an *average* would obscure.

and, in its way, an imaginative working-out of a poet's unique inclinations towards words and texts. The value of examples like these resides in their revelatory power — their capacities to lend us brief but suggestive views of Gower's art in the process of its building. If I am correct in my assumptions about the nature of that art, then cento — both as achieved technique in the Latin poetry and as structuring *idea* elsewhere, usually operative if not always consciously invoked — affords us a revolving point, a center around which to assemble a variety of observations of what Gower did when he made poems.

III

In the pages that follow, I want to use Gower's cento as just such a centering point, to consider further his expectations of readers, of language and of lines. My particular concern will be the poetry in French — the *Mirour de l'Omme* and the two sequences of ballades which Macaulay named *Cinkante Ballades* and the *Traitié pour essampler les Amantz marietz*. The argument I propose to make is simple enough to state. It is that Gower's view of poetry as a powerful tool for moral and social reform brought him to reject all alternative approaches to the art. Writing was for him an accountable act, ultimately subject to the same scrutiny and judgment as other deeds performed by men. A poet (like a preacher — Gower would not have rejected the comparison) thus bears a responsibility, not only for the state of his own soul, but also to others, to keep them on the path with a right use of eloquence. Both 'audiences' could be brought into jeopardy unless the poet did his work well — which for Gower meant taking account of the seriousness of his calling and composing nothing without redemptive purpose. In this I believe Gower resembles Dante, as I shall try to show in some detail here and elsewhere; and in this too he comes (like Dante) to oppose, and to strive to remake, the prominent poetry of his time and place, the courtly models raised by the *Roman de la Rose* and the amorous lyric, by adapting its vocabulary to different ends. Like Dante, Gower sought to speak a fresh 'language of love' in a familiar voice, ultimately turning that voice against itself until the discourse of desire might be cleansed of the secular, to foster the sacred alone.

Having stated this argument, however, it is something else again to make it stick. Doing so will carry us divers ways, and cause us to situate Gower variously among his peers. But the process is also circular, because for Gower poetics began with and returned to the line. As a suitable place to begin we may take an observation of John Fisher's, who called attention some time ago to lines in Gower's ballade sequences which seem borrowed from the French court poets:

> Deschamps' refrain, 'Telle dame estre empereis de Romme' reappears
> in Gower's [*Cinkante Ballades*] XLIIII, spoken by the lady, 'Si jeo de
> Rome fuisse l'emperesse.' The refrain of Gower's XLIII, 'C'est ma
> dolour, qe fuist ainçois ma joie' resembles Machaut's 'C'est ma dolour
> et la fin de ma joie.' The technique of alluding to the names of great
> lovers, found in Grandson's 'Ho! doulce Yseult, qui a la fontaine/ Avec

Tristan, Jason, et Medea' is used in Gower's XLIII, 'Plus tricherous qe Jason a Medée,' etc., and in most of his balades in the *Traitié*.[49]

What ought we to think of details like these? Doubtless initially we should interpret them as Fisher does. 'In the context of the tradition,' he remarks, what is unusual about the shared lines is how few there really are in Gower's ballades. Reasonably we might expect to find more. Not only, as a maker of cento, would Gower seem to have been disposed toward borrowing, but also courtly poetry in French and English was highly stylized by the late fourteenth century, so much so that its poets often incorporated each others' lines. Sometimes this took place in friendly competition (twelve, we know, sought to build the best ballade around the idea, 'Je meurs de soif auprès de la fontaine'); other lines merely seem well-travelled.[50] The refrain of *Cinkante Ballades* XXV, 'Car qui bien aime ses amours tard oblie,' for example, closely resembles Deschamps's 'Qui bien aime a tard oublie' — but it has also been identified as a proverb, and turns up as well in the works of Machaut, Moniot d'Arras, and in the margins of several manuscripts of the *Parlement of Foules*.[51]

Fisher's solution to the problem — that Gower's ballades reflect a strong troubadour influence, congruent with the prescripts of a late-blooming London pui — is helpful, as far as it goes. He points out Gower's 'fondness for the term *fin amour*' (a common locution in Provençal, not courtly, poetry); the evidence, from regulations found in the *Liber Custumarum*, that a pui was active in London until 1320 or possibly after; the 'prevailingly cheerful and philosophical treatment of love' in Gower's ballades, in contrast to the 'languorous, sentimental pose of the broken heart that was conventional for courtly love lyrics;' the similarity of some passages of Gower's to various turns of phrase in extant troubadour poems; and the emphasis, in both the *Cinkante Ballades* and the *Traitié*, on love legitimized by marriage.[52]

These are insightful observations; but, as Fisher readily acknowledges, at last they raise as many questions as they answer. More recent studies of the French tradition have shown that, while *fin amour* is not a favored term of Machaut or Deschamps, it is by no means exclusively a troubadour locution, either.[53] The passages in the *Cin- kante Ballades* and the *Traitié* closest to troubadour work reveal no specific indebtedness for lines or images, and thus remain unconvincing; they

---

[49] Fisher, *John Gower*, p. 76.

[50] See Pierre Champion, *Vie de Charles d'Orléans (1394-1465)*, 2nd edn. (Paris, 1969) 652-53.

[51] Joseph Morawski, ed., *Proverbes françaises antérieurs au XVe Siècle* (Paris, 1925) 67, no. 1835, identifies the line as proverbial; see also Willi Haeckel, *Das Sprichwort bei Chaucer*, Erlanger Beitrage, 2, vii (1890), 3, n. 10. For Machaut, see 'Le Lai de plour,' l. 1; for Moniot d'Arras and the *Parlement*, see the useful note to *PF* l. 677 by Charles Muscatine in Benson, *Riverside*, 1002; and see further E. Koeppel, 'Gowers französische Balladen und Chaucer,' *Englische Studien*, 20 (1895), 155.

[52] Fisher, *John Gower*, pp. 77-83.

[53] See for example the case made by Douglas Kelly, *Medieval Imagination Rhetoric and the Poetry of Courtly Love* (Madison, 1978) 14-22, and further Jean Frappier, ' "D'amors," "Par amors",' *Romania*, 88 (1967), 433-74.

do not (as one French scholar would have it prove) Gower 'comme Petrarque, un chansonnier des troubadours.'[54] Nor is the assumption that Gower belonged to a pui of much help, finally. The records in the *Liber Custumarum* seem to chronicle an organization in decline well before 1320, with fines established for those who defaulted on dues or failed to attend feasts.[55] For Gower to have taken part in its poetic contests, this pui 'would have had to continue into the 1350s' — something of a long shot, as Fisher concedes.[56] And certainly the troubadour poets placed no greater emphasis on moral issues, or the married state, than did the high courtly makers.[57] What seems rather the case is that Gower, always an eclectic reader, sought useful material wherever he could. He *may* have known a little troubadour work, through what source we can only guess; and if so, he merged it with much we readily recognize as courtly, transforming both by this process into a lyrical voice purposefully at odds in its strict moral consistencies with the pliant ethics of the courtly world whence he borrowed the fixed form, and the light resonance, of the ballade. The two lyric sequences are Gower's attempt to subvert the language of courtly poetry from within, to reform (and so to claim) its affective power for moral uses, by fitting it to arguments commonly made in other terms.

If we wonder at the need for such a program, we should perhaps recall the state of amorous language during the later 1300s. The close of the century represents a turning point for Western European societies engaged in a search for new standards of behavior.[58] Distinctions were recognized 'for the first time in our culture' between actions polite and vulgar, alongside simple right and wrong.[59] Style took on emphatic importance — in what one did, and especially in how one

---

[54] Jean Audiau, *Les Troubadours et l'Angleterre* (Paris, 1927) 125. Both Audiau and G. Kar, *Thoughts on the Medieval Lyric* (Oxford, 1933), especially pp. 55-63, cite various examples of passages Gower 'borrowed' from particular troubadours. The following are representative: 'Quant dolour vait, les joies vienont pres' (Gower, *Cinkante Ballades*, II); 'Aissi ven bes après dolor,/ Et après gran mal jauzimen,/ Et rics jois après marrimen' (Rigaut de Barbezieux); 'En resemblance d'aigle qui surmonte/ Tout autre oisel pour voler au dessure,/ Trés douls amis, vostre amour tant amonte/ Sur toutz amantz . . .' (*CB* XLVI); 'Anc tan auta aigla no montet/ Com vostre prez' (Daudé de Pradas); see Audiau, 118, 123. Fisher (*John Gower*, 77) perhaps has the best assessment of Audiau's enthusiasm: 'I must confess that I am not so impressed . . . by the direct similarity. The readings [Audiau] cites are . . . common to the whole troubadour-derived tradition . . . .'

[55] H. T. Riley, ed., *Monumenta Gildhallae Londoniensis: Liber Custumarum* ,3 vols., Rolls Series (1860), II, 222. In his introduction (which includes a fragmentary history of the pui in London) Riley suggests that the concern over defaulted dues and lapsed attendance shows that 'at the date of its Second Series of regulations, [the society] already contained within itself the germs of dissolution;' see lii.

[56] Fisher, *John Gower*, p. 80.

[57] Deschamps, for example, wrote many admonitory ballades, on pious subjects; see A. Queux de St.-Hilaire and Gaston Raynaud, eds., *Oeuvres complètes d'Eustace Deschamps*, 11 vols. (Paris, 1878-1903), I and II, passim, and note 132 below.

[58] The issues and circumstances are admirably laid out by Johan Huizinga, *The Waning of the Middle Ages: A Study of the Forms of Life, Thought and Art in France and the Netherlands in the XIVth and XVth Centuries* (London, 1924) 95-106.

[59] Larry D. Benson, 'Courtly Love and Chivalry in the Later Middle Ages,' in Yeager, *Fifteenth-Century Studies*, 242.

described accomplishment. Froissart exclaims with joy at the gentle skill of the English courtiers at speech; the Household Ordinances of Edward III require of pages and squires (Geoffrey Chaucer among them) that they study 'noble conversation' to fit them for their station: These are signs of a verbal self-consciousness both strong and pervasive.[60] All classes felt it, in isolated circles as well as royal courts — or so it would seem from poetic testimony. The knights and ladies at Bertilak's castle who expect to hear (and remember!) 'the tecchles termes of talkynge noble' present the newly-arrived Gawain with a sensitive audience, doubly so for its wish to learn the gauche from the right, and its consequent insecurity before verbal niceties not yet second nature.[61] Chaucer shows throughout his work a keen awareness of linguistic distinctions and how they matter, from the 'Kek kek! kokkow! quek quek!' of the lower birds in the *Parlement of Foules* (ll. 49 ff.) and their complement in the Miller's 'cherles tale' told 'in his manere' (*CT* I, 3169), to the Franklin's approval of the Squire's eloquence (in contrast to his own son, who 'hath levere talken with a page/ Than to commune with any gentil wight,' (*CT* V, 673-94), to the Host's changes of tone and vocabulary as he addresses pilgrims of different birth (cf. his words to the Miller, I, 3128-35 and to the Prioress, VII, 445-50), and the Manciple's cynical, veristic definitions of 'lady,' 'lemman' and 'wench' (*CT* IX, 210-11), which turn on class distinction.[62] Examples might be further compounded from *Piers Plowman*.[63] Indeed, the theme is so common in verse of the period that it could well serve as a touchstone for Ricardian poetry generally.

At the center of the preoccupation with appropriate language was the specialized idiom of love. 'Luf talkyng,' as Larry Benson reminds us, was so much an art of the upper classes that its proper practice, by itself, gave evidence of nobility.[64] Churls could not speak in its terms, either because they lacked tutoring (a condition the Household Ordinances set out to remedy for Edward III's squires), or — more seriously — because they were thought altogether incapable of the delicate sentiments the language of *courtoisie* describes. The latter was the opinion of Andreas Capellanus — and his judgment that 'vileins know not love,' although delivered two hundred years before, would have won agreement from Chaucer's Miller and the 'hende' Nicholas of his tale, who woos

---

[60] See Frederick S. Shears, *Froissart: Chronicler and Poet* (London, 1930) 16; on the importance of speech, see Richard Firth Green's discussion in his *Poets and Princepleasers Literature and the English Court in the Late Middle Ages* (Toronto, 1980) 73-84.

[61] That is, ll. 91 ff.; see J.R.R. Tolkien and E.V. Gordon, eds., *Sir Gawain and the Green Knight*, 2nd rev. edn. (Oxford, 1967).

[62] On the Manciple's treatment of 'lady,' 'lemman' and 'wench' see Norman E. Eliason, *The Language of Chaucer's Poetry: An Appraisal of Verse, Style and Structure, Anglistica*, 17 (Copenhagen, 1972) 35, 110.

[63] Favel, who weds Lady Meed, and who 'haþ þis folk enchaunted' (B. II, 40 ff.) exemplifies the 'new speechifier.' His 'tonge' is as 'fikel' as his courtier's 'speche' is 'faire.'

[64] Benson, 'Courtly Love,' 243, notes that when Criseyde asks Pandarus if Troilus can 'speke wel of love,' she 'is in effect asking, "Is he a gentleman?" since to speak well of love . . . is to use a class dialect, the first of which we have any clear indication in English.' A page later he quotes Kittredge (*Chaucer and His Poetry*, [Cambridge, MA, 1951] 63) to the same effect: 'Love was the only life that became the gently nurtured, and they alone were capable of love.'

his low-born Alisoun by catching her 'by the queynte,' holding her 'harde by the haunchebones' and threatening, 'Ywis, but if ich have my wille,/ For deerne love of thee, lemman, I spille' (*CT* I, 3271- 87).[65]

Of course what we should notice here is that, discourteous as Nicholas is in his actions and uncouth in his use of words like 'lemman' and 'spille' (with its coarse pun), he nonetheless puts an edge to his demand in terms that shadow courtly speech. His love is 'deerne' ('secret'), and assuredly mortal if left unreturned.[66] Now, it is clear that Nicholas places no faith at all in the persuasive potential of this language — and rightly not, since in the world of the *Miller's Tale* actions speak more efficaciously than words. It is after all the busy Nicholas and not the windy Absolon, for all his stale courtly palaver, who gets the girl; and also that girl herself — of all Chaucer's memorable heroines the least verbal, the most responsive to instinct — who in the end receives no punishment, as if the tale's *moralitas* were the culpability of words instead of deeds.[67]

But Nicholas explains himself in this way because he cannot help it; because, if he is to say anything about what he feels at all, he has at his disposal only some version, more or less proper, of the language of courtly love. Nor are our own choices very much different. Andy Hardy in love, as Benson has noted, is recognizable from patterns of talk and behavior made standard in the Middle Ages and in effect ever since.[68] In fact, the primary difference between amorous language then and now is its extension to cover an increasing range of circumstances, including endearments shared by those in pursuit of, or already bound by, legal marriage. Since 'honest' love is one of Gower's major themes,

---

[65] Capellanus spells out his opinion in Book I, cap. XI of *De arte honesti amandi*: 'We say that it rarely happens that we find farmers serving in Love's court, but naturally, like a horse or a mule, they give themselves up to the work of Venus, as nature's urging teaches them to do. For a farmer hard labor and the uninterrupted solaces of plough and mattock are sufficient.' I quote from the translation of John Jay Parry, *The Art of Courtly Love* (New York, 1941) 149. Shame's words to Daunger in the *Roman de la Rose* are also indicative:

> Yf Bialacoil be sweete and free,
> Dogged and fel thou shuldist be,
> Froward and outrageous, ywis;
> A cherl chaungeth that curteis is.
> This have I herd ofte in seiyng,
> That man [ne] may, for no dauntyng,
> Make a sperhauk of a bosard,
> Alle men wole holde thee for musard,
> That debonair have founden thee;
> It sitteth thee nought curteis to be.

See *The Romaunt of the Rose*, 4027-36, in Benson, *Riverside*, p. 729.

[66] On the pun on 'spille,' see Thomas W. Ross, *Chaucer's Bawdy* (New York, 1972) 207-08. On the supposed mortal nature of unrequited love, see John L. Lowes, 'The Loveres Maladye of Hereos,' *Modern Philology*, 11 (1914), 491-546.

[67] V.A. Kolve has described the world of the *Miller's Tale* as one designed 'to invoke a whole, and wholly attractive, category of life lived outside of morality, in order to locate his young people metaphorically within it: an animal world in which instinct takes the place that reason holds for man, a world in which instinct and necessity are one.' See *Chaucer and the Imagery of Narrative: The First Five Canterbury Tales* (Stanford, CA, 1984) 185.

[68] Benson, 'Courtly Love,' p. 237.

both in the two ballade sequences, where it is the central subject, and in the *Confessio Amantis*, we shall do well to pause a moment over it.[69]

Married couples had never been excluded from the court of love, of course. Capellanus explicitly cited 'Marriage shall be no bar to love' among his list of rules governing lovers; and that he probably did so tongue-in-cheek merely testifies to the absurdity, in his view, of anyone assuming otherwise.[70] Nevertheless, it is clear that marriage complicated matters, doubtless because love at the courtly level — for all the high seriousness of its terminology — was recognized to be an elaborate game, while marriage (which affected bloodlines and property) was anything but. The resultant tension between the demands of real life and those of love's evolving private language became apparent early, at least to poets at the center like Chrétien de Troyes and Dante.[71] Yet the dominant voice, which shaped courtly writing over much of the period, belongs not to them but to the poets of the *Roman de la Rose*, Guillaume de Lorris and Jean de Meun. Since for Jean especially love's activity required no sanctification beyond the procreative urge, this was not a voice Gower could have heard with either pleasure or approval.[72] Doubtless, had he taken part in the famous debate over the ethics of the *Roman*, he would have echoed Gerson's strenuous objections to the indelicacy of Jean's language, and to the amorality of his message.[73]

---

[69] The subject has received the careful attention of J.A.W. Bennett; see his 'Gower's "Honeste Love"' in John Lawlor, ed., *Patterns of Love and Courtesy: Essays in Memory of C.S. Lewis* (Evanston, IL, 1966) 107-21.

[70] Parry translates this as 'Marriage is no real excuse for not loving;' see *The Art of Courtly Love*, p. 184.

[71] Chrétien takes up the question with great clarity in *Cligés*, where marriage is preferred (even by Guinevere!) over adulterous love. He has seen, as R. S. Loomis has put it, 'the humiliation and the debasement of character that went with the *ménage à trois*.' See *The Development of Arthurian Romance* (London, 1963) 47. Dante's feelings are expressed in *Inferno* V, the story of Paolo and Francesca, where significantly the book containing the story of Lancelot and Guinevere is the 'Galeotto' which encourages their adultery. Kelly, *Medieval Imagination*, 19-20 and 263, n. 34, has discovered elements of the tension in Wace.

[72] Opinions of Jean de Meun and his achievement differ widely. For John V. Fleming, 'The *Roman de la Rose* is ironic,' and he cautions us well that 'The danger in writing about archetypal sin in a dramatic way, apparently, is that literary critics some centuries removed may not clearly grasp the moral hierarchies on which dramatic action must be grounded;' see *The Roman de la Rose: A Study in Allegory and Iconography* (Princeton, NJ, 1969) 50, 51. For Fleming, this means that the *Roman* is an ironic poem, a triumph of moral satire. On the other hand, Johan Huizinga characterizes the author and his poem quite differently: 'Jean de Meun is an enlightened man, who believes neither in spectres nor in sorcerers, neither in faithful love nor in the chastity of woman . . . and puts into the mouths of Venus, Nature and Genius the most daring apology for sensuality. . . . Here, then, in the *Roman de la Rose*, the sexual motif is again placed in the centre of erotic poetry, but enveloped by symbolism and mystery and presented in the guise of saintliness. It is impossible to imagine a more deliberate defiance of the Christian ideal.' See *Waning*, p. 101. I confess to finding Huizinga's approach to Jean de Meun more convincing than Fleming's. For other important views on both sides of the issue, see the very useful bibliography Maxwell Luria includes in *A Reader's Guide to the Roman de la Rose* (Hamden, CT, 1982) 235-51.

[73] The major figures in the debate, waged in France apparently between 1399 and 1402,

IV

Seemingly, Gower could not have sounded his trumpet sooner. We are given a
powerful sense of his opposition to the courtly ethos — and by extension to the
Roman's ideas about love — in the first lines of the earliest work of Gower's we
know.[74] The *Mirour de l'Omme* begins:

> Escoulte cea, chascun amant,
> Qui tant perestes desirant
> Du pecché, dont l'amour est fals:
> Lessetz la Miere ove tout s'enfant,
> Car qui plus est leur attendant,
> Au fin avra chapeal de sauls:

were Jean Gerson and Christine de Pisan, who condemned both Jean de Meun and his
poem, and Jean de Montreuil, Gontier Col and Pierre Col, who defended them. Gerson
thought the *Roman* fit only for burning: 'May such a book therefore be put aside and
exterminated without any use in the future, especially in those parts in which he employs
disreputable and prohibited characters, such as the accursed Old Woman, who ought to
be judged to the punishment of the pillory; and Venus, that is, Lechery, which is mortal
sin; and the Foolish Lover, who ought not to be allowed to perform foolishness for his own
pleasure.' (See Joseph L. Baird and John R. Kane, eds., *La Querrelle de la Rose: Letters and
Documents* [Chapel Hill, 1978] 57. Grover C. Furr has argued that Gerson and Christine
knew that the *Roman* was really an allegorical satire, immoral only at the literal level, but
they feared its persuasive style would confuse contemporary readers into believing it (see
his unpublished Princeton dissertation, 'The Quarrel of the *Roman de la Rose* and
Fourteenth-Century Humanism' [1979], p. 205). If Furr is correct, their *true* views, then,
would be more in line with Fleming's (see n. 72, above) and with those of Pierre Col: 'I
say that Master Jean de Meun in his book introduced characters, and made each
character speak according to his nature, that is, the Jealous man as a jealous man, the Old
Woman as an old woman, and similarly with the others. And it is wrongheaded to say that
the author believes women to be evil as the Jealous Man, in accordance with his character,
declares. This is clearly not true of the author. He merely recites what any jealous man
says about women invariably, and Meun does this in order to demonstrate and correct the
enormous irrationality and disordered passion of jealous men' (see Baird and Kane,
Querrelle, pp. 103-04). But the fears of Gerson and Christine were not groundless. The
Roman received a range of readings (on which see Pierre-Yves Badel, *Le Roman de la Rose au
XIVe siècle: Étude de la réception de l'oeuvre* [Geneva, 1980] 55-114). There *were* readers who
took the *Roman* at face value. Guillaume de Deguilleville, for one, is critical of the
doctrines of the *Roman*, and includes Jean de Meun among Venus's servants in his
Pèlerinage de la Vie Humaine. Deguilleville was not unsophisticated, and Gower knew his
poem. My point, however, ultimately concerns not precedents but what I believe the
evidence of *Gower's* work dictates his moral judgment of the *Roman* would have been —
quite negative. On the Quarrel see further Eric Hicks, ed., *Le Debat sur le Roman de la Rose*
(Paris, 1977), and the bibliography in Luria, *Reader's Guide*, pp. 252-53.

[74] It is difficult to date Gower's French poetry accurately. Some scholars (notably John
Fisher, *John Gower*, p. x) judge the *Cinkante Ballades* his earliest works; others (Macaulay,
Works, I, xiii) award that position to the *Mirour*. My sense is that the ballades are a
collection brought together over time, as were Petrarch's *Canzoniere*, and that the *Mirour* is
the first *complete* poem of Gower's we have.

> Lors est il fols qui ses travauls
> Met en amour si desloiauls,
> Dont au final nuls est joyant.
> Mais quiq'en voet fuïr les mals,
> Entende et tiegne mes consals,
> Que je luy dirray en avant.   (*MO*, 1-12)

['Listen to this, every lover, who seems so desirous of sin, whose love is false: Leave the Mother with all her children, for he who is most attendant on them, in the end will have a willow hat [i.e., will weep]. Therefore he is foolish who exerts himself in a love so treacherous from which in the end no one rejoices. But he who wishes to flee evils, let him listen to and keep my counsels, which I shall give him hereafter.']^[75]

I doubt there is a greater contrast with the ironic idiolect of Jean de Meun than the blunt French of these lines, so consciously uncourtly, or a farther remove from the *Roman*'s vernal, venereal world than the uncompromising place whence this voice emanates. In all his works, Chaucer echoes it only three times, in the *Retraction*, the *Parson's Tale*, and when Troilus casts off, with that frozen laugh, 'the blynde lust, the which that may nat laste' (*TC* V, 1824); but — not insignificantly, I think — it is a tone that each time takes him to eternity's brink, and, once, a sphere beyond, to reach.^[76] For Gower, however, this attitude is an obvious constant in the early writing and is present more subtlely, but unremittingly, in the *Confessio Amantis* and the ballades. He pointedly sought inspiration in the penitential and sermonic literatures which focussed on the sins and virtues, and in their primary offshoot, the didactic books of the *speculum regis* tradition. Russell Peck, drawing attention to these aspects of Gower's art, has called him rightly 'the English poet during this period who most systematically studies the ills of his society and theorizes their basis in personal behavior.'^[77]

And yet, for all that, the courtly world initiated by the *Roman* seldom seems far from Gower's mind, in large part I think because it had such hegemony over the poetic idiom he chose to use. For it is an interesting fact about Gower, that while he is closest ideologically to the reformist writers of the alliterative revival — Langland, the authors of *Mum and the Sothsegger* or *Winner and Wastour* — his *formal* peer among his countrymen is none of them, but England's 'grand translateur' (as Deschamps called him), Geoffrey Chaucer instead. And Chaucer of course built his career around the ethos of courtly verse, either in imitation of it, as in the early dream visions, or in measured, often ironic criticism. Gower's problem, in a way, is identical to that of 'hende Nicholas' in the *Miller's Tale*, who can disfigure courtly speech but still must use it if he speaks of love at all.

---

⁷⁵ William Burton Wilson, 'A Translation of John Gower's *Mirour de l'Omme*,' Ph.D. dissertation, University of Miami, 1970.
⁷⁶ See Howard, *Idea of the Canterbury Tales*, p. 132, and further my own ' "O Moral Gower": Chaucer's Dedication of *Troilus and Criseyde*,' *Chaucer Review*, 19 (1984), 87-99.
⁷⁷ Peck, *Kingship and Common Profit*, p. xvii.

As apparently Gower felt he had to do: For he does not avoid love to favor other topics, arguably more 'serious.' This way might have been Langland's, and that of the alliterative moralists, but it was not his. We see a clear example of this in the first dozen lines of the *Mirour* we looked at, above. The audience Gower selects to address is 'every lover' ('chascun amant'). No doubt he meant something like 'Everyman' here. But we should note carefully the non-appearance of 'chascun homme' where appropriately we could expect it, in a work that is a meticulous catalogue of *every* human virtue and vice, and not a 'love' poem at all. Very shortly we see what Gower is up to, of course. 'Amant' in the *Mirour* subsumes anyone who takes delight in the things of this world ('Quanq'en son coer souhaideroit/ Du siecle, pour soy deliter,' ll. 26-27). It is thus against 'l'amour seculer' (l. 31) in general that Gower will harangue, and he means by it any love directed elsewhere than toward God.

To treat love so — to turn it to a metaphor for speciating cosmic good and evil — is no invention of Gower's, certainly.[78] Jean de Meun had anticipated, even practiced it, for his own purposes; and more tellingly, it was Dante's way as well, who carried out his task so grandly in the *Commedia* as to make comparison with the *Mirour* possible only obliquely. Yet to understand what Gower attempted in the *Mirour* it is helpful to bring these two poems, and their poets, together momentarily. The sublimity of Dante's achievement aside, Gower shared with him certain fundamental concerns. Both numbered among their central themes the revelation of just government, and the squaring of physical and spiritual passions in a morally circumfluent world. That these concerns could be moved through poetry neither poet held in doubt. Each believed deeply in the seriousness of the poetic enterprise, and in the calling of the poet to a purpose higher than what the amorous literary tradition allowed.[79]

For clearly, both Gower and Dante felt the limitations of this poetry — the *Roman de la Rose*, the work of the troubadours.[80] But just as clearly they recognized its extraordinary latent power as well. Dante probably chronicled the moment of his own direction in the final chapter of the *Vita Nuova*, where he vows

---

[78] Kurt O. Olsson has studied non-poetic sources in the *speculum* literature, for example; see his helpful essay, 'The Cardinal Virtues and the Structure of Gower's *Speculum Meditantis*,' *Journal of Medieval and Renaissance Studies*, 7 (1977), 113-48. Olsson offers a comprehensive interpretation of the poem, with which I believe my arguments here are compatible.

[79] Howard Schless has made the same point somewhat differently. Responding to J.A.W. Bennett's assertion that Chaucer was 'the first Englishman to share Dante's sense of the worth of poetry and of the act of poetic creation,' Schless notes, 'As given, this evaluation takes too little account of Chaucer's contemporaries — of Langland or Gower or the Pearl Poet, among others;' see *Chaucer and Dante: A Revaluation* (Norman, OK, 1984) 69.

[80] Peter Dronke describes Dante's transformation of the lyric tradition he inherited in these terms; see *The Medieval Lyric*, 2nd edn. (Cambridge, 1977) 161-66. Mark Musa, *Dante's Vita Nuova: A Translation and an Essay* (Bloomington and London, 1973) 171-74, argues similarly, that 'Dante has gone far beyond what he found at hand in the love poetry of the Troubadours and of their followers.' See also Charles S. Singleton's characterization of Dante as one 'who refused to remain a troubadour,' in *An Essay on the Vita Nuova* (Cambridge, MA, 1958) 55-77.

'to compose concerning [Beatrice] what has never been written in rhyme of any woman,' thereby transforming his courtly attachment into a higher devotion, to poetry itself.[81]

Gower has left us no such telling statement as this; yet from the similarity of their responses, we can believe that both he and Dante understood themselves challenged in the same way by the body of vernacular love poetry they knew in common. They each attempted to take back the rich, evocative language of love from secular poets of lower horizons and coarser purposes, in order to convert it to those higher uses for which they believed their art was intended.

To accomplish this, both Gower and Dante also ran a common risk. Audiences, given to hearing what they expect, can misunderstand a new use of a familiar idiom. Might they not assume Gower and Dante held the attitudes their conscript language typically conveyed?[82] It was a danger both poets recognized, and dealt with similarly — by rebutting it directly, within their work. Certainly one of Dante's purposes in the *Vita Nuova* was to leave no doubt as to just how *much* the sentiment of the *dolce stil nuovo* had transformed his *ballatas*, sonnets and *canzoni* into something superior to ordinary troubadour verse. It is a concern he built into the *Commedia* as well, in passages like the Pilgrim's meeting with Bonagiunta (*Purgatorio* XXIV), a conversation between men of letters which explicitly locates Dante's poetry as not only first among love poets but also cosmically, teleologically. For we cannot overlook that the Luccan poet's place is Purgatory, even as we anticipate (and compare it with) Dante's, present and future. Nor are we allowed, in that context, to mistake in Bonagiunta's recognition of what held other poets 'back from attaining the sweet new style of which [he had] heard' the causal connection he draws between Dante's mastery of that style and the privileged vision which the *Commedia* represents.[83]

---

[81] The translation is that of Barbara Reynolds, *La Vita Nuova (Poems of Youth)* (Harmondsworth and Baltimore, 1969) 99. Étienne Gilson develops the argument that 'the *object* of [Dante's] love for Beatrice was to sing of her' in *Dante and Philosophy*, tr. David Moore (New York, 1963) 59-61. And see also Benedetto Croce's still-valuable remarks on Dante's 'consecration' of his 'new style' to Beatrice, *The Poetry of Dante*, tr. Douglas Ainslie (New York, 1922) 42-47.

[82] Reynolds, *La Vita Nuova*, 16-17, represents Dante's circumstances with, I believe, an appropriate measure of concern: 'Looking back, after the death of Beatrice . . . Dante felt impelled to clarify the means by which he had already extended the range of Italian poetry and by which it was now certain he would venture still farther. What innovations had he made? Not in structure: he used mainly the sonnet, *ballata*, and *canzone*, in accordance with metrical rules already laid down by his predecessors. Not in vocabulary: his word-list in the *Vita Nuova* is not extensive and there is much repetition. It was in the gradually increasing admittance of reality into the enclosed garden of poetic convention that Dante made his most original and creative discoveries.' But 'reality' is an elusive element to distinguish, if one uses the language of convention; there leaves much room for clarification.

[83] *Purgatorio* XXIV, 55-57:

> 'O frate, issa vegg'io,' diss'elli, 'il nodo
> che 'l Notaro e Guittone e me ritenne
> di qua dal dolce stil novo ch'i' odo!'

The text is that of Charles S. Singleton, *Dante: The Divine Comedy*, Bollingen Series 80

Bonagiunta speaks for Dante when he suggests that the Pilgrim stands before him in part because he has written well. The extraordinary journey which brings Dante to talk with Bonagiunta is his poetic inspiration, his assurance of salvation — and also his reward.[84]

Gower wrote no critical prose we know of, but he did parallel Dante in building into his works clarifying passages like this of Bonagiunta. His purpose is identical to Dante's. He too wanted to assure against any misperception of how, and why, he might employ the vocabulary and the strategies of courtly poetry. That this was his method from the first is apparent from its presence in the *Mirour de l'Omme* — a poem more carefully put together, and more dependent upon the courtly ethos, than is often noticed.

Lacking space here to give this poem complete discussion, I shall make two points only, to illustrate how Gower effects meaning in the *Mirour* by a careful manipulation of structure and allusion. Were no leaves missing from the front and back of the unique manuscript, the blueprint of the *Mirour* would, very likely, be easier seen.[85] Still, we have enough to be fairly sure of Gower's plan, which will be more readily visible from a review of the *Mirour*'s narrative sequence. The opening address to 'every lover' gives way shortly to an extended personification, first of the Fall of Adam, followed by the Devil's incestuous love for his daughter, Sin, and hers for Death, their son. From this union come the mortal sins.[86] The three join with Flesh and the World to tempt Man again, but he is saved by Reason, Fear and Conscience. To obtain power over Soul, the Devil weds the seven daughters of Sin to the World, who gets upon them a multifarious brood. All of the subordinate sins are named, and their work described. The Devil, well supported this time, succeeds in enslaving Man. Reason and Conscience are driven out, and plead for justice in the high court of God. God marries his own seven daughters — the Virtues — to Reason, 'whereby they too could multiply, so that each in her office might resist a vice, one against the other' ('Dont se pourront multeplier;/ Sique chascune en son mestier/ Doit contre un vice resister,/ Un contre un autre,' *MO*, 10074-77.) Reason and the Virtues have many children, all of which help the Soul in its struggle against Flesh and the sins. The progress of this struggle is described in

(Princeton, NJ, 1970-75). All subsequent quotations from the *Divine Comedy* are taken from this edition.

[84] Thus Bonagiunta acknowledges Dante's divine inspiration (*Purg.* XXIV, 58-60):

> Io veggio ben come le vostre penne
> di retro al dittator sen vanno strette,
> che de le nostre certo non avvenne.

['Clearly I see how your pens follow close after him who dictates, which certainly befell not with ours.'] 'Him who dictates' is Love, initially, but also God. The sense of reward is everywhere implicit, from Bonagiunta's prophecy that shortly 'that will be clear to you which my speech cannot further declare' ('che ti fia chiaro/ cio che 'l mio dir piu dichiarar non puote,' *Purg.* XXIV, 89-90), to the 'Letter to Can Grande;' see especially par. 19-24.

[85] Macaulay, *Works*, I, lxix, points out that four leaves have been lost from the beginning of the unique manuscript.

[86] It is a description which may have had some resonance. See J.S.P. Tatlock, 'Milton's Sin and Death,' *Modern Language Notes*, 21 (1906), 239-40.

terms of the corruption of the Three Estates, because 'Sin generally rules everywhere, at her will, both the schools and the trades' ('Sique Pecché communement/ Par tout governe a son talent/ L'escoles et les artifices,' *MO*, 18418-20). Man, it is concluded, is thoroughly corrupt, and without hope except he repent. The poet himself confesses his sinful life (including the writing of 'foolish love ditties, which I danced about singing' ['les fols ditz d'amours fesoie,/ Dont en chantant je carolloie,' *MO*, 27340-41), and completes the poem with a long (ca. 2,000 line) prayer to the Virgin for grace, in which the life of Christ is abridged as her Joys and Sorrows are rehearsed.

So simplified, the structure of the *Mirour* reveals how central to Gower's poetic imagination were the language and rituals of love. The body of the poem with its diverse antecedents — penitential literature, Prudentian psychomachia, estates satire and complaint, biblical narrative — is developed within an 'envelope' of amorous address, first (as we have seen) to the audience as 'chascun amant' and then, throughout the concluding sections, to the Virgin presented as a *donna* in the manner of lyric.[87] That the *Mirour* is framed so for a purpose becomes clear as we note that its primary metaphors are marriage and generation. By comparison with the two marriages (of the World with the Sins and Reason with the Virtues) and the subsequent naming of the progeny, the combat between the good and evil forces receives perfunctory attention. Now, this seems strange: for it is this battle which provides the *raison d'être* for all the unions. By rights it ought to be cataclysmic, but instead it shrinks steadily in importance as it recedes before its elaborate preparations.[88]

There is in this puzzling recession a key to Gower's treatment of courtly language in the *Mirour*, and to the poem's structure. Essentially the *Mirour* is about desire, good and bad. The moral encyclopedism of the poem, the naming and describing of virtues and vices, is an apparatus necessary because desire is omnipresent in such vast variety in human affairs that it must be adumbrated to be discussed. This enumerative process is the real 'battle' in the *Mirour*, as it is in all didactic literature: the struggle to identify right and wrong, and then to cast what we know of these things into words.

Thus the *Mirour* is, like the *Divine Comedy*, also about language, which Gower and Dante, following Augustine, would have thought resembled desire in its origin and movement.[89] 'Both,' as Warren Ginsberg has remarked concerning Dante,

---

[87] Dronke, *Medieval Lyric*, pp. 48-63, traces the conflation of amorous and religious lyric conventions, with the Virgin at its center.

[88] Olsson, 'Cardinal Virtues,' has sought to explain the absence of pitched battle by reference to the nature of the challenge 'Open warfare would seem to be futile against the continual treachery of the vicious daughters . . . Against such foes, man needs the help of prudence, or of the progeny of Resoun. And warfare, however allegorical, is not in keeping with the medieval definition of the first of the cardinal virtues' (p. 127). Thus, Olsson argues, Gower forces his readers to discover prudence by denying them a battle they have been led by the form to expect. In the same way, I think, he supposed his audience would be brought to meditate on proper and improper love.

[89] My argument here, as elsewhere my readings of Dante, owes most to John Freccero, who has put the case thus: 'The association of language and desire is at least as old as the

are means to an end. We desire the apple because we do not have it, even as the word 'apple' is not the apple itself, but a sign that points to it. In Dante's poem, God is the end-point, the thing signified: He is the peace that satisfies all desires, the eternal Word all temporal language is derived from and refers to. In the fifth canto of the *Inferno*, Paolo and Francesca were brought to satisfy their physical desires by reading a book; neither understood that the words they read and the desire they felt ought to have been signs that mediated between themselves and God.[90]

In the *Mirour*, Gower offers us two kinds of evidence that he also connected language and desire in this way. There is the courtly 'envelope' of the poem's beginning and end. This trains attention on desire by speaking of it as we do most often: using the language of amorous discourse, in which 'desire' itself has an immediate sexual register. And Gower's treatment of his narrator-figure represents proof of another kind. Although he claims to be afflicted by all seven of the sins ('Ce sont les sept, tresbien le sai,/ Qui sont les chiefs de ma folie,' *MO*, 27369-70), he names but one serious offense — the composition ('fesoie') and performance ('chantant') of poetry, of 'fols ditz d'amours' (*MO*, 27340). The suggestion is that wrongful desire, expressed in wrongful language, was the *germe fecondo* of the poet/narrator's plight. Consequently, the narrator realizes that, for him, salvation can come only by reversing this *peccatum* — by turning, that is, his mortal *carole* into 'un chançon cordial,' a truer 'song of the heart' (*MO*, 27351).[91]

That this song turns out to be the long prayer to the Virgin, addressed as a courtly lady, should not surprise us, then. It constitutes a lyrical solution to a problem the poet/narrator presents consistently in lyrical terms.[92] Nor should we

---

Phaedrus and is documented in Dante's poem by the story of Francesca. The transfer of the virtual image of desire from the written text to the human heart and back again is part of the history of all erotic literature, but especially of Dante's writing, where Love's progress is identical with the movement of poetry toward the silence of the ending.' See *Dante: The Poetics of Conversion*, ed. and with introduction by Rachel Jacoff (Cambridge, MA, 1986) 193.

[90] Warren Ginsberg, *The Cast of Character: The Represenatation of Personality in Ancient and Medieval Literature* (Toronto, 1983), p. 80.

[91] The narrator's logic relies on principles familiar to the Middle Ages from Aristotle's *Physics* (I. vii), in which forms of change are assigned to one of three categories — motion, corruption, and generation. Motion is considered a neutral change, from an affirmative state to an affirmative; corruption, a negative change, from an affirmation to a negation; and generation a positive change, from a negative state to one of affirmation. Gower was not the first to poeticize it. Singleton traces the development of the concept through Aquinas, showing the use Dante makes of it in the *Divine Comedy*, to illustrate the spiritual growth of the Pilgrim and to ground his passing from Virgil to Beatrice as guides; see *Journey to Beatrice*, Dante Studies 2 (Cambridge, MA, 1958) 39-71. And see further Freccero, *Poetics of Conversion*, 166-79, who carries Singleton's reading still deeper into the *Commedia*.

[92] Especially the medieval Marian lyric, which commingled courtly and devotional vocabulary from the twelfth century. Rosemary Woolf points out that despite 'quite a long history of Marian piety' lyrics to the Virgin were uncommon in English until the fifteenth

find it strange that Gower elected so to conclude the *Mirour*. For prayer (as Augustine and Dante knew well) uniquely resolves the dilemmas of desire and language — courtly and otherwise — by properly directing both toward satisfaction in the Word of God.[93] Thus Gower's conclusion draws together the multivalent concerns of the *Mirour de l'Omme*. At once a poet's closure well suited to his narrator and himself, it is also theologically sound.

The use Gower makes of the language of courtly love in the *Mirour*, then, is purposeful, and at the center of his poem's meaning. Like Dante, who forced 'the imagery of the *dolce stil nuovo* . . . to undercut its theory of love,' as John Freccero has remarked, so Gower stretches amorous discourse to compass greater issues than it usually allows.[94] In the process he hoped, I think, to turn this language on its head, to reverse its priorities completely.

That he did not entirely succeed in so large a task is scant cause for wonder. The *Mirour* is early work. But reading it, even so cursorily as we have done here, has value. It can teach us much about Gower's ambition, and help us to perceive his basic concerns and strategies. This is particularly true about his control of his manner of expression, and the expectations it reveals he must have had for his audience. For Gower clearly intended to convey a great deal by subtle means. Let us look at one further example from the *Mirour*, before returning to our question of borrowed lines in the ballades.

We have suggested that Gower likely felt a risk of misinterpretation when he converted the familiar language and figures of courtly love to newly-moral uses in the *Mirour de l'Omme*. While to us, perhaps, this poem appears impossible to misunderstand so, yet referential evidence exists that Gower gave some thought to how he might ensure his poem against misreading. The problem once more is the *Roman de la Rose*. Nothing is truly borrowed from the *Roman* into the *Mirour*, but its allegory stands conspicuously behind Gower's characters Reson, Paour and Foldelit, forcing us to recall the *Roman* as their source. (This pressure is doubtless stronger because the *Mirour* is written in French.) Such enforced referentiality is finally to Gower's advantage, since the sensibility and counsel of the *Roman* are among his primary targets; but undoubtedly he knew a special urgency to govern the way his poem might be read, cast up against this backdrop.

His general method in the *Mirour* is to quote extensively (or better, paraphrase) from authorities, primarily the Bible and the Fathers but also ancient moralists like Cicero and Seneca.[95] It is an ordinary enough technique of the penitential and sermonic traditions, and a favorite of Langland's. In Gower's poem its effect is grounding: Here is no lovers' garden. The quotations leave little doubt about the moral imperatives of the fictive world we have entered, and create a kind of

---

century. They were numerous, however, in France; see *The English Religious Lyric in the Middle Ages* (Oxford, 1969) 114-15 and passim.

[93] I have in mind here such connections as Augustine makes between prayer and writing in *Soliloquies*, I.i.

[94] Freccero, *Poetics of Conversion*, p. 193.

[95] On the frequency of Gower's quotations, see Macaulay, *Works*, I, lvi-lviii; also a list of proverbs, lviii-lx.

counter-context within which the borrowed figures from the *Roman* are safely
contained.

Among these standard references, however, one seems singled out for special
attention. It is, in any case, quite different from the others (*MO*, 11404-09):

> Mestre Helemauns, qui fist toutpleins
> Lez Vers du Mort, tesmoigne au meinz
> Qe mort t'ad dist comme tu orras:
> 'Houstez *voz troeffes et voz gas,*
> *Car* tiel *me couve soubz ses dras*
> Q'assetz *quide estre fortz et seins.*'

['Master Hélinant, who wrote *The Verses of Death*, says that death has told
you at least the following: 'Do away with your mockery and your
boasting, for many a man who thinks himself sound and strong has me
already hatching within him'.']

This passage is interesting in several ways. It is, first, close to what we mean
today by quotation — i.e., the acknowledged replication of one text within
another. 'Mestre Helemauns' is Hélinant de Froidmont, the author, as Gower
duly notes, of the *Vers de la Mort*, a poem of wide popularity in the thirteenth and
fourteenth centuries.[96] Medieval writers were seldom so specific. More common
is an approach like Chaucer's 'For after the sawe of the word of the Apostle' (*CT*
VII, 1839), followed by a broad paraphrase of I Tim. 6:10, or Gower's own 'En
s'evangile dieus du ciel/ Dist' ('In his Gospel the God of heaven said,' *MO*,
20593-4), introducing a version of Matt. 15:14. Here, however, Gower copies
Hélinant's lines from the *Vers de la Mort* exactly, as may be seen by comparing
Gower's with Hélinant's own:

> Laisseiez *voz trufes et voz gas!*
> *Car me cueve* desoz *ses dras*
> *Qui cuide estre* tous *fors et sains.*[97]

Quotation of this sort is something we might expect to find in the work of a poet
to whom cento appealed. Yet to speak against our mistaking it for cento, there is

[96] See the edition of Fredrik Wulff and Emmanuel Walberg, *Les Vers de la Mort, par
Hélinant, Moine de Froidmont* (Paris, 1905). In their introduction, the editors describe 24
extant manuscripts of the poem, and note: 'La vogue de ces vers . . . est attestée non
seulement par le grand nombre de copies qui nous en sont conservées, et dont plu siers ont
été executées plus d'un siècle après la composition du poème, mais aussi bien par les echos
qu'on en retrouve dans des ouvrages posterieurs, et par les imitations directes qu'ils
susciterent' (p. iii).
[97] *Vers de la Mort*, XV, 10-12. Wulff and Walberg point out (p. xxiv) that some of the
manuscripts we have exist in a form 'presque inintelligible.' It is impossible to say which,
if any, Gower might have seen, but given the textual variants, a version akin to Bibl. Nat.
lat. 14958 seems probable. The lines quoted above represent a composite based on that
version. See the editors' note, p. 15.

the identification of the lines *as* quotation. With a solicitude oddly modern (and certainly not plagiaristic!) Gower names his source-text and its author.

There are, perhaps, many ways to explain Gower's handling of this passage, but to me only two seem probable.[98] One is that what we see is fortuitous: Gower had the *Vers de la Mort* at hand, wanted a little *auctoritas* to make his point, and — because Hélinant's poem was in the same meter as the *Mirour* — simply transferred the lines. He didn't even need to change the dialect: Late-century Anglo-Norman was an accommodating, all-but-literary tongue.[99] This explanation is attractive for obvious reasons. It suits the usual view of Gower as a haphazard craftsman, and it requires no further thought.

The other possibility is more demanding. It is that Gower quoted Hélinant because he wanted to acknowledge a debt to him, and hoped by so doing to establish his poem within a field of others sharing the moral purposes of the *Vers de la Mort*. Dante's quotations frequently work like this, directing us outside the *Commedia* to a context which serves to gloss the passage. Many of these references are to his contemporaries' poetry; some are to his own.[100] No one has suggested Gower made much use of this technique, but I believe there is cause to suspect him of it here.

His quotation of Hélinant is unusual for reasons other than its exactitude. The monk of Froidmont was, first, a near contemporary, not a classical or early Christian author. Gower could have made no mistake about his *auctoritas*. Mention of his name, and the name of his poem, represents a shift of sorts. Moreover, Hélinant is the only 'modern' named in the *Mirour* — a fact which

[98] Father J.B. Dwyer proposed some years ago in a strong study, 'Gower's *Mirour* and Its French Sources: A Reexamination of Evidence,' (*Studies in Philology*, 48 [1951], 482-505), that Gower borrowed Hélinant's lines from Frère Lorens's *Somme des Vices et Vertus*, where they are also quoted. Because, as Dwyer shows, Gower clearly did rely on the *Somme* for 'parallel ideas and images' (p. 495), it is likely that he knew these lines in the *Somme*. But because of the popularity of the *Vers de la Mort*, Gower's knowledge of that text, and the tradition of moral poetry it initiated, is equally likely — the more so because Gower derived the intricate rhyme scheme of the *Mirour* from Hélinant, not from the *Somme*. However, since my point is the *use* Gower sought from bringing Hélinant's poem before his readers, and the moral poetry which sprang up in imitation of the *Vers de la Mort*, the source of his borrowing is of secondary importance here. Hence, while it seems to me probable that Dwyer has identified the *locus in quo* of Gower's idea, I present the case in its barest form, as if Gower drew directly on Hélinant.

[99] Johan Vising, in *Anglo-Norman Language and Literature* (Oxford, 1923; rep. Westport, CT, 1970), characterizes Anglo-Norman of Gower's time as a *mélange* of French dialects, including northern and south-western influences (p. 32). He remarks that 'during the thirteenth century Anglo-Norman became more and more inconsistent and irregular, and . . . many authors confess their uncertain knowledge of the language' (p. 33). This meant, in effect, that English readers were accustomed to finding broad formal diversity in their French texts, and made the necessary adjustments.

[100] The literature devoted to Dante's quotations is vast. On his references to two central figures — Virgil and Augustine — see Guiseppe Mazzotta, *Dante, Poet of the Desert: History and Allegory in the Divine Comedy* (Princeton, NJ, 1979) 147-91. On Dante's self-quotation, see Freccero, *Poetics of Conversion*, p. 186.

seems less coincidental when we take into account that the intricate rhyme
scheme of the *Vers de la Mort* is identical to the *Mirour*'s, and probably served
Gower as his model.[101] As indeed it served others: for Hélinant's poem seems to
have established its rhyme as a sort of *forme fixe*, appropriate for works with moral
arguments. At least, that is the kind of verse in which we find it most often.
Among others who used it were Rutebeuf, in didactic and satiric pieces, the so-
called 'Reclus de Moiliens,' and Jean Bodel and Adam d'Arras, for *congiés*, or
verses on taking leave of the world.[102]

What might Gower have gained from inclusion in such serious company?
Protection from misinterpretation, certainly; for, set among writers of this order,
there would be no mistaking his poetic stance, or any use of language. Beyond
this, he stood to register yet another corrective against the *Roman de la Rose*.
Gower quotes Hélinant to support the second of four points made by Fear
('Paour'), second daughter of Humility. The points 'recall sinners' to God from
their wickedness ('Tout quatre pointz chante et repelle/ Les peccheours,' *MO* ll.
11354-55.) In describing Fear, Gower is careful to distinguish between kinds:
most are of worldly things, like loss of money or corporal punishment ('soul pour
doubte seculier/ Du corporiel punisement,/ Ou perte avoir de leur argent,' *MO*
10995-97), but 'right Fear' ('Le droit Paour' is to be put 'tout soul en dieu' — in
God alone (*MO* 11234). His portrait of 'Le droit Paour' is worth our notice (*MO*
11246-56).

> Al huiss du chambre il est huissher,
> Qui porte defensable mace;
> Dont, quant ly deable voet entrer
> Pour faire l'alme foloier,
> Paour le fiert enmy la face
> Et le deboute au force et chace:
> Paour auci la Char manace,
> Qe d'orguil n'ose forsvoier:
> Paour est gardeins de la place,
> U il herberge Bonne grace,
> Et laist Pecché dehors estier.

['She is the doorkeeper at the chamber door, bearing the mace of
defense, with which she strikes the devil in the face, when he tries to
come in to make the soul play the fool. She then kicks the devil out and
chases him away. Fear also admonishes Flesh, lest Flesh go off in pride.
Fear is the guardian of the place where she lodges Good Favor; she
leaves Sin outside.']

---

[101] That is, unless other 'moderns' were named in the pages lost from the manuscript.
[102] Twenty-eight poems using this stanza are listed by Gaston Raynaud, 'Les congés de
Jean Bodel,' *Romania*, (1880), 231-32. All are didactic and moral. See Macaulay, *Works*,
I, xliii, on the twelve-line stanza.

Now, 'Paour' is one of the few allegorical figures in the *Mirour* with an antecedent in the *Roman*. There 'Poor' is also female and, in the company of Shame ('Honte'), arouses the churl Dangier to wield his club (a detail Gower has transferred to Paour) to keep Bel Acuel ('Fair Welcome') and the Lover out of the garden of the Rose.[103] Gower strengthens this association with the *Roman* by speaking subsequently of Fear as 'the good treasurer, who guards intact all the treasures which are shut up in the heart' ('ly bons tresorers/, Qui gart tous les tresors entiers/, Qui deinz le cuer sont enserré,' *MO* 11269-71) and as an efficient 'weeder of a garden' ('Du gardin au bon sartiliers') who 'uproots the poisonous nettle from among the rose bushes' ('Qui celle urtie maluré/ Ove la racine envenimé/ Estrepe d'entre les rosiers,' *MO* 11277-80).

These echoes are strong enough to have recalled the figure of Poor for Gower's audience. If we read them with the *Roman* as background, however, we see that Gower has reversed the terms of his source. For in the *Roman* our sympathies are expected to lie with the Lover and Bel Acuel, whose progress toward the Rose is impeded by Dangier, Honte and Poor. The problem they pose requires their defeat as its solution. The Lover must find means to re-enter the garden despite their vigilance. Contextually in the *Roman*, then, Poor is a *negative* character. But in the *Mirour* the opposite is true. 'Right Fear' banishes the devil, 'Char' ('Flesh') and Sin. In effect Gower renders a moral critique of the central *affaire* of the *Roman* — which, in simple terms, is fleshly conquest, sin, the devil's work. He leaves it open to us to complete the equation of the Lover with Char, and 'Bonne grace' ('Good Favor') with a (legitimized) Bel Acuel, who in the righteous universe belongs under the guardianship of a 'droit Paour.'

Borrowing a quotation from Hélinant and interleaving it precisely here, then, strengthens Gower's hand, and give his manipulation of the *Roman* a certain privilege. A brief but telling show of colors, a kind of *segno assoluto* of intent, the lines from the *Vers de la Mort* act in the *Mirour* like a declaration of allegiance to a moral theory of poetics. The flourish is a small one, but significant. It confronts us with the case of Bonagiunta's words to the pilgrim Dante, presented on a less ambitious scale.[104]

V

The *Mirour* can serve us, then, as a suitable introduction to Gower's methods, and to what he expected his audience to notice. At this juncture it might be helpful to look briefly backward over the territory we have covered, before

---

[103] I have used Daniel Poirion's edition of the *Roman de la Rose* (Paris, 1974), as my text; see ll. 363 ff.

[104] Scale is of importance here. When Gower quotes Hélinant, he does so *as an addition* to the larger themes of his poem, which — as Olsson, 'Cardinal Virtues,' has correctly pointed out — relate the generality of sin to absolute salvation and its rewards. For this reason, the placement of the quotation is of little significance (as Dante's location of Bonagiunta is, in contrast, most telling): Its value as a kind of 'insurance policy' would be the same were it found in many other *loci* in the *Mirour*.

proceeding further with these arguments. We began with a question we have yet to answer, about the relationship to his poetics generally, and to his interest in the cento, of the lines Gower borrowed into his ballades from French courtly lyric. I suggested that the ballade sequences illustrate Gower's continuing attempt to develop the moral register of amorous discourse — to 'rehabilitate' the idiom, in effect, by employing it 'against' itself. In the *Mirour de l'Omme*, where his target is primarily the *Roman de la Rose*, he advanced this enterprise structurally, enclosing an anatomy of good and wicked desires inside an 'envelope' of courtly address and lyrical supplication. Gower's method, which in certain ways parallels Dante's in the *Commedia* and elsewhere, is subtle yet timely. He sought to redirect 'luf talkyng' when (as testimony as diverse as Edward III's Household Ordinances and *Gawain and the Green Knight* shows) it was fast becoming manneristic and self-consciously institutionalized.

With this background, we can approach the problem of borrowed lines in the ballade sequences and what they have to tell us about Gower's style by setting out a few conclusions and working backward through the proofs. Language, which we have seen is a major topic in the *Mirour*, plays an even greater role in the ballades. In part this is because lyric poetry — by ancient definition lacking narrative and mimetic force — was thought to depend heavily on verbal polish for success.[105] This dependence is especially noticeable in the courtly love lyrics of Gower's time, which to a high degree refined and conventionalized the rhetorical trope. At worst — the work of courtiers for whom verse was an accessory, like windowed shoes or a long-sleeved gown — such pieces are *only* language, a feckless pushing round of words without life.

Gower's two ballade sequences attempt something very different. Love is offered unconventionally in these poems, as neither a private experience shared to elicit empathy, nor as a *sujet* to showcase bromidic ornament. Instead, Gower chooses love in its practical form, accountable equally to God and Nature, spirit and flesh. Real love has a purpose. It should lead to 'droit mariage,' Gower's

---

[105] The statement presupposes a definition of 'lyric' — a much-vexed question from Aristotle onward, too vast for the present space. Curtius shows us the way, however, by noting that 'The antique system of genres does not correspond with the modern system. For together with genres based on the work as a whole, such as epic, comedy, and tragedy, others, based on versification (iambus, elegy, etc.) are used as classifying principles;' see *European Literature*, p. 248. *Form* — of versification, of expression — thus became the defining element from Horace on. (Dante held this essentially mechanistic understanding of lyric; it dominates Deschamps's *Art de Dictier*, and it would have seemed natural to Gower. See further the discussion of Claudio Guillen, *Literature as System: Essays toward the Theory of Literary History* (Princeton, NJ, 1971), 390-405). Also useful, if rather idiosyncratic, are the remarks of W. R. Johnson, 'On the Absence of Ancient Lyric Theory,' in his *The Idea of Lyric Modes in Ancient and Modern Poetry* (Berkeley and Los Angeles, 1982) 76-95. For Dante's views, see for example *De vulgari eloquentia*, 2.3; on Deschamps, see Kenneth Varty, 'Deschamps' *Art de Dictier*,' *French Studies*, 19 (1965), 164-68; and Glending Olson, 'Deschamps' *Art de Dictier* and Chaucer's Literary Environment,' *Speculum*, 48 (1973), 714-23, especially p. 717, where he points out that in the *Art de Dictier* Deschamps's emphasis is 'on the form rather than subject matter.'

term in the marginal comment beside the fifth of the *Cinkante Ballades*, and his point in the prose headnote to the *Traitié*.

Viewed solely in the context of his work, the decision is unsurprising. As Russell Peck has helped us see, Gower's position on marriage is of a piece with — even emblematic of — his greater promotion of the social ideal of common profit.[106] Both are characteristically mediatory. From the *formal* perspective, however — that of amatory lyric, established by his choice of verse — the insistence on married love is striking. For several reasons, form and content seem bound only to contradict each other.

Now, this is not the case because marriage was forbidden courtly lovers. We have heard already from Andreas Capellanus on that: It is not, he said, a 'real excuse for not loving.'[107] And he makes it his very first rule in a list of thirty-one. But the tone of the voice (like the position, in a way, of the rule on the list) is dismissive. Andreas hurries on, to get to more relevant liaisons. Nor is his treatment idiosyncratic. Three hundred years later it is still the persistent norm, as the fifteenth-century commentator on the *Échecs Amoureux* shows us. Glossing a passage describing the high-minded love shared in Arthur's time, he includes 'the love which is and should be in marriage' ('l'amour qui est et qui doit estre en mariage' as the second of three possible states of affection. The first is carnal love, 'amour folle,' or 'commune au monde,' and clearly unpalatable. The third is 'fin amour,' which resembles conjugal love but which may be shared by unmarried persons ('quelle puist moult bien estre entre personnes frances qui par amours s'entreayment'). This last sort alone holds the commentator's attention.[108]

Married love was seldom a subject, then, for the courtly poets whose lyrics set the style for the kind of ballade Gower wrote. Worse yet, while Machaut and Deschamps (from whom Gower borrowed lines and the ballade form itself) were pious men, the 'innocent' affection they celebrated, 'À l'onneur et à la loange/De toutes dames sans losange,' has troubling implications if one reads very closely in a post-lapserian world.[109] One such fallen reader — Chaucer — recognized the problem in his *Retractions*, when he condemned 'the tales of Caunterbury, thilke that sownen into synne' alongside 'many a song and many a leccherous lay' (*CT* X, 1085-86). Which tales were intended, and which songs and lays, has occasioned much thoughtful guesswork but no consensus, probably because Chaucer's worry here is, like Gower's, a general one.[110] It is that story-telling and 'poetic' — that is to say, amorous — language are slippery fish and risky to entrust to potential (mis)readers. Dante uses Paolo and Francesca to make

---

[106] Peck, *Kingship and Common Profit*, pp. 108-115; and see also his discussion of the story of Mundus and Paulina, pp. 42-45.

[107] *Art of Courtly Love*, tr. Parry, p. 184.

[108] See Ernst Sieper, *'Les Échecs amoreux': eine altfranzösische Nachahmung des Rosenromans und ihre englische Übertragung* (Weimar, 1898) 30 ff.

[109] The collocation is common in Machaut; see for an example his *Prologue*, V, 17-18, in Ernest Hoepffner, ed., *Oeuvres de Guillaume de Machaut*, 3 vols. (Paris, 1907-21) I, 6. All quotations taken from the *dits* of Machaut, unless otherwise noted, are from this edition.

[110] For various views of Chaucer's meaning, see Arthur K. Moore, 'Chaucer's Lost Songs,' *JEGP*, 4 (1949), 196-208, who presents a summary of scholarly opinion.

essentially the same point: Courtly poems all are 'go-betweens' in waiting. Danger of seduction lies latent in the poet's words.

Gower's solution was characteristically direct and, in a way, courageous. Rather than relinquish amorous discourse to writers whose love he found improvident and whose lyrics consequently 'sownen into synne,' he elected I think to open the way for a healthier poetry by composing that poetry himself. To do so, it was necessary both to lay wide the perils of the idiom and to use it, refurbished and reclaimed, in a format which could itself become a model.

The headnote to his second sequence, from which Macaulay extracted the title *Traitié pour essampler les amantz marietz*, prepares us for this program, but subtly, in terms that reward careful scrutiny. Having described 'in English' (i.e., in the *Confessio*, to which the *Traitié* is usually attached) the foolishness of those who affect lovers, Gower says that he

> will now relate hereafter in French, to all the world generally, a treatise according to the authorities, to warn married lovers so that they will be able to preserve the promise of their sacred marriage vows with absolute loyalty, and truly to maintain honor to God.[111]

This introduction is quite unusual. If Gower wrote it — and there is every reason to suppose he did — it represents one of the few declarations we have of his on art, and the only one in prose. Moreover, it suggests that the eighteen ballades to follow were plotted with a suprising thoroughness, beginning with the language in which they were composed. Dante, in *De vulgari eloquentia*, argues that the tongue as well as the idiom and diction should be appropriate to the subject; and while Gower probably took no thought of Dante here, he seems nevertheless to have been similarly concerned.[112] There is, as I have argued elsewhere, good evidence that Gower employed his three languages selectively, matching them to his intended message and audience.[113] But we need no such background to be engaged by what we are told here. To point out that the ballades are in French (or that the preceding *Confessio* is in English) is to call attention to the obvious. No reader, then or now, could miss the change of language. Automatically we must wonder: Why did Gower afford it special mention?

---

[111] 'Puisqu'il ad dit ci devant en Englois par voie d'essample la sotie de cellui qui par amours aime par especial, dirra ore apres en François a tout le monde en general un traitié selonc les auctours pour essampler les amantz marietz, au fin q'ils la foi de lour seintes espousailes pourront par fine loialté guarder, et al honour de dieu salvement tenir.' Text in Macaulay, *Works*, I, 379. The heading as quoted appears in seven of the ten extant manuscripts; of the other three, two are damaged, so that no heading is visible, and the third (MS Hunterian Museum, Glasgow, T.2.17) is headed as follows: 'Cest un traitié quel Iohan Gower ad fait selonc les auctours touchant lestat de matremoine dont les amantz marietz se pourront essampler à tenir la foi de lour seintes espousailes.' See Macaulay's notes, pp. 379 and 470.

[112] I.e., *De vulgari eloquentia*, 2.2; and see further *Convivio* 1.10. 11-14.

[113] ' "oure englisshe" and Everyone's Latin: the *Fasciculus Morum* and Gower's *Confessio Amantis*,' *South Atlantic Review*, 46 (1981), 41-53.

The answer is, I think, that the shift from the English of the *Confessio* to the French of the ballades is intended to signal a difference in the *kind* of poetry we are about to face. The eighteen ballades of the *Traitié* suggest another order of writing from the 'middel weie' of Gower's English poem. In French, at least in the French of an Englishman intended for other Englishmen in the 1390s, they are not 'popular.' Neither are their conventions those of the dream-vision, or the *speculum regis*, or the penitential books, which provide the formal contexts for the *Confessio*. We need different associative gear to read this new poetry properly: The headnote's signal is a timely one. And so Gower introduces his sequence to us, in what is clearly a device to make us better readers. Here and elsewhere he warns us to keep in mind *how* he has written his poems. For we should notice that Gower likes to begin his work with a statement about style. In differing measure we have watched him doing so already, subtly, in the 'envelope' of amorous discourse surrounding the *Mirour*; more clearly, though still refracted by fiction, in the *Confessio*'s opening commentary on its own formation; and here, by way of introduction to a coda of French lyrics, matter-of-factly in French prose. As we saw, this warning in the *Mirour* drew our attention to relationships of language and desire essential to the poem's meaning; and later we shall look at how this discussion of style bears upon our understanding the *Confessio*. Its function here, in the introduction to the *Traitié*, is, first, to invoke the proprietary tradition of these eighteen ballades — the high courtly lyric which, in Gower's lifetime, the French had made their own — and then to announce how the subsequent poems will challenge our expectations.

The lines of this challenge are clear, both from the ballades' proposed subject, married love, and from their description as a 'traitié' composed according to 'authorities.' Let us consider these elements one at a time. To bring together a series of lyrics to form a treatise — that is, to make an *argument* using them — seems very much a strategy the 'moral' Gower might adopt. Yet we should not let its appropriateness to an imaginary picture of the man obscure an underlying originality. 'Argumentative' poetic forms were well established in the Middle Ages: the debate, the complaint, the satire, even (or perhaps especially) the sermon. Most of these Gower had employed already. But I know of no precedent for using a sequence of ballades argumentatively, to set out a moral position.[114]

[114] The question of what constituted a 'traitié' for lyric poets is somewhat muddy. Froissart, who termed six of his longer poems 'trettié' or 'tratiérs,' surely had in mind a generic distinction when he used the word. A 'trettié' was not a 'livre,' a 'dit,' a 'debat,' or a 'plaidoire,' for example; nor was it to be confused with shorter forms such as a lay, a pastourelle, a ballade, etc. This much is clear from the arrangement of poems in the two composite manuscripts whose making we assume Froissart oversaw. Moreover, in describing the collection he presented to Richard II in 1395, Froissart speaks of 'les traittiés amoureux et de moralité' — a distinction emphasized in the manuscripts by descriptive headings prefacing each poem (e.g., 'Ici commence un trettié amourous qui s'appelle Le paradys d'amour;' or 'Ci s'ensieut un trettié de moralité qui s'appelle Le temple d'onnour'). See *Oeuvres de Froissart*, ed. Kervyn de Lettenhove, 29 vols. (Brussells, 1866-77) XV, 141; and *Oeuvres de Froissart: Poesies*, ed. August Scheler, 3 vols. (Brussells, 1870-73), passim. But only the *Temple d'Onneur* is identified as a 'moralité,' and it is written entirely in couplets. Thus nothing in Froissart provides a model for Gower's use of

Nor do 'authorities' figure in lyric poetry — although of course, in a 'treatise' they are a *sine qua non*.

Thus the terms we find in Gower's introduction to the *Traitié* generate questions. Why write French lyrics to make a significant argument about serious matters, when other forms were customary — and familiar to Gower first hand What 'authorities' could suit such an argument, posed in such a form? The questions seem to cut cross-grain against the lyric form itself — and this was, I think, precisely Gower's point, to raise questions about the form. Earlier I suggested that the *Mirour de l'Omme*, with its sights on the *Roman de la Rose*, represents a preliminary attempt of Gower's to reclaim the affective language of courtly love for moral uses by turning it against itself. The ballade sequences are another such attempt, potentially more successful because more thoroughly conceived as literary sabotage. The *Mirour* challenges the *Roman*, but glancingly, as part of a general anatomy of desire. In the *Cinkante Balades* and the *Traitié*, however, Gower is able to make amorous discourse, and the ideals it embodies, his single focus.

These things said, several pieces may be swiftly gathered. Gower announces his eighteen ballades as he does in order to emphasize, at once, the weaknesses of contemporary courtly lyric and how thoroughly he is altering the form. Married love will be his topic because it is both 'honeste' and unsung. Praising it, and it alone, in the courtly voice is to carry lyric to a new and higher register. To insure that we do not overlook the primacy of his moral argument (as well as for another reason we shall examine below) he termed his sequence a 'treatise' and constructed it accordingly. Hence the Latin glosses in the margins, which explain the *moralitas* of the various ballades. They also further our sense of the lyrics as treatise. Hence too the careful ordering of the ballades themselves. And here we need to look more closely, to see how this is so.

The topics of the *Traitié*'s eighteen ballades are arranged to form a persuasive argument. The movement is from the general to the specific, and back to the general again. Thus the first five poems set out the major themes of the sequence — the right purposes of marriage and the evil of adultery; the next ten offer examples of crimes against matrimony; and the last three return to the broad language of the first five to draw conclusions on the whole. Within this larger movement, there are lesser patterns which draw our attention. First among these are the examples themselves. They are an ecclectic lot, taken from equally catholic places: Ulysses and Telegonus. Agamemnon, 'Climestre' and Egistus, Helen, Menelaus and Paris from the *Roman de Troie*; Nectanabus from (primarily) the *Roman de toute chevalerie*; Hercules and Deianera, Jason and

lyric form to carry an argument — although Froissart would seem to set a precedent for the 'trettié' as a poem which comes to a point. See further Daniel Poirion, *Le Poète et le prince: L'Évolution du lyrisme courtois de Guillaume de Machaut à Charles d'Orleans* (Paris, 1965), 205-18. Deschamps maintains similar distinctions of form, separating out 'traictiéz' from lyrics, lays, 'let tres missibles,' 'commissions et autres choses.' For Deschamps, the 'traictié' seems a more argumentative form than for Froissart, and suitable for serious subjects. Again, however, he does not apply the term to sequential ballades. See Queux de St.-Hilaire, *Oeuvres complètes*, I, 1, and Poirion, *Poète et prince*, 218, who finds Deschamps' arrangement of works dependent upon the example of Machaut, and possibly Froissart.

Medea, Tarquin and Lucrece, Tereus and Progne from Ovid; Mundus and Paulina from Vincent of Beauvais; Alboin and Rosamund from Paul the Deacon; Abraham, Pharaoh and Sarah, David and Bathsheba from the Bible; Lancelot, Tristram and Gawain from courtly lyric and romance. One constant binds them all, however In each *exemplum* vengeance provides a central organizing feature. Thus, the sons Alexander, Telegonus, and Orestes slay adulterous parents; the wronged wives Medea and Progne kill their own children by, respectively, the treacherous Jason and the incestuous Tereus (who is fed his son, his crime by that measure worse); the poisoned shirt of Nessus incinerates Hercules, unfaithful with Iole; just punishments (banishment, hanging, burning) are earned by Tarquin and Mundus, Egistus and the false priests of Isis, Rosamund and Elmege. Although usually the agents of this vengeance are human, Gower is specific about its ultimate source: 'God will avenge broken wedlock' ('Freinte espousaile dieux le vengera,' *Tr* VIII, refrain).[115] The omnipresence of God as vigilant judge conjoins all the *exempla*, and directs our reading even of the 'agentless' retributions, displaying them against a vision of justice cosmic and sure: Troy's fall (for housing adulterers); Tereus's metamorphosis ('Dont dieus lui ad en hupe transformée,/ En signe qu'il fuist fals et avoltier,' *Tr* XII, 3.5-6); the humbling of King David ('Merci prioit, merci fuist son desir,' *Tr* XIV, 3.5); the 'purgatoire' Fortune inflicts on Lancelot and Tristan, the punishment awaiting the fickle ('volage') Gawain, 'au fin de son passage.'[116]

Divine outrage and vengeance create a backdrop seemingly intended to invite reflection about the figures the ballades present — a process which, if followed, develops circularly and yields pointed results. Eighteen characters are censured for infidelity in the *Traitié*. Of these, twelve (Climestre, Egistus, Helen, Paris, Nectanabus, Jason, Tarquin, Tereus, Mundus, Rosamund, Elmege, and Pharaoh) are standard examples of vow-breaking and wickedness. They reinforce Gower's moral argument directly, and in familiar ways; for we know them and their stories' meaning as soon as they are named. The other six — Ulysses, Hercules, David, Lancelot, Tristram, and Gawain — have piebald reputations, good and bad. Gower exploited only the negative elements in the *Traitié*, however. He weighted his descriptions to blacken the criminals and emphasize the inevitability of retribution.[117] Thus Ulysses's begetting of Telegonus on Circe forms the center of *Tr* VI, and not Penelope's anxious waiting for her husband's faithful return (told by Gower in the *Confessio* Book IV), for it is Telegonus who will be the agent of vengeance for a sin unknown to Penelope. Thus too it is of

---

[115] The line has special power because it is a refrain. Throughout the sequence, God's role as ultimate judge and avenger is pervasive; see for examples I, II, XII, XIV, etc.
[116] 'Therefore God turned him into a hoopoe, as a sign that he was false and an adulterer,' *Tr* XII, 3.6. It is notable that Gower does not mention the metamorphoses of Procne and Philomena into birds, which would not suit his purpose, i.e., to present the shape-change as a punishment.
[117] Gower's darkening of Nectanabus extends to the *Confessio*; see Peter Beidler's remarks on 'Diabolical Treachery in the Tale of Nectanabus' in his *Literary Transformations*, pp. 83-90.

Hercules's infatuation with Eole (and his unmanly wearing of her clothes — a telling detail, since donning a treacherous shirt will kill him) that we hear in *Tr* VII, rather than about his honorable labors; and similarly, in contrast to his laudatory representation in the *Mirour* (2284 ff.), David's lust for Bersabee and murder of Urie her husband are made our focus in *Tr* XIV.

The examples of Lancelot and Tristram at first glance appear more difficult to classify, although ultimately Gower's strategy is clear. In Ballade XV we learn little about them — only that they remain memorable examples ('en memoire,/ Pour essampler les autres du present,' ll. 1.3-4) of obsession ('sotie'). These allusions are indistinct enough that Gower added a Latin sidenote to spell them out.[118] Gawain's treatment is equally allusive in *Tr* XVII. He is proffered in a general way, as one courteous but fickle, with lovers in different places.[119] Yet on second consideration, Gower's light hand with these three may be just enough. Afforded such scant attention, and placed at the tail-end of so miscreant a company, the knights are stripped of their heroism. Of all their deeds, Gower seems to say, what is important but those that will cost them heaven? It is an off-handed dismissal which suggests the simple clarity of God's view of adulterers — and suddenly we are forced to recall both the motif of divine retribution omnipresent in the sequence, and Gower's announced intention in his introduction to write a 'treatise' in lyric verse, condemning marriage-breakers of every kind, so that married lovers might be fortified to 'keep truly the honor of God.'

There is, then, in Gower's presentation of exemplary figures a kind of circular movement. Having been brought to contemplate ever more deeply the lives of particular figures, we are carried back, by this same motion, to confront again the ballades' moral argument. But this device, while effective, is not the last Gower relied on to achieve his purpose. His introductory concern — to conform his *Traitié* in accord with certain 'auctours' — also works toward this same end, and further objectives.

---

[118] 'Qualiter ob hoc quod Lanceolotus Miles probatissimus Gunnoram regis Arthuri vxuorem fatue peramavit, eciam et quia Tristram simili modo Isoldam regis Marci auunculi sui vxorem violare non timuit, Amantes ambo predicti magno infortunii dolore dies suos extremos clauserunt.' ('Just as the most excellent knight Lancelot foolishly loved Guinevere, wife of King Arthur, even so Tristram in a similar way was not afraid to violate Isolt the wife of his uncle Mark. Both lovers, having been warned, ended their final days in great pain of misfortune.')

[119] Cf. *Tr* XVII, 2:

> N'est pas compaigns q'est comun a chascune;
> Au soule amie ert un ami soulain:
> Mais cil qui toutdis change sa fortune,
> Et ne voet estre en un soul lieu certain,
> Om le poet bien resembler a Gawain,
> Courtois d'amour, mail il fuist trop volage:
> A un est une assetz en mariage.

['He is not a lover who is common to everybody;'/ Only one who loves one is a lover;/ But he who constantly changes his circumstances,/ And is unable to stay in one place,/ That man resembles Gawain,/ Courteous in love, but entirely fickle:/ One is enough for one in marriage.']

Let us think, now, about 'auctours' in that introduction again. Gower seems to apply the word there in its broadest medieval sense, as 'authorities' — venerable names which, when attached to words, had power to ensure those words veracity.[120] In the *Traitié* itself, Gower appeals to an 'auctour' to support his version of Hercules's death: 'Car Hercules, ensi com dist l'auctour,/ D'Une chemise, dont il se vestoit,/ Fuist tant deceu, qu'il soi mesmes ardoit' ('Because Hercules, as the author[ity] says, was completely deceived by a shirt which he put on, and burned himself up,' *Tr* VII, 3.3-5). The 'auctour' here, although he is not named, is Ovid; and he (like Vincent of Beauvais, Paul the Deacon, the *Roman de Troie*, the Bible — most of Gower's other sources for the ballades) would have seemed a qualified 'authority' to Gower's audience. But there is a puzzle about this invocation of 'auctours.' Apart from the single, oblique allusion to (unnamed) Ovid, we hear no more about authorities. No references appear, either in the poems or the marginal glosses — the place where, in a legitimate treatise, we would expect to find them.

Of course (one might say) we are not offered a *real* treatise here, but a sequence of ballades; and perhaps the explanation is that Gower never intended to identify his authorities, or anticipated his readers wondering after his purposes so exactly. Perhaps he had nothing greater in mind than to lend his *Traitié* a little verisimilitude. By referring to 'auctors' in an introduction, he would make his lyric sequence seem more real as a 'treatise.' Yet it is tempting to read 'auctours' in another, more ambitious way, one which subsequently we can turn to hand alongside similar devices to gain a wider view of Gower's design.

'Auctours' has, latent at its center, a play on words which I believe Gower exploited to a purpose here, to point up a difference between his sources — ancient and Christian moralists on one hand, and vernacular, contemporary versifiers on the other. '[Author]ities' reveals the pun readily: Ovid, Vincent of Beauvais, Paul the Deacon and the rest are all 'authors,' 'writers,' albeit ones whose works were granted extraordinary weight by Gower's world. The double meaning was available in Anglo-Norman; Gower reflects knowledge of it in his work.[121] And punning, as we have seen, is Gower's style. The question to be asked of such a reading then, is not whether it was possible but rather what might we, and the poet, gain from pursuing it? To answer this we must turn back to the *Traitié*, and look again briefly at the narratives Gower includes.

With particular exceptions, the *exempla* of the ballades present few 'authoritative' difficulties. Tereus, Tarquin, Pharaoh, Helen, Paris, Clytemnestra, Jason, and most of the rest are 'old' names, from ancient times virtually emblematic of adulterous excess. In a sense, then, Gower lost nothing by raising the issue of 'auctours' and citing none. His moral illustrations were part of a public stock, sufficiently common that he could have counted on the ability of his audience to know relevant authorities, like Ovid, or the Bible, or Dictys

---

[120] On medieval notions of 'authority,' see Alastair J. Minnis, *Medieval Theory of Authorship: Scholastic Literary Attitudes in the Later Middle Ages* (Woodbridge, Suffolk, 1983), 10-15.

[121] Compare Gower's general use of 'auctour' in *Tr* VII, 3.3 with *MO* 1676, where David is referred to as the *composer* of a quoted Psalm.

Cretensis, and to 'read' — or imagine — them back into his text if they wished, to support his stories' 'truth.'

But what 'authorities' stand behind the *exempla* of Lancelot, Tristan and Gawain? These are heroes neither ancient nor Biblical. Among Gower's illustrative figures they represent a different order, of behavior and literature alike. If we follow the pattern established for the others, and 'read' backward to find 'auctours' for these stories, our choices, like those of Gower's contemporary readership, are essentially two: courtly and chivalric romances in both French and English, and the lyrics of French court poets like Machaut and Deschamps.

In one sense, perhaps, we need not choose between these options. To comprehend Gower's references to Lancelot, Tristan and Gawain we can draw usefully on the 'authority' of both poetic types. But it is important to observe the different results we obtain when we do. The poems of the romance tradition are moralistic in their way. Particularly in English they end as does the alliterative *Morte Arthure*, in tragedy brought about by human frailty and the prideful will.[122] Thus like Gower's ballades, they show forth a world in which actions are accountable, and men's choices have predictable consequences. But most vernacular romances are also anonymous. Only Chrétien de Troyes stands out as a significant maker of such poems, and we have no evidence to suggest that his was a name, or an *oeuvre*, Gower knew. Thus, while keeping this tradition in mind as we read the *Traitié* accommodates the tone of Gower's chivalric references, it nonetheless offers us no obvious 'authority' in the medieval sense.

The lyrics of Machaut and Deschamps, however, present an altogether different case. First of all theirs is a poetry which, unlike the vernacular romances, Gower might well have understood to be committed to just those attitudes he opposed with his concentration on rightful marriage, and his condemnation of adultery, in the *Traitié* and the *Cinkante Ballades*. Here, in Machaut's work especially, is an adumbration of love-as-game, an apparent holiday of passion unfettered by moral responsibilities or spiritual consequences. Reading it, we return to the viridescent world of the *Roman de la Rose*, to find the likes of Lancelot, Tristan and Gawain part of a chivalric peopling of the garden of the Rose.[123] Moreover, Machaut and Deschamps stand up as 'auctours,' on several counts deserving close attention. As James I. Wimsatt has carefully established, theirs are names we can be confident Gower knew (unlike Chrétien,

---

[122] That is, I read the *Alliterative Morte Arthur* as does William Matthews: see his *The Tragedy of Arthur* (Berkeley and Los Angeles, 1960), 115-50. Matthews's political reading of Arthur as Edward III (pp. 178-92) would have been especially appreciated by Gower, who probably attacks the king for his pride and sexual indulgence with Alice Perrers in the *Mirour*, ll. 22225-23208; on this see Gardner Stillwell, 'John Gower and the Last Years of Edward III,' *Studies in Philology*, 45 (1948), 454-71. See also K. Holtgen, 'König Arthur und Fortuna,' *Anglia*, 75 (1957), 35-54; and Loomis, *Arthurian Romance*, 151, who argues the contrary position.

[123] On Machaut's return to the *Roman*, see Poirion, *Poète et prince*, 192-205; Kelly, *Medieval Imagination*, pp. 96-154; Kevin Brownlee, *Poetic Identity in Guillaume de Machaut* (Madison, 1984) 3-23; and, with a slightly different purpose, Robertson, *Preface to Chaucer*, 233-38.

and the anonymous composers of romance) as surely as he borrowed their lines
into ballades of his own.[124]

By the end of his life Machaut (who died in 1377) had become the reigning lyrical
presence on both sides of the channel. His work as musician and poet exerted,
Ernest Hoepffner has remarked, 'une influence puissante et durable sur le
développement littéraire du xivᵉ siècle;' he refined and established (if he did not
actually invent) 'les genres à formes fixes, la ballade, le chant royal, le virelai, le
rondeau et le lai, qui, avec quelques variations . . . règneront jusqu'au xvjᵉ
siècle.'[125] Recent studies have placed beyond doubt, too, that Machaut's
achievement was unremittingly self-conscious.[126] A patient reviser, he took pains
to polish his work, selectively combining new material with earlier, and even
overseeing the preparation of his codices.[127] In the view of Kevin Brownlee,
Machaut's purpose was to establish a consistent *persona* for himself as 'poète'
(apparently in the modern sense) and hence as 'auctour.' Brownlee has traced the
semantic field of 'poète,' showing its sudden expansion in fourteenth-century
French from a term with 'reference only to the classical *auctores*' to include
'vernacular, contemporary poets . . . . The idea of *auctor* thus is, as it were, built
into, fused with, the idea of *poète* in its expanded sense.'[128] This new sense was
given voice by Deschamps in two elegiac ballades written in 1377, mourning the
death of Machaut. In one, Deschamps calls Machaut both a poet and a 'maker'
('Noble poète et faiseur renommé'), and applies these terms equally to Ovid; in
the other, he represents Machaut as having drawn inspiration from the same
sources — 'Circe's fountain and the spring of Helicon' ('La fons Circe et la
fonteine Helie') — used by the classical *auctores*.[129] Deschamps treats Machaut 'as
an *exemplum poetae*,' Brownlee demonstrates, in deliberate replication of
Machaut's own carefully constructed, innovative self-image: 'Building on the
Rose, Machaut established a new kind of poetic identity, greatly expanding the

---

[124] Wimsatt has demonstrated Chaucer's extensive debt to Machaut, early and late, in
several detailed studies. See *Chaucer and the French Love Poets: The Literary Background of the
'Book of the Duchess'* (Chapel Hill, 1968), esp. 70-117; *The Marguerite Poetry of Guillaume de
Machaut* (Chapel Hill, 1970), esp. 30-39; 'Guillaume de Machaut and Chaucer's Love
Lyrics,' *Medium Aevum*, 47 (1978), 66-87; and *Chaucer and the Poems of 'CH' in the University
of Pennsylvania MS French 15* (Woodbridge, Suffolk, 1982), passim. I assume Gower's
acquaintance with Machaut from this, if from no other, source.
[125] Hoepffner, *Oeuvres*, I, i.
[126] As, for example, William Calin, *A Poet at the Fountain: Essays on the Narrative Verse of
Guillaume de Machaut* (Lexington, 1974), who notes that 'for the first time in French
literature, poetry and the craft of writing are . . . central themes . . .;' see pp. 239-48.
[127] See Sarah Jane Williams, 'An Author's Role in Fourteenth Century Book Production:
Guillaume de Machaut's "Livre ou je met toutes mes choses",' *Romania*, 90 (1969),
433-54.
[128] Brownlee, *Poetic Identity*, p. 8.
[129] See *Oeuvres completes*, ed. Queux de Saint-Hilaire and Raynaud, 3, 259-60, *Ballade* no.
447, and 1, 245-46, *Ballade* no. 124.

range of the lyric voice, and thus authorized the new sense of the term *poète* as applied to him by Deschamps.'[130]

Deschamps' praise of Machaut as both 'poet and maker' ('poète et faiseur'), logical and easy as it seems now, nonetheless bridges over a distinction of extraordinary importance to thoughtful men of letters five centuries ago. For them, 'making' was a lesser term. It conveyed a craftsman's labors, while 'poetry' reflected higher purpose. Glending Olson has put the case succinctly: 'The court maker is essentially concerned with a limited goal, the perfection of his craft, which meets immediate social demands. Only when he goes beyond this function and writes wisely, too, may he be considered a poet.'[131] Deschamps seems to have been aware of this difference himself. In his *Art de dictier* — a kind of guide for beginning writers of courtly lyric — he avoids 'poète' altogether, and uses only 'faiseur.' Presumably, then, his application of 'poète' to Machaut is a complex matter. It represents a conscious attempt by a younger writer to elevate the achievement of his master to the highest level of verbal art — a level the master had apparently contrived to attain — by applying a term in which moral, as well as merely technical, excellencies are implicit. And, too, it reveals for us most certainly Deschamps's own designs on posterity. A self-proclaimed disciple (and possibly a nephew) of Machaut, Deschamps thoroughly cultivated his master's example. Deschamps's 'lyric voice' is a near echo of Machaut's; like Machaut, he saw fit to leave the world an 'ars poetica,' an enterprise uniformly the business of 'auctores' before. Thus, by finding words to assess Machaut's achievement, Deschamps also predictably described aspirations toward authorship and poetry he held himself.[132]

For our purposes, then, to name one is to speak simultaneously of both. Machaut and Deschamps must have been, in Gower's view, indistinguishably troublesome 'authorities.' On one hand revolutionary and worthily ambitious, yet productive of poems that 'sownen into synne' on another, the poetic 'auctorite' of these French writers both opened the way for, and severely

---

[130] Brownlee, *Poetic Identity*, p. 9.

[131] Glending Olson, 'Making and Poetry in the Age of Chaucer,' *Comparative Literature*, 31 (1979), 276.

[132] There are, of course, significant differences between Deschamps's sensibilities and those of Machaut and Froissart. As Poirion has noted, 'Le poète ne se soumet donc q'uen apparence aux principes de la tradition heritée de Machaut. Le service des dames, tel qu'il se reflète dans ses ballades amoureuses, ses rondeaux et ses virelais, n'a qu'une teinture de courtoisie;' Deschamps instead is much concerned with moral advice, and 'interrompt souvent ses plaisanteries pour se livrer à un didactisme positif et pratique;' see *Poète et prince*, pp. 229, 227. My purpose, however, is to consider Deschamps as Gower probably saw him — that is, not 'whole,' as we do nowadays when we reflect upon his collected works, but in pieces, as Gower most likely read him. From a random selection of poems, Deschamps might easily appear the devotee of Machaut's he himself claimed to be. His *Ballade* 447, for example, in which he offers love service to Péronne, Machaut's 'Toute-belle,' or the *Miroir de Mariage*, with its stringent, satirical attack on the marital state, would have given a rigorous sensibility like Gower's reason enough to judge Deschamps at least ambivalent about moral issues, if not irretrievably compromised. The significant point about Deschamps is that he wrote a great many poems, using more than one voice.

challenged, Gower's own. For Gower too, I think, aspired to be a 'poète:' At least it is difficult to imagine this writer, once aware of the distinction, setting up to be a mere 'maker.' And he, like Deschamps and Machaut, and most other serious men of letters from the 1370s on, certainly knew the difference, as it takes but a little to see.

VI

To the best of my knowledge, Gower has only left us record of applying 'poete' and 'poesie' (one instance excepted, which we shall consider shortly) with reference to Ovid (e.g., 'Ovide the Poete also,' *CA* I, 386; 'Among the whiche in Poesie/ To the lovers Ovide wrot,' *CA* IV, 2668-69), and 'maker' to God, as in 'The hihe makere of nature' (*CA* II, 916). He does, however, use 'makynge' to describe his own writing (cf. *CA* VIII, 3154-55 'Withoute makynge any more,/ Of love and of his dedly hele'), which suggests his understanding of the distinction. Chaucer's practice is identical, and the similarity is instructive about both.

When Chaucer refers to himself he is always a 'maker,' as are most of his contemporaries he mentions (e.g. Oton de Grandson, whom he calls 'flour of hem that make in Fraunce,' 'Complaint of Venus,' 82). Only Dante (a 'grete poete,' *MkT*, VII, 2460, and a 'wise poete,' *WBT*, III, 1125) and Petrarch ('the lauriat poete,' *ClT*, IV, 31) are described otherwise — for obvious reasons, one might say. *Prima facie* the claims seem just, if a bit hard on Chaucer himself, whose modesty amidst the company of the great is nonetheless becoming. But Chaucer's apparent humility here, as elsewhere, is deceptive, I think; it offers no truer indication of what Chaucer thought of himself as artist than does the Pilgrim Geoffrey's disclaimer to Harry Bailly that the *Thopas* is 'the beste rym I kan' (*CT* VII, 928). What we have is a 'modesty *topos*' of a particular kind, probably traceable to, but certainly including, Dante's representation of himself as but one of the illustrious six — *inter pares, sive* (as Christian readers have always known) *primus*, since he alone among Homer, Virgil, Horace, Lucan and Ovid brought back a vision of the true God.[133] The ability both to deny one's worthiness for the laurel and yet in that very act embrace it is characteristic of that class of medieval poets who are demonstrably self-conscious about their poetship. The antique paradigm is Cicero; the medieval, not surprisingly his most vocal, and nuanced, admirer. As 'lauriat' Petrarch knew, one does not give *oneself* the title 'poet;' properly, one conspires to be crowned.[134] Machaut, for this

---

[133] *Inferno* IV, 86-102. As Benedetto Croce has observed, speaking of this passage, 'Dante knew himself to be the depository and executor of a mission, he felt himself to be a poet, to be a prophet or, two in one, a poet-prophet, a poet-seer, whose voice should announce the truth and prepare mankind for judgement.' See *The Poetry of Dante*, p. 235; and further, see Freccero, *Poetics of Conversion*, p. 209.

[134] See Petrarch's letter to Giovanni Colonna (*Familiares* 4.4), and also the analysis of Petrarch's coronation by Ernest Hatch Wilkins, *Life of Petrarch* (Chicago, 1961) 24-29.

reason, created his own 'auctorite' but left it to another to introduce him as 'poète' — Deschamps, who, doing so, found means to take his own place in line.[135] And similarly Boccaccio, in *De casibus virorum illustrium*, a text Machaut might have read, defines a lofty role for the poet, and then wonders — pointedly — how he measures up.[136]

This list could be extended: Boccaccio offers us additional *loci*, as do Villani, Lydgate and others.[137] And it is here among these that we should number Chaucer and Gower. Chaucer tips his hand clearest, perhaps, at the end of the *Troilus*, when he sends his 'little book' to seek its 'betters.' The stanza (*TC* 1786-92), a *tour-de-force* of self-promotional self-effacement, turns upon the distinction of 'making' and 'poesye:'

> Go, litel bok, go, litel myn tragedye,
> Ther God thi makere yet, er that he dye,
> So sende myght to make in some comedye!
> But litel book, no makyng thow n'envie,
> But subgit be to alle poesye;
> And kis the steppes, where as thow seest pace
> Virgil, Ovide, Omer, Lucan, and Stace.

There lacks space here to cover the many ways the terms for writers and writing work, or have been interpreted, in these lines.[138] I want, however, only to draw attention to two points. Chaucer's strict adherence to his 'humble craftsman' persona is obvious immediately: he is a 'makere' who with God's inspiration may 'make' a comedy to balance the *Troilus*. Subsequently (and predictably) this

---

[135] That is, by distinguishing a true poet from the crowd one lays implicit claim to knowing the true nature of poetry; and if one confers the title 'poete' on another writer in poems of one's own, one extends the title implicitly to one's self via that privileged act of creation. This attitude would seem to differ somewhat from the 'makerly' opinions which govern the *Art de dictier* (see *pace* Olson's reading, 'Deschamps' *Art de Dictier*,' p. 721), but of course it, and the poems for Machaut, were composed to fit different purposes.

[136] *De casibus*, III, 16. The chapter, along with early French translations, is printed by Guiseppe Di Stefano in *Il Boccaccio nella cultura francese*, ed. Carlo Pellegrini (Florence, 1971) 41-47.

[137] On Filippo Villani, see *Liber de civitatis florentiae famosis civibus*, ed. G.C. Galletti (Florence, 1847) 31. Lydgate, in the final stanza of *The Chorle and the Bird* (which begins 'Go gentil quayer'), mimics Chaucer's tone in *TC* 1786-92. John Walton, who translated Boethius in 1410, praises Chaucer while similarly dispraising himself; the passage is quoted by Spurgeon, *Five Hundred Years*, I, 20-21.

[138] Views which have been useful in forming my own reading of this passage (n. 76, above, q.v.) are those of E.T. Donaldson, 'The Ending of Chaucer's *Troilus*,' in *Early English and Norse Studies Presented to Hugh Smith in Honour of His Sixtieth Birthday*, ed. Arthur Brown and Peter Foote (London, 1963) 26-45; Peter Dronke, 'The Conclusion of *Troilus and Criseyde*,' *Medium Aevum*, 23 (1964), 47-52; Donald R. Howard, *The Three Temptations*, pp. 149-56 (see his bibliographical note 107, pp. 155-56); and Chauncey Wood, *The Elements of Chaucer's Troilus* (Durham, NC, 1984) 162-63.

modest labor is set in contrast with that lofty product — 'poesye' — of Virgil,
Ovid, Homer, Lucan and Statius. But in between some sleight-of-hand takes
place. The 'litel book' is warned to envy no 'makyng,' but to be 'subgit' [only —
one must read] to 'poesye' of any sort. The lines enforce this meaning: What
writing but that which *improves on* 'makyng' ought never envy it? By implication
Chaucer thus has caused *Troilus* to transcend its 'maker' and its humble origins,
to become — what? Well, 'poesye,' the single option provided by the stanza's
binary structure — with all of the additions that claim entails.

Chaucer's maneuver here is subtle, but no more so than Gower's in the
Prologue to the *Confessio Amantis*, where he intended to achieve the same end.
Although the lines (*CA* Pro., 12-24) are familiar, their several turns require
quoting them at length:

> Bot for men sein, and soth it is,
> That who that al of wisdom *writ*
> It dulleth ofte a mannes wit
> To him that schal it aldai [rede],
> For thilke cause, if that ye [rede],
> I wolde go the middel weie
> And *wryte* a bok betwen the tweie,
> Somwhat of lust, somwhat of lore,
> That of the lasse or of the more
> Som man mai lyke of that I *wryte*:
> And for that fewe men *endite*
> In oure englissh, I thenke *make*
> A bok for Engelondes sake.

Here we have three words for verbal composition: 'wryte' ('writ'), 'endite,' and
'make.' To some degree, the senses overlap, but we should be cognizant also of
the subtle distinctions, since they are being played against each other to a
purpose. Of the three, 'wryte' is the most general. The equivalent term to the
'middel' style Gower proposes here for his poem, it suffices to describe all cases.
His insistence on it for the first three references to composition establishes its
generic value. One may 'wryte' of wisdom, or a book containing 'lust' as well as
'lore:' The term covers the spectrum, 'of the lasse or of the more.' 'Endite,'
however, is a different word altogether, and its appearance alters the tone. While
'endite,' too, has the general sense of 'compose in writing' (from L. 'dictare'), in
Chaucer's usage and in Gower's, 'It implies . . . an intensified and augmented
form of that activity . . . [and] seems to connote rhetorical composition, usually
in a serious manner or elevated style, and often has slightly honorific
overtones.'[139] Thus, while we *can* read 'endite' here as merely 'compose,' there is

---

[139] Anne Middleton, 'Chaucer's New Men and the Good of Literature in the *Canterbury
Tales*,' in *Literature and Society: Selected Papers from the English Insitute, 1978*, ed. Edward Said
(Baltimore) 15-56. The quotation appears on pp. 50-51, at the beginning of a lengthy
excursis on 'endite.'

a strong alternative suggested — that Gower means, not just 'Few men write in English,' but also (and primarily, I think) 'Few men use English to write in a manner appropriate to serious matters.' The difference seems slight, but is in fact quite important. It is a clue, an example *in parvo*, of the way we must read the entire *Confessio*: as a disquisition on serious matters offered in an unprepossessing form.[140]

The change in tone brought about by 'endite' seems immediately overturned in the following two lines, however. Gower proposes to '*make/* A bok for Engelondes sake.' At first the notion sounds absurd. Is the problem not — precisely — that English letters are anemic? How can one more 'maker' hope to cure a malady so profound? The answer Gower provides, I believe, is the ensuing poem. The *Confessio Amantis*, in all its richness of classical story and lore, its sagacity, and (even) its bulk, is no 'maker's' handiwork, but rather the triumph of an Englishman who 'endites' in his native tongue. As it unrolls itself away from the Prologue, couplet by couplet, eight books long, Gower's poem reveals his 'modesty' as *topos*, and his use of 'make' to describe his activity as ironic indeed.

The knowledge that Gower could infuse irony into the terms he applied to his own art prepares us to consider the single case we have in which he uses 'poete' with reference to someone other than Ovid. The instance is important enough to require discussion for its own sake — for the person so titled is Chaucer; but it is also helpful in that it supplies additional evidence of what semantic boundaries Gower could accept around the word. The lines in question come at the end of Book VIII of the *Confessio* (*2941-57). Again, of necessity I quote at length:

> 'And gret wel Chaucer whan ye mete,
> As mi disciple and mi poete:
> In sondri wise, as he wel couthe,
> Of Ditees and of songes glade,
> The whiche he for mi sake made,
> The lond is fulfild overal:
> Wherof to him in special
> Above alle othre I am most holde.
> For thi now in hise daies olde
> Thow schalt him telle this message,
> That he upon his latere age,
> To sette an ende of alle his werk,
> As he which is myn owne clerk,
> Do make his testament of love,

---

[140] Perhaps this is why Gower avoided the obvious *rime riche* 'wryte/ wryte' in the passage above. He is fond of such *rimes*, as we have seen in the preceding chapter, and he makes one here on 'rede rede' (I have marked this in brackets, above which conceivably would have been balanced by a 'wryte wryte' pair. Eschuing the *rime riche* makes sense, however, if Gower had in mind an effect of another kind.

As thou hast do thi schrifte above,
So that mi Court it mai recorde.'

Since we shall have an opportunity to return to this passage in due course, we
need not try to say everything possible about it here. We might now, however,
notice its context. The speaker is Venus, about to take her leave of the recently
enlightened Amans. She it is who calls Chaucer 'poete' and claims him as her
own, offering as evidence of his devotion the 'Ditees' and 'songes' he made for
her sake in his 'youthe.' That it is the Queen of Love who associates the work of a
'poete' with amorous lyrics — for surely ballades, virelais, caroles and so forth
are intended — and not the 'narrative voice' of the Prologue and Epilogue (nor
even that of Amans, revealed to be 'John Gower' in l. 2908, immediately prior to
this passage) cannot be overlooked. Her use of 'poete' is doubly compromised,
once by the message she asks Amans/Gower to carry, and again by her role as
goddess of desire and procreation.[141] For Venus wants Chaucer to realize that his
days of amorous dalliance are past. His 'latere age' is upon him and he must
'sette an ende of alle his werk,' performed for her as 'myn owne clerk.' Just as
Amans/Gower has made his 'schrifte above' — a textual reference, I take it, to
the foregoing *Confessio Amantis* — so now ought Chaucer bid farewell to love by
writing an equivalent 'testament.' This advice should sound familiar. It echoes
Venus's commands to Amans/Gower, with which she opens this same speech
(*CA* VIII, 2910-16, 2924-27):

'This have I for thin ese cast,
That thou nomore of love sieche.
Bot mi will is that thou besieche
And preie hierafter for the pes,
And that thou make a plein reles
To love, which takth litel hiede
Of olde men upon the nede . . .
And tarie thou my Court nomore,
Bot go ther vertu moral duelleth,
Wher ben thi bokes, as men telleth,
Whiche of long time thou hast write.'

[141] Or perhaps thrice compromised, by a recognizable echoing of Machaut. Wimsatt has
argued strongly for the singularity of Machaut's lyric 'voice': 'There is something more
distinctive about xiv c. French love lyrics, notably those of Machaut, than criticism of
them has usually allowed. These works are not mere mass-production items with
interchangeable parts . . . Each love lyric of Machaut, as of Chaucer . . . under scrutiny
displays clear identity, unique essence . . .' Wimsatt concludes that 'with the exception of
the Granson-inspired *Complaint of Venus*, all of Chaucer's independent love lyrics are based
on poems of Guillaume de Machaut' and therefore that 'the lyrics provide additional
strong evidence that Chaucer's French period was lifelong, that he always respected and
profited from the work of his great French master, Guillaume de Machaut.' See
'Chaucer's Love Lyrics,' pp. 84, 66, 85. Venus's references to Chaucer's age may reflect,
perhaps, Gower's weariness with his friend's 'lifelong' devotion to this unique master.

If we read these two admonitory statements together, using one to gloss the other, what Venus wants is plain. Chaucer should amend his writing habits — put aside 'Ditees' and 'songes' and take up books of moral virtue. When he does so, of course, he will cease to be *her* 'poete:' but this loss is inevitable, Venus urges (in fact, has been delayed too long), for the natural course shall be served. Chaucer's matter now must come from better sources — those moral books? — and he himself become, *mutatis mutandis*, a 'poete' of a different, older kind. For, described another way, Venus's plan is to effect the *legitimation* of Chaucer as 'poete' in the primary sense that Gower understood, and used, the term — to designate an 'auctor' whose words derive authority from the wisdom they provide. Her *original* conferral of 'poete' on a youthful Chaucer of ditty and song is, then, ironic. Venus means it to be, from within the fiction, and certainly so did Gower, overseeing his larger poem from without. Indeed, 'Venus's poete' must have verged on oxymoron for Gower, who (striking again at Jean de Meun) had found sufficient provocation in the compound 'Venus's priest' to pen Genius's admission of ignorance about virtue or vice except in love, 'For Venus bokes of nomore/ Me techen nowther text ne glose' (*CA* I, 270-71, and passim). But of course this too has its own keen strain of irony.

One more element concerning the context of 'poete' here should be remarked upon before we set these lines aside, to return to them later. That is, of course, that Gower did not keep them. For reasons we cannot know with any certainty, he saw fit to exclude mention of Chaucer altogether from later copies of the *Confessio*, inserting instead a delicate description of Amans realizing, and coming to terms with, his fate. The lines — as we shall have a chance to see subsequently — are good enough on their own to justify their inclusion as revision of improvement, and perhaps that is the explanation after all. Other reasons have been proffered, the best known being the so-called 'quarrel' between the two poets supposedly provoked by Chaucer's 'digs' at Gower in the *Man of Law's Tale*.[142] Or again, the truth may be that Henry IV's ascendancy caused Gower, always concerned with the state of the commonwealth, to recast his argument, doing away with a 'coterie' reference in favor of matter more suited to advising a king.[143] Another possibility (which belies the 'quarrel' notion, if it truly needs further debunking!) is that Gower remained close enough to Chaucer in 1399-1400 to hear of his final illness and struck the passage in deference, not only to a dying friend, but also to a writer who had rendered Venus's advice obsolete by following it already: for it is striking how the *Parson's Tale* and the *Retraction* correspond, both in tone and in the latter's rejection of 'songs' and 'leccherous lays,' to Venus's program to 'legitimate' Chaucer's poetry, described in these concluding lines, as well as to Amans/Gower's prayer 'for the pes' — the *Confessio*

---

[142] Macaulay discusses the 'quarrel' theory in *Works*, III, xxvi xxviii; see further Fisher, *John Gower*, pp. 286-92; and Derek Pearsall, 'The Gower Tradition,' in *Responses and Reassessments*, ed. Minnis, pp. 180-81.
[143] I borrow 'coterie' from Anne Middleton; see her 'The Idea of Public Poetry in the Reign of Richard II,' *Speculum*, 53 (1978), 94-114, esp. p. 107. See also Paul M. Clogan, 'From Complaint to Satire: The Art of the *Confessio Amantis*,' *Medievalia et Humanistica*, n.s. 4 (1973), 217-22, esp. p. 219.

Amantis, which thus bears affinities with the *Parson's Tale* largely unexplored. Whatever the cause, their exclusion doubtless indicates Gower's ultimate judgment of their value. At last he felt that the business of the *Confessio* could get on well enough without their ironic reference to Chaucer as 'poete' — a term which, the fate of the passage notwithstanding, Gower clearly understood, and could apply in a variety of ways.

VII

The distinction between 'poete' as 'auctour' and as 'maker,' or mere versifier, was of significant importance for Gower, then, for reasons we can probably infer. As we know from the shape taken by his work as a whole, writing for him was an enterprise imbued with formidable responsibility. According to Gower's definition, the moral dimensions of 'authority' were absolute. The honorific title 'poete' was to be earned, and only by strenuous labor of a certain ethical kind. This view underlies Venus's message to Chaucer, that light verse, courtly verse, 'Ditees' and 'songs,' were not the product of a 'poetic' — i.e., a mature or venerable — mind, but rather the more-or-less natural outcome of youthful drives.

But Chaucer was a friend, and a learned man with a side as philosophical as Gower's. His translations included Boethius and Deguilleville as well as the *Roman de la Rose*; he does not seem, from this vantage at least, to have triumphed in his lyricism; he might be turned around with a jibe.[144] Not so the French poets, however. If Machaut represents an 'auctour' in the *Traitié*, then the pun on 'author' and 'authority' is a specially pointed one. The context, created and forced by the designation of the sequence as a treatise, demands we search out the identity of its 'authorities.' The result is that Machaut and the poets he represents must be placed beside conventional 'authorities' from antiquity and theology. When we do this — when we imagine the authorities back into the text — the moral bankruptcy of courtly 'lore' becomes unavoidably apparent. In effect, the strategy is the same we saw Gower employ in the *Miroir* where Jean de Meun became a target, a stand-in for a misuse of language Gower abhorred. In the *Traitié* and the *Cinkante Ballades*, where Gower's concern is to purify exactly the same discourse, it is Machaut (and to a lesser degree Deschamps) whom Gower fits to bear his strokes for an entire class of irresponsible lyricists.

But this is a vast, even a hubristic, claim, it will be objected, and difficult — though not, perhaps, impossible — to document. Let me offer three approaches to the problem which, while not proof *ipso facto*, nonetheless constitute evidence to be accounted for. The first way we might approach the question is through the relationship borne by Machaut's most ambitious poem, the *Livre du Voir-Dit*, to Gower's later writings. By comparing the *Voir-Dit* and Gower's late work in this

---

[144] Or so Gower might have thought; see Fisher, *John Gower*, p. 286. The view is compatible with the Chaucer offered us by Donald R. Howard, 'Chaucer the Man,' *PMLA*, 80 (1965), 337-43.

way I do not mean to imply that this poem of Machaut's was alone in Gower's mind (although I have no doubt that he knew it) when he wrote the *Confessio* and the ballade sequences. But as Machaut himself seems to have been aware, the *Voir-Dit* achieved a kind of quintessence: of his own talent and ideas, and — consequently — of the poetic style to which he was both father and master.[145] It therefore may serve us synecdochically, as representative of a poetry which constraints of space prevent our discussing at deserved length.

According to the narrative of the poem itself, Machaut's *Voir-Dit* (or 'True Story') chronicles the course of a love affair begun in the late summer, 1362, and concluded shortly after May, 1365.[146] The Narrator is a cleric who is also a poet, of bourgeois stock, aged over sixty and subject to gout and sundry infirmities, blind in one eye; his beloved is an extraordinary girl, of less than twenty years, whom he calls 'Toute-belle,' a noblewoman and heiress of great beauty and wit. She it is who begins the courtship, writing the Narrator a rondel admiring his poetry. The *Voir-Dit* combines an explanatory frame (in couplets), the lovers prose letters, and their poems. It traces their courtship, increasing physical intimacies (eventually the lovers enjoy each other, in a bed Venus envelopes with a golden cloud), their growing apart and final reconciliation as warm, if permanently distanced, friends.

The *Voir-Dit* resembles Gower's later poems in certain very general ways. Considered as broad structural entities, the mixture of prose, narrative couplets, and lyric forms in Machaut's sequence is reminiscent of the *Confessio Amantis*, in that the *Confessio* also combines forms: Latin verse and prose, English lyric (Amans's supplication to Venus, Book VIII, 2217-2300, in rime royal stanzas), and narrative couplets in English. This likeness is somewhat stronger if we recall what the bulk of the manuscript evidence suggests: that the *Traitié*, with its French prose and ballades, was intended to be read as in some way of a piece with the *Confessio*. More striking is the chronological relationship of the two pairs of lovers in the *Confessio* and the *Voir-Dit*. 'Guillaume' (as Machaut's Narrator identifies himself in a closing acrostic) is too old for his youthful Toute-belle, as Amans/ Gower is for his unnamed lady.[147] Other points of comparison are less obvious, but suggestive. Both *Confessio* and *Voir-Dit* have first-person narrators who bear the names of their authors. Arguably in each case this creates verisimilitude, since both Machaut and Gower were old when the *Voir-Dit*, the *Confessio* and the *Traitié* were completed. Again, the *Traitié* (like the *Cinkante Ballades*) ostensibly contains the poems of a poet-lover to his lady, and her poems in response. This technique is central (even original) to the *Voir-Dit*. In Machaut's poem, as in Book VII of the *Confessio*, the talk of love is interrupted for

---

[145] That Machaut himself knew the significance of the *Voir-Dit* seems to me the conclusion logically to be drawn from Sarah Jane Williams's study, 'An Author's Role,' especially p. 453, where she points out his interpolation of older materials, 'representing them both to his readers and to Peronelle as newly composed.' See also Poirion, *Poète et prince*, pp. 199-205, and Brownlee, *Poetic Identity*, p. 94.

[146] For the chronology, see Calin, *Poet at the Fountain*, p. 194.

[147] For this acrostic, see the edition of Paulin Paris, *Le Livre du voir-dit* (Paris, 1875) 369-70. All quotations from the *Voir-Dit* are found in this edition.

an excursus on proper kingship. And finally, Machaut calls his *Voir-Dit* a 'traictié' — a term which, as we have seen, must needs have provoked certain expectations in the minds of a medieval audience.[148]

These similarities, as well as the prominence of the *Voir-Dit* at the close of the fourteenth century, may tempt us to wonder whether in his final years Gower was not working to undo precedents set for the tradition by this poem especially. For in the end, when we look closely at the Machaut of the *Voir-Dit* and at Gower, it is their *differences*, rendered the more stark by the correspondences, which are worth our focus. William Calin makes the point directly, in a comparison of the *Voir-Dit* to the *Lancelot-Grail Cycle* and to Dante. In these poems, he notes:

> Profane love is ennobled by contact with the divine . . . In the *V[oir-]D[it]* the opposite takes place: Toute-belle and Venus replace the Virgin, and flesh triumphs over spirit. The Narrator, a man of the cloth, is successfully tempted from the true path and consciously, willfully whores after strange gods. A scholar and a poet, he takes himself seriously as a lover, abandons Reason for Love, and fails miserably.[149]

Calin's description — a fair picture of the *Voir-Dit* — might stand as a catalogue of those things Gower rejected most strenuously everywhere in his work: the preference for earthly over divine love, a resultant idolatry, the (self-) corruption of the clergy, the denial of Reason to embrace passion. There is in addition a claim for the poet's proper role which Gower could only have considered a flagrant abuse. For him Machaut must have seemed a *faiseur*, a maker of verses, and a scandalous one at that. Machaut's *poète* (and by extension the poets of his tradition) is a servant of Amour first and always, charged by Nature to write according to Love's inspiration. Machaut establishes this position in the four-ballade *Prologue* he appended to his carefully collected works.[150] It is a philosophy embodied centrally in the *Voir-Dit*, where poetry serves as aphrodisiac (the Narrator's writing attracts Toute-belle to him), pander (as Calin puts it, in the *Voir-Dit* as in Dante's story of Paolo and Francesca, 'a book causes two people to meditate on love and on each other') and ultimately as sexual fulfillment — for, *mirabile dictu*, the Narrator produces a virelai even as he enjoys Toute-belle in bed.[151] A view less in accord with Gower's, of the poet as 'authority,' can scarcely be imagined. Machaut, moreover, triumphed remorselessly in his art and amoral love-service. Unlike Gower/Amans, who

---

[148] See Paris, p. 17 (vv. 430-32):
>   Le Voir-Dit vueil-je qu'on appelle
>   Ce traictie que je fais pour elle,
>   Pour ce que ja n'i mentiray.
The digression on kingship fills pp. 215-24 (vv. 4990-5243).

[149] Calin, *Poet at the Fountain*, p. 187.

[150] See Hoepffner, *Oeuvres*, I, 1-6.

[151] Calin, *Poet at the Fountain*, p. 199. 'Guillaume's' virelai (which he terms a 'chanson baladee')' is, in Paris's edition, pp. 159-60 (vv. 3798-3842).

recognizes in the end that 'loves lust and lockes hore/ In chambre acorden neveremore' (*CA* VIII, 2403-04) and abandons his unnatural suit to pray for the peace, 'Guillaume' the *senex amans* of the *Voir-Dit* 'remains,' as John Burrow has recently observed, 'unrepentant to the end of the poem.'[152] Worse yet, Machaut exceeded medieval convention regarding the 'truth' of his tales. To assert the historicity of what one wrote was common, even required, practice; but Machaut was greatly skilled at making his works *seem* real, too. (Indeed, so good was Machaut's ruse in the *Voir-Dit* that the fictionality of 'Guillaume' and Toutebelle continues to stir scholarly debate.)[153] Thus the challenge Machaut offered must have broadened, to include for Gower the personal as well as the theoretical. In his 'traictié' — the *Voir-Dit* — and his other works, Machaut would have appeared to present both a life and a poetic tradition fundamentally flawed and antagonistic to all Gower valued, as a poet, as a Christian citizen, and as a man.

The ballade sequences, then, show Gower deeply engaged in a struggle involving the highest stakes. The reference he makes to this struggle characteristically requires language to convey meaning of multiple kind: for a second indication of Gower's intention is a group of puns in Ballade XVIII of the *Traitié*. This, the final ballade of the sequence, is also unique in that it has an added (fourth) stanza:

> Al université de tout le monde
> Johan Gower ceste Balade envoie;
> Et si jeo n'ai de François la faconde,
> Pardonetz moi qe jeo de ceo forsvoie:
> Jeo sui Englois, si quier par tiele voie
> Estre excuse; mais quoique nulls en die,
> L'amour parfit en dieu se justifie.

A standard translation of these lines might be: 'To the community of the whole world John Gower addresses this balade; and if I have not fluency in French, forgive me if I go astray; I am English, and seek in this way to be excused; but whatever anyone says of it, perfect love is justified in God.'[154] But it is also possible to take the stanza differently. Elsewhere in his work Gower used 'François' to mean 'French*man*,' and 'facounde' to mean 'speech' or 'eloquence' — both grammatically possible readings in the context.[155] Incorporating these

[152] John Burrow, 'The Portrayal of Amans in *Confessio Amantis*,' in Minnis, *Responses and Reassessments*, p. 19.
[153] See the summary of opinion in Calin, *Poet at the Fountain*, pp. 167 ff.
[154] The translation is that of M. Dominica Legge, *Anglo-Norman Literature and Its Background* (Oxford, 1963) 358.
[155] E.g., 'françois' for 'Frenchman,' see *MO* 22965, 26128; 'facounde' for 'speech' or 'eloquence,' see *MO* 1202, 4046.

alternatives, the sense of the third and fourth lines becomes: 'If I have not the smooth speech of the French, forgive me.' The result is a stanza acidulously ironic in its apology for 'clumsy' English habits, when measured according to 'sophisticated' French standards. The final line, ('L'amour parfit en dieu se justifie') which poses the contrast between diverse human *talk* of love ('mais quoique nulls en die') and love's actuality as it exists in God, presses the point home. As does the retrospective reference in the second line: For there 'ceste Balade' asks us to look back to the preceding three stanzas for help with the sense of the fourth and last. When we do so we find two voices juxtaposed in the poem's opening stanza, one the moral intonation of the ballades' 'auctour,' the other the familiar lyrical voice 'of those who sing ('Tiels chante') 'c'est ma sovereine joie' (ll. 1-7)':

> En propreté cil qui del or habonde
> Molt fait grant tort s'il emble autri monoie:
> Cil q'ad s'espouse propre deinz sa bonde
> Grant pecché fait s'il quiert ailours sa proie.
> Tiels chante, 'c'est ma sovereine joie,'
> Qui puis en ad dolour sanz departie:
> N'est pas amant qui son amour mesguie.

['He who (has) by right abundant gold does much great wrong if he steals the money of others. He who has contracted a proper spouse does great sin if he seeks other prey. Many a one sings, 'It is my sovereign joy,' who afterwards has unending sadness: He is not a lover who misguides his love.']

Gower's use of quotation here reminds us of the central role discourse plays in love affairs. More specifically, by presenting a lover's 'line' (in two senses) which we recognize as generic to courtly verse, it cautions us to test the truth of amorous language — especially the language of lyric, which lovers 'chante,' or 'sing' — for evidence of sincerity beneath. The result is heightened contrast between the typical 'voice' of lyric discourse, which may deceive and bring grief, and the narrative, or authorial, voice of the *Traitié*, a collection of lyrics set to restore the language of love to a higher purpose. Put another way, what we are asked to compare is the 'normality' of one with the 'inconsistency' of the other and, having pondered the disparity, to effect a reversal of terms.

The point is registered a third time in the two Latin marginalia accompanying Ballade XVIII. The second side-note (in order of appearance) refers to the final stanza only, and raises once again the issue of an English poet writing French: 'Here at last Gower, who is an Englishman ('qui Anglicus est'), excuses his French words ('sua verba Gallica'), if they will have been *incongrua*' — a word meaning both 'ill-suited' and 'inconsistent.' The ambiguity recalls the double 'voices' of the ballade, and helps us to identify the unnamed 'authorities' whose views, the first *marginalis* tells us, the ballade itself reflects: 'Nota hic secundum *auctores* quod sponsi fideles ex sui regiminis discreta bonitate vxores sibi fidissimas conseruant' ('Here it is noted following the *auctores* that faithful husbands keep their good wives very faithful by their discrete behavior'). No 'auctores' are mentioned in the ballade — an absence which by now should neither surprise us, their omission having been Gower's technique throughout the sequence, nor leave us much in doubt about which 'voice' they support. It is the predominant, moral voice inveighing against adultery which speaks with 'authority,' and not the courtly, lyric voice conjured up by the quoted line. The dichotomy thus amounts to a comparison and subsequent rejection of conventional lyric style in favor of one more 'authoritative' in the classical sense. And it brings into tighter focus what elements Gower found *incongrua* in the 'French words' he used his ballades to indict.

<h1 style="text-align:center">VIII</h1>

If we turn now to the third approach to the problem of how Gower regarded the French courtly lyric, we will be able to bring a wheel full circle. Early in this chapter I suggested that, the line being Gower's primary unit of thought and composition, his writing of Latin cento in the *Vox Clamantis* could be understood as paradigmatic of his style there, and in other quarters. Consideration of lines borrowed into the *Cinkante Ballades* was deferred until a later moment, when a basis would have been prepared for their discussion. It is to take up this material that the present question directs us — a task for which we are at last equipped.

To go forward, however, let us start with a half-step back, to think again about the generic courtly fragment 'c'est ma sovereine joie' in Ballade XVIII. We noted above that the line functions in the poem as a kind of *locum tenens* for a way of writing — and living — Gower opposed. Now, as a technique, this handling of quotation shares much with cento. The same requirements exist for readers of both, for example. Both involve language we are expected to recognize as borrowed. Lacking this recognition the poems make sense, but in less resonant ways. And both are techniques similar enough that a poet employing one would reasonably find appeal in, and application for, the other. As we consider the lines of Machaut, Deschamps and other French courtly writers which Gower incorporated into his ballades, it is useful to keep such similarities before us. They remind us that Gower could borrow passages for many reasons — and they help us take the measure of that borrowing, both according to its purpose and to its artistic success.

For the *Cinkante Ballades*, Gower adopted the same strategy he applied in Ballade XVIII of the *Traitié*: that is, he used quotations selectively, not to build his poems, as the 'patchwork' of cento dictates, but rather as place-holders through which to identify and supercede the courtly *ethos* whose poetry he quoted. We can see this well if we look closely at how quotations appear in Gower's sequence. Like the *Traitié*, the *Cinkante Ballades* have a functioning structure. Five ballades at the beginning celebrate mutual affection. A marginal note explains that these were written particularly for lovers ('sont fait especialement') who look forward to legitimate marriage ('ceaux q'attendont lours amours par droite mariage'). The final three ballades, including LI, in praise of the Virgin, are also normative. They describe the role of 'proper love' ('bon amour') which, as 'the mother of honor' ('d'onour la droite miere,' *CB* XLIX), teaches us the laws of marriage ('nous aprent/ Soubtz matrimoine de les seintes lois,' *CB* XLIX), harmonizes the natural impulses with reason ('Amour s'acorde a nature et resoun,' *CB* L), and is itself either governed by reason or else it is not love at all, but foolishness ('sotie'): 'Si resoun le governe et justifie/ . . . N'est pas amour, ainz serra dit sotie' (*CB* ⟨LI⟩). In between, forty-three ballades describe the 'properties and conditions of those lovers who are diversely troubled by the fortunes of love' ('les propretés et les condicions des Amantz, qui sont diversement travailez en la fortune d'amour'), as we are told in the margin beside *Ballade* VI. These ballades are not arranged arbitrarily, however. References to the revolving seasons and the shifting hopes of the primary narrative voice sketch for us a love affair covering approximately two years.[156] This voice, a man's, reveals his devotion, frustration, his fears and ultimately his celebration when his lady accepts him at last. A certain drama is created as well when the lady herself composes (or at least *speaks*) *Ballades* XLI-XLIIII.

Even so cursory a summary as this one provokes several observations. Putting aside the normative poems of beginning and end, Gower's sequence bears a circumstantial resemblance to the *Voir-Dit*. To be sure, there are no prose epistles in the *Cinkante Ballades*, and no narrative in couplets; nor are Gower's nameless male and female voices the unique, memorable characters Machaut gives us in old 'Guillaume' and Toute-belle. Moreover, the outcome of the 'affair' Gower describes differs radically from that of the *Voir-Dit*. Machaut has his lovers bed, then drift apart; Gower leads his to a union which will be permanent — or so we must presume, since it is forged under the watchful eye of 'bon amour,' informed by reason.

Yet again, as we saw in the *Traitié*, it is just these differences between Gower's work and Machaut's which render the superficial similarities more interesting, and vice-versa. In both the *Voir-Dit* and the *Cinkante Ballades* the course of a love affair of some duration is described in the first person, through the poetic 'correspondence' of a man and a woman. There are not many examples of this sort of thing before 1400. Froissart wrote several major collections mixing narrative and lyrics, but of these only his *Prison Amoreuse* and *Joli Buisson de Jonece* concern us.[157] The *Prison* includes prose epistles, ballades and virelais and probably took its form from the *Voir-Dit*. Although the talk is often of love and poetry, the content of the *Prison* is finally quite different from Machaut's poem,

---

[156] That is, the poems begin in the winter (*CB* II), and progress according to seasons XIII — March; XXIII — May; XXXII — winter (January?); XXXIIII (sic), XXXV — February (St. Valentine's day); XXXVI, XXXVII — May. In between come poems without time references. They give the impression of extended time — perhaps filling another year or more.

[157] In fact, the majority of Froissart's longer works are formal mixtures. In addition to the *Prison* and the *Joli Buisson*, see *Le Livre du Trésor Amoreux*, *Le Joli Mois de May*, *Le Paradys d'Amours*, and *L'Espinette Amoreuse*, in Scheler, *Oeuvres de Froissart*.

for the correspondents are not a man and a girl but Froissart and his patron Wenceslas of Luxembourg and Brabant, during the latter's imprisonment (1371) in Niedeck Castle. Froissart's adaptation provides, nonetheless, an indication of the influence of the *Voir-Dit* on contemporary poetry.

The *Joli Buisson* offers a more significant example of this influence, as the poem bears both directly and indirectly on Gower's later work.[158] Its direct effects we must lay aside for study in a subsequent chapter, when we shall consider Book VIII of the *Confessio Amantis*. Indirectly, however, the influence of the *Joli Buisson* is felt strongest on Gower's ballades. For, if Gower had the *Voir-Dit* in mind when he composed the *Cinkante Ballades*, it was not with the intention of following in its direction that he did so. Quite the contrary, in fact. As we have seen, the moral positions ultimately achieved by the two sequences are opposite. The effect of recalling one when reading the other is to become impressed afresh with their irreconcilable differences. And this, I believe, was Gower's purpose: to 'echo' Machaut's poetry enough to bring it to mind for his audience when his own was read, as quintessentially the kind of writing, expressing the kind of error, which he hoped the alternative example of his own ballades would transform and reclaim.

For this somewhat radical idea Gower might well have found support and comfort in a precedent set by Froissart's *Joli Buisson*, which stands less self-consciously in similar opposition to Machaut of the *Voir-Dit*. Central to both poems is the difficulty imposed on lovers by the passage of time, and the aging of the principals. In the *Voir-Dit*, as throughout his work, Machaut 'solves' this problem by seeking to ignore it: A *senex amans* should serve love (and a young mistress) as long as the spirit moves him. But as John Burrow has observed,

> this very high courtly position proved extremely difficult to defend, even by writers otherwise ready to entertain claims for the transcendent character of human love. For one thing, it was open to attack from learned athorities of every sort, especially the *medici* with their doctrine of the diminution of bodily heat, and the moralists with their prescription of wisdom and piety as the proper business of old people . . . Hence we find some courtly writers setting out to portray that delicate transitional stage in the life of a lover at which, recognizing that he is no longer young, he bids farewell to love and composes the lover's equivalent of a last will and testament.[159]

---

[158] Gower doubtless knew Froissart's work, given the French poet's frequent presence in England, his association with Chaucer (on which see Wimsatt, *French Love Poets*, pp. 118-33), and possibly even through Froissart's gift of his collected poems to Richard II; see Shears, *Froissart*, p. 233, n. 1. In any case, one of the two complete manuscripts of Froissart's works resided for a time in England, and was the property of the Earl of Warwick.

[159] John A. Burrow, *The Ages of Man: A Study in Medieval Writing and Thought* (Oxford, 1986), 179.

The 'courtly writers' Burrow has in mind are Petrarch and Froissart, specifically in the *Joli Buisson de Jonece* where he takes as his subject an aging lover coming to terms with his future. In a dream he is led by Venus and Youth back in time, into the 'joli buisson de jonece' ('fair arbor of youth'). There he meets his lady again and once more feels lyric inspiration, but he also recognizes time cannot stand still, even for lovers. He awakens and, in an activity appropriate for his age, turns his lyric talent to composing a hymn to the Virgin.

Apart from their similar endings (the *Cinkante Ballades* also conclude with a paean to Mary) there is little directly connecting Gower's sequences with the *Joli Buisson*. But the corrective applied by Froissart's poem to Machaut and the *Voir-Dit* is extremely supportive of the project in which Gower engages. Froissart takes the same moral position Gower does — and indeed, the 'lover's equivalent of a last will and testament' that Burrow finds in the *Joli Buisson* suggests another lens through which to read Venus's message to Chaucer, in the final Book of the *Confessio*, to 'make his testament of love.' Indirectly, then, the *Joli Buisson* provides a moral context for the radical revision of amorous discourse Gower proposes.

The lines Gower borrows from Machaut, Deschamps and Grandson also reflect this approach to the tradition. We see this from their placement: for what few there are we find clustered in three ballades, all of which variously raise questions about the behaviors urged by the courtly *ethos*. Two of these are the 'work' of the lady, whose five ballades address, first, a false lover, dismissing him (XLI-XLIII), and then her 'tresdouls amis,' complimenting him and pledging her love (XLIIII, XLVI). In Ballade XLIII, the third of the poems, she brings the rejections to a kind of climax by removing her own betrayal by her false lover from a contemporary context and placing it among those of ancient stature. The initial two stanzas tell the story and illustrate the tone:

> 1. Plus tricherous qe Jason a Medée,
>   A Deianire ou q'Ercules estoit,
>   Plus q'Eneas, q'avoit Dido lessée,
>   Plus qe Theseüs, q'Adriagne amoit,
>   Ou Demephon, quant Phillis oublioit,
>   Je trieus, helas, q'amer jadis soloie:
>   Dont chanterai desore en mon endroit,
>   C'est ma dolour, qe fuist ainçois ma joie.
> 2. Unqes Ector, q'ama Pantasilée
>   , En tiele haste a Troie ne s'armoit,
>   Qe tu tout nud n'es deinz le lit couché,
>   Amis as toutes, quelqe venir doit,
>   Ne poet chaloir, mais q'une femne y soit;
>   Si es comun plus qe la halte voie.
>   Helas, qe la fortune me deçoit,
>   C'est ma dolour, qe fuist ainçois ma joie.

['More treacherous than Jason to Medea,/ Or Hercules was to Deianira,/ More than Aeneas, who deserted Dido,/ More than Theseus,

who loved Ariadne,/ Or Demophon, when he forgot Phillis,/ I find, alas,
him whom I was wont to love:/ Thus for my part I will sing henceforth,/
My sadness is that which was once my joy.

Never did Hector, whom Penthesilea loved,/ Arm himself in such
haste for Troy,/ Than you, completely naked, lie down in bed;/ You
love all women, whoever should come,/ It matters not at all, save only
that she be female;/ Thus you are more common than the highway./
Alas, because fortune deceived me,/ My sadness is that which was once
my joy.']

Strong stuff, certainly — from the lady or from Gower. But of equal
significance here is the role played by quotation. The poem is indeed built
around lines borrowed from the tradition. For, as we noted earlier, Fisher has
pointed out how closely Gower's naming of great lovers (and these lovers, Jason,
Medea, and the others, in particular) resembles Grandson's 'Ho! doulce Yseult,
qui a la fontaine' Avec Tristan, Jason et Medea;' and that the refrain 'C'est ma
dolour, qe fuisst ainçois ma joie' recalls Machaut's 'C'est ma dolour et la fin de
ma joie.' The result is a poem of extraordinary resonance, the most referential of
the sequence. Its intended effect, I think, is a kind of double cancellation, first of
the unfaithful lover and next of the poetic tradition which sometimes sanctioned
his 'type.' For one corollary of the lady's invocation of literary figures to
characterize her 'real-life' plight is an inevitable comparison of the fictive and the
actual. As the bitterness of her tone makes clear to us, she has discovered the
border dividing a world of bright lies from a harsher ontology, where risks must
be run at a price. Thus it should come as no surprise that, in her following poem,
addressed to her faithful lover (he of the forty-plus ballades and the devoted years
of service), she stresses *deeds* as the cause for his acceptance:

Vailant, courtois, gentil et renomée,
Loial, verrai, certain de vo promesse,
Vous m'avetz vostre corps et coer donné,
Qe jeo rescoive et prens a grant leesce.

['Valiant, courteous, gentle and renowned,/ Loyal, true, certain in your
promises,/ You have given me your body and heart,/ Which I receive
and take with great delight.']

Essential here is the language of exchange — bodies and hearts given and
received, adjectives transformed into 'facts' by consistent performance. The
metaphor is expanded in the rest of the stanza:

Si jeo de Rome fuisse l'emperesse,
Vostre ameisté refuserai jeo mie,
Q'au tiel ami jeo vuill bien estre amie.

['If I were the empress of Rome,/ Your friendship I would not refuse,/
For to such a friend I wish to be a good friend.']

Gower's 'Si jeo de Rome fuisse l'emperesse' recalls Deschamps' refrain, 'Telle
dame estre empereis de Romme.' Here again, a quotation represents the highest
courtly world, both in its imagery and its origin. It brings that world before us,
holds it in place for our consideration. But Gower has revised the line, apparently
to emphasize its conditionality ('*If* I *were* the empress of Rome . . .'); and in the
lady's poem, it is made to contrast with her lover's friendship, a 'hard fact' the
stanza has just established. Exchange — of a sort by now familiar — is thus suggested: an empery of words in trade for concrete, selfless acts. It is a bargain
which the refrain 'To such a friend I wish to be a good friend' underscores, and
opens into a broader context.[160]

The quotations borrowed into the lady's poems, then, echo and 'correct' the
traditional 'voice' of French courtly lyric by calling its implications to account. At
the same time, they raise effectively one of the central problems of language: how
one separates materially verifiable discourse — words backed by fact — from
empty talk.[161] In Ballade XXV, Gower takes as a refrain the much-travelled 'Car
qui bien aime ses amours tard oblie' ('Because he who loves well forgets his love
but late') to help establish this question as being at the core of the *Cinkante
Ballades*. The male lover explains that he must absent himself from his lady
because his visits to her, made with her permission ('a vo plesir'), have set wicked
tongues wagging. Thus, to save her honor, he leaves:

> Ma dame, si ceo fuist a vo plesir,
> Au plus sovent jeo vous visiteroie;
> Mais le fals jangle et le tresfals conspir
> De mesdisantz m'ont destorbé la voie,
> Et vostre honour sur toute riens voldroie:
> Par quoi, ma dame, en droit de ma partie,
> En lieu de moi mon coer a vous envoie;
> Car qui bien aime ses amours tard oblie.

At its basic level, the lover's troubles spring from the autonomy of language and
truth. 'Fals jangle' is possible because deeds and descriptions do not have to
correspond. The lover's response — to *do* something (i.e., stop visiting) —

---

[160] The importance to love relationships of real exchange, unfettered by falsehood or
obligation to return, needs no elaboration; but Gower's treatment of the idea here, in a
context pointedly concerned with what it means to be a *poet*, as well as an appropriate
lover, suggests the wider conclusions of Lewis Hyde, who finds the essence of poetry in an
'economy of giving.' The inspiration, and then the poem itself as passed on to society, are
gifts in a special form of exchange. See *The Gift Imagination and the Erotic Life of Property*
(New York, 1979).

[161] Gower's linguistic focus here has its counterpart in Machaut. As Calin, *Poet at the
Fountain*, notes (p. 199): 'The *V[oir]-D[it]* is a tale of language — speech, poetry, prose

confirms his intentions actively. It constitutes 'truth' by bringing together word and deed. As did the lady's poems, this reaction predicates exchange. The lover expects his leaving to replace 'fals jangle' — to trade deeds for (untrue) speech. It is thus a form of interpretation, a 'critique' of the 'text' of the 'mesdisantz,' based upon a text of proverbial kind, that 'Actions speak louder than words.'

In a curious reversal, however, it is by rejecting language of one sort that the lover establishes his right to apply its powers himself. As he does in the two final lines of the stanza: for when he claims that 'In place of myself I send my heart to you' ('En lieu de moi mon coer a vous envoie') he describes an exchange which cannot be literally true. Because, however, to this point the lover has anchored his statements in the literally true — that is, in action — we are willing to accept this impossible promise as a metaphor. We read on, to discover in the refrain a justification The lover's promise to 'leave his heart with his lady' means 'he will not forget her.'

Now, at first glance this appears to be a different use of quotation than we have been examining. Instead of 'standing in' for the French tradition of courtly lyric, and so providing critical access to it, the borrowed refrain in Ballade XXV seems rather to accept the line — and, in consequence, the tradition — at face value. But the affirmation (for it is, I think, a special affirmation Gower offers here) is extended, not in isolation, but in the context of the testing of language realised by the surrounding ballade. Emerging as the conclusion to this process, as the justification for the lover's venture into metaphor, the quoted line represents amorous discourse employed as Gower believed it could and should be that is, as an *earned* discourse, morally consistent and approvable, its promises backed by deeds. Language *not* so supported by action is specifically excluded. It is 'le tresfals conspir' that works to universal dishonor.

Thus the refrain Gower borrowed for Ballade XXV serves the same purpose as similar lines in the poems written for the lady. All point, in individual ways, to the dangerous writing of the courtly lyric; and all seek to turn that writing to a better end by using it against itself. Moreover, there is a logic guiding the selection of these particular ballades as *loci* in which to question conventional amorous discourse. The lady's recent deception by a false lover's words lends her critique a dramatic sharpness, and emphasizes actual human costs. Coming naturally at the end of the narrative, her judgement affords us a backward look at — and a vantage whence to assess — all that has gone before. Similarly, the placement of Ballade XXV, at the exact center of the sequence, dictates its importance.[162] That it offers a kind of general reading of the ways a love affair can

correspondence — in which words and the poetic art impede rather than encourage physical action.'
[162] Depending on how one counts them, the total number of ballades in the sequence can be as high as 54 or exactly 50. The problems are the two dedicatory pieces to Henry IV at the beginning, the double numbering (there are two ballades marked 'IIII'), and the final poem to the Virgin, LI. My own feeling is that Gower would not have included the dedicatory poems in his 'official' count of the sequence, would have eliminated one of the two marked 'IIII,' and allowed the poem to the Virgin to stand, outside the sequence, at LI.

be described is not, I think, to be ignored. In effect, it bares the deeper concerns of the sequence which the lady's poems will finally confirm — truth and falsity, the relationship of promise to act, legitimate and illegitimate languages of love.

IX

Ballade XXV takes aim at Deschamps, then, but in a more general way than do the lady's at Machaut. And this is fitting, since the refrain Gower quotes there Deschamps shared with Moniot d'Arras, with Machaut himself, with Chaucer and with French proverb, as well. One might argue the suitability of such a representative quotation in its place, in a poem intended to establish a general method for criticising a set of poetic conventions, and perhaps be right to do so. Yet what ought to draw our attention finally is the broader outline of Gower's poetic which emerges from the scrutiny we have applied to his French and Latin poems. That Gower should be revealed by this a comprehensive moralist is surprising only in its degree. For we find, when we press him, his sensitivity for verbal nuance and the multiple uses of the poetic line sharing power and purpose with his beliefs. Each informs the other, each gives the other shape. Thus it is that Gower's 'cento,' once perceived, can guide is through his work diversely, connecting his major themes, his plenitude of learning and of story, with the finest minutiae of technique.

Chapter III: TRANSFORMATIONS

I

The primary enterprise of all 'strong' poets, the critic Harold Bloom would have us believe, is an act of transformation. By substantially 'misreading' the work of their predecessors, they hope to 'clear imaginative space' for their own writings to flourish.[1] Now, having devoted most of two lengthy chapters to describing aspects of John Gower's poetry which Bloom could claim showed 'strength' (the concern to alter fourteenth-century readings of French love poetry being salient among them), it might do here to imagine quickly what a resurrected Gower would make of himself, confronted with a Bloomian portrait. Assuming he kept his bearings through an unfamiliar thicket of Freud and Oedipus, 'misprision' and anxiety, Gower might finally come to appreciate what Bloom calls 'a major aesthetic consciousness' — somewhat more, at least, than he would N. F. Blake's view that medieval English authors conceived of texts 'quite fortuitously, without past or future,' or A.C. Spearing's argument that only Chaucer 'was aware of the work of earlier writers . . . as the property of individual precursors,' available for incorporation into his own writing with the intent 'to produce recognizable quotation or allusion.'[2] For, as we have seen, Gower was thoroughly aware of himself in relation to earlier poets. As much as Chaucer's, his poetic too depends on his readers knowledge of literary context for its success. Beyond this, we may even notice an anxiousness underlying his attack on Jean de Meun and Machaut, and a general *measuring* of himself against other 'auctours' amounting, *de facto*, to competition.

But in the end, Gower is no anachronism. He built his poetic around a medieval moralist's imperative to hone his lessons and drive them home, not in response to pressures — Oedipal or otherwise — to supplant his literary ancestors. Hence a Gower brought to life would quarrel bitterly with Bloom on all the major points: those, that is, which define what literature is *for* in the world. In their modern extremity, however, Bloom's notions of the poet's inner struggle contrast with, and so ultimately help us absorb, Gower's complex aesthetic to the better appreciation of his art. For it is right to say that Gower felt a challenge in

---

[1] Harold Bloom, *The Anxiety of Influence: A Theory of Poetry* (London and New York, 1973), p. 5.
[2] Ibid., p. 6; Norman F. Blake, *The English Language in Medieval Literature* (London, Totowa, N.J., 1977 14-15; A.C. Spearing, 'Lydgate's Canterbury Tale: *The Siege of Thebes* and Fifteenth-century Chaucerianism,' in Yeager, *Fifteenth-Century Studies*, p. 332.

other poets' work. When he read, it was always with a look-out for what he could transform, if we take 'transform' to mean adapt more precisely to edifying use.

To conceive this clearly, we must pay attention to Gower's sources and the changes he made in them as he turned them to hand. In the pages to follow I shall focus on the *Confessio Amantis* for examples, as it is Gower's best poem, and also the most accessible. Conclusions are applicable to his other work as well, however, for — as Fisher often reminds us — Gower is technically and ideologically a consistent writer.[3]

By way of connecting what we have already said about style and language, let us begin with two adaptations Gower made to his sources which, reasonably, might have found their way into either of the foregoing chapters. Since the thought process followed to produce them tells us much about Gower's narrative concerns, however, I include them here. The first involves a technique John Burrow has referred to as 'light pointing.'[4] 'To point,' as Burrow notes, is one of the few terms we can recover from the working vocabulary of Ricardian poets. He connects it with the *via brevitatis*, the 'short way' of writing classified by rhetoricians like Geoffrey of Vinsauf among figures of abbreviation.[5] It meant 'to describe in detail.' Light pointing is thus a feature of spare style, associated either with brief narrative or with 'low' or 'plain' writing. Chaucer's *Legends of Good Women* exemplifies the former; the 'middel weie' as Gower applies it in the *Confessio Amantis* (where his tales are both short — the average length is 15 lines — and simply told) illustrates the latter. An instance occurs in Book I, 2508-11, in the 'Tale of Albinus and Rosamund':

> The grete stiedes were assaied
> For joustinge and for tornement,
> And many a *perled* garnement
> Embroudred was ayein the dai.

[3] Fisher, *John Gower*, p. 135.
[4] Burrow, *Ricardian Poetry*, pp. 69-78, especially p. 74.
[5] On the *via brevitatis*, see Faral, *Les artes poétiques*, pp. 61-85, for the views of Geoffrey of Vinsauf, John of Garland, and Eberhard the German. Geoffrey's comment is (*Poetria Nova* 206-10):
> Curritur in bivio: via namque vel ampla vel arta,
> vel fluvius vel rivus erit; vel tractius ibis,
> vel cursim salies; vel rem brevitate notabis,
> vel longo sermone trahes. Non absque labore
> sunt passus utriusque viae.
['The way continues along two routes: there will be either a wide path or a narrow, either a river or a brook. You may advance at a leisurely pace or leap swiftly ahead. You may report the matter with brevity or draw it out in a lengthy discourse. The footing on either path is not without effort.'] See further Curtius, *European Literature*, Excursus XIII (pp. 487-94), on 'Brevity as an Ideal of Style.'

Burrow comments that 'the abstract, generalizing manner, marked by Gower's special use of definite and indefinite articles, creates a context in which the epithet *perled* produces an exquisite effect.'[6] Specific and visual, the single adjective vivifies a generic scene of 'joustinge,' 'tournement,' and 'grete stiedes' with a sudden conferral of sensory depth. Sometimes the result is a synaesthesis almost Keatsian. When Almeene, deceived by Amphitrion, hears her actual husband Geta pounding on the door (*CA* II, 2484-87),

> . . . sche ansuerede and bad him go,
> And seide how that abedde al warm
> Hir lief lay naked in her arm;
> Sche wende that it were soth.

The narrative is spare and straightforward, with only two sensory details: a lover's nakedness, and a warm bed. Yet with this economy an irrevocable gulf of difference is opened between Geta, cold and locked out in the night, and Amphitrion, at ease and skin-to-skin in the arms of Almeene.[7]

Deftness aside, however, what makes these passages valuable as examples of Gower's art is their moral resonance. Burrow has astutely juxtaposed the tournament sketch with another, 25 lines further along in the tale, in which the same technique is applied. The tourney is part of a celebration planned by Albinus to impress his wife Rosamund, daughter of Gurmond, whom Albinus has decapitated in battle. At the feast, Albinus commands Rosamund to 'drink with your father,' handing her a goblet (*CA* I, 2535-45),

> Which made was of Gurmondes hed.
> As ye have herd, whan he was ded,
> And was with gold and riche stones
> Beset and bounde for the nones,
> And stod upon a fot on heihte
> Of burned gold, and with gret sleihte
> Of werkmanschipe it was begrave
> Of such werk as it scholde have,
> And was policed ek so clene
> That no signe of the skulle is sene,
> But as it were a Gripes Ey.

---

6 Burrow, *Ricardian Poetry*, p. 76.
7 One might compare Keats' image of Madeline unclasping her 'warmed jewels one by one' from 'The Eve of St. Agnes;' see *Keats: Poetical Works*, ed. H. W. Garrod (London, 1956), p. 202.

Again, Burrow's analysis is worth quoting: 'Gower's vagueness about the workmanship of the cup ('Of such werk as it scholde have') prepares for the startling precision of the last detail: a spot of exposed bone the size of a griffin's egg. A modern reader will be reminded of the sudden close-up which may, in films, create a similar horrific effect.'[8] But unlike many filmmakers, Gower had no interest in horrific effect *per se*. Intended to illustrate 'avantance,' or boasting, 'Albinus and Rosamund' turns not only narratively but morally also on this moment when the girl discovers both the fate of her father and the monstrous character of her new husband. Since the lesson of the tale is to look below the surface — to perceive the skull-scrap stark amidst the gold — it is imperative that we share Rosamund's revelation and raise it to a higher plane. For this crucial observation the lightly pointed 'perled garnements' serves as preparation: It is an exercise in how we ought to read. In 'Geta and Amphitrion' the light pointing similarly illuminates unnatural inversions brought about by sin: What deception does Amphitrion's 'nakedness' disguise? For whom (and in what sense) should Almeene's bed be 'warm'?

Each of these examples represents an addition Gower made to his sources, to render a special effect. In none of them, however, was he following his original closely. Let us look, then, at a case in which he 'points' a near translation. In the 'Tale of Virgil's Mirror,' Gower speaks of a bloody defeat of the Romans by Hannibal (*CA* V, 2201-04):

> So gret a multitude [he] slowh,
> That of goldringes, which he drowh
> Of gentil handes that ben dede,
> Buisshelles fulle thre, I rede.

The incident Gower found in the *Secretum Secretorum* of Jofroi de Watreford and Servale Copale:

> Et tant ocis des romains que un jour fist emplir trois muis d'aniaus d'or,
> qui furent az princes et az hauz homs.

This in turn derives from Eutropius, whose account Gower might have known also:

> et tres modios aureorum annulorum Carthaginem misit, quos e
> manibus equitem Romanorum, senatorum, et militum dextraxerat.[9]

---

[8] Burrow, *Ricardian Poetry*, p. 77.
[9] Texts printed by George L. Hamilton, 'Some Sources of the Seventh Book of Gower's *Confessio Amantis*,' *Modern Philology* 9 (1912), 326, 337, n. 1.

What is revealing here is not that all three writers tell the same story, but rather the ways in which they envision the scene. In each case, the Carthaginian victory produces a large number of dead Romans and three measures of golden rings. Eutropius takes an historian's interest in the slain, carefully categorizing them according to social class 'equitum . . . senatorum, et militum.' Jofroi, less specifically concerned with whose rings filled the containers than with the magnitude of the Roman losses, states generally 'az princes et az hauz homs.' Gower however seems to have sensed that, beyond the blunt enormity of the victory, there was a poignancy in so swift a passing away of a national nobility, and he chose to emphasize this. For him the senators and princes become a light synecdoche: 'gentil handes,' viewed even at the moment of despoilage. It is delicate work, as it has to be to catch the tone, which is itself a moral comment on the awful costs of war.

Light pointing, then, is one sort of transformation Gower worked on his sources. A second, which could also be classified as stylistic but for its didactic implications, is in a way light pointing's close relation. It too is an approach to description. What I want to talk about has been portrayed by C.S. Lewis as singularities of Gower's imagination. Specifically, Lewis felt that what Gower 'saw' with his mind's eye was 'movement, not groups and scenes, but actions and events.'[10] As a result, Lewis found Gower's poetry psychologically reluctant ('It is almost a rule with him not to tell us what his people thought') and short on imagery ('The pictorial imagination finds little to feed on in the *Confessio Amantis*').[11]

To be fair, Lewis understood both absences to be characteristics of the plain syle, and he recognized also that Gower did choose to apply 'the pictorial touch' from time to time. A passage that Lewis singles out for praise in this regard appears at Book V, 3731-34, in the 'Tale of Jason and Medea.' Jason, having survived his ordeal,

> The Flees he tok and goth to Bote,
> The Sonne schyneth bryhte and hote,
> The Flees of gold schon forth withal,
> The water glistreth overal.

Although Lewis conflates the details a little in his enthusiasm (what he likes is 'the glittering of the golden fleece bright and hot as Jason rows back with it'), nonetheless we can see what he means.[12] Gower seldom devotes much room to how the sun shone or the water glistened, even when such information is provided him by his sources. And in this case, placing the lines here is original to him: neither Benoît de Ste. Maure nor Guido della Colonna, on whose works

[10] Lewis, *Allegory of Love*, p. 206.
[11] Ibid., pp. 203, 205.
[12] Ibid., p. 205.

Gower drew for the story, includes this passage here.[13] So, one might ask, why did he add them? The answer takes us beyond Lewis's aesthetic response to pretty poetry and back to Gower the craftsman. He has a particular use for the fleece, the sun and the bright water. We find, within the next ten lines, that Medea is 'upon a Tour alofte,' praying and watching for Jason's return. She knows instantly that 'al is wonne' when she sees on the horizon 'The Flees glistrende ayein the Sonne' (*CA* V, 3735-44). The 'Sonne hot' is made to shine later on Jason's men who, with the 'nobles alle' and 'the comun of the toun,' are also waiting on the shore. In the bright light, they see his boat, and rejoice (3752-72). At last the king, Medea's father, learns of Jason's success. Like his daughter, he 'sih the Flees, hou that it schon,' even as Jason makes toward land (3773-75).

What is significant here is the way the fleece is developed. It functions not only as the end of Jason's quest, but also as a sign, first telegraphing, then standing for, his triumph. The 'pictorial' description that Lewis liked is part of Gower's plan to achieve this double effect. This passage calls our attention to the bright weather (good for reflecting beams long distances) and the light-throwing qualities of the fleece. That Medea should first catch sight of its golden gleam in the distance thus has an apparent ontological rightness which comes from our having been prepared by the added descriptive passage: *Naturally* (so to speak) she picks out the glistening fleece. But there is more to it than this. Medea's father also sights Jason by the fleece. The royal pair thus stand in contrast to the townspeople and Jason's crew. No brilliant flash for them: *They* become aware of Jason's coming only when they see 'the bot, which thei wel knowe.' It is a mundane observation, of a piece with other 'mob' attitudes they hold — that Jason must be a 'faie ('fairy') kniht' (3769) to have achieved so much, that the fleece is a 'proprete' (a 'property') around which they crowd, laughing and (presumably) jostling to get a view (3781-83).

Our recognition of this contrast is important, for it opens an avenue into the center of the tale. We should remember, in reading it, that Genius tells 'Jason

---

[13] See Leopold Constans, ed., *Le Roman de Troie*, 6 vols. (Paris, 1904-1912) I, 99 (ll. 196 ff.); and Nathaniel Edward Griffin, ed., *Historia Destructionis Troiae* (Cambridge, MA, 1936), p. 31. Although Guido has no passage similar to Gower's lines, Benoît includes the following couplets (ll. 1883-86):

> Les bues choisi e le serpent
> E le mouton, qui mout resplent:
> Grant clarte done l'or vermeil
> Contre la raie del soliel.

['The bulls he saw, and the serpent, and the ram, which shone dazzlingly: the red gold gave off a great brilliance in the sun's rays.' This possibly was Gower's inspiration for his passage, unnoticed before since it appears 80 lines ahead of where Lewis was looking. Finding it there and transporting it to a more significant locus would have been typical of Gower's 'centonic' work habits. For Gower's use of Guido and Benoît, see Karl Eichinger, *Die Trojasage als Stoffquelle für John Gowers Confessio Amantis* (Munich, 1900); George L. Hamilton, 'Studies in the Sources of Gower,' *JEGP* 26 (1927), 491-52 (who shows how Gower has interwoven material from Guido, Archpresbyter Leo, Walter Map, Albericus of London, and Thomas of Kent); and also Dwyer, 'Gower's *Mirour*, 482-505.

and Medea' to illustrate 'Perjury,' which he has classified as a type of Avarice, the sin discussed in Book V. But the richness of the fleece must not mislead us. More specifically still, it is 'Avarice in love' that the priest exemplifies, not garden-variety greed. This difference Gower manifests by various means throughout the tale, including the divers sightings of Jason. Like Podsnap's dinner-guests before his great epergne, the Greek crewmen and the townsfolk eye the fleece as if it were 'so many ounces of precious metal worth so much an ounce.'[14] To them, it is 'proprete,' gold. And why not? Their lives do not change by Jason's winning it. Jason's life, and those of Medea and her father, however, *are* changed — irrevocably and inextricably. For Jason, the fleece is equivalent to identity. Seizing it, he becomes who he 'is' for all time — an exceptional man, the Hero of the Golden Fleece.[15] This exceptionality the townsfolk and crewmen attempt to explain by attributing 'faie' powers to Jason. Their perspective renders the fleece symbolic of these powers, the *je ne sais quoi* of heroism.

Yet we readers know otherwise. We have been inside the bedchamber of Medea when the fateful bargain was struck, Jason promising (*CA* V, 3487-92)

> That if Medea dede him helpe,
> That he his pourpos myhte winne,
> Thei scholde nevere parte atwinne,
> Bot evere whil him lasteth lif,
> He wolde hire holde for his wif.

Jason's 'edge' has been love, not magic. Hence the tale is aptly part of Gower's larger program in Book V — a conjuror only of hearts, Jason transmutes *love* with his perjured vow, not cosmic laws.[16] On this level, then — of Medea and, through her, her father — the fleece 'means' a congeries of things: Jason himself, his victory and heroism, but also love (which, in Gower's metaphysics, entered the heart like light, beamed through the eye), and subsequently loss as well.[17] Inexorably, albeit in ways Medea and the king neither sense nor can predict, the

---

[14] Charles Dickens, *Our Mutual Friend*, ed. E. Salter Davies (London, 1952), p. 131.

[15] Gower's audience would have been familiar with the figure of Jason made identifiable by the visible fleece. In this sense, the fleece represents Jason iconographically. But there is another way the fleece is Jason's sign, i.e., the manner in which the pentangle on Gawain's shield (cf. ll. 619 ff.) 'stands for' Gawain on several levels simultaneously. In *Sir Gawain and the Green Knight* there appears to be an awareness of heraldic device equalling inner man which I think Gower is approximating here.

[16] That Gower has Jason swear to marry Medea on an idol of Jupiter, not Venus, heightens the importance of the scene. This statue he found 300 lines away in Benoît (i.e., ll. 1625 ff.), and brings it forward to solemnize the oath.

[17] Eyes as 'windows to the soul' is a Neoplatonic commonplace much in vogue; see the useful discussion by Leonard Forster, in *The Icy Fire: Studies in European Petrarchism* (Cambridge, 1978), 10-11 and 27. Gower emphasizes the role of sight by pointedly denying Jason and Medea any verbal communication: they only gaze, and fall in love (see ll. 3378-92).

golden flash in Jason's approaching boat already has begun to redesign their lives.

Development of this kind has much in common with light pointing as Gower used it. In 'Jason and Medea' the descriptive alterations he made to his sources are slight, but morally telling. That is, like light pointing they bring about a subtle advance in our understanding of the lesson of the poem. And, as Lewis noticed, such passages are visually evocative. But because the descriptions Gower worked into his spare style are both uncommon there, and more extensively wrought than a single 'pointed' word, so may we expect more from them than either most description or light pointing usually tells us. As is the case here: for Gower has one further tune to play on the heat and brilliance we have learned to associate with fleece of gold. At the end of the tale (*CA* V, 4175-89) Genius sums up the marvels that Medea has performed for Jason. Winning him the fleece, restoring his father's lost youth, bearing him two children — indeed, 'Medea hath fulfild his wille' and has the right to expect the honorable marriage Jason promised long ago. Gower's narration emphasizes this element of exchange (4190-93):

> Bot whanne he scholde of riht fulfille
> The trouthe, which to hire afore
> He hadde in thyle of Colchos swore,
> Tho was Medea most deceived.

In the context of exchange, 'pointed' by legalistic language ('scholde of riht,' 'trouthe'), the catalogue of Medea's services frames Jason's perjury and supports our outrage as he rejects her for Creusa.[18] As well, these privilege Medea's sanguinary response, so that we approve it as justice much deserved.

But Gower has other strategies working in these lines, too. Recounting Medea's marvels and Jason's bedchamber promise effectively recalls their early love and the glistening image of the fleece itself, in Jason's boat under the hot sun. No mention of the fleece is made in the closing lines of the tale, but it is present nonetheless, disguised but scantly amid the details of Medea's revenge. 'With hire art,' Gower tells us (4200-01, 4206-09) Medea

> . . . hath wroght
> Of cloth of gold a mantel riche . . .
> And whan that yonge freisshe queene
> That mantel lappeth hire aboute,

---

[18] Jason's unjust refusal to complete his bargain with Medea — to exchange fairly what she has so clearly earned — is affirmed and condemned by the legalistic phrasing of the subsequent narrative. As Medea kills their sons, she tells Jason, 'Lo, this schal be thi *forfeture*' (4214).

Anon therof the fyr sprong oute
And brente hir bothe fleissh and bon.

After the fascinating but emotionally uncharged accounts of Medea's sorceries which fill the middle of the tale, passion suddenly is reintroduced. By now, however, it is a love gone dark, and — predictably, in this story of balances and transformations — we find the central symbols fitted with new shapes. The unselfconscious 'joie' of the young Medea, metonymically pictured in the gleaming fleece, by Jason's perfidy now becomes the all-consuming flame; and the fleece itself, its gold strands 'by arte' now wrought into a mantle, the instrument needed to close the moral of the tale.

Lest we find such a reading ingenious, we should consider two details. First, none of the three writers Gower used for most of 'Jason and Medea' — Benoît, Guido, and Ovid — relates the story of Creusa's death.[19] To include it Gower went to a fourth source, we do not know which; and while this may have been serendipity, it would seem more reasonable to infer purpose.[20] Second, whether or not there was in Gower's unknown source a *golden* mantle, he clearly is responsible for specifying 'cloth of gold' as the material in the *Confessio*. This is a medieval product, usually made by interweaving gold and wool.[21] Since many of

[19] Benoît, and Guido who followed him, stop their narratives when Jason leaves Colchis; Ovid tells of Medea's restoration of Aeson's youth, and of the killing of Peleus. See *Roman de Troie*, ed. Constans, ll. 2045 ff. and *Historia*, ed. Griffin, p. 33; for Ovid's version, see *Met.* VII, 169-349.

[20] Macaulay, *Works* III, in his note to *CA* V, 417 ff., says only that Gower 'of course knew the [Creusa] story from other sources' — but lists none specifically. Such imprecision is unusual from Macaulay, and undoubtedly reflects the difficulty of identifying Gower's original. It is not Ovid, who omits the events of Corinth from both the *Metamorphoses* and the *Heroides*; nor is it either Benoît or Guido. Apparently Gower depended on a fourth source for the conclusion of his tale, a procedure noteworthy for its thoroughness and erudition. What that source was, however, remains obscure. The details of Gower's version are closest to those in Euripides' play, unknown and unread in fourteenth-century England. Hyginus's account (*Fabulae* XXV), which Gower likely knew, differs in nearly every significant detail, save only that Creusa dies in flames of Medea's making. The dramatic cento *Medea* of Hosidius Geta is too obscure, both in its description of the death and probably in its provenance (only a single manuscript, Parisinus 10318, is now known), to warrant consideration; see the edition of Rosa Lamacchia (Leipzig, 1981), and further Nathan Dane, 'The *Medea* of Hosidius Geta,' *Classical Journal* 46 (1950), 75-78. Of other ancient *Medea* versions we know too little to judge: those of Lucan and Curiatus Maternus exist only in title; and of Ennius's work (while interesting in that what we have seems to be a translation of Euripides) and Ovid's only fragments remain. Of course any of these, or an unknown text, might have been Gower's source; but the more likely possibility is Seneca's *Medea*, of which more than thirty manuscripts known to have been in England in Gower's time are now extant. A number of these include the commentary written by Nicholas Trivet, on whose other work Gower drew elsewhere. See the edition of C.D.N. Costa, *Seneca: Medea* (Oxford, 1973), and Theodor Dürling, *Zur Überlieferung von Senekas Tragödien* (Leipzig, 1913), for a description of English manuscripts, and Trivet's commentaries.

[21] *OED*, s.v. 'cloth,' II. 9c. Less often the base material was silk.

Gower's readers would have known this, his specificity seems again to be purposeful, to remind us of the fleece with its multivalent meanings, and help us see what it — and they — have become.[22]

'All that glitters is not gold,' then, is one moral we might draw from the account of Medea's love for the perjuror Jason. It is also wisdom applicable to Lewis's opinion about the visual poverty of the *Confessio*. For, by comparision with many flashier but less thoughtful poets, Gower provides — when he provides — pictorial imagery enriched by controlled moral connection. Nearly the same point may be made too in response to Lewis's second assessment, that Gower reveals little about his character's thoughts, preferring to show us action instead.

Now, it is true that Gower frequently passes over moments another poet (Ovid, for example) would make more of. Lewis himself cites several; and like him, we would wish to know more when Alceste, resolved to die to save her husband, takes him in her arms 'and spak unto him what hire liste' (*CA* VII, 1940); or when Lucrece, about to be raped by Tarquin, 'unwaked/ Abedde lay, but what sche mette,/ God wot' (*CA* VII, 4966-68), and so on.[23] But despite these tantalizing silences, the fact is that we seldom feel out of touch with the inner workings of Gower's characters. We can derive their thoughts from their actions quite satisfactorily — and it is important that we see this as a *method* Gower employed to *present* or *portray* — not as a failure to acknowledge — introspection.

Florent in bed with his hag-wife in Book I, 1774-1800, offers a clear example. I quote it in full, because its length is an essential part of the effect.

> His body myhte wel be there.
> Bot as of thoght and of memoire
> His herte was in purgatoire.
> Bot yit for strengthe of matrimoine
> He myhte make non essoine,
> That he ne mot algates plie
> To gonne to bedde of compaignie:
> And whan thei were abedde naked,
> Withoute slep he was awaked;
> He torneth on that other side,
> For that he wolde hise yhen hyde
> Fro lokynge on that foule wyht.
> The chambre was al full of lyht,
> The courtins were of cendal thinne,

---

[22] *À propos* of this transformation, there is irony in Medea's specifying that she sent the mantle to Creusa as a gift 'for Sosterhode hem was betuene' (4205). The primary sense of 'Sosterhode' must be 'friendship' (for to think that Gower believed, from his source or generally, that Medea was related to Creusa is improbable); but the resonances the kinship term sets up are ironically suggestive: Medea recognizes that she and Creusa have both been betrayed by Jason, that a 'golden fleece' has been perpetrated on them both.
[23] Lewis, *Allegory of Love*, p. 203.

> This newe bryd which lay withinne,
> Thogh it be noght with his acord,
> In armes sche beclipte hire lord,
> And preide, as he was torned fro,
> He wolde him torne ayeinward tho;
> 'For now,' sche seith, 'we ben bothe on.'
> And he lay stille as eny ston,
> Bot evere in on sche spak and preide,
> And bad him thenke on that he seide,
> Whan that he tok hire be the hond.
>   He herde and understond the bond,
> Hou he was set to his pennance,
> And as it were a man in trance
> He torneth him al sodeinly . . .

Florent's mental conflict (which Gower intensifies by drawing out) could not be more apparent. Caught between what he perceives to be his duty to fulfill the marriage debt and its odious nature, he functions stiffly, like a man turned to wood. His mind rejects what his body will have to do, and this stiffness, like his turning away from his wife's hideous (or so he expects) nakedness is another way of saying so. Actively he does what he can to be somewhere else, while remaining constrained to be where he least wants to be; just so, his consciousness strives unsuccessfully to desert the body which it is well aware will soon become involved in an unpalatable act. The brilliantly lighted room is another purposeful touch, with obvious intellective overtones: Florent knows well that when (not if) he turns over, it will be to embrace his future. 'Al sodeinly' he does this — the way we resignedly rip off an adhesive bandage — and the abrupt maneuver speaks volumes. It is a detail true to life, and psychologically revealing.

The fullest example of actions indicating thought in the *Confessio Amantis* is given us, however, not by Florent, but through the person of Amans. For it is toward Amans, the central character of the complex, integrated fiction that Gower directs his greatest attention. He scrutinizes the Lover's acts, screening them for us to lay out the secrets of his heart. The *Confessio* is, in fact, Amans's poem, and though it transforms itself into much more than a personal odyssey of love, it is through Amans's mental and emotional revelations and metamorphoses that the change must be brought home to Gower's audience.

The poem's confessional frame is well suited to convey Amans's innermost thoughts through action. Confession requires the penitent to describe deeds done or considered, and so by intent probes private feelings by way of acts. Because he often discusses his behavior with candor (or prominent naïveté, depending on one's point of view), Amans proves an apt subject for such analysis. Consider his self-portrait under the influence of Melancholy (*CA* III, 82-83, 87-92):

> Whan I ne may my ladi se,
> The more I am redy to wraththe . . .
> And am so malencolious,

That ther nys servant in myn hous
Ne non of tho that ben aboute,
That ech of hem ne stant in doute,
And wenen that I scholde rave
For Anger that thei se me have..

This passage reveals two important things, about Amans and about Gower himself. First it shows us that Amans can analyse. He is aware of himself as the middle link in a chain of events, and can connect his lady's treatment of him, his resultant melancholy, and how he abuses his servants. He recognizes clearly that a delicately-set emotional compass controls his behavior. Should he come upon his lady and she 'speke a goodli word' to him, his anger would evaporate: 'For al the gold that is in Rome' he could no longer be 'wroth' (*CA* III, 99-101). Yet just as quickly his ire can return (108-15):

Ayeinward if that it so befelle
That I at thilke time sihe
On me that sche miscaste hire yhe,
Or that sche liste noght to loke,
And I therof good hiede toke,
Anon into my ferste astat
I torne, and am with al so mat,
That evere it is aliche wicke.

More significant than Amans's recognition that actions reflect internal states — are, in a sense, psychological 'texts' — is the identical sensitivity these examples reveal was Gower's own. The admissions he concocts for Amans illustrate the kind of 'reader' Gower could be of human affairs. To take another instance: In Book IV, (2826-30), Amans describes how he bids his lady good night after a visit. According to custom, he embraces her on his way 'forth withal.' But:

Er I come fulli to the Dore,
I torne ayein and feigne a thing,
As thogh I hadde lost a Ring
Or somwhat elles, for I wolde
Kisse hire eftsones, if I scholde.

The tarrying, the fabricated 'lost ring,' the finessing for a second parting kiss, are descriptive light pointing. As always, they are details put to a purpose. All portray with accuracy a state of mind which, if common among lovers, is rendered no less complex or individual by its familiarity. Indeed, precisely by means of such 'readable' actions Gôwer 'brings Amans out' beyond his *typus* as generic lover. As Amans reveals a self-awareness, conventional material is transformed into something deeper, fresh and new.

When Gower does have Amans talk about his thoughts, the insight we acquire can be startling, the more so because such passages are infrequent, and because they are offered dramatically. (That is, Amans is made to reveal more to Genius and to us than probably he knows, as does a character on stage.) An excellent example of both is Amans's response to Genius's query in Book II, whether he was guilty of detraction. The passage is carefully contrived, and establishes Amans's contradictory mental state. The lover begins by justifying his backbiting on the grounds that his rivals (notably termed 'this yonge lusty route') 'al day pressen [his lady] aboute,' waiting for a moment to interject a false tale, 'Al to deceive an innocent' (454-65). The argument has a certain initial plausibility: Without him to uncover their plots, his lady might be overwhelmed. But Gower purposefully interjects elements which disturb this comfortable image of lover-to-the-rescue. Amans 'hauntes' behind the others (481-89), saying 'what evere comth to mowthe, . . ./ And ay the werste in special;' indeed, he wishes he knew more 'dirt' ('And worse I wolde, if that I cowthe'). The result is a self-presentation rich with irony and some real humor. Amans again condemns his rivals 'double entente' (490-93), but this time, his motives obviously suspect, he undermines himself. Gower brings the irony to a head with a pun on 'green' (494-95):

> Thus toward hem that wicke mene
> My wicked word was evere grene.

Literally, the lover means that his retaliatory words have always flourished against those who intend to deceive — but green is a loaded color in the Middle Ages, and suggests that Amans has some thought that his efforts to save his lady are not entirely innocent.[24] His next statement seems to confirm this for, as a man will who recognizes that perhaps he has gone too far, he immediately reverses himself with what sounds like a sheepish admission (496-506):

> And natheles, the soth to telle,
> In certain if it so befelle
> That althertrewest man ybore
> To chese among a thousand score,
> Which were alfulli forto triste,
> My ladi lovede, and I it wiste,
> Yit rathere than he scholde spede,
> I wolde swiche tales sprede

---

[24] Green as the color of inconstancy, envy and sexual passion is well attested; see *MED*, s.v. 'grene,' adj., 1.c, and 'grene,' n., 2.

> To my ladi, if that I myhte,
> That I scholde al his love unrihte.

Amans is doing what most have also done at one time or another: presenting his actions in a light favorable to himself while knowing all along how different his true motives are. As is commonly the case, he is only temporarily successful. Gower's modulation of the speech as it unfolds is subtle, and psychologically astute. Gradually he allows contradiction to impinge on Amans's narrative until, in an overweighted moment, resolution breaks to the surface.

The dramatic manner of this presentation is worthy our underlining with a related example. In part this is so because it will contribute to my larger point that, *contra* Lewis, Gower actually represented intellection in several ways. But, more pertinently, it introduces an additional treatment of sources which can help us conceptualize the range of Gower's art. Here we must take 'sources' in a broad sense, to include influences and analogues that stand behind and beside a work's large design — drawn upon, albeit indirectly, as reflections or ideas of what things language might be made to do. Gower had access to several exhibitions of the engaged mind and heart, in Ovid's *Metamorphoses* and *Heroides* — and in the figures of thought and apostrophe in rhetorics like Geoffrey of Vinsauf's, and of their application by Boccaccio and Chaucer.[25]

When Criseyde debates with herself the relative merits of taking Troilus as a lover (*TC* II, 694-875) Chaucer gives us a magnificent example of what we are looking for in Gower. The lines are too numerous to quote in their entirety, but the following illustrate the dramatic approach Chaucer takes. After putting the case pro and con, Criseyde seems at first to have resolved the issue (757-63):

> 'What shal I doon? To what fyn lyve I thus?
> Shal I nat love, in cas if that me leste?
> What, par dieux! I am naught religious.
> And though that I myn herte sette at reste
> Upon this knyght, that is the worthieste,
> And kepe alwey myn honour and my name,
> By alle right, it may do me no shame.'

But then, as the March sun suddenly can dip into shadow, 'A cloudy thought gan thorugh hire soule pace' (768, 771-77):

> That thought was this: 'Allas! syn I am free,
> Sholde I now love, and put in jupartie

---

[25] I have in mind figures such as those Geoffrey lists under 'Amplifi cation' ('Prosopopoeia,' Faral, *Les Artes poétiques*, pp. 211-12), and 'Ornaments of Style' (Faral,

My sikernesse, and thrallen libertee?
Allas! how dorst I thenken that folie?
May I naught wel in other folk aspie
Hire dredful joye, hire constreinte, and hire peyne?
Ther loveth noon, that she nath why to pleyne.'

As Chaucer with Criseyde, so Gower with Amans. In Book IV of the *Confessio*, we are given a portrait of the lover in the act of reasoning, contrasting courses to pursue and admonishing himself for temerity. He has written an address to tell his lady of his passion, but her presence so distracts him that he cannot make out his text. Later, 'in other place al one,' he makes what he calls 'a wofull mone/ Unto miself' (597-617):

'Ha, fol, wher was thin herte tho,
What thou thi worthi ladi syhe?
Were thou afered of hire yhe?
For of hire hand ther is no drede:
So wel I knowe hir wommanhede,
That in hire is nomore oultrage
Than in a child of thre yeer age.
Whi has thou drede of so good on,
Whom alle vertu hath begon,
That in hire is no violence
Bot goodlihiede and innocence
Withouten spot of any blame?
Ha, nyce herte, fv for schame!
Ha, couard herte of love unlered,
Wherof art thou so sore afered,
That thou thi tunge soffrest frese,
And wolt thi goode wordes lese,
Whan thou hast founde time and space?
How scholdest thou deserve grace,
Whan thou thiself darst axe non,
Bot al thou hast foryete anon?'

Here Amans is, as he says, visibly 'betwen tuo stoles.' The approach Gower takes to showing this indecision is not, perhaps, removed as far from rhetorical set-pieces as is Chaucer's handling of Criseyde, but in its context it is dramatic and effective, and it lets us view directly Amans's thoughts. It is a different kind of transformation from either light pointing or active description. Like them, however, it particularizes Gower's style and extends his working range.

pp. 231-34). The French romances supply other examples; see for example Guinevere's soliloquy in Chrétien's *Lancelot*.

II

In addition to these changes, Gower made others to his sources more extensive and predictable. That is, he looked for, and then shaped, narrative material to fit his purposes, drawing on reading unusually broad and deep. These purposes, and consequently his use of sources, differ from poem to poem. The most challenging transformations occur in the *Confessio*, where the fiction requires a large collection of exempla. To see what Gower could do with story, then, we need to look to his English poem.

As we do so, it is useful briefly to place Gower beside Chaucer once again. V. A. Kolve, speaking of the Canterbury pilgrims, has argued that

> Chaucer clearly understood that one possible entry into any man's most hidden self is to ask him to tell you a story. The story that he chooses to tell, along with the way he chooses to tell it — his language, tone, emphasis, and choice of detail — can sometimes constitute a communication that goes beyond the story itself, and is not inferior in terms of interest.[26]

'By turning his central characters into narrators,' Kolve notes further, 'Chaucer was able to investigate human personality in its fullest and richest detail.'[27] We moderns, of course, like such revelations and rightly acknowledge Chaucer's genius for showing us so much of his characters' inner lives. But this, beyond a certain point, was never Gower's concern. Neither in the *Confessio* nor elsewhere does he approximate Chaucer's emphasis on revealing the human personality. Usually this is deemed a failure of Gower's, either of the imagination or of poetic skill. It is high time now, however, to take a more sophisticated approach. Without denigrating Kolve's observation (for he is certainly correct about Chaucer's eye for what makes men tick) we should see that *The Canterbury Tales* is a poem as much about literary genres as it is about psychology, and that the *Confessio Amantis*, while it probes Amans's deeds and drives, and those of various characters, does so according to a formula.[28] At bottom, this formula is the one by which God orders creation: it is with a

---

[26] Kolve, *Imagery of Narrative*, p. 218.

[27] Ibid.

[28] Helen Cooper makes the point concisely in *The Structure of the Canterbury Tales* (Athens, Ga., 1984), p. 55: 'If "all of human life is there" in the *Canterbury Tales*, so is all of literature, all artistic interpretation and formulation of human experience.' See further Northrup Frye, *Anatomy of Criticism: Four Essays* (Princeton, N.J.), 1957, p. 122, for the view that life for Chaucer was 'the seed-plot of literature, a vast mass of potential literary forms;' and also the recent argument of C. David Benson against 'dramatic readings' of the tales, *Chaucer's Drama of Style: Poetic Variety and Contrast in the Canterbury Tales* (Chapel Hill, 1986).

clearer vision of this order that we are to come away from a reading of Gower's poem.

Such a plan enforces certain economies on the ultimate shape of the work. These in the past have led to mistaken assessments of what Chaucer and Gower were capable of achieving as poets. For, as we have seen in the pages above, Gower did indeed take an interest in revealing the thoughts of his characters, of showing them to us as 'real people' with complexities of mind, contradictions and blind spots all their own. But only up to a point: thereafter the lesson might be lost beneath the surface of a strong character's personality, which could usurp our focus. If, then, it is a measure of Chaucer's genius that his combination of *doctryne* with psychological exposé suited the poems he chose to write, it is similarly a testimony to Gower's good judgment that, in his poems with very different purposes, he restrained his experiments accordingly, to fit a different plan.

To illustrate what Gower's poetic dictated he do with story, I want to present two approaches to the exempla of the *Confessio*. Broadly speaking they might be called 'external' and 'internal' views, although both ultimately describe the relationship Gower's narratives bear to their original sources. The first — an 'external' classification — concerns the ways in which the narratives differ from each other in performing their exemplifying tasks. While these differences might be accounted for in more than one manner, five 'types' seem basic to Gower's handling of tale after tale.

The first approach is the simplest — almost deceptively so. It involves a direct transference of a narrative from its source into the *Confessio Amantis*, bringing with it an established development and interpretation. Of this, the 'Tale of Capaneus' (*CA* I, 1977-2009) is an example. Gower probably found the story in Statius's *Thebaid*, where Capaneus is the supreme example of heroical power and size rendering a man blind to forces yet larger and stronger than himself.[29] Statius presents Capaneus as a blasphemous victim of his own vain-glory, and it was as such that he became a kind of rhetorical set-piece for the Middle Ages.[30] Gower's description (1980-88) is true to his models:

> The proude knyht Capaneus
> He was of such Surquiderie,
> That he thurgh his chivalrie
> Upon himself so mochel triste

[29] Macaulay, *Works* III, 474, note to ll. 198 ff., points out that the details of Gower's account mesh only with those of Statius.
[30] Geoffrey of Vinsauf, for example, uses Capaneus to illustrate how a proud man might be defamed; see *Poetria Nova* IV, 1808-09, in Faral, *Les Artes poétiques*, p. 252.

That to the goddes him ne liste
In no querele to beseche
Bot seide it was an ydel speche,
Which caused was of pure drede,
For lack of herte and for no nede.

Gower here draws directly on Statius's account of Capaneus's rebuff of the soothsayer Oeclides's warning that to make war is against the wishes of the gods.[31] Similarly the *Confessio* account follows Statius for the details of Capaneus's death.[32] 'Whan he was proudest in his gere,' Gower says (1998-2003),

[31]   Illum iterum Capaneus: 'Tuus o furor uni
ista tibi, ut serves vacuous inglorius annos
et tua non umquam Tyrrhenus tempora circum
clangor est. Quid vota virum meliora moraris?
Scilicet ut vanis avibus natoque domoque
et thalamis potiare iacens, sileamus inulti
Tydeos egregii perfossum pectus et arma
foederis abrupti. Quodsi bella effera Graios
ferre vetas, i Sidonios legatus ad hostes:
haec pacem tibi serta dabunt. Tua prorsus inani
verba polo causas abstrusaque nomina rerum
eliciunt? Miseret superum, si carmina curae
humanaeque preces! Quid inertia pectora terres?
Primus in orbe deos fecit timor!

['To him Capaneus yet once more: "To thyself alone utter thy raving auguries, that thou mayst live empty and inglorious years, nor ever Tyrrhenian clangour resound about thy temples. But why dost thou delay the nobler vows of heroes? It is forsooth that thou in slothful ease mayst lord it over the silly birds and thy son and home and women's chambers, that we are to shroud in silence the stricken breast of peerless Tydeus and the armed breach of covenant? Dost thou forbid the Greeks to make fierce war? Then go thyself an envoy to the Sidonian foe: these chaplets will assure thee peace. Can thy words really coax from the void of heaven the causes and hidden names of things? Pitiable in sooth are the gods, if they take heed of enchantments and prayers of men! Why dost thou affright these sluggish minds? Fear first created gods in the world".'] Text and translation by J.H. Mozley, Loeb Classical Library (Cambridge, MA, London, 1928) I, 498-500.

[32]   Iam sordent terrena viro taedetque profundae
caedis, et exhaustis olim Graiumque suisque
missilibus lassa respexit in aethera dextra . . .
'Hac' ait, 'in Thebas, hac me iubet ardua virtus
ire, Menoeceo qua lubrica sanguine turris.
Experiar, quid sacra iuvent, an falsus Apollo.'
. . . Utque petita diu celsus fastigia supra
eminuit trepidamque adsurgens desuper urbem
vidit et ingenti Thebas exterruit umbra,
increpit attonitos: 'Humilesne Amphionis arces,
pro pudor! . . . 'nunc totis in me conitere flammis,
Iuppiter! An pavidas tonitru turbare puellas
fortior et soceri turres exacindere Cadmi?'
. . . Talia dicentem toto Iove fulmen adactum

> Ful armed with his schield and spere
> As he the Cite wolde assaile,
> God tok himselve the bataille
> Ayein his Pride, and fro the sky
> A fiery thonder sodeinly
> He sende, and him to pouldre smot.

Even Gower's conclusion, that 'The strength of man is sone lore,/ Bot if that he it wel governe' (2008-09), has precedent in the *Thebaid*, although in Statius's poem it is stated more obliquely.[33]

Gower principally alters Statius's account in two ways. First, he has shaped his version to bring out the story's inherent *moralitas*. Statius's description of Capaneus's exploits appears not in one place but two in the *Thebaid*, in Books III and X. In 'centonic' fashion Gower brought together details from each locus for his passages, revealing thereby an intentional selectivity even as he seems to borrow most dependently. Second (and more particularly), Gower has 'groomed' what he says, not by adding or subtracting details, but rather by changing what Statius merely suggested into direct statement. The moral is thus rendered explicit and unavoidable for his audience. On the fictive level such changes have a pointed efficacy, for the form suits the didactic tone of Genius, and helps to complete the portrait of the Confessor essential to the final direction of the poem.

Yet for all this, the point remains that, application and all, whatever appears of the nature and *moralitas* of 'Capaneus' devolves from Statius. In this — which we may term his 'borrowed model' — Gower's eye for a useful story has accomplished the lion's share of the task by recognizing in the writings of another author a piece suitable to a new context. For the literate and learned in Gower's audience, such an exemplum would have had the additional attraction of

> corripuit: primae fugere in nubilia cristae,
> et clipei niger umbo cadit, iamque omnia lucent
> membra viri . . .

['Now earthly battles grow mean in the hero's eyes, he is tired of the endless slaughter; long ago have his own weapons and those of the Greeks been spent, his right arm grows weary, he looks up to the sky . . . 'By this road,' he cries, 'By this road my lofty valour bids me go to Thebes, where yonder tower is slippery with Menoeceus's blood. I shall try what sacrifice avails, and whether Apollo be false . . .' And when he stood out high above the long-attempted summit, and in towering height looked down upon the trembling city, and terrified Thebes with his huge shadow, he taunted the astounded folk: 'Are these Amphion's insignificant towers? For shame! . . . Come thou and strive with all thy flames against me, thou Jupiter! or art thou braver at frightening timid maidens with thy thunder, and razing the towers of my father-in-law Cadmus? . . . Even as he spoke, the thunderbolt struck him, hurled with the whole might of Jove: his crest first vanished into the clouds, the blackened shield-boss dropped, and all the hero's limbs are now illumined.'] Text and translation in Mozley, II, 380-86.
[33] With this, compare *Thebaid* XI, 1-20.

familiarity.[34] But like other examples of this 'borrowed model,' the tale is so perfect an illustration of 'Surquiderie,' Pride's third division, that prior acquaintance would be unnecessary for 'Capaneus' to support Genius' argument, and make his point.[35]

The second 'type,' or model, is much akin to the first, in that both involve close following of stories in Gower's sources. Here, however, instead of a direct transportation of material, Gower adds a detail or two from his own imagination to adapt the tale more precisely to his needs. In the 'Tale of Narcissus' (*CA* I, 2274-2366) we can see this process at work very clearly. Like Ovid, from whose *Metamorphoses* he took the story, Gower presents Narcissus as the beautiful youth who 'thoghte alle women lothe.' Mistaking his own reflection for a nymph, he pines away by a wooded spring. Both Gower and Ovid attribute Narcissus' death to his scorning of proffered loves, finding in that refusal a hubris which renders his punishment apt.[36]

Certainly this is the aspect Gower chose to highlight with his imaginative addition to Ovid. After Narcissus's death, Ovid says that the nymphs and dryads who went to bury him could find no body, but only a yellow flower with white 'leaves' (*Met.* I, 161):

> Nusquam corpus erat: croceum pro corpore florem
> Inveniunt, foliis medium cingentibus albis.

['In place of his body they find a flower, its yellow center girt with white leaves.'][37]

Gower's version is somewhat different (2349-58):

---

[34] Chaucer may have given us some idea of its popularity with a possible reference to Statius in *Troilus and Criseyde* IV, 1408: 'Eke drede fond first goddes, I suppose — .' This line, though something of a commonplace (it also appears in Petronius, for example), is nonetheless a translation of Capaneus's words to the priest Oeclides, 'primus in orbe deos fecit timor;' see *Thebaid* III, 661.

[35] Other good examples of 'borrowed model' tales in the *Confessio* in clude 'Medusa' (Book I, 389-445) and 'Eneas and Dido' (Book IV, 77-146).

[36] As Ovid puts it (*Met.* III, 353-55):
> multi illum iuvenes, multae cupiere puellae;
> set fuit in tenera tam dura superbia forma,
> nulli illum juvenes, nullae tetigere puellae.

['Many youths and many maidens sought his love; but in that slender form was pride so cold that no youth, no maiden touched his heart.'] Text and translation by Frank Justus Miller, rev. G.P. Goold, Loeb Library (Cambridge, MA, London, 1977). Gower makes the point more explicitly; see *CA* I, 2275-82.

[37] Miller translates 'foliis albis' as 'white *petals*.' While this seems true to nature, and to subsequent ages' identification of the flower as a species of daffodil, it is not what Ovid wrote. This translation may obscure the silver leaf of the crocus; see note 399, below.

> And thanne out of his sepulture
> Ther sprong anon per aventure
> Of floures such a wonder syhte,
> That men ensample take myhte
> Upon the dedes which he dede,
> As tho was sene in thilke stede;
> For in the wynter freysshe and faire
> The floures ben, which is contraire
> To kynde, and so was the folie
> Which fell of his Surquiderie.

The yellow flower Ovid described has, since the sixteenth century, been identified with a species of daffodil, the *Narcissus poeticus*, or 'poet's lily.'[38] Ovid himself may have had this plant in mind or, quite possibly, the *Crocus sativus*, which produces the spice saffron.[39] Whichever Ovid intended, it seems apparent that Gower at least was thinking of a crocus as the bloom springing from Narcissus's grave. The crocus was a flower familiar to Gower's England and — as in Gower's description — it often blooms when snow is still on the ground.[40] Of course, (as Macaulay suggests, in a dissatisfied way), Gower's winter-blooming plant could have been a fabrication, a magical growth to emphasize miraculous events, but this would have been something of a departure from his poetic habits.[41] What Gower does best as a writer is not create elaborate fantasies of his own. Rather, he finds in old stories, and in everyday objects and events, a new meaning which is the more effective as a lesson because we realize suddenly it has been there all along, unnoticed beneath our noses. Thus for him the possibility of centering an exemplum around a flower known to all, from which 'men ensaumple take myhte,' would have had a strong attraction. Not only would it allow him to make his story that much tighter and more credible, thus going Ovid one better, but it also would help to clarify and make more memorable his smaller and larger points: that 'Surquiderie' in love will produce its own, apt punishment; and that one man's unnatural love is scarcely an isolated happening in the microcosmic/macrocosmic world. Instead, it is integrally connected with everything

---

[38] *OED*, s.v. 'crocus,' 'daffodil,' and 'narcissus.'

[39] Ovid's *croceum florem* is difficult to interpret. It could mean either 'saffron (i.e., 'yellow') flower' or '*the* saffron flower' (i.e., that particular plant from which we obtain the spice saffron). See Lewis and Short, *A Latin Dictionary*, s.v. 'crocum, crocus,' (a) and (b). The 'foliis albis' may be a clue, at least to Gower's thinking about it, since there are varieties of crocus with silver (or 'white') leaves, and leaves with silver stripes.

[40] The properties of crocus used for saffron were known to the Anglo-Saxons; see Joseph Bosworth and T. Northcote Toller, *An Anglo-Saxon Dictionary* (Oxford, 1921), s.v. 'croh.' John of Trevisa speaks of it ('Saffron hyghte "crocus" and is an herbe'), *De Proprietatibus Rerum* XVII, xli, 626; Isidore of Seville also describes the plant in his *Etymologies*, XVII, 5-6.

[41] For Macaulay's remark, see his note, *Works* II, 474-75.

readable in the great 'book' of Nature.[42] By adding the detail of the winter-blooming crocus, Gower molds Ovid's tale to his poem.

A third 'type' to which Gower turned frequently, both in its simple form and in combination with other approaches, we may call the 'object model.' It was shown in the previous pages how skillfully Gower could manipulate objects to give them symbolic value and psychologically revealing significance. His use of them to heighten the effectiveness of his exemplifying stories is an extension of that practice. An excellent illustration of this is the 'Trojan Horse' (*CA* I, 1077-1189), told to clarify the workings of Hypocrisy, the first minister of Pride. The tale is the familiar one: the Greeks, frustrated in their attempt to conquer Troy by strength, resort to the ruse of a feigned departure, leaving on the beach the great horse which the Trojans draw into their city, to their destruction. In keeping with his theme of Hypocrisy, Gower in his description emphasizes the guile involved. The first thirty lines of the tale are linguistically loaded with *double entendre* to make the point (1077-1106):

> Of hem that be so *derk withinne*,
> At Troie also if we beginne,
> Ipocrisie it hath betraied:
> For whan the Greks hadde al assaied
> And founde that be no bataille
> Ne be no Siege it myhte availe
> The toun to winne thurgh prouesse,
> This *vice feigned* of simplesce
> Thurgh *sleyhte* of Calcas and of Crise
> It wan be such a maner wise.
> An Hors of Bras thei let do *forge*
> Of such entaile, of such a *forge*,
> That in this world was nevere man
> That such an other werk began.
> The *crafti* werkman Epius
> It made, and forto telle thus,
> The Greks, that thoghten to *beguile*
> The kyng of Troie, in thilke while
> With Antenor and with Enee,
> That were bothe of the Cite
> And of the conseil wiseste,
> The richeste and the mythieste,
> In *privy place* so thei trete
> With fair beheste and yftes grete
> Of Gold, that thei hem have *engined*;
> Togedre and when thei be *covined*,

---

[42] Curtius gives a succinct discussion of the 'book of nature' *topos* in *European Literature*, pp. 319-26.

> Thei *feignen* forto make a pes,
> And under that yit natheles
> Thei schopen the destruccioun
> Bothe of the kyng and of the toun.

Troy was 'betraied' by those 'derk withinne,' using a 'vice feigned of
simplesce;' the Horse was built by 'crafti' (i.e., both 'skillful' and 'sly') Epius; to
'beguile' the Trojan king, Antenor and Aeneas were 'engined' in a 'privy place,'
and so on. The patterning of linguistic underlay is effective throughout the tale,
but particularly so in the opening lines where the notion of deception is
introduced and then reinforced by the exclusion of other methods of taking the
city 'be no bataille/ Ne be so Siege,' nor by any form of 'prouesse' might Troy be
won. This concentration of puns culminates in the first appearance of the 'Hors
of Bras,' in lines connected by the *rime riche* 'forge/ forge.'[43] This introduction
collects the force of the language and focusses it on the Horse, which becomes, in
effect, the emblem of deceit and hence of the entire tale, the object interpretable
as the abstract condition.[44] It is to get the Horse into the city that the Trojans
themselves tear down the walls, making a breach for the Greeks to enter. This is
paradigmatic of the way in which Hypocrisy works in the human breast. By
believing the hypocrite the individual makes an 'opening' through which the
disaster may pass.[45] Our reaction to the 'Tale of the Trojan Horse' is thus
double-staged. We take away first an image of the great brass beast itself, and
then, recalling and pondering that, we confront Genius's admonitions about the
vice. Thus, the 'object model' serves to provide a focus to retain and learn from
Gower's point. It is a method to which he turned often in the *Confessio*, and
elsewhere in his work.[46]

The three approaches, or models, discussed so far have all been 'positive'
exempla: that is, they illustrate directly the vice being described. However,
Gower makes use also of two sorts of what may be called 'negative' exempla —
tales which demonstrate against a vice by showing its opposing virtue, or by

---

[43] It is worth noting that 'forge' had a sinister meaning in Middle English. See *MED* s.v.
'forgen,' (a): 'To compose or invent (a story, falsehood),' with examples cited from the
fourteenth century.

[44] It is possible that Gower intended a learned — though false — pun here, connecting
'hypocrisy' (from ὑποκρισις with 'hyppos' (ἱππος), 'horse.' Isidore of Seville isolates
the Greek elements of 'hypocrisy' and 'hippocentaurus' in the *Etymologies* (see X. 118,
I.40.5, and XI.3.39), a text Gower apparently knew.

[45] Probably this contributed to the presence of the 'Trojan Horse' and Hypocrisy under
Pride, since it is through pride of one individual that the hypocrisy of another can take
root. Already having a high opinion of themselves, the proud are more than ready to
believe hypocritical flattery and slander.

[46] Other salient examples of the 'object model' include 'Demetrius and Persius' (Book II,
1613-1861), where the dog appears archetypally as as an image of Envy; 'Tristram' (VI,
440-84), where the drink is the governing emblem of the point at issue, 'Love-
Drunkenness,' a subdivision of Gluttony.

presenting a character avoiding its pitfalls. The 'Tale of Florent' (*CA* I, 1407-1861) falls into this latter category of 'negative' illustration. The general outline of Gower's plot is familiar from Chaucer's *Wife of Bath's Tale*, which 'Florent' closely resembles. As many recent studies have noted, however, Gower's story differs importantly from the analogue versions. Russell Peck, for one, has pointed out the emphasis Gower placed on Florent's integrity; and, to be sure, Gower's young hero is upright and guiltless.[47] His initial 'transgression,' which places him in jeopardy, is killing another knight in self-defense. Kidnapped by the knight's vengeful kinsmen, Florent is forced to promise by his devotion to honor first to seek an answer to the purportedly unanswerable question, 'What alle wommen most desire' (1481), then to return to his captors' court at an appointed hour to divulge what responses he can. In Gower's tale, it is apparent no one doubts Florent's sincerity. Integrity, indeed, is the lever used to maneuver Florent into this fix. He will return and, since the question is so difficult, he will apparently submit to death, thereby allowing his enemies their revenge without risk of retribution from 'themperour,' Florent's uncle.

On the way back to the castle, with no adequate solution to offer, a grim Florent discovers the inevitable hag in the forest.[48] She alone has the answer — that women wish to 'Be sovereign of mannes love' (1609) — and will give it to him if he promises to marry her. This proves correct; Florent must then keep a second bargain. Arriving again at his uncle's court, Florent has his new bride arrayed as gaily as possible and marries her at night. In lines we have examined for a different purpose in an earlier chapter, she rushes him to bed. He lies horror-stricken as she tries to kiss him. At last he turns to face her, and discovers not an ugly old woman but a lady 'Of eyhtetiene wynter age,' of rare beauty and grace (1803-05). As the enraptured Florent attempts to embrace this unexpected vision, the lady stops him, saying that 'He mot on of tuo thinges chese,' to have her beautiful at night, or during the daytime only 'For he schal noght have bothe tuo' (1810-13). After painfully rolling the choice around, Florent puts all in his new love's hands, asking 'Ches for ous bothen, I you preie.' In the story, the response is perfect. By granting the lady that sovereignty over her lover which she herself had claimed women desire above all things, Florent inadvertently releases her from an enchantment. She resumes her former beauty permanently — much to Florent's delight and our edification. Structurally, the tale is symmetrical, with Florent acting out in the latter half the lesson provided in the first.

In a larger context too, Florent's response is perfect. At this point in Book I, Gower wishes to illustrate 'Murmur and Complaint,' two divisions of 'Inobedience,' the second minister of Pride. Through Florent, who in the course of the narrative learns not to argue but to accept his love's directives, Gower

---

[47] Peck, *Kingship and Common Profit*, pp. 46-47.

[48] One of the so-called 'Loathly Lady Group,' Gower's 'Tale of Florent' has connections of varying closeness with the romance 'The Wedding of Sir Gawen and Dame Ragnell' and the ballad 'The Marriage of Sir Gawaine,' as well as Chaucer's 'Wife of Bath's Tale.' For the general classification, see Stith Thompson, *Motif-Index of Folk-Literature* (Bloomington, 1955-58), D732; and also B.J. Whiting's discussion in W.F. Bryan and Germaine Dempster, eds., *Sources and Analogues of Chaucer's Canterbury Tales* (Chicago, 1941; repr. New York, 1958), pp. 223-68.

outlines a course for each member of his audience to follow. The connection with
Pride is detailed in the Confessor's introduction to the tale. Murmurers and
complainers, Genius says, are never happy with their lot (1348-51):

> For thogh fortune make hem wynne,
> Yit grucchen thei, and if thei lese,
> Ther is no weie forto chese,
> Wherof thei myhten stonde appesed.

The odium is directed at those prideful ones who are satisfied only by what
they themselves have imagined. The model here is certainly Lucifer, who sinned
most in believing he was his own origin. To undercut this attitude, Gower was
careful in presenting Florent from the first as a chivalric paragon, unselfish,
unjustly attacked, and above all, true to his word. He is thus from the beginning
a very different character than Chaucer's unnamed knight in the *Wife of Bath's
Tale*, who gets into his predicament through a rape. Some readers have found this
more psychologically satisfying than Florent's innocent act of self-defense, but
when viewed more closely it becomes difficult to make the comparison.[49] The
intentions of the narrators concerned — Alison of Bath and Genius — are wholly
dissimilar, and should render impossible any simple preference. For Florent to
have committed such a crime as rape is unthinkable in Gower's context, and
would have upset the careful development of the tale.

This contrast between Chaucer's version and Gower's becomes clearer when
Florent's real situation is examined. The tale contains three tests of Florent's
obedience, and it is hardly coincidental that none of these seems to offer any
possibility of conventional reward. As a man of integrity, Florent endures them
all, honor constraining him more than personal risk. Yet pointedly Gower refuses
to present his hero as romantically unaware of the stakes. On the contrary,
Florent appears pragmatic throughout, one who 'worthi was *and* wise' (italics
mine). We see this first when he asks to have the terms of his bargain put into
writing 'and have it under Seales write' (1474), so that on his return its
dimensions may not be altered by his enemies. This is not just the lawyer in John
Gower speaking (though perhaps Gower's legal training would have suggested
it); rather, it is a central manifestation of Florent's character. Again, when faced
with the hag's demand of matrimony in exchange for the answer which will save
his life, Florent's pragmatism is apparent. Gower does not make his choice too
easy. The young knight is not so 'worthi' that his wisdom lacks a self-protecting
side. In one of his direct presentations of a character's thoughts, Gower shows
what moves Florent to agree to the hag's proposal. His reasons are suspect, if
humanly understandable (1575-80):

[49] See for example Derek Pearsall, 'Gower's Narrative Art,' *PMLA* 81 (1966), 483. Peck,
Kingship and Common Profit, pp. 47-49, takes a more positive view.

> . . . sche was of so gret an age,
> That sche mai live bot a while,
> And thoghte put hire in an Ile,
> Wher that noman hire scholde knowe,
> Til sche with deth were overthrowe.

Gower breaks his usual silence about his character's motivations here in order
to make a point. Although he always follows through with his promises, Florent
does not do so without 'murmur and complaint' in his heart, if not on his tongue.
The 'pragmatism' which he shows at every juncture until the last is in reality an
impediment, not shrewdness. But Florent must wait to find this out — as must
the reader — until his uncontested surrender of control to his wife on his
wedding-night. In the enemy castle, Florent at first tries every solution but the
one offered by the hag. Gower tightens the suspense here, so that the audience
may share in Florent's discomfiture. The development is both effective and
psychologically sound. Driven finally to the hag's alternative, Florent (in a
manner foreshadowing his sudden, all-or-nothing confrontation in their wedding
bed of his wife's ugliness) even grasps at it with some pleasure, because he
recognizes his all is now in the balance (1650-55):

> And thanne he hath trewly supposed
> That he him may of nothinge yelpe,
> Bot if so be tho wordes helpe,
> Whiche as the womman hath him tawht;
> Wherof he hath an hope cawht
> That he schal be excused so.

The crux of Gower's narrative is not here, however. Florent — although he
does not yet know it — still has one more bargain to make, and two to keep. In
the process, he will discover that the *true* pragmatism is identical with that staunch
integrity which, from a conventional viewpoint, seems the source of his dilemmas
for most of the tale. Now freed from the threat of death, Florent significantly does
not question that he must do as he has promised. Returning to the woods, he
brings home his repulsive bride-to-be. In the scenes that follow, the 'pragmatist'
reasserts himself continually, for Gower stresses the lengths to which Florent goes
to satisfy the letter and not the spirit of his promise: the wedding is at night, with
no company assembled. Installed together abed, Florent avoids his wife, facing
toward the wall. Nonetheless, it is the exemplary Florent, he whom Gower's
audience is to emulate, who wins out over the pragmatist, going with the
agreement to the bitter dregs, turning at last — albeit woodenly, 'as it were a
man in trance' — to make love to the hag according to her wifely right, and so
fulfill his second bargain truly.

Florent's mistaken pragmatism, then, is as essential to the success of Gower's
tale as is his strong sense of honesty. Worked out with believable vacillation, in
the end Florent's discoveries drive home the lesson and make the story a success

psychologically as well as an exemplum. If it had been any easier, if Florent had not been at once pragmatic and 'worthi,' the instruction would have been valueless. He would not have been enough 'like us' to make the wisdom stick. As it is, however, Florent's uncomplaining acceptance of his lady's sovereignity in his third and final test underscores how much he has learned from his experience. At the same time, it sets out for those listening the boundaries of aspiration. Gower causes us to find in Florent familiar weakness and admirable strength, both kept at human scale. Vice — specifically a branch of Pride — is faced and ultimately negated by a man good but hardly perfect, whose virtues as a consequence are not out of reach.

The 'Tale of Florent,' then, represents one kind of 'negative' exemplum discoverable in the *Confessio Amantis*, and in Gower's work generally.[50] There is also a second sort, involving not merely vice avoided, but presentating as well its offsetting virtue. The 'Tale of the Three Questions,' which concludes Book I (3067-3402), is designed to perform such a task. It illustrates 'Humility,' Pride's opposite, as it does in the *Mirour de l'Omme*, where the story is briefly told (12601-13). In outline, the tale proceeds as follows: young King Alphonse of Spain, who 'sette of his wit gret pris,' was fond of testing his courtiers by questioning them in abstruse manners on arcane subjects. At last none was able to answer his questions consistently save Danz Petro, a poor knight who always responded immediately with the correct solution. Petro's wits nearly prove his undoing, however, for the King 'somdiel hadde an Envie' and decides to confound the knight so that he alone would have 'of wisdom the hihe fame' (3083-89). King Alphonse requires Petro to answer three questions at a date three weeks hence, on pain of losing both his head and his possessions (3099-3106):

> The ferste point of alle thre
> Was this: 'What thing in his degre
> Of al this world hath nede lest,
> And yet men helpe it althermest?'
> The secounde is: 'What most is worth,
> And of costage is lest put forth?'
> The thridde is: 'Which is of most cost,
> And lest is worth, and goth to lost?'

Greatly depressed, Petro goes home, where he ponders the questions but finds no answers. Petro's daughter Peronelle, fourteen years old, asks that she be entrusted to answer for him. Having no better option, Petro agrees. Peronelle of course solves the King's riddles perfectly: That thing which needs it least but men help most is the earth, since it would produce abundantly without human tillage;

---

[50] Other examples of the 'negative' model include 'Leucothoe' (Book V, 6713-83) and the lengthy 'Tale of Custance' (II, 582-1612) which, like 'Florent,' is often called one of Gower's best.

what is worth most but costs least is Humility; what costs most but is worth least is Pride. King Alphonse, much smitten by Peronelle's charms, forgets his former anger, and 'al his pris on hire he leide' (3329). He regrets that her father is only a 'Bachilier,' since were Danz Petro a great lord Alphonse might make Peronelle his wife. As it is, however, he can only reward her by granting her what she has requested — an earldom for Petro. This done, Peronelle with all her wits about her points out that, since her father is now an earl, she has become daughter of a peer and so is eligible to marry royalty. Alphonse is thus unexpectedly trapped by his rash statement, as 'A kinges word it mot ben holde.' But, fully enraptured by 'hire beaute and hir wit withal,' Alphonse gladly marries Peronelle, and the story ends in joy.

There are several ways in which Humility is exemplified in the 'Tale of the Three Questions.' Most striking is Petro's willingness to place his fate in his untested daughter's hands. This is analogous to Florent's permitting his newly-beautiful bride to decide for both of them what shape she should have, and when. The similarities between Florent and Petro are useful to pursue, for they show us the difference between the two kinds of 'negative' models the tales represent. Gower introduces both knights through their salient characteristic, which will also prove to be the structural hinge of each story. Florent's 'worthinesse,' which includes elements of goodness and devotion to keeping his word, has its counterpart in Petro's wisdom. Both attributes get them into trouble, but both ultimately also provide a way out. Thus, with particular emphasis, Petro is shown to stand apart from his colleagues by his extraordinary quickness (3077-82):

> To him was every thing so liht,
> That also sone as he hem herde,
> The kinges wordes he answerde;
> What thing the king him axe wolde,
> Therof anon the trowthe he tolde.

Again, when Petro explains to the court that he will allow his daughter to answer for him, it causes great consternation, since he was 'so wys a knyht.' This wisdom, like Florent's integrity, is essential to the success of Gower's lesson. Had Petro *not* been presented as wise initially, and on his own, his turning to his young daughter for help would have demonstrated no humility. Similarly, the important tests for Florent — the last two — actually require him to trust in 'worthinesse' other than his own. He 'fails' the test of the hag's answer, because he refuses to see beyond her ugliness and the apparently repugnant price he must pay to use that answer; he triumphs later when he places all his trust in her choice.[51] At that moment, he illustrates with his behavior the virtue, obedience,

---

[51] There are certain interesting parallels between Florent and Gawain in the way that each falsifies trust. Gawain, by keeping the girdle given him by Bertilak's wife, seeks to preserve his life at the price of breaking his agreement with his host and hedging his faith. In each case, the heroes (as the *Gawain* poet notes of his) 'lakked a lyttel;' see *GGK* 2366.

which is the purpose of the tale. So too with Petro, a wise man without arrogance: his willingness to entrust his life to the wits of an untried girl is a humble act, precisely exemplifying the point Gower wishes his story to make.

The 'Tale of the Three Questions' goes farther to portray Humility than does 'Florent,' however. Another way it presses its argument is via the contrast between Petro and King Alphonse. While both are said to be highly intelligent, their attitudes toward their own abilities differ radically. For Petro, cleverness represents a kind of natural outgrowth, like an arm or a leg. But for the King, wisdom is serious — and competitive — business. It is of extreme importance to Alphonse that he be considered not wise *simpliciter* but the wisest. Gower's emphasis on fame as the King's motive for seeking to destroy Petro gives the youthful Alphonse away as one infected by Pride, the subject of Book I. For, while Gower would be the first to stress the necessity of wisdom for a ruler (indeed, in many ways the *Confessio Amantis* was intended to offer just that for Richard II and Henry IV), he distinguished carefully between knowledge possessed to serve others, and when it simply enhanced reputation. Alphonse's opposition to the humble Petro and his subsequent 'defeat' by Petro and Peronelle is thus a paradigm of the way Pride will always be overcome by Humility. By this and other means, the tale thus makes a perfect 'cap' to the Book as a whole.

The didacticism of the tale is not limited to this contrast of king and subject, however. It is also presented through the character of Peronelle. In typical romance fashion, this heroine is the younger of Petro's daughters. While she is pointedly identified as being fourteen years old — a highly marriageable age — she has not lost any of her childlike innocence or freshness. Gower stresses the child/woman duality in Peronelle's nature in several ways, and for a specific purpose. While Peronelle calls herself a 'womman' (3206), for example, Petro thinks of her as a 'child' (3172). This is fatherly, and a nice bit of psychological verisimilitude — but the courtiers share his attitude when they react against Petro's entrusting life-and-death matters to 'so yong a wyht.' Too, like a good child (and like her father) Peronelle is humble, and justly respectful. While she does not sell short her legitimate abilities, speaking up both to her father and to the King when she has something important to say, she does not flaunt her wisdom as does Alphonse. Despite her beauty and her sense of her own cleverness, she knows how to treat her father properly (3145-46):

> Upon hire knes sche gan doun falle
> With humble herte and to him calle.

Similarly, she addresses the King 'knelende,' as does her father (3228).

Behind this combination of childishness, learning, and humility is a biblical model. Peronelle is meant to recall that sage and unselfconscious innocence much praised by Christ when he claimed, 'Of such is the kingdom of God.'[52] Her

---

[52] Compare Matt. 19:13-14; Mark 10:15; Luke 10:21.

presentation is clear and direct, as is its purpose. With Peronelle as with Petro, Gower wishes to establish a paragon of humble virtue 'wisely' to offset a foolhardy Pride: for Humility, not overbearing conceit, shows wisdom according to Gower's standards.

Other examples of Humility are in the tale, alongside Petro and Peronelle. Like Gower himself, Peronelle is a bit of a preacher. To support her answers to King Alphonse's last two questions, she contrives illustrations of her own. Thus, she defends her choice of Humility as that which costs least but is worth most by explaining that (3276-82):

> . . . the highe trinite
> As for decerte of pure love
> Unto Marie from above,
> Of that he knewe hire humble entente,
> His oghne Sone adoun he sente,
> Above alle othre and hire he ches
> For that vertu which bodeth pes.

So it is that the most priceless 'thing' ever created — God's earthly body — came as a reward to his mother for her perfect Humility. In the same way, Peronelle's examples of Pride are the most evocative she, or Gower, knew (3296-3306):

> What lest is worth of alle thinges
> And costeth most, I telle it, Pride;
> Which mai noght in the hevene abide,
> For Lucifer with hem that felle
> Bar Pride with him into helle.
> Ther was Pride of to gret a cost,
> Whan he for Pride hath hevene lost;
> And after that in Paradis
> Adam for Pride lost his pris;
> In Midelerthe and ek also
> Pride is cause of alle wo.

The force of these examples would hardly have been lost on Gower's audience, and they affect the King, as well. But it is important to notice how, in the context of the tale, Peronelle's exempla operate. Pride in his own intellect, which is Alphonse's major flaw, was also Lucifer's. Similarly, Peronelle's wise, reverent humility has several recognizable parallels with Mary's.[53] What Peronelle has

---

[53] On the features of the Virgin, see Marina Warner, *Alone of All Her Sex: The Myth and the Cult of the Virgin Mary* (New York, 1976), esp. chapters 10 and 11; and Penny Schine Gold, *The Lady, and the Virgin: Image, Attitude, and Experience in Twelfth-Century France* (Chicago and London, 1985) 62-75. The same figure of the wise maiden (who is also compounded

done, in effect, is to encapsulate the major dichotomy of the larger tale within her two final answers. This becomes clearer when we examine the last illustration of Humility offered by 'Three Questions.' When King Alphonse expresses his admiration for Peronelle's many good qualities but declines to marry her he is showing signs of wisdom, in that he is drawn to virtue when he sees it even though he remains too much the proud monarch taken up by earthly appearances. She is an unsuitable bride in the opinion of the world only because her birth is lowly. Alphonse must yet learn to humble himself, and this occurs when he changes his mind. Peronelle's argument — that now she is an earl's daughter — is strictly true to the letter, but it completely skirts the issue of power and money on which marriages of kings are commonly decided. Alphonse, whom Gower has shown is at least worldly 'wys,' could scarcely have been fooled by Peronelle's cleverness. Indeed, Gower lets us know exactly what transpires after the girl's speech (3377-80):

> This yonge king, which peised al,
> Hire beaute and hire wit withal,
> As he that was with love hent,
> Anon therto yaf his assent.

'Peised' ('to weigh,' 'to feel by weight') is an important word, since it portrays the King considering all the angles of the case. Although Alphonse makes his decision with all the objectivity of a man in love, it is significant that the qualities which convince him are arrived at via a process of thought. It is also significant that these qualities are legitimate and pure. Though on a different, and lesser, plane, they are analogous to Mary's virtues which drew to her the King of Heaven. As a result, Alphonse's abandonment of his proud, mistaken values — including his rancor with Petro and his materialistic preconditions for marriage — takes on within the tale a certain approximation of God's recognition of Mary's vast worthiness, as Peronelle presented it earlier.

So understood, the 'Tale of the Three Questions' gains both richness and didactic significance. More than a simple, single lesson in Humility, it actually compounds four individual but interconnected illustrations which, taken together, form one of Gower's best tales. As such, it puts a fitting conclusion to Book I, summing up Genius's various arguments about Pride with a 'cap,' or 'antidote,' the vice off-set by its opposing virtue.

III

Another view we may take, to observe Gower transforming his sources into exempla, we might call an 'internal' one. To see it requires an extended close reading of a tale, juxtaposing particular passages against their originals in order

amorously) is, of course, central to *Pearl*; see Muscatine's perceptive discussion, *Poetry and Crisis*, pp. 52-55.

to understand Gower's finer-grained changes, exclusive of tale models, or types. 'Albinus and Rosamund,' which we have already begun to consider, and 'Tereus' from Book V, amply reward examination of this sort. They thus may serve us as suitable illustrations of Gower's range, and practices.

As we have seen, Gower tells 'Albinus and Rosamund' in Book I to illustrate the dangers of 'Avantance,' or boasting. Although some evidence exists that Gower knew the accounts of both Paulus Diaconus and Godfrey of Viterbo, it seems more likely that he took the story from the latter's *Pantheon*.[54] In order to fit the story to his love-confession structure, however, Gower had to alter his source narrative in several ways. In the *Pantheon*, Albinus's marriage to Rosamunda is given short shrift. The king's wife Glodosunda (whose name Gower appropriates to Glodeside, Rosamund's maid) dies. With excellent political sense though no special affection, Albinus marries the daughter of the man whose kingdom he has conquered and successfully rules:

> Interea sua sponsa prior moritur Glodosunda,
> Filia regis ei Gepidi fit sponsa secunda,
> Haec Rosimunda fuit.[55]

But Gower sets his narrative in an entirely different context from the beginning. His Latin verses to open the section are indicative:

> Magniloque propriam minuit iactancia lingue
>   Famam, quam stabilem firmat honore cilens.
> Ipse sui laudem meriti non percipit, unde
>   Se sua per verba iactat in orbe palam.

['The vanities of a boastful tongue diminish renown, which silence would have established as permanent in honor. A boaster does not perceive the praise of his merit; therefore he values himself publicly, in the words of the world.']

Genius then refines this general point, first by restating it metaphorically. 'Avantance,' he says (*CA* I, 2401-06):

---

[54] Macaulay, *Works* II, 476, note to ll. 245 ff. There are strong similarities of plot and character in Godfrey's account and Gower's which distinguish both from Paulus Diaconus's: Helmege's position as 'boteler' rather than 'shield-bearer' and foster-brother of Alboin; the absence of Paulus's character 'Peredeus;' even certain similarities of language found in a marginal gloss to a manuscript of Godfrey, as cited by Macaulay, p. 476.

[55] 'Meanwhile, his first wife Glodosunda having died, he made Rosimunda, daughter of the king of the Gepi, his second.' All quotations from the *Pantheon* are taken from Migne, *Patrologia Latina* CXCVIII, cols. 936-38; the lines above appear at col. 937.

> . . . his oghne pris he lasseth,
> When he such mesure overpasseth
> That he his oghne Herald is.
> That ferst was wel is thanne mis,
> That was thankworth is thanne blame.

Then the Confessor recasts such boasting into a lover's fault by the form of his question to Amans (2419-27):

> Whan thou hast taken eny thing
> Of loves yifte, or Nouche or ring,
> Or tok upon thee for the cold
> Som goodly word that thee was told,
> Or friendly chiere or tokne or lettre,
> Wherof thin herte was the bettre,
> Or that sche sende the grietinge,
> Hast thou for Pride of thi likinge
> Mad thin avant wher as the liste?

The introductory formula is common to Gower's exempla: a broad definition of the vice is presented, embracing real as well as amorous sin, and then is redefined specifically as an act against proper behavior in love. In this case, the new application works particularly well, since secrecy is requisite for amorous dalliance in a society where loss of a woman's honor is the necessary price of a discovered love affair. Thus, the test of silence was also a test of love. A man who tried to love a woman truly would not risk her honor, even though by letting others know he had enjoyed her he might gain increased respect from his masculine peers. The focus of the 'avantour' is thus quite backwards, for it is trained not on the source of the lover's worthiness — the beloved whose affections he/she has won — but on the self which, for all its glorying and preening, is of little value without the beloved.

These changes, then, initiate the process by which Gower transformed his general source into a love story.[56] In keeping with this plan, Gower makes his Alboin much less the designing monarch, and more the courtly lover, than is Godfrey's Albinus. Alboin is captivated by Rosamund at first sight ('anon') with 'such a love' that 'he hire weddeth ate laste' (2480-86) — apparently with Rosamund's approval, since for long thereafter (2488-89):

> With hire he duelte, and to the beste
> Thei love ech other wonder wel.

[56] See the discussions of Fisher, *John Gower*, p. 195; Arno Esch, 'John Gowers Erzählkunst,' in *Chaucer und seine Zeit: Symposion für Walter F. Schirmer*, ed. Esch (Tübingen, 1968) 219; and Gallacher, *Love, the Word, and Mercury*, pp. 44 ff.

Love is the motivating force in this union, and it is love, pointedly portrayed by Gower in chivalric terms, which prompts Alboin to call the disastrous feast (2499-2503):

> Tho thoghte he wolde a feste make;
> And that was for his wyves sake,
> That sche the lordes ate feste,
> That were obeissant to his heste,
> Mai knowe.

A tournament precedes the banquet, completing the romance formula 'of armes and of love' (2528). As Gower has Alboin imagine it, the feast is a stage from which he may demonstrate to Rosamund the compass of his warrior's 'pru.' Because Gower casts the pragmatic *Pantheon* account in the language of romance, this conclusion makes a certain traditional sense; and initially we, like Alboin, are left to draw a connection between his strength at arms and the love Rosamund bears him. But as Gower further develops the context, Alboin's feelings — and his circumstances — are more precarious than he knows. Indeed his wife *has* been the result of his prowess: By defeating his enemy, Alboin at once found love and enabled his marriage. The difficulty of course is that the king he defeated and killed was Rosamund's father — a detail irrelevant in the *Pantheon*'s loveless account but so obviously a problem for Alboin the lover that we wonder how he could have forgotten it.

Gower's revisions, however, provide an answer both subtle and omnipresent. The lines describing Alboin's state of mind when he first envisions the celebration are inconspicuously ominous (2495-98):

> This king, which stod in al his welthe
> Of pes, of worschipe and of helthe,
> And felte him on no side grieved,
> As he that hath his world achieved . . .

Barely disguised beneath the surface here is the familiar image of Fortune's wheel, on which Alboin is occupying the highest seat. It was a medieval commonplace that whenever man 'felte him on no side grieved' a precipitous fall was imminent — Alboin has nowhere to go but down.[57] That he fails to recognize his danger is an index both to his conflicting motives and to the use Gower has for the tale. In another addition to his source, Gower lays bare what blinds Alboin. As at the feast the rest all regale their exploits at war and *fin amour* (2532-33):

---

[57] In the iconography of Fortune, and often in literary renderings, four positions are recognized, termed by application to kings as (from the lowest position) 'sum sine regno,' 'regnabo,' 'regno,' 'regnavi.' The pattern of ominously felicitous times is standard — it is, for example, the major pattern in Boccaccio's *De casibus virorum*. On the whole matter

> The king himself began to glade
> Withinne his herte and tok a pride.

Godfrey twice narrates this scene, once in prose and once in verse. In neither does he offer pride as the force driving Alboin.[58] Gower's addition thus adapts the *Pantheon* story to his specific concern in Book I, where his subject is Pride. And it plausibly explains why Alboin overlooks the glaring fact that the king he slew in triumph and his wife's father were the same man.

For Alboin is offered us in illustration of how the proud are incapacitated readers of essential 'texts.' Gower's tale contains two central symbols — the cup made from Gurmond's head and Rosamund herself. Both establish Alboin's 'pru,' but in antithetical ways. The cup is evocative of the harsh realities of a militaristic society, and of the coarse and humiliating forms its triumphs could exact on the defeated. Rosamund, on the other hand, is evidence as Gower presents her of a gentler reward for a more refined masculinity. Her affections might be won by valor, an attribute of manliness not to be boasted of, or confused with ferocity. Alboin, surrounded by evidence of his own glory, does confuse them nonetheless, and the mistake has deadly consequences.

Gower's presentation of the crucial scene reveals a shrewd psychology (2532-5; 2549-62)

> The king himself began to glade
> Withinne his herte and tok a pride,

see Howard R. Patch, *The Goddess Fortuna in Medieval Literature* (Cambridge, MA, 1927) chapter 5.

[58] Godfrey's prose and verse descriptions are as follows: 'Albinus rex in quadam sua magna solemnitate in convivio solemniter residens, cum scypho illo, quem de capite Cunimundi, regis Gepidorum, soceri sui, sibi fecerat praeparari, imperat, ut in prasentia omnium, reginae propinetur: quae dum fecti sceleris ignara, poculum bibitura tulisset, dicit ei rex Albuinus, "Bibe cum patre tuo . . .".' ['Solemnly sitting at a certain great feast, King Albuinus commanded in the presence of all that that goblet (which he himself had caused to be made from the head of his father-in-law Cunimundus, king of the Gepides) be brought before the queen. She, until that time when the cup had been borne to her to drink, was unaware of the crime. King Albuinus said to her, "Drink with your father . . .".'] *Pantheon*, in Migne, col. 937. Compare with this the following:

> Ipse caput soceri, quem fecerat ense necari,
> Arte scyphum fieri statuens, auroque ligari,
>   Vina sua sponsae praecipit inde dari
> Femina nescisset quod testa paterna fuisset,
> Vina nec hausisset, nisi diceret impius ipse:
>   Testa tui, patris est, cum patre nata bibe.

['He himself had the head of his father-in-law, whom he had caused to be put to the sword, artfully turned into a cup and inlaid with gold. He ordered wine to be given to his wife from it. The woman would not have known that it was her father's head, nor would she have drunk the wine, had not the wicked man said, "It is the head of your father. Drink with your father, daughter." '] *Pantheon*, col. 938.

And sih the Cuppe stonde aside,
Which mad was of Gurmondes hed . . .
The skulle is fet and wyn therinne,
Wherof he bad his wife beginne:
'Drink with thi fader, Dame,' he seide.
And sche to his biddinge obeide,
And tok the Skulle, and what hire liste
Sche drank, as sche which nothing wiste
What Cuppe it was: and thanne al oute
The kyng in audience aboute
Hath told it was hire fader Skulle
So that the lordes knowe schulle
Of his bataille a soth witness,
And made avant thurgh what prouesse
He hath his wyves love wonne,
Which of the Skulle hath so begonne.

Clearly, being able to command the daughter of his fallen enemy to drink from her father's skull is acceptable to the tradition of martial triumph understood by Alboin and his knights. Within *this* framework the act enhances the king's image. On the other hand, as Gower underscores, Alboin 'hath his wyves love wonne' by that 'bataille,' and such a diminution of her honor is a gross sin against love. Alboin, forgetting himself, attempts to bring together antithetical symbols on the same plane, without realizing that to do so he must reduce his wife to the level of an object. Rosamund recognizes the insult, however. During the remainder of the feast 'sche was softe/ Thenkende on thilke unkynde Pride' (keeping a silence Gower adds to his source with brilliant light pointing); but later her understanding is made explicit. She will (2578-81):

> . . . vengen hire upon this man,
> Which dede hire drinke in such a plit
> Among hem alle for despit
> Of hire and of hire fader bothe.

The greater part of what remains in Gower's version is devoted to Rosamund's preparations for her revenge — primarily sleeping with Helmege who, as Alboin's 'boteler' in Gower's version has close access to the royal person. The seduction is effected with a ruse: Helmege believes he is in bed, not with the queen, but with the maid Glodeside, whom he 'loveth hote.' Later, when she reveals her identity, the choice Rosamund offers Helmege in both *Pantheon* and *Confessio* is similar (2615-19):

> . . . it schal sore ben aboght,
> Or thou schalt worche as I thee seie.

And if thou wolt be such a weie
Do my plesance and holde it stille,
For evere I schal ben at thi wille,
Bothe I and al myn heritage.[59]

But Gower has greatly exaggerated the role of love in prompting Helmege's decision. No sooner, apparently, does Rosamund make herself known than Helmege transfers his passion from maid to mistress (2620-23) and joins the plot for love:

Anon the wylde loves rage,
In which noman him can governe,
Hath mad him that he can noght werne,
Bot fell al hol to hire assent.

Nor is the shift a hapless one. Helmege's 'wylde loves rage' for the queen is thematically correlative in the *Confessio*, where Rosamund's use of sex to implement her revenge acquires an aptness missing from the *Pantheon*. There, political expediency alone directs Albinus's marriage: Were Rosamund not Gurmond's daughter, she would be meaningless to him. But in Gower's context Alboin sins first against love, then against social values, here represented by family honor. (Rosamund's word-order, indeed, puts the case for us directly: her revenge will be for Alboin's 'despit/ Of *hire*, and of hire *fader* bothe.') Such exaggeration is thus in keeping with other changes Gower instituted to strengthen the tale's force as an exemplum both amorous and moral.

Gower shortens the conclusion of his narrative for similar reasons — to keep the essential elements in direct view. Godfrey goes on to explain that after decapitating the sleeping Albinus ('Rege soporato sustulit ille caput') the two regicides flee to Ravenna where Rosimunda plots with the prefect Longinus to poison Helmechis, who, though dying, retains sufficient strength to force Rosimunda to drink from the cup also, and perish herself. Gower, on the other hand, cares little about the method of Alboin's death, saying only that Helmege and Rosamund 'shope among hem such a wyle,/ The king was ded withinne a whyle' (2627-28). The murderers are also summarily dispatched. In Ravenna the Duke first grants them asylum; but later, in terms, and with a swiftness, echoing the death of Alboin (2644-46):

[59] Unde nisi meis dictis parueris, ipso Albuino te feriente, peribis. Elige igitur magis illum occidere, mecumque regnare feliciter, quam illo vivente, meque te accuante, perire . . . .Aut regem perimes, inquit, vel rex perimet te. ['For this reason, unless you obey my counsels, you will perish with Albuinus beating you. Choose therefore to kill him and to reign with me contentedly, rather than to die with him living and me accusing you. Either you will kill the king,' she said, 'or the king will kill you.']

> This Duk let schape for hem so,
> That of a puison which thei drunke
> Thei hadden that thei have beswunke.

Gower's near-neglect of the final details of the *Pantheon* story has a profound effect on the rest of the tale. It forces the emphasis to fall unavoidably on Alboin's act of 'Avantance.' Unlike Godfrey, for whom all names, places and events have an equivalent importance, Gower is concerned to make specific points about love and universal morality. Therefore he is selective about what he retains. He leaves no question that he is shortening his source for a purpose, nor confusion as to what that purpose might be.

This purpose explains other details Gower added in places where the *Pantheon* account is thin. At two crucial points in the narrative Gower brings in the unperceived working of Fortune's 'blinde whel,' spun significantly here by Venus. The first instance (2490-94) comes just after we have been told that Alboin and Rosamund have lived happily for some time:

> Bot sche which kepth the blinde whel,
> Venus, what thei be most above,
> In al the hoteste of here love,
> Hire whiel sche torneth, and thei felle
> In the manere as I schal telle.

What follows is the description, examined earlier, of Alboin's sense of himself at the pinnacle of peace and 'pru,' and his decision to give the feast. The second such allusion is equally significant. It prefaces Alboin's murder, and separates the actual commission of the deed from Helmege's agreement to enter into the conspiracy (2624-25):

> And thus the whiel is al miswent,
> The which fortune hath upon honde.

Gower thus positions the wheel at the two turning-points of the exemplum. Just as its first appearance signaled Alboin's having moved beyond his depth, so here we see Helmege about to do the same, well on his way to becoming the thoughtless instrument of another's will. The union of the two goddesses Venus and Fortuna is not an idea original to Gower — its analogues are myriad — but his combined addition of them to his source is the structural masterstroke of the piece.[60] In so far as he is a lover, Alboin's fate is totally dependent on Venus's whimsy; yet in this case his sin of boasting results not only in the alienation of his

---

[60] Patch, *Goddess Fortuna*, pp. 90-98, gives many examples of Venus in combination with Fortune.

beloved but also in his own death, and the overturning of his kingdom — events under the power of Fortuna. Ultimately the combination emphasizes the role played by love in human affairs, since Alboin so obviously had no notion of what he was about to forfeit by his act of amorous 'Avantance.' In fact, the king's death is implicit from the moment his treatment of Rosamund turns selfishly loveless (and hers and Helmege's as well, who misuse or misconstrue love's powers). Gower can exclude details of their dying, in order to shorten the tale to draw his point more sharply.

Thus as Gower has transformed it, 'Alboin and Rosamund' declares one of the *Confessio*'s major themes. For, among other things, the poem like the tale illustrates that those who attempt to live without love are 'dead' from the moment love passes out of their grasp, usually through misinterpretation born of selfishness. The tale contains much borrowed action but, as is often the case in Gower's work, the exterior events are so modelled, shortened and lengthened appropriately, as to focus on the ongoing life of the heart.

These features are all present in the 'Tale of Tereus' from Book V. There is no difficulty determining Gower's source as he notes himself, 'The clerke Ovide telleth thus' (5570). Yet Gower has transformed his source to serve his purposes through excisions and additions. Let us look first at what Gower saw fit to remove.

In general, Gower seems to have been at pains to delete from Ovid's account the more exotic or lurid passages. Thus we are not told by Gower of Theseus's lustful fantasies (*Met*. VI, 47 ff.), of Philomela's severed tongue 'murmuring on the stained earth' ('terraeque tremens immurmurat atrae,' *Met*. VI, 558), or of the bacchanal which provided cover in Ovid's account for Procne's rescue of her sister. What takes thirteen lines in the *Metamorphoses* (587-600) is accomplished matter-of-factly with three in the *Confessio Amantis* (5803-05):

> Hir Soster was delivered sone
> Out of prison, and be the mone
> To Progne sche was broght by nyhte.

Similarly, we are spared most of Ovid's bloody details of the murder and dismemberment of Itys.[61] What interests Gower about the murder is not the horrific aspect of a mother and an aunt slaughtering a child, but the cause underlying it. In fact, in Gower's version Philomela takes no part in the process; and the actual killing is 'withouten noise or cry' (5896). Other deletions include Tereus's descent from Mars ('genus a magno ducentem fort Gradivo'), Philomela's first appearance, her beauty rivalling that of the wood nymphs ('Divitior forma: quales audire solemus/ Naidas et Dryades mediis incedere

---

[61] Ovid shows Itys and his mother in sudden confrontation, her double change of heart, the boy's tearful pleadings in the face of what he knows will be his death; see *Met*. 638-46.

silvis'), and the lengthy description of Tereus persuading Pandion to part with Philomela (*Met.* VI, 467-85).

Several of these excisions gain resonance in the context of Gower's additions to Ovid. Briefly, Gower has fleshed out the sketchy figures of Ovid's account; his characters are more clearly individuals. The process is most elaborately applied to Tereus, through the subtle development of a 'split' in his personality. Ovid from the beginning uses a list of omens to signal the dark nature of coming events. In his version, there is no question that disaster will occur. Gower on the other hand offers initially a vision of Tereus as a 'worthi king,' a 'noble kniht' unspotted by exploitable or characteristic vice. His marriage to Progne has endured happily; the two are particularly portrayed as comfortable in their domesticity. As if to stress this, Gower has the idea to fetch Philomela occur to Progne while she is in bed with Tereus (5572-77):

> A lusti lif with hire he hadde;
> Til it befell upon a tyde,
> This Progne, as sche lay him besyde,
> Bethoughte hir hou it mihte be
> That sche hir Soster myhte se,
> And to hir lord hir will sche seide.

In keeping with the mood of this conjugal scene, Gower (unlike Ovid) has Tereus embark upon his journey with selfless motives (5587-89):

> 'I wole,' he seide, 'for thi sake
> The weie after thi Soster take
> Miself, and bringe hire, if I may.'

Still innocent of base desire, Tereus takes Philomela onto his ship. Here he feels lust for her — suddenly, Gower says, like 'fyr, whan it to tow aprocheth' (5623) — and not at first sight of her, as Ovid has it. Only at this point, when Tereus has lost all ability to control himself, does Gower criticize him, calling him (in carefully chosen words) a 'tirant raviner' (5627).[62] The moment marks a transformation of Tereus's personality, a complete shift of shape. Gower accentuates the change by his subsequent handling of the rape itself (5628-32):

> And he therto sawh time and place,
> As he that lost hath alle grace,
> Foryat he was a wedded man,

---

[62] *OED*, s.v. 'ravener,' 2, 'A deforcer, ravisher, destroyer,' lists examples of first use from the *Confessio Amantis*. In applying the new word to Tereus, then, Gower may have had the most particular purposes in mind.

> And in a rage on hire he ran,
> Riht as a wolf which takth his preie.

These lines describe a carefully staged alteration. Since within the compass of the tale Tereus's 'selfhood' has been defined wholly through his relationship with Progne, his abandonment of grace here leads first to lost identity and thence to a loss of humanity altogether. We should observe too that the change affects both Tereus *and* Philomela. *Qua* wolf, Tereus no longer can distinguish a sentient girl from a dish of flesh and, as he rages, she is reduced to 'preie.' In the end, he falls on her not even sexually, but as a beast on meat. Gower goes on to heap other animal similes on Tereus: he is a 'lyon wod' (5684) and a 'wode hound' (5701), epithets he did not find in Ovid, although they work well alongside the image of the king as wolf. Such similes have particular relevance in Gower's poetic lexicon. Reason — the faculty overcome in Tereus by 'rage,' or madness — separated man from brute beasts. It is this idea which underlies the allegory of Book I of the *Vox Clamantis*, where the peasants in revolt take on the appearance of animals in Gower's dream. Its use here has just this implication.[63] From the onset of his mad infatuation, Tereus is to be understood as a person wholly different from the 'noble kniht' of the opening lines, a man unlike his comfortable, unselfish and rational former self. The split, in Gower's version, is calculated and thorough. Tereus dehumanizes himself completely, thereby illustrating how dangerous an emotion is love.

Tereus's madness creates powerful resonances, then. But it has other implications for the story, too. It provides the means by which Gower absolves Progne and Philomela of blame for killing Itys. Ovid accomplishes this by fanning our hatred for Tereus because of his savage treatment of the girl. But Gower, while sacrificing none of our outrage at Philomela's rape and mutilation, leads us as well to consider these events on a higher, more thoughtful level. For Gower, the problem is not that the crime was too bloody to go unavenged; rather, he draws our attention to a solid marriage betrayed, and the desertion of a loyal wife at the core of the story. As we have seen, Tereus enjoys a 'lusti lif' with Progne, and we find them chatting comfortably in bed. This is one of the tale's strategies. Another is Progne's prayer to Venus, Cupid and Apollo, a lengthy addition Gower makes to Ovid. Here the deceived wife and sister fixes all blame on her renegade husband (5825-29; 5835-42):

> Ye witen wel that evere yit
> With al mi will and al my wit,
> Sith ferst ye schopen me to wedde,
> That I lay with mi lorde abedde,
> I have be trewe in mi degree . . .

---

[63] See for example *Vox Clamantis* I, 177-78:
> Qui fuerant homines prius innatae racionis
> Brutorum species irracionis habent.
['They who had been men of reason before had the look of unreasoning brutes.']

Bot nou allas this wofull strif!
The most untrewe and most unkinde
That evere in ladi armes lay.
And wel I wot that he ne may
Amende his wrong, it is so gret;
For he to lytel of me let,
Whan he myn oghne Soster tok,
And me that am his wif forsok.

These lines call attention to the basic values on which a society must be built: loyalty, recognition of and respect for kinship and domestic roles, personal and social commitment. Such things are not sensational, but their significance ultimately transcends the emotional shock of rape and dismemberment, to address the crime as sin on a higher moral, or cosmic, level. This handling of the tale fits well with Gower's larger purposes for the *Confessio*, and points prophetically toward the conclusion, when Amans's love will be rejected because of its unsuitability on the impersonal plane of natural law.

Working toward a similar conclusion is the treatment of Philomela. In the *Confessio Amantis* she appears as a character more sentient, and thus more deeply pitiable, than is her original in the *Metamorphoses*. Gower affects this by a subtler presentation of her, as a being with thoughts, rather than as a focal object for scenes of lust and abuse. When, for example, after the rape, she prays in prison to Jupiter, it is her desire for answers about divine involvement in evil events, and not for revenge, that Gower dwells on (5741-52):

'O thou, almyhty Jupiter,
That hihe sist and lokest fer,
Thou soffrest many a wrong doinge,
And yit it is noght thi willinge.
To thee ther mai nothing ben hid,
Thou wost hou it is me betid:
I wolde I hadde noght be bore,
For thanne I hadde noght forlore
Mi speche and mi virginite.
Bot, goode lord, al is in thee,
Whan thou therof wold do vengance
And schape mi deliverance.'

Beneath her bewilderment at circumstances here, Philomela shows flashes of an attitude almost Boethian. It helps her resolve the problem of divine complicity in evil events, and contrasts sharply with her sister's harsher view: 'Of suche oultrages/ . . . wepinge is noght the bote' (5792-93). Importantly also, by trusting Jupiter to provide for her 'vengance' and 'deliverance,' Gower's Philomela further removes herself from blame for the bloody deeds her sister Progne perpetrates alone (in the *Confessio Amantis*) on Tereus and the child Itys.

Characterizing Philomela in this way of course heaps additional odium onto Tereus, whose crime seems much the worse in contrast to her unspotted goodness, innocence, and philosophical cast of mind, preserved even after such savage mistreatment.

Another addition, representative of the kind Gower made to his sources, can be seen at the conclusion of the tale. The fate of all three characters in both the *Confessio* and the *Metamorphoses* is to be turned into birds. Ovid does this succinctly, if with some obscurity of allusion, specifying Tereus as a hoopoe because of his helmet and sword ('prominet inmodicum pro longa cuspide rostrum; nomen epops volucri,' *Met.* VI, 673-74) and the two sisters only as birds which fly one to the woods, the other to the roof ('Quarum petit altera silvas,/ Altera tecta subit,' 668-69). Gower expands Ovid's eight-line description into 112, making it clear that Philomela became a nightingale (5998), Progne a 'swalwe' (6005), and Tereus — in a direct departure from Ovid — a 'lappewincke' (6046), or lapwing, a bird more familiar to Englishmen than the hoopoe. The changes are apparently slight, but nonetheless significant. As Bruce Harbert has noted:

> Where Ovid had seen only superficial resemblances between the human characters and the birds into which they are transformed, Gower continues to look more deeply into their minds. Metamorphosis does not really change their character: it reveals it more clearly for what it is. The depiction of them and their actions throughout the tale has led up to this final judgment.[64]

Whereas Ovid has Tereus become a hoopoe because the bird's crest and long beak are comparable to the Thracian king's warlike plumage and sword ('facies armata videtur,' 674), Gower's lapwing is like Tereus inside and out — at once crested, and proverbially perfidious.[65] Similarly Progne, who in the *Confessio* is presented as a woman of temper and direct speech, is made a swallow (6011-14):

> And chitreth out in hir langage
> What falshod is in mariage,
> And telleth in a maner speche
> Of Tereus the Spousebreche.

The choice of bird is implicit in Ovid's account (she is the one who flies to the roof-top), but Gower's specificity enriches the passage by making the metamorphosis more internally revealing. Philomela's transformation too is carefully

---

[64] Bruce Harbert, 'The Myth of Tereus in Ovid and Gower,' *Medium Aevum* 41 (1972), 213.
[65] Gower reveals his attitude toward lapwings at *CA* II, 329-30:
> A lappewinke has lost his feith
> And is the brid falsest of alle.

handled. Describing her, Gower is notably selective in his choice of metaphors — much more so, indeed, than Ovid, who in painting Philomela's helplessness before Tereus compared her first to a hare caught by an eagle ('quam cum pedibus praedator obuncis/ deposuit nido leporem Iovis ales in alto,' 516-17), then to a lamb bloody from the mouth of a wolf ('velut agna pavens, quae saucia cani/ Ore excussa lupi,' 527-28), and at last to a dove set free from a preditor's talons ('utque columba, suo madefactis sanguine plumis/ Horret adhuc, avidosque timet, quibus haeserat, ungues,' 529-30). In the *Confessio Amantis*, however, Philomela is compared exclusively to birds. During the rape (5643-46) she

> . . . lay oppressed and desesed,
> As if a goshauk hadde sesed
> A brid, which dorste noght for fere
> Remue . . .

Afterwards, when Tereus has cut out her tongue, Gower pointedly transforms Ovid's snake metaphor ('utque salire solet mutilatae cauda colubrae,' 559) into another avian one (5697-5700):

> Bot yet whan he hire tunge refte,
> A litel part therof belefte,
> Bot sche with al no word mai soune,
> Bot chitre and as a brid jargoune.

Characteristically, Gower has seen through to the tale's essentials, and has simplified them in his own version to create a deeper, differently illuminating narrative.

Thus, in the tale of 'Tereus' (as in 'Alboin and Rosamund' and throughout the *Confessio Amantis* especially) we can observe Gower judiciously amending his source materials, both 'internally,' to render them psychologically and artistically satisfying as stories, and also 'externally,' to adapt them to the broad framework of his design. Gower remade 'raw' narratives, modelling them to fit his didactic measures, translating even lilaceous styles such as Ovid's into his own, of 'low' diction, light pointing, and clear moral purpose. That he achieved this by being aware of the potential of actions and objects to express interior states is an indication of his poetic perspicacity; that he could make such a method — so different from the work of his contemporaries — function successfully is another measure of his talent's range.

CHAPTER IV

EXCEPTIONS PROVE
THE RULE

I

My argument presented in the preceding pages — that a consistent poetic
directed Gower's work — has not, of course, been universally approved. From
time to time even G. C. Macaulay expressed doubts about his poet's power over
his materials. The unity of Book II of the *Confessio Amantis*, it seemed to
Macaulay, was 'very seriously impaired by digressions;' and in the last four
Books of the same poem he found 'much irregularity of plan . . . by which the
. . . construction is seriously marred.'[1] This view of Gower as an artlessly
digressive — even formless — writer has been variously echoed, and requires
careful attention. In this chapter, then, I want to take a close look at five 'hard
cases' — apparently anomalous departures from the logical pattern of illustration
in the last Books of the *Confessio*: the description of 'Labor' in Book IV, on Sloth;
the section 'Religions of the World' in Book V, on Avarice; the inclusion of
'Sorcery' under Gluttony, Book VI; Book VII in its entirety; and the decision to
focus in Book VIII, not on Lechery in general, but on Incest alone. Properly
explicated, I believe these 'exceptions' confirm that Gower composed according
to rule.

I

At its simplest level, Gower's discussion of 'Labor' serves the same purpose in his
Book on Sloth that the 'Tale of the Three Questions,' about Humility, does in
Book I, devoted to Pride. Both are counterexamples, intended to illustrate right
action relative to sin. All the Books of the *Confessio* but one indeed are built

---

[1] Macaulay, in his article on Gower in the *Cambridge History of English Literature* (New
York, 1927), II, 169, remarks '. . . in general, there is much irregularity of plan in the
last four books [of the *Confessio*] by which the unity of construction is seriously marred.'
Again, in his exemplary summary of Book II, he comments: 'The plan of the work is not
ill-conceived; but unfortunately, it is carried out without due regard to proportion in its
parts, and its unity is very seriously impaired by digressions which have nothing to do
with the subject of the Book.' *Works*, II, 171.

according to this contrasting pattern. (Book VII, because it deals *inter alia* with sin but takes education as its focus, has no opposing virtue to present.) In each case, along with the exempla showing the fate of those entrapped by a vice, there is an illustration of its corresponding virtue. Four Books, in addition to the first, have this virtuous tale at the end, where it puts a kind of 'cap' to the lesson. Thus, Book II concludes with 'Constantine and Sylvester,' concerned with portraying Charity, the virtue balancing Envy; Book III, assigned to Ire, finishes with 'Telephus and Theucer,' a story about Mercy; Book V presents in conclusion first 'Prodigality,' Avarice's opposite extreme, and then is completed with 'Largesse,' the antidote to both extravagance and cupidity; Book VIII, devoted to Lust, concludes with two examples of Chastity in the 'Tale of Apollonius of Tyre.'

Books IV and VI also contain counterexamples, but they appear otherwhere than at the last. At first glance, these cases thus seem evidence of the kind of carelessness which so troubled Macaulay. But on second consideration, Gower may have had sound reasons for arranging his work as he did. Let us take up the example of Book VI first. It is less complicated and will help clarify the circumstances of Book IV.

Book VI ends with 'Nectanabus' and the brief narratives of 'Zoroaster' and 'Saul and the Witch' — tales demonstrating the evils of sorcery, hardly a virtue offsetting Gluttony. Earlier in Book VI, however, Genius tells the tale of 'Bacchus in the Desert' to exemplify the power of prayer. This, as we shall see subsequently, represents a positive counterweight to Gluttony, one aspect of which is 'Evil Speech,' which Gower envisions according to a tradition partly Biblical, partly secular.

Very likely Gower put the sorcery tales, rather than 'Bacchus in the Desert,' at the end of Book VI for a reason both germane and instructive. 'Nectanabus' creates a neat bridge to Book VII through their mutual focus on the life of Alexander the Great. Recalling what he has just heard in 'Nectanabus,' Amans asks Genius about Alexander's education, ostensibly the subject of Book VII. The 'digressive' seventh Book, then, is tightly bound to the sixth and appears to result from it naturally, following the course of conversation between Amans and his confessor. Such a jointure is hardly unique in the *Confessio*. At every opportunity, Gower sought to connect his Books smoothly, and to preserve the illusion of spontaneity. Indeed, we have noted another example already. In the 'Tale of the Three Questions' the pride of King Alphonse drives him to envy Don Petro. Alphonse's envy thus looks ahead to, and sparks, Envy's appearance as the major sin of Book II, and provides a credible transition from one Book to the next. Structural foreshadowing of this kind functions well on a didactic level, too, since it presents sins as insidiously interconnected, like shoots from a single stalk.[2]

---

[2] Gower's habit is to link his Books by suggesting this interconnection of sins. Thus, at the end of Book II, the dread felt by the Christians before Constantine's angry pursuit of them foreshadows Wrath, the subject of Book III; or, in a more general way, the active tales Gower chooses to illustrate Wrath lead directly into those of Sloth in Book IV.

Book IV, in so far as it has its counterexample 'Labor' roughly in the middle rather than at its conclusion, is very much like Book VI. Here, too, a concern for keeping the impression of discursive spontaneity doubtless played a part in the development of the Book. Several readers have noticed that Book IV breaks the pattern of five subsections per vice which characterized Books I-III, and also the entire *Mirour de l'Omme*.[3] Apparently, having established a pattern that had served him well, Gower saw fit to overturn it in favor of variations, much in the manner of a musical composition built upon a theme and sundry ornaments. It is a desire to interrupt order with the unexpected we notice in much of the best late Ricardian poetry — in the crustaceous bursting and shedding of texts in *Piers Plowman*, of the Miller's intrusion, and the Canon's Yeoman's, into the *Canterbury Tales*, of the entry of the Green Knight into the formal banquet of Arthur and his knights. Coming where it does, Gower's section on 'Labor' lends a certain air of verisimilitude to the poem's fictive frame.

There are, however, other purposes served by a section on 'Labor.' These also have to do with its placement, but on a much higher plane. As the following chapter will demonstrate in greater detail, Gower's poem proceeds contrapunctally, sometimes in apparent opposition — an amorous, and a less obvious but omnipresent Christian moral dimension. Far from being confused by this duality, Gower capitalizes on it, incorporating its tension into the heart of his poem. By the conclusion, these elements have been merged to give the *Confessio Amantis* a single meaning.

To accomplish this, Gower takes special care both with his introduction of the issues raised in 'Labor' and with their subsequent delineation. While 'Labor' explicitly opens at IV, 2363, in fact Gower has begun preparing us for the topic somewhat earlier. His treatment of 'Gentilesse' (IV, 2204-2363) is in fact a prolegomenon for the topics of 'Labor.' By way of providing 'negative' examples of men whose deeds overcame Sloth in love, Gower points out that (2196-99):

> For communlich in worthi place
> The wommen loven worthinesse
> Of manhode and of genilesse,
> For the gentils ben most desired.

---

[3] One such is Donald G. Schueler, 'Some Comments on the Structure of Gower's *Confessio Amantis*,' in *Explorations of Literature*, ed. Rima D. Reck (Baton Rouge: Louisiana State University Press, 1966). As an explanation of Gower's behavior, he offers the following: 'The main reason why Gower departed from this geometric kind of pattern was that he had discovered there was no need for it; the structure of his poem did not have to depend on so mechanical a device and would have been actually weakened by it . . . A didactic monologue, such as the *Mirour*, may permissibly sound rehearsed; but the supposedly spontaneous confession of a lover to a priest of love cannot . . . What does seem certain is that [Gower] soon realized that the structure of his work depended, not on this geometric approach, but on whatever naturalness he was able to inject into the conversation and the characters of his two speakers' (p. 17).

Amans claims not to know 'What gentilesce is forto seie,' and Genius proceeds to explain. While many consider it a product of 'richesse' and 'hih lignage,' these things are worldly and passing.[4] True gentility is enthroned in the heart, Genius says — thereby taking a side in a traditional debate having many participants.[5] Yet regardless of the internal nature of gentility, in Gower's view it must be transformed ultimately into deeds (2288-91):

> Bot yit to putte himselve forth
> He moste don his besinesse,
> For nother good ne gentilesse
> Mai helpen hem whiche ydel be.

Such a treatment is characteristic: As we have seen from the ballades and in tales like 'Jason and Medea,' virtue, like promised love, was meaningless to Gower until manifested in deeds. Only then could it be considered 'real,' through action and — ideally — reciprocal exchange. True gentility thus requires effort; achieving it becomes a kind of work. Hence, the discussion of 'gentilesse' leads to one of 'Labor,' with its particularly non-courtly forms of human action. For the first time since the Prologue, we are asked to see the love-fiction in a broader moral context.

Much of Gower's description in the 'Labor' section points back to Jean de Meun, who has Dame Nature discourse on forms of physical and mental exertion in the *Roman de la Rose* — and before looking further at the *Confessio*, it is helpful to review what it was that Gower rejected.[6] Like Gower, Jean discounts any relationship of true gentility ('noblece') and birth: Nature casts all men from the same mold; their lineage and property are gifts of Fortune and consequently meaningless. What matters for Nature is 'bon corage' — a good heart — which, she suggests, should be apparent in the behavior of men (18494-96):

[4] The idea is hardly original to Gower, of course; versions receive utterance from as diverse a group as John Ball, Dante (*Convivio* IV, 10), and the Wife of Bath (D 1109-16), to name but three.
[5] Genius' views are put succinctly at *CA* IV, 2257-68:
> For lacke of vertu lacketh grace,
> Wherof richesse in many place,
> Whan men best wene forto stonde,
> Al sodeinly goth out of honde:
> Bot vertu set in the corage,
> Ther mai no world be so salvage,
> Which mihte it take and don awaie,
> Til whanne that the bodi deie;
> And thanne he schal be riched so,
> That it mai faile nevermo;
> So mai that wel be gentilesse,
> Which yifth so gret a sikernesse.
[6] Perhaps significantly, her audience is Genius, one of the literary ancestors of Gower's Confessor.

> Ne gentillece ne valeur,
> S'il ne font tant que gentill saient
> Par sans ou par vertuz qu'il aient.

['Neither gentility nor valor, unless they act appropriately, through their sense or their virtue.']⁷

Vice makes men base, and vice knows no class (18607-18). Pressing her point, Nature names fieldworkers as the opposite of nobility ('qui les terres coutivent, 18613), who nonetheless have the same chance to live noble lives, before passing on to her primary contrast — that of knights and clerks, the 'lerned and the lewd.' In an extensive argument (18635 ff.) Nature in the *Roman* claims for the clerks the better opportunity to achieve gentility, for their books provide extensive examples from the past. Nature's discourse is wandering, however, and carries her to speak of the heavenly bodies, the elements, plants, animals and finally man, whom, of all creation, she accuses of disobedience (19021 ff.).

⁷ Nature's descriptions come in her discussion of Gentility, 18589-946. The quoted lines conclude a passage it is helpful to know in full:

> Noblece vient de bon courage,
> Car gentillece de lignage
> N'est pas gentillece qui vaille,
> Por quoi bonté de queur i faille,
> Par quoi doit estre en li paranz
> La proece de ses paranz
> Qui, la gentillece conquistrent
> Par les travauz que granz i mistrent,
> Qui, quant du siecle trespasserent,
> Toutes leur vertuz amporterent,
> Et lessierent as airs l'avoir,
> Qui plus ne porent d'aus avoir,
> L'avoir ont, riens plus n'i a leur,
> Ne gentillece ne valeur,
> S'il ne font tant que gentill saient
> Par sans ou par vertuz qu'il aient.

['Nobility comes from an upright heart;
Gentility of birth is nothing worth
If he who has it lacks goodheartedness.
In him the prowess should be shown of those
Who were his forebears, and their name achieved
By the good works to which they set themselves.
When from the world they went, they with them took
Their virtues, leaving only to their heirs —
Who nothing more could claim — their property.
These have their fathers' wealth, but nothing more —
No nobleness or worth — unless they do,
By reason of their virtue or good sense,
That which discloses true nobility.']

French text from *Le Roman de la Rose*, ed. Lécoy; translation by Harry W. Robbins, *The Romance of the Rose*.

Gower's development of 'Labor' recalls this speech of Nature's in several important ways. At first there are the obvious structural similarities: Gower's Genius and Jean de Meun's Nature come to their topic amidst broad attempts to define gentility. For both it is a virtuous disposition made concrete by virtuous action. Each account in some way speciates human business, and touches upon a wide range of subjects: the sciences, the structure of the universe, the uses and abuses of learning. But here the similarities cease; and we may see readily that, as usual, Gower began with the *Roman* only to bring forward ends of his own.

Unlike Jean, who organized Nature's speech according to the three estates — plowman, knight and clergy — with emphasis on the latter two, Gower seems to have had in mind to represent the 'two lives' familiar in the Middle Ages from theological and secular writings: the so-called 'vita activa' and 'vita contemplativa.'[8] Thus the English verses near the opening of the section (*CA* IV, 2383-87):

> That on the plogh hath undertake
> With labour which the hond hath take,
> That other tok to studie and muse,
> As he which wolde noght refuse
> The labour of hise wittes alle.

Here 'labor of the hand' seems a synecdoche for all physical exertion including the work of knights — a group which, while it deeply concerned Nature, generally occupied Gower but little. This dichotomy is repeated in the Latin verses introducing the 'Labor' section — albeit with a clear preference for the work of the mind:

> Expedit in manibus labor, ut de cotidianis
>   Actibus ac vita vivere possit homo.
> Set qui doctrine causa fert mente labores,
>   Preualet et merita perpetuata parat.

['Manual labor is useful, so that by daily activities and regular life a man may live. But he who, for the sake of learning, carries out mental labor is stronger, and prepares for perpetual honor.']

---

[8] The origin of the 'two lives' is Luke 10:42, where Christ prefers Mary over Martha, representing contemplation and labor. Augustine's important discourse on the lives is based on this passage; see his Sermo 10 (a), 'Rursus in illud evangelii Lucae, ubi de Martha et Maria,' *PL* XXXVIII, cols. 616-18. Other influential medieval interpretations also exist. Aquinas (*Summa Theologica* III, Q. 40, A. 1) argues for a kind of 'mixed' life, of active good works following a period of contemplation, as being the most like Christ's example ('sed vita activa, secundum quam aliquis praedicando et docendo contemplata aliis tradit, est perfectior quam vita quae solum est contemplativa'). Such a mixed life is also preferred in the *Meditationes Vitae Christi*, a popular work thought in the fourteenth century to be by Bonaventura.

The verses which follow offer a rich compendium of major themes. The sequence of human activities, seemingly arbitrary, nonetheless has an observable progression, which, because of its complexity, we should recall before considering its interpretation. Gower begins with writing and those who, by discovering it, made possible the transmission of all knowledge (2388-90):

> And in this wise it is befalle,
> Of labour which that thei begunne
> We be now tawht of that we kunne.

This approach recalls the very first lines of the Prologue, in which 'hem that writen ous tofore' were raised up as examples guiding the composition of the *Confessio* itself. In Book IV, the progression of written language is likewise historically sketched, and forms an envelope around other significant 'arts and sciences.' In 'Croniqes' appear the names of 'Cham' who first wrote Hebrew, 'Cadmus,' the father of Greek script, and then a list of (presumably Greek and Hebrew 'Enditours/ Of old Cronique and ek auctours' (2407-10):

> Cladyns, Esdras, and Sulpices,
> Termegis, Pandulf, Frigidilles,
> Menander, Ephiloquorus,
> Solins, Pandas and Josephus.[9]

The history is completed two hundred lines later (2633 ff.) at the conclusion of 'Labor,' with a discussion of Latin letters, again presented systematically: first script, (the discovery of one 'Carmente'), then grammar (formulated by 'Aristarchus,' 'Donat,' and 'Dindimus'), rhetoric (by 'Tullius *with* Cithero'!), translation (Jerome) and poetry (Ovid).[10]

In between, Gower catalogues an oddly diverse congeries of human achievements. Yet these too, on reflection, show evidence of order. As with Latin letters, the progressive sophistication of the Greek and Hebrew languages culminates in the invention of poetry. It was 'Heredot' who (2413-15):

> . . . in his science
> Of metre, of rime and of cadence,
> The ferste was of which men note.

Gower's stress on the aural elements of the 'science' of versification creates a neat bridge to music, his next topic. The *riche rime* 'note/ note' ('The ferste was of

---

[9] These names, and Gower's source(s) for them, are obscure. Macaulay finds some of them in Godfrey of Viterbo's *Pantheon*; see his note to *CA* IV, 2396 ff., *Works* II, 508.
[10] Chaucer also transforms Cicero into two people; see *CT* F 722.

which men note./ And of Musique also the note,' 2415-16) enforces this jointure. Two inventors are named, in order of the probable sequence of their discoveries: a Jew ('Jubal'), said to be patriarch of choral song, and a Greek ('Poulins,' or Apollo), craftsman of the first harp.[11] Music is succeeded by the other fine arts — painting (the contribution of 'Zenzis') and sculpture, 'wroghte' (2424) initially by 'Promotheus' — and these in turn by the life-sustaining crafts. Again, Gower smoothes the path with verbal and logical connectives. 'Tubal,' who perfected the forge, also first 'wroghte' (2426), like the sculptor Zenzis, albeit in iron and steel: although not a *riche rime*, the repeated verb with but a line between helps emphasize the related 'arts' of sculpting and forging tools. Next 'Jedahel,' called father of net-making, fishing, hunting and tents, presumably employs Tubal's handiwork — and both are the brothers, in Gower's biblical source, of Jubal the musician.[12] Jedahel's discoveries necessitate cookery (developed by 'Verconius,' 2433) and put to use the products of 'Minerve' and 'Delbora,' women 'of gret engyn' who created cloth from wool and linen. Farming — our other source of sustenance besides the chase — is attributed to 'Saturnus,' also the originator of 'Chapmanhode,' or commerce (that is, what one does with surplus food and crafts), and its *sine qua non*, coinage (2447-50).

In turn, coinage opens the way for the largest *amplificatio* of the 'Labor' section, and — at first glance — the most puzzling. Before closing the linguistic 'envelope' with the discussion of Latin language and letters, Gower devotes 175 lines to defining, describing and tracing the history of alchemy. Its linkages to preceding topics are easily seen: coins being made of metal leads to discourse on metals' origins; and the double sense in which 'philosopher' could be taken in the Middle Ages — as learned man and alchemist — relates Cham, founder of both the Hebrew alphabet and 'naturel Philosophie' (the first inventor named, at the beginning of 'Labor,' 2399-400) to the 'Philosophres wise' (2453) who initiate mining and alchemy as alternative means of obtaining metals. Thus Gower strives to lend his disquisition a simple, visible cohesion.

Beneath this surficial jointure, however, lies a unity of idea quite close to the center of Gower's poetic. What we should notice is the logocentric approach Gower takes toward intellectual discovery. In 'Labor' he offers us a narrative of history beginning — not, as historians teach us, with an evolving agriculture — but with the acquisition of letters. This is scarcely arbitrary. Gower gave great weight to the biblical description of creation as a verbal act (Gen. 1) and evolved his own assessment of language accordingly. He defines his position in Book VII (1545-49):

[11] This treatment of Jubal is somewhat unorthodox. The son of Lammech and Adah (Gen. 4: 19-20), Jubal is 'the ancestor of those who play the harp and the pipe.' Gower must have had this passage of the Bible in mind, since in the next few lines (2425-32) he identifies Jabal ('Jedahel') and Tubal, both brothers to Jubal, by their respective crafts. (But see n.12, below.) By ascribing a Greek origin to the harp, however, Gower maintains his dual structure and — probably — follows the better-known of the two traditions.
[12] Gen. 4: 19-21. Again, Gower alters material here: In the Bible Jabal is only a tentmaker. The better-known ancestor of hunting is Nimrod; see Gen. 10: 9.

> In Ston and gras vertu ther is,
> Bot yit the bokes tellen this,
> That word above alle earthli thinges
> Is vertuous in his doinges,
> Wher so it be to evele or goode.

By 'vertuous' Gower means *powerful*. All events in Gower's universe are, or have been, wrought by divine words — or man's, in approximation of the Word of God. For efficacious 'vertu' is not confined to the *Logos*. Using his gift of language, man can directly alter his world, as Book VII makes plain (1574-80):

> The wordes maken fo of frend, and pes of werre,
> And werre of pes, and out of herre
> The word this worldes cause entriketh,
> And reconsileth whan him liketh.
> The word under the coupe of hevene
> Set every thing or odde or evene.

The last couplet, above, sums it u:p *every thing* 'under the coupe of hevene' devolves from words. Significantly, man may preserve life through speech (VII, 1567-69):

> Of word among the men of Armes
> Ben woundes heeled with the charmes,
> Wher lacketh other medicine

and even create *ex nihilo*, through 'Sorcerie the karectes' (1571). (In Medea's restoration of Eson's youth, and Nectanabus's magic, we have narrative examples of both ideas put to work.)[13]

Obviously such power comes encumbered with significant responsibility. Proper use of language is perhaps Gower's most insistent theme, with unambiguous consequences for his view of poetry. Understandably, given the stakes, he situates upon poetry the highest potential for accomplishing good or ill. Hence his urgent concern, discussed in an earlier chapter, to 'correct' what he perceived as the detrimental poetics of Jean de Meun and the French courtly lyricists; hence here poetry culminates the linguistic histories of Hebrew, Greek and Latin offered in 'Labor;' hence too its development precedes his description of the other civilizing discoveries of man.

[13] See *CA* V, 4064-66, and VI, 1966. Medea and Nectanabus use many devices, including astronomical configurations and 'herbes' to bring about their results — but significantly it is only when the proper 'charmes' or 'carectes' (cf. VI, 2005-06) are recited that the magic takes effect.

Against this background, it is easier to see and understand the role played by the *amplificatio* on alchemy in 'Labor.' It is, I believe, intended to fit into four contexts. We have seen how, in the development of the passage, it evolves naturally from the discourse on coinage, and the production of money from metals. But in a broader way it anchors Gower's thesis that, of the two 'lives' active and contemplative, the latter is the more important. Gower's logocentric presentation of alchemy illustrates that, for him, it is both a 'trewe' (IV, 2598) and a mental science. In the ancient days of its discovery, its 'karectes' were properly applied, and 'hem that whilom weren wise' (2579) successfully produced precious metals. The alchemists of his own day, however, are failures (2580; 2592-93):

> Bot now it stant al otherwise . . .
> I not hou such a craft schal thryve
> In the manere as it is used.

The problem, not surprisingly, is linguistic, at least on the surface. The antique texts 'Of Grek, of Arabe and of Caldee' (2627) exist, but can no longer be deciphered (2613-25):

> [These] bokes, pleinli as thei stonde
> Upon this craft, fewe understonde;
> Bot yit to put hem in assai
> Ther ben full manye now aday,
> That knowen litel what thei meene.
> It is noght on to wite and weene;
> In forme of wordes thei it trete,
> Bot yit they failen of beyete,
> For of tomoche or of tolyte
> Ther is algate founde a wyte,
> So that thei folwe noght the lyne
> Of the parfite medicine,
> Which grounded is upon nature.

Modern alchemists follow the 'forme of wordes' but lack the insight to evoke their inherent power. Typically in Gower's righteous universe such weakness has a moral cause, and in the context of Book IV we are asked, I think, to perceive it as a concomitant of intellectual sloth. The Latin note in the margin beside the opening of 'Labor' directs our reading of the whole section, and bears this out:

> Hic loquitur contra ociosos quoscumque, et maxime contra istos, qui excellentis prudencie igenium habentes absque fructu operum torpescunt.

['Here he speaks against the slothful of all sorts, and particularly against
those who, although they have superior natural intelligence, are
unproductive of fruitful works.']

Contemporary alchemy thus provides Gower with a pointed example of 'Labor'
gone wrong, betrayed as it were by mental lapse. Its sterility — the result of
intelligence ineffectually applied to words potentially powerful — is of a sort
compatible with the risks run by all language users, especially poets. Hence its
placement inside an 'envelope' beginning and ending with histories of classical
letters which themselves culminate in the invention of, first, Greek, then Latin,
verse. The 'word above alle erthli thinges/ Is vertuous in his doinges' (VII, 1547-
48): alchemists (properly) and poets create through language, despite the
former's mistaken reliance upon 'ston and gras' (VII, 1545).

It is the similarity of poetic and alchemical creation as verbal acts (singularly
appropriate in a section devoted to arts *and* sciences) which illuminates a third
context of 'Labor.' This is Nature's speech in the *Roman de la Rose*. As I pointed
out earlier, this passage stands behind 'Labor,' providing a basic structure that
Gower reactively reshapes. The section thus continues and expands the
adversarial rewriting of the *Roman* which we find in varying degrees throughout
Gower's work.

Several of the major points shared by 'Labor' and Nature's speech were
mentioned above: the concern to locate true gentility in behavior rather than
lineage or property; the consequent insistence that poor men and fieldworkers
can act nobly; the defence of clerks and learning.

Despite these similarities, however, the different methods of Gower and Jean
at last have signally divergent consequences. Nature's speech juxtaposing knights
and 'philosophers' allows for measured approval of chivalric figures real and
imagined (e.g., Robert of Artois and Gawain, 18697 ff.); but it is apparent
balance bought at a price. Nature's windy decrying of a lapsed chivalry leads her
to deny the possibility of reform (she portrays *all men as corrupt simpliciter*, 19225
ff.). Gower, by enfolding the warrior class within the *activa vita* alongside
chapmen and laborers, takes a clear position. As the antithesis to a certain aspect
of Sloth, intellectual industry in the *Confessio* is endowed with a primary moral
obligation. Gower thus provides a *reason* for clerkly labor to receive the highest
value — something Nature, for all her talk of giving poets towns (e.g., Naples to
Virgil, 18719 ff.), of Albumazzar, Plato, and the Virgin Birth (19113 ff.) — does
not supply.[14] This contrast of texts is thoroughly carried out, including even the
lesser levels. Gower's alchemical descriptions supply an integrated answer to
Nature's *digressio* on the operation of heavenly bodies and the manufacture of
weather (18897-966); and his presentation of the three alchemist's stones —
'vegetabilis,' 'animalis,' and 'Minerall' (IV, 2531-79) — balance Nature's
excurses (18967-19020) on, first, the 'obedient' elements, then on plants, birds,
fish, and higher animals.

---

[14] Possibly because she can't, as an allegorical figure of limited moral understanding. But
Jean obviates this defense by having Nature preach on Christ's example — see 19191 ff.

The net — and neat — result of Gower's management of 'Labor' is a context which permits him to foreshadow, and subtly justify, the call to poetic labor which concludes his poem. The umasking of Amans *senex* and his subsequent exclusion, as one who can no longer procreate, from Venus's court starts a chain of the most original transformations in Ricardian poetry. The previously anonymous lover gains a name — John Gower — and a commission from Venus, to 'preie hierafter for the pes' (VIII, 2908 ff.). As he does so, 'Amans/Gower' creates a kind of epilogue to the *Confessio*, hearkening back to the concerns, and the authorial voice, of the Prologue. He thus ends his poem — in one sense at least — where he began, standing before us no longer as 'just' a character, but also as John Gower, poet of moral and political reform. The charge of Venus is consequently laid upon him as well. From this vantage the *Confessio* is self-reflexive: in telling it the poet has fulfilled his eponymous lover's obligation to deliver a prayer.

Thus the 'labor' of the *Confessio* is quite complex. By its end it seeks resolution and synthesis for a fictive love affair, a poetic history (i.e., the narrative of its own making), a moral metaphysics and what one might call a 'theology of art' — the approximation, that is, of the Divine *Logos* in the creative acts of men. All of these, we have found, are touched upon *in parvo* in the 'Labor' section of Book IV: all, indeed, but the solution to Amans's amorous dilemma. But in fact this too is present, made plain as the fourth context woven into the concluding lines of 'Labor.' Genius brings to a close his history of the growth of Latin letters with a single illustration (2668-71):

> . . . in Poesie
> To the lovers Ovide wrot
> And tawhte, if love be to hot,
> In what manere it scholde akiele.

This is a curious passage on several counts. It is an odd way to characterize Ovid, as the author of (only) the *Remedia Amoris* — which in any case seems an unusual choice to represent all of Latin poetry. Nor do Genius' next remarks make matters easier (2672-74):

> Forthi, mi Sone, if that thou fiele
> That love wringe thee to sore,
> Behold Ovide and take his lore.

What, we might well ask, is a priest of Venus up to, pointing out love-cures to a devotee? Especially in a Book describing (we suppose) ways to avoid Sloth-in-love, the example and the application appear misplaced. But if we recall that Genius speaks with knowledge we at this point lack — for he can *see* Amans, and his old age — the passage takes on new shape. It represents in fact a look ahead, to the *Confessio*'s conclusion when in Venus's mirror gives him Amans will recognize himself as Genius decorously hints he sees him now, a lover with a hopeless suit, and sore in need of Ovid's cure. Amans fails of course to understand; his response is, he will read Ovid's books if they 'mihte spede/ Mi love' (2675-76). But this reply, for Amans at this stage, is apt. Like the gentle nudge of his confessor to think, and learn to disengage his heart, it reveals much about how carefully Gower drew these characters, with how pressing a sense of personality and life. Properly understood, the passage challenges us to imagine Amans as a physical (and hence *actual*) being, a gentleman with a real problem in confession with a 'real' priest, to gain a real absolution through the penitential labor represented by the poem we read.[15]

Beyond this, the interchange also hearkens back to Nature's speech in the *Roman*, where her scattered references to Virgil and Ennius serve no structural purpose. She merely mentions the poets, as worthy recipients of property, as foretelling (Virgil) the Virgin Birth. In Gower's world, however, where poetry is labor of the highest kind, it must justify itself whenever it is named. Thoroughly integrating his writing into every context here, including the framing fiction, Gower goes Jean de Meun one better and fulfills the demand for structural resolution his poetic placed upon him.

II

If 'Labor' fits purposefully within the *Confessio*'s greater plan, so also does Genius's outline of the 'Religions of the World' in Book V, 738-1959. Modern readers of the *Confessio* have labelled these lines needlessly digressive. Macaulay, for example, comments at length that the section is 'very ill-advised,' and argues:

> There is no more reason why this should come in here than anywhere else; indeed, if the question of false gods was to be raised at all, it ought to have come in as an explanation of the appearance of Venus and Cupid in the first Book. Many stories have been told . . . which required the explanation quite as much as this one [i.e., of 'Vulcan and Venus'] and the awkwardness of putting it all into the mouth of the priest of Venus is inexcusable.[16]

---

[15] It thus stands as evidence supporting those readers who have argued for the steady, planned revelation of Amans' age. See especially Donald G. Schueler, 'The Age of the Lover in Gower's *Confessio Amantis*,' *Medium Aevum* 36 (1967), 152-58.

[16] Macaulay, *Works*, II, 515. A similar view is aired by Schueler, 'Some Comments,' 20: 'The confessor not only contradicts the laws of courtly love when they contradict the laws of nature, but, in the fifth Book, after failing to bypass a discussion of Venus, he also admits . . . that she is by no means omnipotent or even virtuous. The confessor's attempt here to extricate himself from the narrower role of priest of Love is not a fortunate device on Gower's part; it is the one point in the poem when Genius's dual meaning becomes noticeably dichotomized.'

Far from being digressive, however, the 'Religions' section, like that on 'Labor,' seeks to establish the inseparable duality of fleshly and spiritual love, as we have been describing it. On reflection, it seems odd that Macaulay, whose wisdom is generally consistent, should have misunderstood so absolutely Gower's inclusion of the 'Religions of the World' under Avarice — particularly since he had himself lighted the key to its placement here. At the conclusion of the subsection on Christian faith, which follows the beliefs of the Chaldeans, the Egyptians, the Greeks, and the Hebrews, Genius accuses modern clergy of eschewing 'gostli labour,' in favor of (1951-55):

> . . . the worldes Avarice;
> And that is as a sacrifice,
> Which, after that thapostel seith,
> Is openly ayein the fieth
> Unto thidoles yove and graunted.

The lines give the impression that Gower had in mind a particular text, as indeed he did; Macaulay has found it, in Colossians 3:5, where 'thapostel' Paul cautions his listeners to mortify the flesh against a collection of sins, including 'avaritiam, quae est simulacrorum servitus.'[17]

'Avarice, which is the service of idols': At issue is the misdirection of human worship away from God, and the consequent 'deification' of materiality. The idea that Avarice represented a form of idolatry found frequent expression in the Middle Ages. Alan of Lille, for example, put the case succinctly, through the mouth of Nature in his *De planctu naturae*. The second of Idolatry's daughters, Alan's Nature says, is 'Avarice, through whom money is exalted in the human breast, and the authority of divine worship is extended to a coin.'[18] Gower expresses the matter more abstractly, but to the same point in his section on 'Religions of the World' (*CA* V, 777-80):

> And who that takth awey thonour
> Which is to the creatour,
> And yifth it to the creature,
> He doth to gret a forsfaiture.[19]

---

[17] 'Mortificate ergo membra vestra, quae sunt super terram; fornicationem, immunditiam, libidinem, concupiscentiam, malam, et avaritiam, quae est simulacrorum servitus' ['Mortify therefore your members which are upon the earth fornication, uncleanness, lust, evil concupiscence and covetousness, which is the service of idols'].

[18] 'Haec est Avaritia, per quam in animis hominum pecunia deificatur nummo divinae venerationis exhibitur auctoritas.' *Liber de Planctu Naturae*, ed. Nikolaus M. Häring. *Studi Medievali*, 3rd series, 19.2 (1978), 797-879. For the line quoted, see prosa 6. Augustine and Dante use the same idea; see *De Magistro* IX, 26 and *Inferno* XXVII, 54-57.

[19] The Latin verse heading to the section makes the same point: 'Nulla creatori racio facit esse creatum/ Equiperans, quod adhuc iura pagana fouent' ['Reason esteems not at all a created thing fitted out as a creator, which heretofore the pagan laws fostered'].

For Gower, then, Avarice was a suitable place for a disquisition on idolatrous religions. But this answers only the easier half of Macaulay's objection, which of course extends farther than a concern for the mere location in Book V of 'Religions of the World.' What Macaulay really wanted to know is whether, in a lover's confession, the issue of the world's religions ought to be raised at all. Now, this is a much larger problem. To discuss it we must take two approaches, one general, one specific.

We must begin by reminding ourselves that Gower's poem is a good deal more than a fictional romantic confession. Despite what the framework dialogue about a love affair implies, in the *Confessio* as in his other poetry Gower was concerned to articulate a coherent view of the universe, and of man's special place within it. Macaulay, in limiting his objection to fictive 'inconsistencies,' thus also limited the field of inquiry — and unprofitably. Gower's poem continually challenges us to seek beyond the amorous narrative, here as elsewhere. The 'Religions of the World' section forces us to recall the Christian perspective and — taking one step back — apply it to the fiction. Man's place in the cosmic order we know only from our proper relation to God. Lest this relation be obscured by the *dénouement* of Book VIII, the error of pagan theologic systems must be explained. To this end, the 'Religions of the World' section finds a necessary place, and advances the larger argument.

Looked at specifically, the arrangement of the religions suggests what is occurring. Gower has ordered them according to an intelligent Christian's notion of sophistication.[20] To do so, he had to modify the way they appear in the *Vita Barlaam et Iosaphat*, his major source for the 'Religions' section which in other respects he followed closely.[21] Both the *Vita Barlaam* and Gower thus begin with the Chaldeans, who worshipped the inanimate world, including the astrological signs. Such foolishness was patent to Genius, and (we must assume) to Gower's audience also. As the priest points out (*CA* V, 759-67):

---

[20] The progression is a commonplace, originating in Plato but codified for the Middle Ages by Aristotle, *De animalibus historia*, VII, i, 588b, and also *De partibus animalium*, IV, 5, 681a. (On the availability of both works in Latin translation from the thirteenth century, see A.O. Lovejoy, *The Great Chain of Being: A Study of the History of an Idea* [New York], 1960, 340, n. 41.) Nature's speech in the *Roman de la Rose*, considered above as central to Gower's treatment of 'Labor' in Book IV, follows this order in praising the heavenly bodies and the elements, the plants, the fish, birds, and animals, before upbraiding man; see ll. 18947-19334. And see further the useful discussion by C. S. Lewis, *Discarded Image*, 92-97.

[21] As Macaulay notes (*Works* II, 515), the sources of the 'Religions' section are quite complex. The *Vita Barlaam* is a major source, but others including Fulgentius's *Mythologia*, Godfrey of Viterbo's *Pantheon*, and the *Historia Alexandri Magni de Preliis* seem also to have been consulted. The pastiche typefies Gower's 'centonic' use of sources. For the *Vita Barlaam*, see Migne, *PL* 73, cap. xxvii; all quotations are taken from the Middle English edition of John C. Hirsh, *Barlam and Iosaphat: A Middle English Life of Buddha*, EETS O.S. 290 (London, 1986).

In thelementz and ek also
Thei hadden a believe tho;
And al was that unresonable
For thelementz ben servicable
To man, and ofte of Accidence
As men mai se thexperience,
Thei ben corrupt be sondri weie;
So mai no mannes reson seie
That thei ben god in eny wise.

'These elementz ben creatures' (i.e., 'created things') Genius says a bit further along (773): to worship them, and not their creator, is (like all idolatry) contrary to reason.[22]

The Egyptians, who worshipped 'divers bestes' (791), exhibit a similar rational failure. They, too, served creations, not the creator. Gower describes them after the Chaldeans, doubtless because along the creational 'chain' 'Unresonable beestis' rank between inanimate objects and men.[23] *Mutatis mutandis*, man-centered idolatries and misbeliefs (the Greeks) should follow descriptions of, first, astrological (the Chaldeans) and then animalistic religions (the Egyptians) — as they do, in Book V. Gower's acceptance of this schema can be judged from the way he altered his source. In the *Vita Barlam* the Egyptians are presented as the worst of a worsening series of three pagan nations, Chaldea, Greece, Egypt:

Thes Egipcianes . . . erren worste of al peple. For þey holde hem nat contente with þe goddis of Caldees and of Grekys, but alone aboue al hem þei maken of vnresonable beestis of þe erthe and of þe watere, trees and herbis, and callen hem here goddis. And þei done moste synne of al þe peple in erthe.[24]

Instead of reproducing this order, however, Gower transposed the Greeks and Egyptians. His order in Book V thus conforms to his earlier statement of the theme, in the Prologue (949-56):

For man of Soule resonable
Is to an Angel resemblable,
And lich to beste he hath fielinge,

[22] The *Vita Barlaam* makes the same point about the irrationality of worshipping corruptible 'elementis and planettis'; see Hirsh, *Barlam*, p. 121.
[23] See for example Augustine, *City of God* XI, 16: 'Among living things, the sentient rank above the insensitive, and animals over trees. Among the sentient, the intelligent take precedence over the unthinking — men over cattle.' Trans. Henry Bettenson, in *Augustine: Concerning the City of God Against the Pagans*, ed. David Knowles (Harmondsworth: Penguin, 1972), p. 447.
[24] Hirsh, *Barlam*, p. 125.

> And lich to Trees he hath growinge;
> The Stones ben and so is he:
> Thus of his propre qualite
> The man, as telleth the clergie,
> Is as a world in his partie.

That he continued to term the Egyptians 'the worst of alle' (789) despite the
oddity, from a purely structural point of view, of according 'the worst' second
place, is only momentarily puzzling. Gower would seem to be maintaining the
moral assessment of his source while asserting in his order of the religions the
different, 'scientific' logic of the Great Chain of Being. His treatment of the
whole subject here attests both to his faith in the *Vita Barlaam* as a 'true' text to be
respected on all points, and his thorough commitment to the hierarchy of Being.

Having established that the Egyptians were animal worshippers, Gower edits
the more elaborate list of 'gods' in the *Vita Barlaam* to focus on the four major
deities.[25] All of these have human shapes (798-801):

> Tho goddes be yit cleped thus,
> Orus, Typhon and Isirus:
> And the goddesse in hir degre
> Here Soster was and Ysis hyhte.

Moreover in a significant alteration of his source, Gower specifies that the central
relationship among the four was incestuous (802-03):

> [Ysis] Isirus forlai be nyhte
> And hield hire after as his wif.[26]

---

[25] The *Vita Barlaam* account provides a list of animals (and 'oþer creaturis') the Egyptians
propitiated: sheep, kids, calves, hogs, hawks, eagles, 'cokedrylles', cats, dogs, wolves,
dragons, adders, an onion, a garlic, and a thorn (!); see Hirsh, *Barlam*, 126.

[26] The *Vita Barlaam*, however, says nothing about the incest of Isis and Osiris; see Hirsh,
126. In Egyptian myth, Osiris and Isis are indeed an incestuous pair, being the offspring
of the same mother, Rhea (Nut), but of different fathers (Osiris of Ra, the Sun; Isis of
Hermes). They were both in the womb at the same time, however, and in one version of
the tale fell in love and copulated there. Our best source for this story is Plutarch, *Isis et
Osiris*, 12-19; see Harold P. Cooke, *Osiris: A Study in Myths, Mysteries and Religion* (London:
Daniel, 1931), 7-9, who includes a translation. Gower, of course, could have had no
knowledge of Plutarch. The incest story may have come to him from other sources, if
indeed he did not institute it for his own purposes: Diodorus Siculus and Macrobius both
give versions of it (though less complete than Plutarch's); and a third version, in which
Typhon is the husband of Isis and kills his brother Osiris when he finds that the two have
become lovers, is related in a work probably of the first half of the 4th century A.D., *De
Errore Profanorum Religionem*, attributed to Julius Firmicus Maternus. (See E.A. Wallis
Budge, *Osiris and the Egyptian Resurrection*, 2 vols. [London: Warner, 1911], I, 12-17). The

The next seven lines (804-10), linked to those above by the rhyme 'wif/ strif,' detail other passions darkened by this incest:

> So it befell that upon strif
> Typhon hath Isre his brother slain,
> Which hadde a child to Sone Orayn,
> And he his fader deth to herte
> So tok, that it mai noght asterte
> That he Typhon ne slowh,
> Whan he was ripe of age ynowh.[27]

Gower's apparent originality in presenting the Egyptian pantheon as undone, at the root, by incest is especially noteworthy in light of its prominence in his treatment of the Greek gods and in Book VIII, where the sin figures synecdochically for Lechery. Here in Book V, however, the horrific crimes of the Egyptian deities — seduction, incest, fratricide — serve to justify their dismissal as false apprehensions of unlearned intelligences (832-34):

> Lo, hou Egipte al out of syhte
> Fro resoun stant in misbelieve
> For lacke of lore, as I believe.

The Greek gods are a more serious problem. Gower was clearly aware that to describe the religion of Greece was to confront the origins of what the medieval West knew of arts and science. He points out, for example, that 'The Romeins hielden ek the same' beliefs (V, 1303 ff.), and he 'cross-references' information about various deities (Minerva, Saturn) here and in the 'Labor' section in Book IV.[28] In consequence, Gower is walking a fine line in this subsection. One measure of his concern is the number of sources he used to inform the discussion here, and the resultant lengthening of the Greek subsection.[29] His attempt seems to have been to get every fact 'right.' The painstaking effort to separate the false

---

work is probably not by Firmicus, however, and certainly rare; the *editio princeps* is a Strasbourg blackletter of 1562, taken apparently from a Minden manuscript now lost. See the account of William Ramsay, ed., in *A Dictionary of Greek and Roman Biography and Mythology*, 3 vols. (New York: AMS Press, 1967), II, 152-54.

[27] The *Vita Barlaam* gives no reason for the killing of Osiris by Typhon, mentioning only that it took place; see Hirsh, pp. 125-26.

[28] Cf. IV, 2435-36 and 2439 ff. with V, 1203-04 and 1226-30.

[29] For the Greeks, Gower draws not only on the *Vita Barlaam* but also on Godfrey of Viterbo, Fulgentius, the *Historia Alexandri Magni*, and possibly Guido della Colonna. There may be other sources as well; see Macaulay's notes, *Works* II, 516-18, passim. The Greeks' religion occupies nearly 700 lines of text (i.e., 835-1946), as compared to about 40 for the Chaldeans (747-86), and 50 (787-834) for the Egyptians.

gods themselves from their associations was obviosly difficult. The case of
Mercury (V, 945-54) is revealing:

> A gret spekere in alle thinges
> He was also, and of lesinges
> An Auctour, that men wiste non
> As other such as he was on.
> And yit thei maden of this thief
> A god, which was unto hem lief,
> And clepede him in tho believes
> The god of Marchantz and of thieves.
> Bot yit a sterre upon the hevene
> He hath of the planetes sevene.

Gower's careful distinction of the true and the misbegotten ideas of the Greeks
offers us a key to his handling of an even more delicate task, the separation of the
classical apparatus of his poem from an undesirable paganism. This he will do in
part through Genius' renunciation of Venus; but here and earlier he has been
preparing the groundwork for that dramatic occasion. What we must notice is the
manner in which the Greek deities are finally dismissed. His approach is two-
fold. As he introduces each deity (with the interesting exception of Venus, who
sprang up from Saturn's severed genitals 'be weie of kind,' 859) he stresses that
all were human beings who, for various reasons, were worshipped by later
generations. Thus, Saturnus was the king of Crete (845), and Jupiter, Juno,
Neptune and Pluto his children by wives Rea and Sibeles (849, 852, 1135-46);
Mars, a Dacian, was deified by the military exploits of his two sons, Romulus
and Remus (883-84; 900-08); Apollo was a hunter, an idle harper and a
wandering fortune-teller (915-36); Mercury, a thief, a murderer, a sorcerer, and
a common liar (938-40; 946-47); Eolus the king of Sicily (967-68); Pan a skilled
Arcadian herdsman, from the 'Cite Stinfalides' (1007; 1016-19; 1038-42);
Bachus the offspring of adulterous Jupiter and Semele (1044-45); Esculapius a
surgeon slain by Jupiter in a quarrel over a girl (1058-64); Hercules 'a man was
full of sinne' (1098); Minerva an orphaned child (1189-94); 'Pallas' the daughter
of Pallant, 'a cruel man, a bataillous' (1211); Ceres the second wife of Saturn
(1232-33) and mother of Proserpina (1277-78); Diana another child of Jupiter's
philandering (1249-51); Manes, a group of 'men also that were dede/ Thei
hadden [as] goddes' (1361-63); and the 'Satiri,' the 'Nimphes,' the 'Driades,'
and 'Naiades' either imaginary or, like the 'Nereides' (the drowned daughters of
'Dorus whilom king of Grece,' 1337-42), more human beings worshipped by
ignorant folk.

Gower's insistence on the humanity of the Greek gods permits him to develop
a parallel strategy for dismissing them based upon their behavior. The so-called
gods of the Greeks, Gower takes care to demonstrate, were many of them no
more than flagrant criminals: adulterers (Jupiter), liars (Mercury), killers
(Jupiter, Mercury), rapists (Mars), mountebanks (Apollo), pirates (Neptune),
drunks (Bacchus), even cannibals (Saturn) and perpetrators of incest (Jupiter,

Venus, Cupid). Being men, all are of course culpable, and subject to God's condemnation in specifically Christian terms. This justifies Gower's application of pejorative Christian vocabulary, such as 'dampnacion,' 'sinne,' 'lecherie,' etc., to the Greek deities — an important consideration, since it is primarily through this vocabulary that Gower succeeds in bringing the troublesome Greek beliefs within contemporary moral reach. One comment is particularly telling (1318-19):

> And thus the Greks lich to the bestes
> The men in stede of god honoure.

This we should interpret as both a *précis* of his description of the Greek pantheon and as a deliberate echo of the 'worst' animal worship of the Egyptians. (Gower's elaboration of the incestuous marriage of Jupiter and Juno assists here, by recalling the similar relationship of the Egyptian central pair Isis and Osiris.) The connection invokes Gower's approach to the entire 'Religions' section. It is after all on the Greeks that the origin of idols is blamed (V, 1523-28):

> . . . Promotheus was tofore
> And fond the ferste craft therfore,
> And Cirophanes, as thei telle,
> Thurgh conseil which was take in helle,
> In remembrance of his lignage
> Let setten up the ferste ymage.

When the bible swells with references to the idolatry of the Egyptians and the Chaldeans, this is curious; but, given Gower's program for the 'Religions' section, it makes sense. Serving false gods of *every* form has the same cause and will yield the same results. While men occupy a higher place on the Chain of Being than either elements or beasts (and so might be, in some way, more appropriately deified than lower orders), they are still 'creatures,' not the creator. Man acts irrationally when he fails to separate what has been made from its maker. In doing so, man descends the Chain, becoming (like the Egyptians, or the Greeks in the lines above) 'lich to the bestes,' to which reason is foreign. Moreover Gower suggests that in worshipping his own image man repeats the fall of Lucifer, whose deception is pointedly blamed for the Greeks' mistakes (1586-90):

> And thus the fend fro dai to dai
> The worschipe of ydolatrie
> Drawn forth upon the fantasie
> Of hem that weren thanne blinde
> And couthen nought the trouthe finde.

Ultimately, Gower would appear to be saying, the Greeks and the 'fend' outsmarted themselves, blindly taking 'fantasie' for 'trouthe.'

The approach has much value in the *Confessio*. With it Gower deflects questions of pagan involvement in the arts and sciences, and particularly in the fiction of his own poems. All that he uses, he might claim, is the grain of Greek discovery (the art and figures of poetry, for example) shaken clean of what he demonstrably understands is the chaff of misbelief. Thus he is able to turn the Greeks to hand as the righteous do Lucifer, to build a lesson upon the very act of distinguishing the helpful mythologies from the corruptive; for he clearly accepts the fact that the Greeks, if they were deluded about much, nonetheless had much to offer, particularly as sources for the language of medieval learned discourse. The problem is knowing truth from delusion — and (for poets like himself) showing your readers that you do.

Thus, even if Gower had no larger purposes with the entire 'Religions' section, his poem might have included a discussion of Greek theogony. But Gower did have other purposes. Having shown the error of the Chaldeans, the Egyptians and the Greeks, he goes on to illustrate how God enlightened mankind successfully, first through revelations to the Jews and then finally by taking human shape. Here the figure of Lucifer, introduced in the discussion of the Greeks, is developed more fully. Like Lucifer, first of the angels, the Jews began as God's chosen people (1599-1600), only to fall into condemnation through an obstinate refusal to accept Christian mysteries (V, 1701-06; 1712-25):

> Whan Lucifer was *best* in hevene
> And oghte most have stonde in evene,
> Towardes god he tok debat;
> And for that he was obstinat,
> And wolde noght to trouthe encline,
> He *fell* for evere into ruine . . .
> And riht be such a maner weie
> The Jwes in here *beste* plit,
> Whan that thei scholden most parfit
> Have stonde upon the prophecie,
> Tho *fellen* thei to most folie,
> *And him which was fro hevene come,*
> And of a Maide his fleissh hath nome
> And was among hem bore and fedd,
> As men that wolden noght be spedd
> Of goddes Sone, with o vois
> Thei hinge and slowhe upon the crois.
> Wherof the parfit of here lawe
> Fro thanne forth hem was withdrawe,
> So that thei stonde of no merit.

This is a lengthy passage, but it tells us a great deal in several ways. Gower's emphasis (1717 ff.) on the incarnation is particularly efficacious. It clarifies the Jews' resemblance to Lucifer, in that both he and they had the opportunity to look on God 'in the flesh,' and turned away. It also calls attention once again to Gower's central objection to pagan religions. Christianity is unique in its insistence on the living presence of the creator amongst the world of his creation.[30] The corporeality of Christ is consequently stressed here in Gower's description of the roots of Christianity — Jesus's engendering in a human mother, his birth and feeding as a baby, his torment and death on the cross. This miraculous humanity of the Christian deity contrasts sharply with the mistaken attempts of the pagan religions to embody God. Their best attempts — pantheism, anthropomorphism, obstinancy — are false incarnations, and hence failures.

Gower's description here is subtly crafted to establish and illuminate this contrast. Puns on 'best' and 'beast' in the lines above (1701, 1713) draw the Jews into the controversial vortex also, casting them among the idolatrous with an oblique reminder that they too failed to recognize the creator among created things.[31] The pun again connects the Jews with Lucifer, who was 'best' in heaven before his irrational pride made him 'bestial;' and it receives support from the repeated 'fell/ fellen' used to describe both Lucifer's decline (1706) and that of the Jews into 'most folie' (1716). Together, these 'falls' contrast with the (glorious) descent of 'him which was fro hevene come' (1717) — Christ, not Lucifer, whose journey from above (1718) accomplishes the incarnation ('And of a Maide his fleissh hath nome,' etc.) and leads to a second corporeal miracle, the crucifixion, by which man is able to regain his forfeited place in heaven. Christ's 'fall' is thus an ascent. As such, it reverses Lucifer's downward path (he also 'came from heaven'), just as Christianity's message will finally restore the 'parfit' to the now-meritless 'lawe' of the Jews (1723). Looking backward over the entire 'Religions of the World' section from this vantage, the economy and effectiveness of Gower's development is striking. By ordering his religions according to the Great Chain of Being, Gower's various descriptions present theologic history as evolutionary, a steady growing away from the grosser pagan attempts at incarnation, toward a Christian wisdom which is 'man-centered' in the truest sense. Looking forward too, we can see that this treatment has significance also for the design of the *Confessio* as a whole.

---

[30] John T.A. Robinson makes the case lucidly; see his *The Human Face of God* (Philadelphia, 1973), pp. 19-32, 102-113. Medieval attitudes toward the doctrine, from Ambrose to Ockham, Duns Scotus and Trivet, are traced thoroughly by Johannes T. Ernst, *Die Lehre der hochmittelalterlichen Theologen von den völlkommenen Erkenntnis Christi: Ein Versuch zur Auslegung der klassischen Dreiteilung: Visio Beata, Scientia infusa und Scientia acquisita* (Freiburg, 1971). And see further Paul Ricoeur, *The Symbolism of Evil*, trans. Emerson Buchanan (New York, 1967), pp. 259-78, on 'The "Adamic" Myth and the "Eschatological" Vision of History.

[31] Intended here also may be a reference to Old Testament errors like the golden calf and the regression of the Danites. On Jewish distinctions of creator/created with reference to Lucifer, see Ricoeur, *Symbolism of Evil*, p. 259.

This may be understood a bit more clearly if we now turn to Genius' rejection
of Venus and Cupid. As we noted earlier, this treatment is often cited as an
example of Gower's inability to handle architectonic matters with competence.
Certainly at first glance the case seems strong against him. Genius himself
appears aware of his tenuous position, replying to Amans's query, why he has
omitted Venus and Cupid from his descriptions of the Greek gods (V, 1381-82):

> Mi Sone, I have it left for schame,
> Be cause I am here oghne Prest.

Genius explains that Venus 'fond to lust a weic.' With Jupiter, 'hire oghne
brother,' she got Cupid — and he, 'Whan he was come unto his Age,' 'his moder
dorste love.' Not content with incest, Venus went on to invent prostitution and
sow wantonness among women of rank, including Semiramis and 'faire
Neabole.' As a result (1441-43):

> . . . men hire clepen the goddesse
> Of love and ek of gentilesse,
> Of worldes lust and of plesance.

Genius's portrait of his goddess is thus a far cry from Christ's mother, with
whom Venus is contrasted as a mother herself — but with what consorts, and of
what children?[32] Here Gower's poem seems dangerously close to splitting
asunder between opposing pressures, amorous and Christian.

Yet the work of several modern scholars — C. S. Lewis, E.C. Knowlton,
George D. Economou and Jane Chance among them — have given us reason to
look again, and more closely, at what Gower means when Genius takes Venus to
task.[33] The Middle Ages recognized two Venuses, one good and one sinful, as

---

[32] Gower makes a point of spelling out Venus's waywardness; 'in sondry place,' he says
(V, 1390-95):
> Diverse men felle into grace,
> And such a lusti lif sche ladde,
> That sche diverse children hadde,
> Nou on be this, nou on be that.

[33] C.S. Lewis, in *The Allegory of Love*, pp. 361-63, takes up the issue of the two Geniuses.
E.C. Knowlton has dealt with Genius, Nature, and Venus in several articles, including
'The Allegorical Figure Genius,' *Classical Philology* 15 (1920), 380-84; 'Genius as an
Allegorical Figure,' *Modern Language Notes* 39 (1924), 89-95; and 'The Goddess Nature in
Early Periods,' *JEGP* 19 (1920), 224-53. George D. Economou has looked particularly at
Genius and at Nature in two publications, 'The Character Genius in Alan de Lille, Jean
de Meun, and John Gower,' *Chaucer Review* 4 (1970), 203-10; and *The Goddess Natura in
Medieval Literature* (Cambridge, MA, 1972). Jane Chance (Nitzsche) has produced the
most helpful and extensive study of Genius to date, *The Genius Figure in Antiquity and the
Middle Ages* (New York, 1975). See further Maureen Quilligan, *The Language of Allegory:
Defining the Genre* (Ithaca, NY, 1979), pp. 242-46.

well as two equally dissimilar Geniuses. Because men do not consistently follow their reason, it was believed, these good and wicked figures were often mixed up. Indeed, Amans' condition, an old man pursuing a young girl, is evidence that he himself has done so. The origins of the two Venuses and Geniuses are of course very old, and for the most part do not concern us until late Roman times. By then, as Chance has shown, both deities represented aspects of procreative worship, with Venus understood as a generative force, and Genius as a 'birth-god,' or living essence of human nature.[34] For the Christian allegorists of the Middle Ages, the figures of Venus and Genius became a splendid raw material, to be molded afresh for different service. Suggestions of how the tradition will develop are clear in the work of both Bernard Silvestris and Claudian; but it is to the *De Planctu Naturae* of Alan of Lille that we must look for the first key to Gower's treatment of Venus.[35]

Alan portrays the great figure of Nature, 'Dei auctoris vicaria,' confessing her lot: Venus, her assistant in the never-ending task of universal generation, has deserted her and, instead of encouraging a wholesome fertility, has turned to idleness and fruitless lust.[36] Worse, man has been caught up in this change of Venus from *pronuba* and *genetrix* to *luxuria*.[37] Sexual adventurism and all types of perversity now occupy human energies. After a lengthy presentation of the case against man, Nature decides he has rejected the dictates of reason, and deserves excommunication. She summons her other assistant, Genius. For Nature, Genius fills a priestly office ('qui mihi in sacerdotali ancillatur officio'), and is a figure of much authority. (In her summoning letter, she addresses him as her double — 'Genio, sibi alteri' — and as one bound to her by the knot of love ('nodo dilectionis praecordialis astringer').[38] When Genius arrives, he excommunicates the sinners, and the poem is ended.

Alan's version is the source of Gower's two Venuses. So great was the influence of *De Planctu* that its authority could only stand behind any subsequent work limned in its tradition as both a support and a shadow, simultaneously to be

---

[34] See Chance (Nitzsche), *Genius Figure*, pp. 15-17 and 21-41.

[35] Knowlton, 'Allegorical Figure,' is the first to point out the use by Claudian of Genius in a manner leading to the later tradition. On Bernard Silvestris, see particularly Chance (Nitzsche), *Genius Figure*, pp. 65-87, and E. R. Curtius, *European Literature*, pp. 106-13.

[36] Alan presents Natura as God's vicar, and a kind of 'coiner' of all living things: 'Me igitur tanquam sui vicariam, rerum generibus sigillandis monetarium destinavit . . . ' (*Liber de Planctu*, Prosa 4, ed. Häring). About Venus he leaves no doubt. Bored with her daily task of initiating the business of creation ('cotidianique laboris ingruentia exequendi propositum appetitus extinguitur'), she left her husband Hymenaeus and 'began to live in fornication and concubinage' with one 'Antigamus' ('coepit cum Antigamo concubinarie fornicari'); see *Liber de Planctu*, Prosa 5, ed. Häring.

[37] 'Homo autem qui fere totum divitiarum mearum exhausit aerarium, naturae naturalia denaturare pertemptans, in me scelestae Veneris armat iniuriam' ['Man, however, who has all but drained the entire treasury of my riches, tries to denature the natural things of nature and arms a lawless and solecistic Venus to fight against me']. Text from *Liber de Planctu*, prosa 4, ed. Häring, trans. by James J. Sheridan, *Alan of Lille: The Plaint of Nature* (Toronto, 1980), p. 163.

[38] *Liber de Planctu*, Prosa 8.

acknowledged and accounted for. It was not Gower's only model, however. As he did on other occasions, Gower turned also to the *Roman de la Rose* for his gods of love. Jean de Meun extracted a great deal from the *De Planctu*, including the characters Venus, Natura and the priest Genius. Nonetheless, his outlook was less sanguine than Alan's. For Jean, human virtuous proclivities seemed an opportunity for satire. Thus, while the names of characters in the *Roman* are familiar from *De Planctu*, their roles and relationships have been altered significantly.

On first glance, Nature in the *Roman* seems very much like Natura in Alan's work. She still occupies her forge, hammering out the multitudinous shapes of creation, and she has an opinion of man similar to that in *De Planctu*, which leads her to excommunicate the sinners.[39] Again, it is man, of all creation, who is acting unnaturally. The differences, however, are more numerous than the likenesses. No longer is reason a gift of Nature to humanity; she gives man life and body, but not his understanding which, since it not subject to corruption, can only come from God.[40] Man's rational powers are thus presented in the *Roman* as decidedly 'other': because they are not engendered in the same way, they are often at odds with the physical. The stage is set, in short, for the war between mind and body, the terms in which Jean understood the world.[41]

Having separated the natural from the rational, Jean was free to alter further Alan's cosmos. He did this by strengthening Venus in her role as concupiscent goddess and by modifying the functions of Nature and Genius. No longer have they any involvement with the spiritual side of man, but only with the body, with the procreative. As John Fisher has pointed out:

> Jean de Meun's presentation in the *Roman de la Rose* is largely deterministic. Nature is God's vicar on earth. Genius, her priest, is potency. Venus is sexual passion. In their amoral view, the only sin is shirking Nature's work.[42]

---

[39] Jean shows nature occupied at her forge, 'An forgier singulieres pieces/ Por continuer les espieces' (*Roman*, ed. Lecoy, 15867-68). Her attitude toward mankind is clear from her confession: Man alone of all creatures has betrayed her ('Cist me fet pis que nus louveaus,' 19024).

[40] See *Roman*, ed. Lecoy, 19025-28:
>   San faille de l'antandemant,
>   Connois je bien que vraiemant
>   Celui ne li donai je mie,
>   La ne s'estant pas ma baillie

['Man's understanding I know very well, believe me, is something I do not provide him; it is outside my power'].

[41] It is this attitude which has led readers like John Fleming to see Jean's extension of the *Roman* as a satire critical of human behavior and opinion represented by the various figures. See Fleming, *Roman de la Rose*, 19 ff. Similar attitudes are held by Rosamund Tuve, *Allegorical Imagery* (Princeton, NJ, 1966), 268-330, and Charles Dahlberg, *The Romance of the Rose by Guillaume de Lorris and Jean de Meun* (Princeton, NJ, 1971), in the preface to his translation.

[42] Fisher, *John Gower*, p. 161.

Nature and Genius thus find no distinction between man and the lower animals: man must depend upon himself. Judging from the outcome of the *Roman*, it is clear that Jean de Meun had little faith in human ability to make and maintain such a distinction either. Like Nature herself in this respect, humanity is too easily separated from reason by fleshly desire. Of course, so negative a view is a perversion of what Nature and Genius are arguing, and although they fail to see it, Jean himself did not. Indeed, it is a measure of his cynicism that Nature and Genius, by fulfilling their roles as 'deterministic' procreators, can be led so easily astray by Venus and Amor, whose purpose is not generation but sexual intercourse for its own sake. In this regard it is telling that while in *De Planctu* Genius removes his secular robes to don his vestments before invoking the excommunication ('post vulgaris vestimenti depositionem, sacerdotalis indumenti ornamentis celebrioribus honestius infulatus'), in the *Roman de la Rose* he leaves behind his religious garments, putting on worldly garb, as if he were going to a dance.[43] Later, it is Cupid, Venus son and aide, who gives Genius rudimentary vestments just before he exhorts the barons in an address corresponding in position and importance, if not content, to his excommunication speech in *De Planctu*.[44] As George Economou suggests, the refrocking of Genius by Cupid is 'an instance of Jean's ironic use of details from Alan,' and also something more.[45] It signifies the enlistment of Nature's priest into the service of love, a transformation which is completed when a laughing Venus thrusts into Genius grasp a burning candle ('ardant cierge' specifically made from non-virgin wax ('qui ne fu pas de cire vierge'). Ostensibly the taper is intended to reinforce his diatribe ('por plus enforcier l'anatesme'), but in the context of the *Roman* the phallic symbolism is blatant.

Gower, then, inherited a tradition at once familiar in its broad outline, and perplexingly compounded in detail. Nor did the work of his contemporaries make matters simpler. In the *Parlement of Foules*, Chaucer describes Nature, Cupid and Venus in complex relation to each other. (Genius does not appear.) Since it is reasonable to assume Gower knew the *Parlement*, Chaucer's version ought to be mentioned in a list of Gower's probable antecedents.

---

[43] See Häring, *Liber de Planctu*, Prosa 9; compare with *Roman* 19404-08:

> Lors va tout pandre a un crochet,
> Et vest sa robe seculier
> Qui mains anconbreuse li ere,
> Si con s'il alast queroler,
> Et prant eles por tost voler.

['He hung his vestments on a hook and put on less confining secular clothing, as if he were going to a dance, and took flight swiftly.']

[44] 'Tantost li dieux d'Amours affuble/ A Genius une chasuble . . . .' *Roman*, 19447 ff.

[45] Economou, 'The Character of Genius,' p. 207. He goes on to point out that at this moment, 'The priest of procreation has unwittingly become the priest of Love, and his message and promise of paradise becomes the means through which Venus and Cupid inspire the barons to begin their victorious assault,' p. 208.

Chaucer's Nature is straight out of the *De Planctu*. She is for him as for Alan the 'vicaire of the almyghty Lord' (*PF* 316). For his characterization of Venus, however, Chaucer clearly drew much from Jean de Meun. Although there is possibly in the presence of Bacchus and Ceres at Venus's either hand in the *Parlement* a slight suggestion that she was once Nature's good assistant as in *De Planctu*, there is no doubt whose version of the tradition Chaucer was following. In a temple filled with 'sykes hoote as fyr/ . . . engendered with desyr' Venus is kept close company by 'the bittere godess Jelosye' and by Priapus, 'hys sceptre in honde' (*PF* 246-56). Venus herself appears with loose hair, bare bosom, and transparent garments (*PF* 267-73). On the walls of her temple are the broken bows of maidens, no longer followers of chaste Diana, who 'here tymes waste In Venus servyse;' and frescoes of the unhappy lovers of antiquity and chivalric romance:

> Semyramis, Candace, and Hercules,
> Biblis, Dido, Thisbe and Piramus,
> Tristram, Isaude, Paris, and Achilles,
> Eleyne, Cleopatre, and Troylus,
> Silla, and ek the moder of Romulus . . .[46]

In the *Parlement* as in the *Roman*) then, Venus is a deity of sexual passion, not procreation. This latter function — seemingly to Chaucer the more worthy — is Nature's and Nature's alone, as in Alan's poem. Chaucer thus has combined elements of both earlier works to create a version with which he could feel philosophically compatible. His reworking also sets a precedent which Gower in his own manner may have followed.

Gower's most obvious deviation from all these antecedents is his apparent elimination of Nature from the pantheon. In the *Confessio*, Cupid is present as Venus's consort, Genius is her 'oghne Clerk' (*CA* I, 196), and it is in her name, not Nature's, that the priest pursues Amans's shrift. The initial impression left by the *Confessio*, then, is of its dependency on the *Roman de la Rose*, where Venus Luxuria replaces Natura as chief motivating force. This interpretation seems at first confirmed when, in Book VIII, the shriven Amans offers up his prayer to Venus, not Nature. Yet Nature is not in fact removed from the sphere of the *Confessio*. In his lengthy complaint, Amans draws her into the proceedings by addressing her first, before appealing to Venus or Cupid. His treatment here

---

[46] *PF* 288-92. Significantly, Cupid is placed outside this temple, 'Under a tre, besyde a welle,' and it seems likely that Chaucer, correctly reading Jean de Meun's intentions for Amor, substituted Priapus as a less ambiguous and tradition-laden representative of potency. This allowed Chaucer to maintain an implied connection of Cupid and Nature within the lines laid down by Alan — an important factor in the poem which may have established the tradition of St. Valentine's Day in England. See Jack B. Oruch, 'St. Valentine, Chaucer, and Spring in February,' *Speculum* 56 (1981), 534-65.

shows how fully Gower understood her function within the pattern established by
Alan. Nature, Amans states (VIII, 2232-33), 'techeth me the weie/ To love,' for
(2225-28):

> . . . every creature
> Som time ayer hath love in his demeine,
> So that the litel wrenne in his mesure
> Hath yit of kind a love under his cure.

Nature here corresponds to the generational urge present in every living thing,
undifferentiated along the Great Chain of Being. Her command represents the
'lawe of kinde,' or the *lex naturali*, distinguished from other binding powers by
canon law.[47] Venus rules the amorous with Cupid, and employs Genius as an
assistant. Echoes of Jean de Meun's division of responsibility are strong here — it
is apparent how closely Gower read the *Roman* — yet the *Confessio*'s synthesis of
ideas finally rejects Jean's cynicism and dark irony. Gower's Venus establishes
this unequivocally as she banishes lovers whose vices have offended Nature, those
'wherof that sche fulofte hath pleigned.' Such lovers violate natural law. They are
unwelcome in Venus' court (2346-49):

> Mi court stant alle courtz above
> And takth noght into retenue
> Bot thing which is to kinde due,
> Or elles it schal be refused.

[47] Possibly because of his legal training, the concept of natural law was extremely
important to Gower, and figures prominently in all of his works, including the *Confessio*.
In the *Institutiones* of Justinian, and in Gratian's *Decretum* (I, Dist. i-ii), the *lex naturali*
figures at its simplest level to be the call to generation to which all living creatures
respond. In Justinian's words (*Lib.* I, tit. ii 'Natural law is that which Nature teaches all
animate creatures: for that law is not peculiar to humans, but [extends] to all animate
creatures, those born in the heavens or in the sea' ('. . . quod natura omnia animalia
docuit: nam jus istud hon humani generis proprium est, sed omnium animalium, quae in
caelo, quae in mari, nascuntur'). Kurt Olsson, in a recent study of the question, has
identified five different meanings for *Jus naturae* in the *Confessio Amantis* alone; see his
'Natural Law and John Gower's *Confessio Amantis*,' *Medievalia et Humanistica*, N.S. 11
(1982), 231-61, where he argues that the notion is ultimately replaced by divine grace, as
an integral pattern of the poem. What Gower is up to, however, he elegantly states in the
second poem of the *Traitié*, ll. 1-4:
> De l'espirit l'amour quiert continence
> Et vivre chaste en soul dieu contemplant;
> Li corps par naturele experience
> Quiert femme avoir, dont soit multipliant.

['Spiritual love seeks continence, and to live chastely, contemplating God alone; the body,
guided by natural experience, seeks to have a woman, so that it may multiply.']

Venus's role in the *Confessio Amantis* then is precisely that intended for her by Natura in *De Planctu*. Again, she is Nature's 'subminister,' Venus Genetrix to a Natura Pronuba, who has been all along the great shape in the background of Gower's poem.

Gower thus overcomes the problem of duality in the traditional amorous imagery he inherited. Even in *De Planctu* there were two Venuses, and consequently two Cupids.[48] This plurality was emphasized for subsequent writers by Jean de Meun's focus on the fleshliness of Venus and Cupid, and by his presentation of Genius as their dupe. Chaucer, who by keeping Cupid apart from Venus' temple to suggest how some of the onus might be removed from the gods of love, nonetheless also separated the goddess from Natura in the *Parlement*, thereby perpetuating Jean's Venus. Against such a series of precedents, it was impossible for Gower to use Venus, Cupid or Genius 'straight.' By the late fourteenth century their characters — and amorous discourse generally — were too ambiguous. As a result, Gower had to separate these dual personalities, and keep them strictly apart, in order to rectify, and restore meaning to, the language applied to love.[49]

What he needed to accomplish this was a device, and he found it in the section on 'Religions of the World' in Book V. Convenient precedent for a condemnation of the Greek deities existed in the *De Planctu*.[50] There, in response to a query about the many wanton loves of the gods, Natura retorts that only one unified ruler exists. All accounts of pagan gods and goddesses are the creation of irresponsible poets and heretics.[51] The conjunction of blame is fortuitous, for it reflects Gower's own concerns with false religions and with false poets, epitomized by Jean de Meun. This passage may very well have been the *germe fecondo* of Gower's 'Religions' section. He would have been aware, in any case, of the problem of Greek mythology raised and answered in *De Planctu*, and, as we have seen, attempted to dispel it. Following Alan's example, Gower circumvented the difficulty of denying some gods while accepting others as

---

[48] I am indebted to George Economou's insights (especially *The Goddess Natura*, pp. 125-50) for much of this discussion, and also to D.W. Robertson, Jr., 'The Doctrine of Charity in Medieval Literary Gardens: A Topical Approach through Symbolism and Allegory,' *Speculum* 26 (1951), 24-49.

[49] Cupid's role has been studied extensively by Thomas R. Hyde; see his unpublished Yale dissertation, 'Love's Pageants: The Figure of Cupid in the Poetry of Edmund Spenser' (1978).

[50] For discussion, see Winthrop Wetherbee, *Platonism and Poetry in the Twelfth Century* (Princeton, NJ, 1972), pp. 187 ff.

[51] Alan is working from the classical mistaking of 'true' poets by false mythologizers, e.g.: 'Quid ergo, ut poetae testati sunt, si plerique homines praedicamentalibus Veneris terminis ad litteram sunt abusi? Narratio vero illa, quae vel deos esse, vel eos in Veneris gymnasiis lascivisse, mentitur, et in nimiae fasitatis vesperascit occasum' ['Because, then, many men, as we know from the testimony of the poets, have misused, by a literal interpretation, the terms applied to Venus, this account of theirs which falsely states that there is a plurality of gods or that these gods have wantoned in the playgrounds of Venus, comes to the evening and sunset that await extreme falsehood']. Text from Häring, *Liber de Planctu*, Prosa 4; trans. Sheridan, *Plaint*, pp. 141.

'necessary' parts of the fiction. He equated Nature, Cupid and Venus with procreative forces, labelled them servants of God. The figure Genius undercuts in the *Confessio*, then, is also repudiated by Alan and (implicitly) by Chaucer as well — Venus Luxuria, the renegade double so prominent in the *Roman de la Rose*. What Gower is saying through Genius is, in effect, 'Be careful. Sexuality is a pluralistic force. When wrongly understood it is sinful since it drives men to lust. In broader terms it is heretical too, in that like a false religion it contravenes the *lex naturali* of God.' The entire section on 'Religions of the World,' then, is crowned by Genius's rejection of the 'other' Venus. This 'excommunication,' like the whole section, plays an integral role in the multifaceted poem that is the *Confessio Amantis*. Far from being a digression, or a contradiction of the poem's fictive premises, Gower's development of the world's religions past and present demonstrates instead an intricate learning and a masterful control.

III

Reference to the surrounding tradition lets us understand Gower's Venus and Genius, and their places in the *Confessio Amantis*. To feel the same confidence about the structure of Book VI, we must approach the problem similarly, taking note not only of how Gower handled his material, but also of the conventions informing it. Only about half of the sixth Book is devoted to what most of us expect when we learn that its subject will be Gluttony, i.e., the first 126 lines on 'Dronkeschipe' and 'Delicacie' in eating. The latter portion of Book VI condemns 'Sorcery and Witchcraft' — and surprises many. A man in love, Gower says, is comparable to a drunkard or a gormandizer, driven by appetite. Such a one will not stop short even of the black arts to satisfy his craving (VI, 1307-10):

> For rathere er he scholde faile,
> With Nigromance he wole assaile
> To make his incantacioun
> With hot subfumigacioun.

Now, since there is no apparent necessity for the love-besotted to turn exclusively to magic to gain his or her ends (why not murder, say, or extortion?), the linkage seems contrived. Three approaches to the predicament suggest themselves. The first is authorial ineptitude: Gower thought little of coherent structure, preferring to cobble in a good story or two when — or wherever, regardless of larger effects. But this, while adopted by several puzzled readers in the past, is not Gower's way as I understand it.[52] A second approach is that

---

[52] I have in mind here such readers as Donald G. Schueler; see his 'Some Comments on the Structure of John Gower's *Confessio Amantis*', in *Explorations of Literature*, ed. Rima D. Reck, Louisiana State University Studies, 18 (Baton Rouge, 1966), pp. 15-24.

Gower created a purposeful digression here. Perhaps (like Chaucer's Pardoner) he was accumulating a *mélange* of sins for rhetorical effect, sins not strictly connected but which, with the power inherent in their naming, could foster a productive climate for a lesson to take hold. A bit of merit adheres to such a reading (it at least acknowledges Gower's otherwise-deliberate habits of composition), although it too presents problems. It presumes that Gower trusted his audience to seek no firm connections between the two halves of Book VI — that they would be sufficiently fascinated, or daunted, by the *outré* tales to follow as to raise no objection to their placement. The Pardoner pulls this off, such an argument might run; why not Gower's Genius? But there are obvious differences between the Pardoner and Genius as narrators we cannot ignore. We have seen enough in five and a half Books to know the Confessor no master of the dazzling con. To find a Pardoner in him now would cast into doubt all the delicate portraiture built up before. And it would mark as well a significant departure from Gower's own authorial practice established over the same expansive distance. Elsewhere when he 'digresses,' Gower has forewarned his readers with explanations built into the fiction. We might compare the fictive justification for Book VII (Amans asks to know 'Hou Alisandre was betawht,' VI, 241 ff.), or the *apologia* offered in Book I for writing in a new style about a new subject (1-9):

> I may noght strecche up to hevene
> Myn hand, ne setten al in evene
> This world, which evere is in balance:
> It stant noght in my sufficance
> So grete thinges to compasse.
> Bot I mot lete it overpasse
> And treten upon othre thinges.
> Forthi the Stile of my writinges
> Fro this day forth I thenke change . . .

What seems truer, then, given such precedents, is that Gower like the Pardoner assumed a context which would have rendered his remarks clear for his audience without further explanation. This context, I believe, was a tradition which included, under Gluttony, not only excessive eating and drinking, but also great oath-taking and blasphemy, sorcery, witchcraft, and devil worship as well.[53]

For clues to the source of such a tradition, we might turn to one more of the Canterbury Pilgrims, the Parson. Both Pardoner and Parson draw their imagery and language from the same general body of background literature, the group of penitential treatises which sprang up after the decision of the Lateran Council of

---

[53] Morton W. Bloomfield suggests this connection, but does not bring together, or draw conclusions from, the evidence of his sources. See *The Seven Deadly Sins: An Introduction to the History of a Religious Concept, with Special Reference to Medieval English Literature* (East Lansing, 1952), pp. 183-84.

1215 to require confession. Gower too is dependent on these treatises for the structures and vocabulary of the *Confessio Amantis*, which betrays its origins even with its title. Modern scholarship has shown, further, that sermons and homiletic materials shaped the utterances of Parson and Pardoner, and of Gower's priest Genius.[54] Here was a fertile relationship between art and theological necessity bearing fruit of many kinds. We should not therefore be surprised to discover broad areas of agreement of ideas amongst the *Confessio*, the Parson and the Pardoner, manuals of religious instruction, and selected sermons.

An examination of this background material suggests that to penitential writers and preachers Gluttony was a chief cause of loose speech. Raymond of Pennaforte for example notes in a work which Gower and Chaucer knew, his *Summa casuum poenitentiae*, that *ventris ingluvie* leads to, among other evils, *scurrilitas* and *multiloquium*; and similarly in the Anglo-Norman *Compileison* (which shares many features with the 'Parson's Tale,' whether or not Chaucer actually used it as a source) we find that 'gule' is a primary cause of 'ueine parole,' one form of which is swearing.[55] And we possess sermons by various hands (including John Bromyard) in which 'blasphemyng God with many grett othes' and 'swerynge and slaunderynge' are represented as versions of, respectively, *Ebrietas* and *Gula*.[56] In these sermons too, and in penitentials, we find the image of the devil's church, chapel, or schoolhouse. This is defined explicitly in *The Book of Vices and Virtues*, a fourteenth-century English translation of the *Somme le Roi*, written a hundred years earlier by the Dominican friar Lorens d'Orleans:

þe tauerne is þe deueles scole hous, for þere studieþ his disciples, and þere lerneþ his scolers, and þere in his owne chapel, þere men and wommen redeþ and syngeþ and serueþ hym, and þere he doþ his myracles as longeþ þe deuel to do. In holy chirche is God ywoned to do

[54] Several recent studies have joined Chaucer's two preachers. See Daniel Knapp, ' "The Relyk of a Seint': A Gloss on Chaucer's Pilgrimage,' *ELH* 39 (1972), 1-26; Susan Gallick, 'A Look at Chaucer and His Preachers,' *Speculum* 50 (1975), 456-76; Frank Cespedes, 'Chaucer's Pardoner and Preaching,' *ELH* 44 (1977), 1-18; and Judith Davis Shaw, 'Gower's Illustrative Tales,' *Neuphilologische Mitteilungen* 84 (1983), 437-47. Shaw's 'Gower's Art in Transforming His Sources into Exempla of the Seven Deadly Sins,' Diss. Pennsylvania (1977), is also a valuable resource; and see further Owst, *Literature and Pulpit*, pp. 229 ff.
[55] For views of Chaucer's knowledge of the *Summa* and similar sources, see Bryan and Dempster, *Sources and Analogues*, pp. 72 ff.; H.G. Pfander, 'Some Medieval Manuals of Religious Instruction in England and Observations on Chaucer's Parson's Tale',' *JEGP* 35 (1936), 243-58; R. Hazelton, 'Chaucer's Parson's Tale and the *Moralium Dogma Philosophorum*,' *Traditio* 16 (1960), 255-64. An opposite argument is made by Siegfried Wenzel, 'The Source of the "Remedia" in the "Parson's Tale",' *Traditio* 27 (1971), 433-54, and 'The Source of Chaucer's Deadly Sins,' *Traditio* 30 (1974), 351-78, who shows that while Chaucer probably knew other sources, his major dependence in the *ParsT* was on the two texts Wenzel identifies. On Gower's acquaintance with, and possible use of, the *Somme le Roi*, see Fowler, *Une Source Française*, 2 ff.; and Dwyer, 'Gower's *Mirour*,' 482-505.
[56] Owst, *Literature and Pulpit*, pp. 436-37.

myracles and schewe his vertues: þe blynde to seen, þe croked to gon
riȝt, brynge wode men into here riȝt wytte, doumbe men to speke, deue
men to here herynge. But þe deuel doþ þe contrarie of al þis in þe
tauerne. For whan a glotoun goþ to þe tauerne he goþ riȝt ynow, and
whan he comeþ out he ne haþ no fot þat may bere hym; and whan he
goþ þidre he hereþ and seeþ and spekeþ and understandeþ , and whan
he comeþ þannes-ward alle þes ben y-lost, as he þat haþ no witt ne
resoun ne understondynge. Þes ben þe miracles þat þe deuel doþ.[57]

When the Pardoner condemns drunkards for doing 'devel sacrifise/ Withinne
that develes temple,' his language has its roots in this image of the tavern
common to all penitential tracts, including the *Ayenbite of Inwit*, *Pricke of Conscience*,
and *Handlyng Synne*, which base themselves on the *Somme le Roi*. (As far as I know,
the tavern/temple image, with the glutton doing his 'devel sacrifise,' does not
appear in tracts derived from the *Summa* of Pennaforte, the Anglo-Norman
Compileison, or Peraldus's *Summa de viciis et de virtutibus*.)

The distinction is important, as may be seen if we look more closely at what
'services,' or lessons, take place in the tavern. The author of *Jacob's Well*, a tract
based on the *Somme le Roi* and written about 1440, includes the passage quoted
above from the *Book of Vices and Virtues*, and goes on immediately to observe:

Now hereþ þe what lessoun he techyth his clerkys in þe scole of þe
tauerne. he techyth hem glotonye, leccerye, for-sweryng, slaunderyng,
bakbyting, to scorne, to chyde, to dyspyse, to reneye god, to stel, to
robbe, to fyȝte, to sle, and many oþere swich synnes. And þus he
heldyth hem be þe throte of glotonye in þe scholehus of his tauerne. he
techyth his dyscyples to mysgouerne here tungys.[58]

To 'mysgouerne here tungys' represents a key phrase in the differentiation of
the two groups of penitential books. Pennaforte, Peraldus and the author of the
Compileison consider Gluttony primarily in terms of eating and drinking. In the
Somme le Roi and its derivatives, however, the sin is handled quite differently. It is
itself made a part of a section entitled 'Sins of the Mouth':

Þe sevenþe heued of þe best is þe synne of mouþ. And for þe mouþ haþ
tweie offices, wher-of þat on serveþ to þe swelewyng of mete and drynk,
þat oþer serueþ to speche, and þerfore is þis pryncipally departed two:
þat is to seye, in þe synne of glotonye, þat is in mete and drynke, and in
þe synne of wikked tonge, þat is to speke folye.[59]

[57] *The Book of Vices and Virtues*, ed. W. Nelson Francis, EETS o.s., 217 (London, 1942), p.
53
[58] *Jacob's Well: An Englisht Treatise on Cleansing of Man's Conscience*, ed. Arthur Brandeis,
EETS o.s., 115 (London, 1900), p. 148.
[59] Francis, *Book of Vices*, p. 46.

The division into Gluttony, 'þat is in mete and drynke,' and 'wikked tonge, þat is to speke folye,' is very close to Gower's treatment in the *Confessio*. Indeed, Gower would seem to have had the *Somme* in mind when he says that, the branches of Gluttony being so many (VI, 12-14):

> . . . of hem alle I wol noght trete,
> Bot only as touchende of tuo
> I thenke speke and of no mo.

By these two he means 'Dronkeschipe' (VI, 15) and 'Delicacie,' or gormandizing (VI, 629) — that is, the familiar abuses 'in mete and drynke.' But what of Sorcery and Witchcraft, with which he completes the Book? If Gower were applying the *Somme*'s model of 'Sins of the Mouth,' and if these sins included witchcraft, the awkward yoking is transformed. It is therefore important that we see what Friar Lorens meant by 'wikked tonge.'

On one level, evidently, Lorens had in mind the *scurrilitas, multiloquium* and 'ueine parole' we have found attributed to drunkards by the Parson, the Pardoner, and other penitential sources. His reference to speaking 'folye' tells us that. But the *Somme* describes additional 'sins of the tongue':

> . . . we wole sette ten chef braunches þat comeþ of þis tree of wikkede tonge: udel, auantyng, losengerie, apeyre a man bihynde hym, þat is bakbityng, lesynges, forswerynges, stryuynges, grucchynges, rebbelynges, blasphemye, þat is to speke euele of God.[60]

Most of these sins are predictable. It is hardly surprising that an evil tongue should be guilty of lying, back-biting, or idle complaint. 'Blasphemye', however, Friar Lorens saw fit to define in detail:

> Blasphemye is a word, as seynt Austeyn seiþ, whan a man bileueþ or seiþ of God þing þat a man scholde not bileue ne holde ne seye, or whan a man ne bileue nouȝt þat he scholde holde. But propurly we clepen blasphemye whan a man mysseiþ of God or of halowen or of þe sacramentes of holy chirche, and it is also as it were to scorne God. Þis synne is ydo in many maneres, as when a man seiþ it as to-fore þou ȝt, as bougres and mysbileued folke, or as iogelours, or nygremancers, or enchauntours, or wycches, þat do it for couetise to wynne þerwiþ[61]

At the center of the *Somme*'s notion of blasphemy is a perversion of belief, to which the abuse of sacred language stands witness. Necromancy, enchantment

---

[60] Ibid., p. 55.
[61] Ibid., p. 67.

and witchcraft were forms of blasphemy and therefore — like Gluttony — sins of the mouth. The glutton who swears in his cups transgresses the same law as the heretic and witch because, like them, he uses powerful verbal symbols improperly. In so doing, he, like heretic and witch, debases the eternal truth extant behind the symbol.[62]

[62] The position is consistent with the Church's treatment of witchcraft from the seventh century. Until then, most Church dicta linked acts of magic to idolatry and pagan worship rather than heresy. (See for example the *Liber Poenitentialis* of Theodore of Canterbury, I, xv, 1-5, and the Penitential of St. Columban, no. 24 [both trans. John T. McNeill and Helena Gamer in *Medieval Handbooks of Penance* (New York, 1938), pp. 198 and 256, respectively]; also the *Lex romana Visigothorum*, or *Breviarum*, of Alaric II, IX, xiii, 3 [ed. Gustavus Haenel (Leipzig, 1849), pp. 18 ff.]. This latter passage is probably behind Isidore of Seville's subsequent interpretation of magic as incantations to demons; see *Etymologiarum sive originum*, ed. W.M. Lindsay [Oxford, 1911], VIII, 9, 9 ff.) As overt paganism disappeared, distinctions between it, heretical beliefs, and sorcery and witchcraft diminished. This is apparent in the conflation of terms in the *Canon Episcopi* of Regino of Prüm, ca. A.D. 900:

> Bishops and their officials must labor with all their strength to uproot thoroughly from their parishes the pernicious art of sorcery and malefice invented by the devil, and if they find a man or woman follower of this wickedness to eject them foully disgraced from their parishes . . . It is also not to be omitted that some wicked women perverted by the devil, seduced by illusions and phantasms of demons, believe and profess themselves, in the hours of the night, to ride upon certain beasts of Diana, the goddess of the pagans . . . and to obey her commands as of their mistress, and to be summoned to her service on certain nights. But would it were they alone who perished in their faithlessness and did not draw many with them into the destruction of infidelity. For an innumerable multitude, deceived by this false opinion, believe this to be true and, so believing, wander from the right faith and are involved in the error of the pagans when they think there is anything of divinity or power except the one God . . .

('Ut episcopi episcoporumque ministri omnibus viribus elaborare studeant ut perniciosam et a diabolo inventam sortilegam et maleficam artem penitus ex parochiis suis eradant, et si aliquem virum aut feminam hiuiscemodi sceleris sectatorem invenerint, turpiter dehonestatatum de parochiis suis eiciant . . . Illud etiam non omittendum, quod quaedam sceleratae mulieres retro post Satanam conversae, daemonum illusionibus et phantasmatibus seductae, credunt se et profitentur nocturnis horis cum Diana paganorum dea et innumera multitudine mulierum equitare super quasdam bestias, et multa terrarum spatia intempestate noctis silentio pertransire, eiusque iussionibus velut dominae obedire, et certis noctibus ad eius servitium evocari. Sed utinam hae solae in perfidia dus perissent, et non multos secum in infedelitatis interitum pertraxissent. Nam innumera multitudo fac falsa opinione decepta hae vera esse credit, et credendo a recta fide deviat et in errorem paganorum revolvitur, cum aliquid divinitatis aut numinis extra umun esse arbitratur.' See J.P. Migne, *Patrologia latina*, CXXXII, 352-53; and further Joseph Hanse, *Quellen und Untersuchungen zur Geschichte des Hexenwahns und der Hexenfolgung im Mittelalter* [Bonn, 1901; rpt. Hildesheim, 1963], pp. 38-39, and Henry C. Lea, *Materials toward a History of Witchcraft*, ed. Arthur Howland [Philadelphia, 1939; rpt. New York, 1957], I, 178-80.)

The *Canon Episcopi* had wide dissemination. It was incorporated in the tenth century into the *Corrector* and, later, the *Decretum*, of Burchard of Worms, in which form it probably reached Alexander of Hales, Aquinas, Gratian, and others. (See Lea, *Materials*, I, 187-92; Jeffrey Burton Russell, *Witchcraft in the Middle Ages* [Ithaca, N.Y., 1972], pp.

Following this theological tradition, then, are the poets Chaucer and Gower. Manuscripts of the *Somme le Roi* in French are numerous, and at least nine separate English translations of it have survived in copies datable before 1500.[63] So we may assume that Friar Lorens's classification of wicked magic and Gluttony as related sins would have been familiar to the audience of the Pardoner, Parson, and the *Confessio*. Set against the larger backdrop of this tradition, Gower's treatment of 'Sorcery and Witchcraft' alongside Gluttony in Book VI appears less arbitrary than commonly has been supposed. He was working with a convention his audience, and his fellow poet, would have understood and appreciated.

291-93, prints variations of the *Canon Episcopi* and Burchard's *Corrector*; and Migne, *Patrologia latina*, CXL, 949-1014.) It is therefore an essential document, because it formed a basis for much of what, in the later Middle Ages, was held most dangerous about witches: that they would lead believers first to 'wander from the true faith,' and thence to commit atrocious acts. It is not surprising therefore that in the great trials of the thirteenth and fourteenth centuries charges of heresy and witchcraft were intermingled with each other, and with suspected abominations of the flesh. This is the case in the prosecution of the Knights Templars, carried out between 1306 and 1314 by Edward II; and such charges played so major a role in the condemnation of the Cathars and Waldensians that two names for witches — 'gazara' (or 'gazarius') from 'Catharus' and 'wadensis' from 'Waldensis' — were derived from them. (On the trials of the Templars and the charges against them, see Jules Michelet, ed., *Le procès des Templiers*, 2 vols., in *Collection de documents inédits sur l'histoire de France* [Paris, 1841-51] and Julius Gmelin, *Schuld oder Unschuld des Templerordens: Kritischer Versuch zur Lösing der Frage*, 2vols. [Stuttgart, 1893], who gives and excellent summary of the trials. On 'Gazerius', see D. Ducange, *Glossarium mediae et infirmae latinitatis* (Graz, 1954), s.v. 'Gazara'; on 'Waudensis', see Frederic Godefroy, *Dictionnaire de l'ancienne langue française et tous ses dialects du IX au XV siècle* [Paris, 1938], s.v. 'Vauderie'; and further *MED*, 'bougre, bougeron' and *OED* 'bugger'.) By 1485, the connection of witchcraft with heresy and other crimes was complete. The *Malleus Maleficarum*, 'Hammer of Witchcraft,' a central edict of the Inquisition, cited as the first among the four essential characteristics of witchcraft the renunciation of the Christian faith. (See *Malleus Maleficarum*, trans. Montagu Summers [London, 1928; rpt. London, 1971], p. 225: 'Now the method of profession is twofold. One is solemn ceremony, like a solemn vow. The other is private, and can be made to the devil at any hour alone. The first method is when witches meet together in conclave on a set day, and the devil appears to them in the assumed body of a man, and urges them to keep faith with him . . . and they recommend a novice to his acceptance. And the devil asks whether she wlll abjure the faith, and forsake the holy Christian religion and the worship of the Anomalous Woman — for so they call the Most Blessed Virgin Mary — and never venerate the Sacraments . . .') Somewhat earlier witchcraft and swearing had become a commonplace pair, as species of blasphemy. Thus, the author of *Jacob's Well* (p. 156) records:

X. braunche of blasphemy is slandryng of god & of his seyntys, or to speke aȝens þe sacramentys of holy cherch; as charmeris, or wytches, or swererys, that wyth othys dyspysen godys body.

[63] Francis, *Book of Vices*, p. xix ff. lists 81 French manuscripts of the *Somme* (a dozen of which were in English libraries), and notes that 'Although the lists are twice as long as any I have seen, they are probably still incomplete.' He discusses English translations on pp. xxxii-xl.

Moreover, it is a convention wholly compatible with his poetic; of which, as if through a window, it offers us a helpful view. The similarities are especially revealing if we place them in the context of the Gospel of Matthew, where several passages suggest the appropriate relationship of deeds to speech and are, very probably, the biblical source for Friar Lorens' 'Sins of the Mouth.'

> Not that which goeth into the mouth defileth a man, but what cometh out of the mouth, this defileth a man . . . . Do you not understand, that whatsoever entereth the mouth, goeth into the belly, and is cast out into the privy? But the things which proceed out of the mouth, come from the heart, and those things defile a man. For from the heart come forth evil thoughts, murders, adulteries, fornications, thefts, false testimonies, blasphemies. These are the things that defile a man. (Matt. 15, 17-19)[64]

Christ's anger was stirred by the Pharisees's condemnation of the disciples for not washing their hands before they broke bread. His point is that eating, or the manner of eating, has nothing *per se* to do with sin; rather, it is the *cause* of the eating that may be sinful, depending upon what desire is in the heart. A subsequent passage makes this plain (Matt. 12: 34-37):

> O you generation of vipers, how can you speak good things, whereas you are evil? For out of the abundance of the heart the mouth speaketh. A good man out of a good treasure bringeth forth good things; and an evil man out of an evil treasure bringeth forth evil things. But I say unto you, that every idle word that men shall speak, they shall render an account for it in the day of judgment. For by thy words thou shalt be justified, and by thy words thou shalt be condemned.

Salient is the state of the human heart, which we learn appears as readily through speech as deeds.[65] Christ's pronouncement thus effectively eliminates all distinction between language and action by making them equally judicable. It is a position with obvious appeal to Gower — in fact, we have found it commanding the center of his quarrel with 'amoral' French poetry in his lyrics and in the

---

[64] The translation is Douai-Rheims.

[65] Interestingly, the author of *Jacob's Well* independently backs his argument about blasphemy, witchcraft, and swearing with a paraphrase from the same section of Matthew. Compare (p. 156):

> [Witches and swearers] faryn as a wood hound þat knowyth nouȝt his mayster, but byteth hym. god seyth in þe gospel he þat synneth aȝens þe holy god in slaundryng his god, it schal noȝt be forȝouyn him in þis world ne in þe oþer . . .

with Matt. 12: 32:

Mirour de l'Omme.[66] It would be surprising indeed if we could not discover its presence here.

As of course we can: almost ubiquitously, so that even so small an item as the Latin margin-note at the beginning of 'Sorcery and Witchcraft' provides a case in point. The note reminds us that a difference exists between proper ('naturalis') and improper ('execrabilis') magic.[67] But Sorcery in the *Confessio*, like alchemy as we have seen Gower present it in 'Labor', is (we might say) 'logopotent': i.e., despite their paraphernalia, Gower's sorcerers and alchemists rely on incantations — words — to achieve their effects. So to speak here of 'natural' and 'execrable' magic is to call attention in another way to language, first, and then (through its 'goodness' or 'badness') to the purposes, moral or not, buried in the user's heart. The *marginalium*, seemingly a hollow flourish of erudition, in fact brings us face-to-face with the theological tradition we have been examining.

And on: for it is difficult to imagine that the self-conscious logocentric Gower could have meditated on this tradition and failed to find in it a single imperative for alchemy, sorcery and poetry — arts which both 'create' and 'transform' with words. A rational chain links all together, fast to the moral anchor of Christ's pronouncements about language and intention in Matthew 12. Indeed, one is tempted to speculate that the halving of Book VI into Gluttony and 'Sins of the Mouth' reflects Gower's earnestness about both language and poetry, structurally transcribed. Thus this 'digression' too may be seen to take its place as part of a thoughtful plan.

> And whosoever shall speak a word against the Son of Man, it shall be forgiven him; but he that shall speak against the Holy Ghost, it shall not be forgiven him, neither in this world, nor in the world to come.

Several other loci are also revealing of the dependence of the *Somme* and its derivatives on Matthew. The comparison in Matt. 7: 15-20, of false prophets to trees bearing evil fruits, is behind Friar Lorens's remarks (p. 55) that 'euele tunge is þe tree þat God curseþ in þe gospel for he ne fond noþing but leues; and leues are take in holy writ wordes, and riȝt as it is hard to telle alle þe leues of a tree, wel hardere is it to telle or to noumbre alle þe synnes þat come of wikkede tonges.' Also suggestive in a general way are the many references connecting right eating, right speech, and consequently right faith, which appear throughout Matthew. Friar Lorens would hardly have felt on dangerous ground using this gospel as a source for condemning those lacking, or mis-stating, the faith and Gluttony. Consider, for example, Matt. 11: 16-19:

> But whereunto shall I esteem this generation to be like? It is like to children sitting in the market-place. Who, crying to their companions, say: we have piped to you, and you have not danced: we have lamented, and you have not mourned. For John came neither eating nor drinking, and they say: he hath a devil. The Son of Man came eating and drinking. And they say: Behold a man that is a glutton and a wine-drinker, a friend of publicans and sinners. And wisdom is justified by her children.

[66] Patrick J. Gallacher has argued that the entire *Confessio Amantis* is designed to present the appropriate relationship of man and the word of God; see his *Love, the Word, and Mercury*, pp. 2-4.

[67] 'Nota de Auctorum necnon et de librorum tam naturalis quam exe crabilis magice nominibus.' The note is opposite l. 1293.

IV

For modern readers, the 'problem' of Book VII was set out first by Macaulay in the introduction to his edition. Here we are told that the *Confessio Amantis* has, alongside its several beauties, 'most serious faults [of] plan and execution.'[68] Of these the worst is:

> the deliberate departure from the general plan which we find in the seventh book, where on pretence of affording relief and recreation to the wearied penitent, the Confessor, who says that he has little or no understanding except of love, is allowed to make a digression which embraces the whole field of human knowledge, but more especially deals with the duties of a king, a second political pamphlet, in fact, in which the stories of kings ruined by lust or insolence . . . are certainly intended . . . as an admonition of the author's royal patron. The petition addressed to Rhehoboam by his people against excessive taxation reads exactly like one of the English parliamentary protests of the period against the extravagant demands of the crown.[69]

After noting that such digressions seem to stand 'apparently for no reason except to show the author's learning,' Macaulay concludes: 'All that can be said is that these digressions were very common in the books of the age — the *Roman de la Rose*, at least in the part written by Jean de Meun, is one of the worst offenders.'[70]

Here we have both the best and the worst of Macaulay as a critical reader of Gower: the former most evident in his ability to perceive the probable implications of the verse, the latter in that Victorian censoriousness, and narrow sense of what shape a courtly love-poem *ought* to take, which prevented him from trusting what he perceived. For, as more recent scholarship has made clear, Macaulay's eye was true, despite his negative evaluation.

Essentially Macaulay's quarrel with Gower over Book VII rests on four concerns:

1) that the *Confessio Amantis* is, or should be, a poem about courtly love — but it sometimes forgets its subject;

2) that eight Books are an unintentional overgrowth, the result of authorial failure to recall, or perhaps to understand, the economy of an 'originally planned-for' seven;

3) that the resemblance of Book VII to parts of Jean de Meun's *Roman de la Rose* represents an accident, unfortunate but typical of an age when writers held precedent in great awe;

---

68 Macaulay, *Works* II, xix.
69 Ibid., xix-xx.
70 Ibid., xx.

4) that 'a digression which embraces the whole field of human knowledge' could have had no value, either for Gower as poet or for an English audience at the end of the fourteenth century.

Most of these objections have been answered in one way or another by various scholars over the last fifty years, and it is helpful to consider what they have said. The first direct challenge to Macaulay's characterization (and by this time C.S. Lewis's, too) of the *Confessio* as a courtly poem came in 1937 from Wilhelm Kleineke, who placed Book VII, the *Vox Clamantis* and the *Mirour de l'Omme* in a context of English advice to princes.[71] Kleineke's case was established subsequently by two Americans, George R. Coffman and John H. Fisher. Their work showed themes of love and social order interwoven throughout the *Mirour*, the *Vox* and the French ballades as well as the *Confessio Amantis*. Coffman and Fisher thus repositioned the *fürstenspiegel* of Book VII from the periphery to 'the heart of the discussion' in the *Confessio*, carefully prepared for and concluded by the Prologue, and 'coda' in Book VIII.[72] Recently Russell A. Peck and A. J. Minnis have refined the argument for the centrality of Book VII.[73] Each has shown at length, and with substantial learning, the widely recognized affiliation of politics and ethics in Gower's society.[74]

Macaulay's second claim, that a poem representing a confession could not accommodate a format of eight Books, has been similarly questioned by John Burrow. Citing the 'commonplace' nature of ' "numerical composition" . . . in medieval book-poetry,' Burrow argues that the *Confessio*'s penultimate Book

. . . can be justified even from a strictly formal point of view. The effect of a single unlike member in a series of like ones is not necessarily

[71] Wilhelm Kleineke, *Englische Fürstenspiegel vom Policraticus Johanns von Salisbury bis zum Basilikon Doron König Jakobs I*, Studien zur englischen Philologie, 90 (Halle, 1937), esp. pp. 132-34. For Lewis's views, see *Allegory of Love*, pp. 213-14.

[72] See Coffman, 'Gower in His Most Significant Role', p. 60, and Fisher, *John Gower*, pp. 196-9 and passim. The quotations are from Fisher, p. 198.

[73] Peck's primary argument is of course supported by Book VII, which he presents as the most important in the poem; see *Kingship and Common Profit*, pp. 139-59. Minnis, both in 'John Gower, *Sapiens* in Ethics and Politics,' *Medium Aevum* 49 (1980), 207-29, and in *Medieval Theory of Authorship*, pp. 184-85, treats Book VII as a *de regimine principum*, tracing its approach from the *Nichomachean Ethics* through Brunetto Latini and linking it firmly to the courtly tradition as a *principalis materia* of love. This position receives full treatment in the volume of essays edited by Minnis; see *Responses and Reassessments*, especially Minnis's own chapter (pp. 62, 71-74) where he demonstrates that political theory was a logical outgrowth of late medieval *compilatio*, and explores the influence on Gower of the work of Giles of Rome.

[74] Several other recent studies have made the same points with recourse to different sources: see C.A.J. Runacres's essay, 'Art and Ethics in the "Exempla" of the *Confessio Amantis*', and that of Elizabeth Porter, 'Gower's Ethical Microcosm and Political Macrocosm', both in *Responses and Reassessments*, ed. Minnis, pp. 104-3 and 135-62, respectively; and further Kurt O. Olsson, 'Rhetoric, John Gower and the Late Medieval Exemplum', *Mediaevalia et Humanistica*, N.S. 8 (1977), 185-200; and Gerald Kinneavy, 'Gower's *Confessio Amantis* and the Penitentials', *Chaucer Review* 19 (1984), 144-61.

unpleasing; and a medieval reader would not have been surprised to find
a series of seven so raised to eight. The seven planetary spheres were
enclosed within the sphere of fixed stars. According to Macrobius, the
monad is especially praiseworthy in conjunction with the number seven;
and according to St. Gregory, the raising of seven to eight signifies that
this temporal state is brought to an end and closed by eternity. Gower's
extra book may therefore be meant to point beyond the temporal state
represented in the other seven.[75]

Burrow's argument gains persuasive force from his recognition that a
numerological awareness such as he projects for Gower is characteristic of
'bookish' poets, among them Dante, Chaucer — and Gower himself.[76]
    As for Macaulay's distaste for the resemblance of Book VII to the discursive
'excessess' of the *Roman de la Rose*, George G. Fox had an explanation often
overlooked in its simplicity: there was a popular demand for the 'rimed
encyclopedia,' which found obvious satisfaction in the garrulity of Jean de
Meun, and must have done so in Book VII as well. Thus for Fox, while Gower's
science was limited and second-hand, there was sufficient *literary* validity for its
exhibition to explain its presence in the *Confessio*.[77] With this assessment J.A.W.
Bennett concurred, although he followed a different route to make essentially the
same point. Bennett judged Gower's 'speculum of knowledge' scarcely a
digression at all by comparison with the 'long cyclopaedic excursuses' of Jean's
Roman; moreover, Bennett suggested that, because Book VII reminds us how
much 'instruction was always part of [Gower's] purpose,' it cannot be dismissed
as unintended, or an afterthought.[78]
    Fox's observation that encyclopedism was not always met with aversion in the
Middle Ages also stands as an answer to the fourth of Macaulay's charges, i.e.,
that presenting the 'whole field of human knowledge' was a gross tactical
mistake. Quite the contrary. As Fox recognized, the diverse scholarship in many
works afforded a specific kind of delight to a learned audience — a pleasure not
unlike what we ascribe to noble hearers of those detailed scenes of arming and
animal dismemberment endemic to chivalric romances.[79] Another contemporary
scholar who views Book VII as deliberately flourished erudition is Maurice
Hussey. Like Fox, Bennett, and other recent readers, Hussey believes the Book's
lore was designed to broaden enjoyment of the *Confessio*, and by that means
inspire us with Gower's wider vision of human and celestial love.[80]

---

[75] Burrow, *Ricardian Poetry*, p. 60. See further Curtius, *European Literature*, excursus xv (on
'Numerical Composition').
[76] Burrow, *Ricardian Poetry*, p. 61.
[77] Fox, *Medieval Sciences*, pp. 156-57.
[78] Bennett, ed., *Selections from John Gower*, p. xvi.
[79] E.g., in *Sir Gawain and the Green Knight* or *Ipomedon*, both produced for noble audiences;
see Dieter Mehl, *The Middle English Romances of the Thirteenth and Fourteenth Centuries*
(London, 1969), pp. 58-86 and 193-206; and Derek Pearsall, *Old English and Middle English
Poetry*, Routledge History of English Poetry, I (London, 1977), 146, 171-76.
[80] Maurice Hussey, *Chaucer: An Introduction*, 2nd ed. (London, 1981), p. 202.

Given such learned voices in opposition, it should by now be valueless to cite Macaulay's criticisms, or make them any further the focus of a defense of Book VII. Yet opinions forcefully stated and long accepted die hard (especially when they appear in the only complete edition of the author's works); and in contrast to the scholars noted above, other prominent readers of Gower recently have echoed Macaulay, thus keeping his assessments before us as open questions.[81]

Nor, it should be said, has every argument been made that might be, regarding these matters, or been gathered in one place. So let us, having brought together the major voices in the debate, look once more at Macaulay's objections, and add what we can. We may begin by noticing that all of Macaulay's disagreements with Gower's inclusion into a fictive lover's confession of an encyclopedic 'regiment of princes' in fact have two parts. He wants to know not only *could* Gower have done it (was there precedent?), but also a harder thing — *why*. would a poet unshape a work with so clear a structure to develop connections, even if theoretically it was possible? Kleineke, Coffman, Fisher, Peck, Minnis and others, in showing us that medieval literary and political theory supported Gower's practice, have ably attacked the question of 'could;' and Burrow, Fox, Bennett, and Hussey have done so as well, even as they focussed on different problems.

But while all have also suggested something about Gower's possible motivations — the 'why' behind the work — the implicit half of Macaulay's objections remains essentially unanswered. Not without reason, perhaps: For the question *why* a poet writes what he does (in the words of Donald R. Howard) 'at once invites and eludes' since it seeks to assemble, from out the dumb *bricolage* of the work alone, the poet's 'genius . . . the part of a subject's mind we can least hope to grasp or understand.'[82] Daunting as the task is, however, it seems to me that with Gower (more, certainly, than with Chaucer) we are offered a chance to supply an answer to the difficult questions Macaulay raised, and so effectively put them behind us at last.

To do so we need first to recall briefly the backdrop of the age. While this might be helpful in understanding all poets' concerns, it is especially so with Gower, a more *reactive* writer than most, whose verse seems to have come in response to people and events around him. His times were parlous, replete with natural catastrophe, disease, famine, religious and social unrest, war. These were the years of the Black Death (beginning in 1349-50, when close to a third of the population died); the Great Schism, which exposed the worldly weaknesses of

---

[81] I am thinking here of readers the likes of Derek Pearsall, who finds Book VII 'an encyclopaedic digression on Education' (*Old and Middle English Poetry*, pp. 210-ll) and Michael D. Cherniss, to whom the Book seems digressive, contrived, and diffuse (*Boethian Apocalypse: Studies in Middle English Vision Poetry* [Norman, OK, 1987], pp. 103-04, 113-14); and see also Michael G. Sargent, 'Three Notes on Middle English Poetry and Drama' in *A Salzburg Miscellany: English and American Studies 1964-1984* (Salzburg: Institut für Anglistik und Amerikanistik, 1984), 2. 171, who portrays Book VII as an attempt to prolong suspense with prolixity, before telling us about the prime sin of a lover's confession — lechery.

[82] Donald R. Howard, *Chaucer: His Life, His Works, His World* (New York, 1987), p. xi.

Peter's See and cast the Christian world for recourse either into cynicism, mysticism, or (in Wyclif's England) radical reform; of enervating, increasingly ruinous hostilities between England and France; of widening extremes of rich and poor, a riven commonality perhaps most visible in its products, the French Jacquerie, the English Peasants' Revolt, and ubiquitous class struggle; of intellectual discovery in the universities (Ockham and his followers) with great, but unsettling, consequences; at home in London the spectacle of a doddering king led about by an unscrupulous mistress and ministers, the news from abroad of the heir-apparent's death, and the subsequent, vertiginous rule of Richard, boy and man.[83] It was these times (probably the 1380s) that Chaucer lamented in the closing stanza of 'The Former Age':

> Allas, allas! Now may men wepe and crye!
> For in oure dayes nis but covetyse,
> Doublenesse, and tresoun, and envye,
> Poyson, manslauhtre, and mordre in sondry wyse.[84]

And we know even more clearly Gower's response to those dark days. Unlike Chaucer, Gower attacked their ills directly and at length. Indeed, the extraordinary consistency of themes in the *Mirour*, the *Vox*, the *Cronica Tripertita*, and in the Middle English poem addressed 'To King Henry IV, In Praise of Peace' prompted John Fisher to throw the *Confessio* in with them and address Gower's writings as a unity, as parts almost of a single poem. But did Gower *really* write that way? Perhaps; though probably the consistency we see occurred to him the way it does to us, *post terminum*. When the three major books were finished and the titles could be viewed together, *then* (for example) the *Mirour de l'Omme* became *Speculum Hominis*, not before.[85]

It is useful to speak of Gower's consistency in this way because much has been made of it without, I believe, striking the main point it has to teach us. And that is that the thematic unity of Gower's writings reveals choices bred first of conviction, if given form by art. The portrait sketched by Fisher, for instance, presents Gower as an initially 'contemplative spirit' steadily coming to political consciousness, and conscience — a progress Fisher sees in 'Gower's development from the casual composition of love ballades for an audience such as the Pui to

---

[83] Charles Muscatine, in *Poetry and Crisis in the Age of Chaucer* (Notre Dame, IN, 1972), pp. 16-26, offers an excellent overview of the period; see also Gordon Leff, *The Dissolution of the Medieval Outlook* (New York, 1976), on the philosophical background, particularly Ockham and his followers; and May McKissack, *The Fourteenth Century: 1307-1399*, Oxford History of England V (Oxford, 1959), pp. 328-48.

[84] Howard, *Chaucer: His Life*, pp. 37 ff., dates 'The Former Age' as work of what he terms 'the worst of the times — the 1380s.'

[85] As Fisher, *John Gower*, pp. 88-92, points out, the name 'Speculum hominis' for Gower's French poem first appears in the colophon attached to the finished *Confessio*, probably in 1390, and retrospectively describes Gower's three primary poems. In subsequent revisions of the colophon, the title is further emended to 'Speculum meditantis'.

literature in a more serious vein.'[86] *This* Gower 'undertook [the *Mirour*] more or less for his own edification,' and without a sense of himself 'as speaking to the public, as he did when he wrote his later poems.'[87] But Fisher's supposition, derived from the survival of the *Mirour* in but a single copy and a reading of the colophons appended to the *Confessio Amantis*, is more ingenious than evidentiary. We have no accurate means to date the individual ballades. Who is to say whether some we know as part of the *Traitié* were not composed simultaneously with the *Cinkante Balades?* Or both collections could represent late work, although it hardly seems likely. Nor should it be automatic to assume, along with Fisher, that a poet accustomed to taking part in poetry contests (if, indeed, he did so) like those we believe a London Pui once sponsored would embark upon his most ambitious project to date, anticipating no audience to whom it could be presented beyond himself. Writing in the Middle Ages was not a private act, and the ten thousand-plus couplets of the *Mirour* are too many to ascribe to anyone's urge for meditation.

In fact, the testimony of Gower's work might well be read another way, to show (as Minnis, Peck and Porter suggest) that public ethics and poetry were never unrelated in Gower's estimation, the one functioning as the well-spring of the other. What variations we find in his work, composed in response to the tumultuous final twenty-five years of the fourteenth century, reflect, not a changeable poetic stance, but rather two things: shifting English political and social conditions, and differences in the audiences Gower conceived for each piece. Both influence form and, as causes, both are often inseparable.

Examples of this are not difficult to find in Gower's work. If I have read the ballade sequences accurately, as correctives to a style of love and poetry Gower hoped to redeem, then these furnish one such illustration. Their number, their order, the play they exhibit with imagery and style, even the choice of the ballade sequence itself, illustrate attempts to influence a specific audience — a particularly sensitive, enculturated group — to respect worthy writing of more than one kind.

Another example, closer kin, perhaps, to *Confessio Amantis* Book VII, is the opening 'Visio' section of the *Vox Clamantis*.[88] This Macaulay identified as a late addition, superceding the 'original' beginning, now in consequence relegated to Book II. What happened, as Macaulay saw it, was that Gower had completed most of a Latin poem about the responsibilities and present corruption of the Three Estates when the Peasants' Revolt broke out in June, 1381. (The date is mentioned in the version of the poem recorded in the Laud MS.) Gower was then so moved by the anarchic violence he saw around him that he appended to his otherwise-conventionally admonitory poem an account of macabre dreams, of talking animals hunting men, the fall of Troy, a storm-tossed journey by ship —

---

[86] Ibid., p. 88.
[87] Ibid., p. 92.
[88] The term 'visio' was first applied to this section by Maria Wickert; her *Studien zu John Gower* remains the most extensive discussion of the poem.

all thinly-veiled allegory of the rampant mob. Unfortunately, in Macaulay's view, the splicing was crudely done so that, while this 'Visio' was 'in itself the most interesting part of the work,' it retained 'something of the character of an insertion' because 'the plan of the remainder seems to be independent of it . . .'[89]

Now, much of this criticism is just. Movement from part to part is never seamless in the Vox Clamantis, and the Visio's jointure to Book II is scarcely an exception. But as our concern at present is to uncover motive, let us temporarily reserve judgement on craft. The question Macaulay raises grows out once again of an addition made to a poem 'planned' to include six Books. Or did the original blueprint call for five? For as Macaulay himself remarks, the variable numbering of the Books in the different manuscripts of the Vox suggests that at one time Gower 'proceeded on the principle of making five books, beginning with the third, the second being treated as a general prologue to the whole poem.'[90] If true, this guess convicts what is now Book VII as well as the 'Visio' of having been 'something of an insertion.' And then there is the Cronica Tripertita, which seems to have been made to follow the Vox in late manuscript copies. Are we to think of it as yet another addition? Indeed, it all makes rather tempting the recent opinion that:

> Gower was quite ready to add an 'afterthought' to the Vox Clamantis . . .
> Such a practice is medieval: Langland must keep adding to Piers Plowman
> . . . Jean de Meun must quintuple the length of the Roman de la Rose.
> Sheer length and extensive form are impressive.[91]

But in the end I believe we can find an alternative way to read this evidence without resorting to all-too-familiar charges of 'medieval' formlessness. The Cronica Tripertita was never intended by its author to be an 'eighth Book' of the Vox Clamantis. Gower states very clearly in a prose paragraph separating the two works that 'the book which is entitled The Voice of One Crying has ended' ('Explicit libellus qui intitulatur Vox Clamantis . . . .'), and that what follows is something different, a 'chronicle, which is in three parts' ('in hac consequenti cronica, qui tripertita est').[92] The works are not unrelated, however, since each was inspired by the woeful government of Richard II. The thematic similarity must have caused both to seem to Gower, not parts of the same poem, but simply 'comments old and new I have made on an inept king.' Quite likely political acumen played a part in their grouping, too. By our best guess the Cronica Tripertita was composed about 1400. The manuscripts in which it joins the Vox thus all post-date the ascension to power of Henry IV. The finest of these

---

[89] Macaulay, Works IV, xxxii.
[90] Ibid., p. xxxi. Macaulay continues: 'In connexion with this we may take the special invocation of divine assistance in the prologue of the third book, which ends with the couplet, "His tibi libatis novus intro nauta profundum,/ Sacrum pneuma rogans ut mea vela regas".'
[91] Stockton, Major Latin Works, p. 12.
[92] See Macaulay, Works IV, 313.

manuscripts were prepared, possibly under Gower's eye, for presentation to prominent churchmen, at least one of whom — Thomas Arundel, Archbishop of Canterbury — had little reason to love Richard II.[93] Such men, especially in such times, well might be reminded of a poet's early courage, criticizing an enemy. Placing together the old and the new in the same manuscripts, tail-to-head, would lend current loyalty the persuasive force of long-held truth.

This is of course a simple, practical logic to use, and I take a good deal at face value when perhaps I ought not do so. But as a method it suits what I know of Gower's character, which is to call a spade a spade, and it resolves the 'problem' of the *Vox-Cronica* connection. The same logic may be turned as well on the relationship of the 'Visio' to the 'plan' of the *Vox*, with similar results. Probably the manuscript record shows what happened. When the rebellion erupted, Gower had nearly completed a Latin poem of some length, perhaps to include five sections. Their sequence was yet in flux, because their subject — the unhappy state of English society — could be approached in more than one way. Possibly, like his narrator in the 'Visio', Gower witnessed bloody deeds while hiding in fear for his life. (I admit to finding an urgency in the 'Visio' that suggests first-hand experience, even if, as we have seen, much of the opening is *cento*.) But observed or no, the anarchic cruelty of the Revolt clearly affected Gower, and drew from his pen a powerful response.

This response took the shape of two Books added to the Latin poem he had at hand, entitled already (in the Prologue to what was soon to be Book II) the *Vox Clamantis*. He connected these new Books using the device of warnings we receive in dreams. In what would become the last Book he incorporated, from the Book of Daniel, Nebuchadnezzar's famous statue with golden head and feet of iron and clay.[94] In the new first Book, the 'Visio,' after a Prologue citing the authority of Daniel's dreams and Joseph's ('Ex Daniele patet quid sompnia significarunt,/ Nec fuit in sompnis visio vana Ioseph,' *VC*, 7-8), Gower presented a 'dream' of his own making. The form and meaning of this 'dream' — and its relationship to the rest of the ensuing poem — he made plain with a prose *incipit* worth considering in full:

> In huius opusculi principio intendit compositor describere qualiter seruiles rustici impetuose contra ingenuos et nobiles regni insurrexerunt. Et quia res huiusmodi velut monstrum detestabilis fuit et horribilis, narrat se per sompnium vidisse diuersas vulgi turmas in diuersas species bestiarum domesticarum transmutatas: dicit tamen quod ille bestie domestice, a sua deuiantes natura, crudelitates ferarum sibi presumpserunt. De causis vero, ex quibus inter homines talia contingunt enormia, tractat vlterius secundum distincciones libelli istius,

---

[93] See Gower's dedicatory epistle in Macaulay, *Works* IV, 1-2. Arundel was badly treated by Richard; see Anthony Steel, *Richard II* (Cambridge, 1962), p. 272.

[94] The Book of Daniel had unusual significance for Gower, as an historical and an apocalptical touchstone; see Russell A. Peck, 'John Gower and the Book of Daniel,' in R. F. Yeager, ed., *John Gower: Recent Readings* (Kalamazoo, MI, 1989), 159-87.

qui in septem diuiditur partes, prout inferius locis suis euidencius apparebit.

['In the beginning of this work, the author intends to describe how the lowly peasants violently revolted against the freemen and nobles of the realm. And since an event of this kind was as loathsome and horrible as a monster, he reports that in a dream he saw different throngs of the rabble transformed into different kinds of domestic animals. He says, moreover, that those domestic animals deviated from their true nature and took on the barbarousness of wild beasts. In accordance with the separate divisions of this poem, which is divided into seven parts (as will appear more clearly below in its headings), he treats furthermore of the causes for such outrages taking place among men.']⁹⁵

The *incipit* shows that, whatever his idea may have been for the 'original' *Vox*, Gower had a very clear plan for the poem he completed. Moreover, this final structure is both logical and significant. It is logical because, hard at work on a forward-looking admonition — the five-Book *Vox* — Gower found himself overtaken by events of the sort he had hoped, through his writing, to ward off. For what was the Peasants' Revolt but precisely the nightmarish end he was predicting for his nation unless it found reform? Under such circumstances, that Gower would 'change his plan' to comment directly on these events is less surprising than that he should stick unwaveringly to it as the chickens came home to roost.

But (Macaulay has asked), how skilled a job did he make of it? Well, Gower's structure is significant also in two other ways. With the addition of the 'Visio' the *Vox* gains dramatic power, in approximately the same way that classical epic does, from a beginning resembling *in medias res*. For despite its dreamlike machinery, the 'Visio' occupies *present* time, both historically (as an immediate response to the Peasants' Revolt) and rationally, that is, within the progression of the poem's argument. But Gower has structured his poem so that the 'Visio' poses the requisite epic question, 'How have you (or we) come here, in this place?' To answer this the classical hero — Odysseus, Aeneas — tells his story, temporarily diverting narrative focus from the present onto the past. In just this way Books II through VI offer us answers by moving backward on both levels: historically, since the conditions they describe antedate the events of the 'Visio'; and logically too since these conditions in fact are the causes of England's nightmare.

Subsequently the present is re-established in classical epic. The hero's tale ends and past time converges with the current moment — Odysseus silent at last in

⁹⁵ For Gower's prose, see Macaulay, *Works* IV, and 20; the translation is by Stockton, *Major Latin Works*, p. 49, with my revisions.

Alcinous's silent hall, Aeneas before Dido.[96] Just so, in the *Vox Clamantis*, Book
VII recovers the present on both its levels. Historically we rejoin a contemporary
society still enduring conditions which led to the Rebellion; rationally the
summary of these at the beginning of Book VII (and a brief recollection, in the
prophecy of Nebuchadnezzar's statue, of the Danielesque dream of the 'Visio')
reminds us of the cost of continued moral obduracy. And then, as in epic, we
proceed through the present toward a future foreshadowed but not, without
struggle, to be achieved.[97]

The nature of this struggle is defined in the final Book of the *Vox*. Gower
accomplishes this, first, by the representation of life as battle (*VC* VII, 375-76):

> Vita quid est presens temptacio, pugna molesta;
> Hic acies semper, semper et hostis adest.

['What is this present life? Temptation, a threatening struggle; The
battle-line is always here, always the enemy is at hand.']

The enemy is the Seven Sins, each of which is described in conflict for man's
soul. But, as the venue for this battle is the death-bed, with victory determined in
the eternal, on the other side of time, Book VII steadily bears us, in epic fashion,
away from the here-and-now into time yet to come. Thus Gower briefly invokes
the Last Judgment in Book VII. But, because his ultimate concern in the *Vox* is
temporal reform, he does not close his poem with the eternal. Its final lines,
replete with the rhetoric of struggle, hold us firmly in the here-and-now (*VC* VII,
1475-81):

> Mundus non ledit iustum, bene dummodo credit,
> Quando set excedit, mundus ad arma redit:
> Mundus erit talis, fuerit viuens homo qualis;
> Obstet vitalis quilibet ergo malis.
> Culpa quidem lata, qua virtus stat viciata,
> Cum non purgata fuerit set continuata,
> Que meruit fata sunt sibi fine data.

['The world does not harm the righteous man while he keeps good faith,
but it takes up arms as soon as he transgresses. The world will be just as
a man was while living. Thus every man should, during his life, oppose
evil. For when guilt, which corrupts virtue, is hidden, not purged but
continued, it merits the fate which it is given.']

---

[96] Comparable moments in epic are Odysseus's description of his travels to Alcinous
(*Odyssey*, VII, 215-347) and Aeneas's tale to Dido (*Aeneid* II-III). These recitations tell us
'how we got here' in the narrative, just as Gower's Books II-VI explain, on a moral rather
than a fictive/historical plane, the pattern of our arrival.
[97] Thus, while Odysseus and Aeneas are aware of their destinies, they must act
themselves to bring prediction to fruition.

Thus, by forming a kind of 'epic envelope' around the five Books 'original' to
it, Books I and VII provide a structural cohesion to the 'new' *Vox* and enhance its
didactic power. Of course, we have no unassailable way to know that the epic
model was in Gower's mind as he wrote. But the borrowings from the Book of
Daniel at front and end are unmistakably thoughtful work, as is the decision to
open and close with vivid, cautionary dreams. These elements suggest that
Gower was shaping his poem purposefully. Taken together, they represent one
reply which might be made to charges that the 'expanded' *Vox Clamantis* lacks
poetic craft.

We may respond in another way by calling attention to the symbolic advantage
gained when two Books were added to the five of the 'original' *Vox*. While five is
a meaningful figure according to medieval number theory, much greater
significance would have been attributed to a work comprised of seven.[98] For
seven, according to Augustine, recalled the final day of creation, on which God
'rested' by casting a backward look over his work, to find that 'It was good.'[99] In
consequence seven came to represent the universe of created things, and also the
act of their assessment. (So Hugh of St. Victor took seven, as the number 'of this
present life'; and Aquinas, commenting on Augustine's analysis, interprets the
'rest' of the seventh day as 'not opposed to labor or to movement but to . . . the
desire tending to an external object'.)[100] Thus for man, attaining 'God's rest,
which has no evening' (in Augustine's fine phrase) required no cessation of
labor. On the contrary; it meant coming to terms with the fragmented world of
created objects. For, as Augustine held:

> In this whole, in this complete perfection, is rest, whereas in the part is
> labour. Therefore we labour, as long as we know in part; but when
> perfection is reached, what is partial will vanish'.[101]

To pierce 'what is partial' to find the 'complete perfection' of the whole is,
then, man's incumbent duty. So much is implicit in the number seven. For
Gower to raise the five Books of the 'original' *Vox* to seven would make, in this
context, strategic sense. The poem he has crafted examines 'this present life' in
various detail — the duties of the Estates, of the judiciary, of the king — and

[98] By 'greater significance' I mean, in general, more holy, since 5 was equated with
animality and the flesh in the Middle Ages; see Vincent Foster Hopper, *Medieval Number
Symbolism: Its Sources, Meaning, and Influence on Thought and Expression* (New York, 1938);
and more recently two studies of Russell A. Peck, 'Numerology and Chaucer's *Troilus and
Criseyde*', *Mosaic* 5 (1972), 1-29 and 'Number as Cosmic Language', in *By Things Seen:
Reference and Recognition in Medieval Thought*, ed. David L. Jeffrey (Ottawa, 1979), pp.
47-80.
[99] Augustine discusses 7 and the seventh day in *The City of God* XI, 31.
[100] For Hugh of St. Victor on 7, see 'De arca Noe morali' in *Selected Spiritual Writings*,
trans. 'A Religious of C.S.M.V.,' intro. Aelfred Squire, O.P. (London, 1962), pp. 120-
21; for Aquinas, see *Summa Theologica*, O. 73, art. 2. res. 2, in *Basic Writings of Saint Thomas
Aquinas*, 2 vols., ed. and trans. Anton G. Pegis (New York, 1945), I, 671 and passim.
[101] *City of God*, trans. Knowles, p. 466.

concludes with man on the horn of choice, face-to-face with England and the world. A 'new', seven-Book structure directly reinforces the political, practical message of the *Vox*. And just as importantly, perhaps, to its intended audience — high ranking ecclesiasts, fluent in Latin and conversant with the theological implications of number — that strategy would be clear.[102]

What even so brief a reconsideration of its structure has to tell us, then, is that there may be more legitimate judgments to reach than Macaulay's on the 'formlessness' of the *Vox Clamantis*. Different audiences, and changing social conditions — the Peasants' Revolt and its aftermath — both may have played shaping roles in the finished *Vox*, as they did in the ballade sequences — and, I believe, in the *Confessio Amantis* as well. Let us look back at that poem now, and take up again the 'problems' posed by its seventh Book. We saw earlier that objections to Book VII could be reduced basically to four: that the appearance in the *Roman de la Rose* of a similar excursus on the panoply of human knowledge must have been coincidental; that such a discourse on learning as Book VII brings to the *Confessio* would have conveyed no special message to its audience, nor held one for Gower; that eight Books could only represent an ill-considered overflow of a superior seven-Book 'plan'; that politics have no place in a poem about love. Considering these in light of what has been said thus far of Gower's working habits should give us a fresh start.

To Macaulay's first concern, that somehow the precedent of the *Roman de la Rose* eluded Gower's notice as he composed Book VII, our study of the *Mirour* and the ballade sequences has furnished a ready reply. Certainly the model of Jean de Meun's Nature at confession (*RR* 16707 ff.), describing the operation of the universe, the properties of glasses, free will and destiny, dreams, frenzies, mirrors, animals, birds, insects, fish, mankind, gentility, and on and on, stands behind Book VII; indeed, we are *expected* to recognize, and use, this comparison as we read. For in the *Roman*, Nature's rambling discourse ultimately serves as summons to Genius to rouse Love's barons for the final assault on the Rose. The message of this is unmistakeable. Learning is implicated — dragooned, as it were — into the battle waged and won in the name of amoral fecundity. (The speech of the 'jealous husband', as related by Ami, 8437 ff., illustrates how this works. In a thoroughly contrary reading, he gives credit to Héloise's education for her 'sensible' opposition to matrimony and her preference for 'whoredom' with Abelard.)[103]

In the *Confessio Amantis*, however, learning produces antipodal results. It is an enlightened 'John Gower', his inappropriate *persona* Amans laid aside at last, who

---

[102] Fisher identifies a number of probable recipients: William of Wykeham, Bishop of Winchester; William Courtenay, Bishop of London; Simon Sudbury, Archbishop of Canterbury; Thomas Brunton, Bishop of Rochester; Ralph Enghum, Bishop of Salisbury; and of course Arundel; see *John Gower*, pp. 105-06.

[103] See especially 8786-8802; the jealous husband compliments Héloise for preferring to be Abelard's whore ('putain') than the crowned empress of Rome. This attitude, the husband claims, derived from her education ('lestreure').

turns away from carnality to pray for peace. Nor (as Russell Peck has shown) is the *speculum regis* of Book VII incidental to this transformation. The analogies of rule, over nations or the individual soul, were broad and binding in the Middle Ages. For Gower and his audience, successful 'kingship' began most intimately 'at home'.[104]

Thus, if we ask *why* Gower included Book VII in the *Confessio*, we might frame one answer in terms of the importunity of the cause. What indirect recollections of the *Roman* we find in Book VII are not without function. They furnish additional evidence of Gower's unrelenting opposition to misuses of learning and poetry which the French, in his view, were particularly prone to commit. In just this way, in response to perceived crisis, the 'original' *Vox Clamantis* grew to include the 'Visio' and its own seventh Book. Seldom, it would seem, did Gower turn away from challenges when so much that he admired with such passion was at risk, and the stakes were so high.

With its clarity as an illustrative image, the transformation of the lover Amans into the penitent, 'John Gower', memorably asserts the positive value of learning. And in so doing it directs us as well toward a reply to Macaulay's second objection, that neither Gower nor his audience would have valued, or been impressed by, a learned display. Here however we must be cautious with our terms. 'Learning' requires pinning down before we use it, or it will carry us astray. Certainly what Gower and his readers thought of 'learning' differed from contemporary Italian ideals. Boccaccio, in fact, alluded disparagingly to English 'learning' in his *De Genealogia deorum gentilium*.[105] And undoubtedly Beryl Smalley is correct in her suspicion that, to Petrarch, the audience of the *Confessio Amantis* 'would have seemed . . . legend-hungry louts.'[106] Yet there is also that in Gower which has provoked other voices. J.A.W. Bennett, for one, has argued that Gower's classical accomplishment 'stands [him] at no great distance from later humanists and translators,' such as Ben Jonson. (Indeed, to Bennett, Gower's excursus on ancient religions in Book V of the *Confessio* provided 'an English equivalent to Boccaccio's more elaborate *Genealogia Deorum*'.)[107] For Bennett, an appreciative audience is implicit.

---

[104] See Peck, *Kingship and Common Profit*, pp. 139-60; and further, for a learned general description of the analogies present, Ernst H. Kantorowicz, *King's Two Bodies: A Study in Mediaeval Political Theology* (Princeton, NY, 1957), chapters III, IV, V (pp. 43-271). The connection is actually inherent in Aristotle's own sense of *politikē*. As T.A. Sinclair notes, 'For Aristotle, as for Plato, the subject of political philosophy . . . embraced the whole of human behaviour, the conduct of the individual equally with the behaviour of the group. Ethics was, therefore, a part of politics; we might also say that politics was a part of ethics.' See *Aristotle: The Politics* (Harmondsworth, 1962), p. 21.

[105] Boccaccio apparently considered Britain beyond the civilized pale, treating its inhabitants as did Virgil (*Eclogue* 66), Horace (*Odes* I. 35.29; IV. 14.47), and Catullus (XI.11); see *De genealogie deorum gentilium libri*, ed. Vincenzo Romano, 2 vols. (Bari, 1951), I, (Preface, 9b), and 33 (VI, 73d); and compare *De casibus virorum illustrium* IX.27.

[106] Beryl Smalley, *English Friars and Antiquity* (Oxford, 1960), pp. 26-27.

[107] J.A.W. Bennett, *Selections*, xi.

But in the end it is difficult, if not futile, to try to place Gower precisely in the continuum these opinions suggest.[108] I submit that this is because his learning — what it meant to him, and why it mattered, both to acquire and to share — is anachronistic in the purest sense of 'out of time.' Uniquely among Middle English writers, Gower partakes simultaneously of the future and the past. His manner of moralizing, his major sources, his attachment to Anglo-Norman, even his preferred verse-forms the balade, the tetrameter couplet, the Ovidian elegiac, all bespeak a sensibility formed in an age gone by. But if Gower is not yet the 'compleat humanist' Bennett would have him be, on the matter of learning he is even less the 'legend-hungry lout.' Concerns of his we have examined above — for authorship in a near-classical sense, for technical effects which, like *cento*, inspire pleasure proportionate to classical learning — seem eloquently to sound the contrary.[109]

More evidence of Gower's attitude toward learning — what Bennett would call his 'humanism' — appears from a closer look at the sources Gower used for Book VII as well. These, as Macaulay noticed, were primarily two: Brunetto Latini's *Li Livres dou Trésor* and the Psuedo-Aristotlean *Secretum Secretorum*.[110] Significant as these works are to the finished shape of Book VII, however, neither they nor the abundant scholarship they have generated tells us the full story of Gower's knowledge, or of his making. For this we must attempt to look *behind* the texts whose marks imprint themselves so clearly, to glimpse, if we can, dimmer shapes, and the process by which Gower chose as he did among the available sources.

Not that, for the task Gower had before him, the *Trésor* and the *Secretum* were exceptionable choices. Between them they easily contain argument and exempla sufficient to ground the Book he projected, the more so because, on specific points, he apparently had both the library and the adaptable willingness to

---

[108] The difficulty is apparent in Janet Coleman's recent attempt to place Gower's political vision. She finds him at once 'hopelessly behind the times' and 'more in touch with the spirit of his age . . . than any other writer of the times.' See *Medieval Readers and Writers, 1350-1400* (New York, 1981), pp. 13 and 138, respectively.

[109] Indeed, most recent critical studies support Bennett's optimistic assessment of Gower's prescient humanism. Both A. C. Spearing (*Medieval to Renaissance in English Poetry*, Cambridge, [1984]) and Lois A. Ebin (*Illuminator, Makar, Vates: Visions of Poetry in the Fifteenth Century*, Lincoln and London, [1988]) argue strongly that the kind of audience requisite for a 'modern' reading of Gower's learning existed during the late fourteenth century. As Spearing remarks, 'What is most characteristic of the Renaissance . . . is not a rediscovery of lost material, but a new sense of the historical distance and difference inherent in classical texts . . . together with a sense of the possibility of overcoming that distance and difference by creative imitation' (p. 13). It is precisely because he was so full of that possibility, and from such a learned base pursued 'creative imitation' so aggressively, that Gower often outstrips even Chaucer as a harbinger of a new age. For a similar view, see further Alastair Minnis, 'From Medieval to Renaissance,' *Proceedings of the British Academy* 72 (1987), 205-46.

[110] *Works* III, 521-22. On Gower's use of the *Secretum*, see especially M.A. Manzalaoui, 'Nought in the Registre of Venus: Gower's English Mirror for Princes,' in P.L. Heyworth, ed., *Medieval Studies for J.A.W. Bennett Aetatis Suae LXX* (Oxford, 1981), pp. 159-83.

supplement them with other topical texts.[111] But it is instructive to imagine what Book VII would have been, had Gower selected different models. Other *encyclopaediae* were certainly available; of which none is more prominent than the *Speculum Maius* of Vincent of Beauvais.

In certain ways the *Speculum Maius* seems the most obvious *locus* to which Gower might have turned, to find a model and resources for Book VII. The *Speculum* was immensely popular in the Middle Ages, judging from the numerous copies yet extant.[112] Chaucer knew to look to 'Vincent in his Storial Mirour' for narrative matter; and Gower himself, while never giving the Dominican credit, apparently relied on his *Speculum* for sections of the *Confessio Amantis*.[113] Moreover the *Speculum* contained, among its 'four' parts (*Naturale*, *Doctrinale*, *Historiale*, and the spurious *Morale*, long thought to be, but probably not, by Vincent's hand), just the sort of information Gower hoped to supply in Book VII: descriptions of the universe, its elements, workings, and various populations finned, furred, feathered and leaved; all the arts, including what he calls the 'logical' (beginning with language and proceeding through grammar, logic, rhetoric and *poetica*, illustrated chiefly by fables), the 'practical' (including ethics, 'economics' in the broad sense of family life, education, householding and husbandries, such as chicken-keeping), the 'mechanical' (treating, among others, wool production and clothing, agriculture, architecture, armaments and combat, sports, naviga-tion, hunting, alchemy and applied medicine); politics; law; the sciences, such as medicine, physics, mathematics, metaphysics, and theology, treated theoreti-cally; a chronological story of the world, interweaving secular, biblical and cultural history; and (in the spurious *Morale*) theology and ethics presented afresh.[114] Indeed so much is there, and so obviously, that one wonders why Gower looked to Brunetto and the *Secretum Secretorum* at all.

To be sure, he might not have had a complete *Speculum* readily at hand. Manuscript evidence attests to the independent circulation of the four parts of Vincent's book, and to many bastardized compilations and excerpts.[115] (Thus Chaucer's reference to the 'Storial Mirour' may indidicate his reading only of the *Historiale*, by far the *Speculum* best known.) But Vincent apparently foresaw this difficulty, and (as he describes in the twentieth chapter of his Prologue) attempted to alleviate it for his readers. In each of the individual *specula* he summarized the others, so that, possessing a copy of the *Naturale*, the *Doctrinale* or the *Historiale*, one would be aware of the general arrangement and contents of the

---

[111] On Gower's use of additional sources in Book VII, see two studies of George L. Hamilton, 'Some Sources of the Seventh Book of Gower's *Confessio Amantis*,' *Modern Philology* 9 (1912), 323-46, and 'Studies in the Sources of Gower,' *JEGP* 26 (1927), 491-520; see further Macaulay's notes, passim.

[112] On the textual history of the *Speculum Maius*, see the essay of B.L. Ullmann, 'A Project for a New Edition of Vincent of Beauvais,' *Speculum* 8 (1933), 312-326.

[113] This, at least, is Macaulay's judgment; see his remarks *Works* III, 523, 535.

[114] On the authorship of the *Speculum morale*, see Ullmann, 'A Project,' pp. 319-20.

[115] Ullmann, 'A Project,' p. 326, records 'over fifty complete manuscripts' of the *Historiale*, 'twelve or thirteen' of the *Naturale*, seven of the *Doctrinale* and two of the *Morale*. His search, he points out further, was not exhaustive and he excludes partial manuscripts from his count.

Maius entire. With independent copies so common, Gower could have acquired and used the whole *Speculum*, then, had it appealed to his sense of design.

That he did not do so suggests another strategy at work. For this we have several clues. One is that Vincent's *Speculum* is the major source for form (or apparent lack of it) and for detail of Nature's speech in the *Roman de la Rose*.[116] Now, Gower need not have known this, with the scholarly assurance we can summon today, to have remarked the similarity; Jean de Meun scarcely rendered his debt invisible to those familiar with both texts. In such circumstances, Gower's poetic dictated the same response: 'correct' the flawed worldview of the *Roman* by offering alternatives.

It is unfortunate we cannot know the process, serendipitous or deliberate, that brought Gower together with Brunetto's book. However, had he been directly seeking an alternative model to the *Speculum Maius* and Jean de Meun's adaptation of it, he could not have found a better than the *Trésor*. For Brunetto, crafting his own work in Vincent's shadow, undoubtedly balanced the *Trésor* against the *Speculum*, drawing on it as a source while attempting another kind of book entirely.[117] As Francis J. Carmody, Latini's modern editor, has pointed out:

> . . . plus ambitieux, peut-être moins judicieux dans son choix, Vincent a rassemblé en latin toutes les connaissances humaines, bien rangées, bien documentées; Latini, au contraire, n'a reproduit que les détails importants, et il a évité les répétitions et les contradictions de Vincent. Le *Speculum Naturale* est donc un livre de référence d'une grande valeur, mais le *Trésor* a disseminé ses connaissances parmi les hommes du monde aussi bien que parmi les étudiants.[118]

Carmody's observation has particular relevance when applied to Gower's use of Brunetto. For we might say that the *Trésor* is to the *Speculum* what a delivery van is to an eighteen-wheel diesel: a cargo-carrier still, but fleeter, leaner, and more readily handled by that 'new' audience Gower projected for the *Confessio Amantis*. The French *Mirour* and the Latin *Vox* were surely written for what Carmody would call 'les étudiants,' men of letters, educated clerics high and low; but the *Confessio*, Gower tells us in its Prologue, was composed to reach the English-speaking 'hommes du monde' as well. Other factors may have drawn Gower to the *Trésor* — Brunetto's pointed use, for example, of the vernacular

---

[116] Ibid., p. 323.
[117] The point is made by Francis J. Carmody in the introduction to his critical edition of Brunetto; see *Li Livres dou Trésor de Brunetto Latini* (Berkeley and Los Angeles University of California Press, 1948), p. xxiii. All passages of Brunetto's are quoted from this edition.
[118] Ibid.

when Gower himself was writing in his native tongue, perhaps for the first time; or the contrast of Jean de Meun's garrulous, independent Nature with Brunetto's unpersonified, 'obeissant' primal force. but what Gower would have perceived 'à premiére vue' in Brunetto's book was a better way to organize the important materials Gower composed Book VII to convey — better, that is, because the structure and execution of the *Trésor* promised to help clarify complex issues for Gower's broadest audience yet.[119]

For what Brunetto did by removing the 'repétitions et les contradictions de Vincent,' as Carmody puts it, was to create a book more visibly indebted than the vast, amorphous *Speculum* to Aristotle's three categories of human knowledge, *theōrētikē* ('theoretical', called 'theorique' by Brunetto and Gower), *poiētikē* ('productive') and *praktikē ('practical'*, or *'pratike' in the Trésor).*[120] *To these Brunetto added another topic, 'la doctrine de retorike.' The result is a book of great range — in its first livre alone we learn of the origin of the world and the history of the Bible, of astronomy, geography, and natural history — an encyclopedia, truly, but also something else. For always civil government, and the uses of language on which political power depends, provide the nexus of discussion in the Trésor. Thus even in the first, and most heterogeneous, of livres, among the lives of saints and descriptions of animals, we are shown how the European nations (including England) have been ruled, with their sovereign families and traditions traced to Biblical and ancient lines.*[121]

If, however, Brunetto's political interests remain somewhat muted amidst the diversity of the first livre, primus inter pares as they are with a half-dozen significant subjects, they dominate the remainder of the Trésor. Livre two nominally presents the Aristotlean categories 'productive' and 'practical' science, but in effect it is a treatise on how the virtuous state may be achieved and governed.[122] *'Practique' here is translated initially into Christian terms, as concerned with the vices and virtues; then, Aristotle's politikē* (from the *Ethics*) is taken to mean 'De governemens de cités', and discussed using the vocabulary just established.[123] *Livre* three (loosely translating Cicero's *De Officiis*) anatomizes rhetoric as the vehicle for successful rule — 'la science de bien parler et de governer gens.'[124] That Brunetto should interpret these categories in such ways is hardly surprising; he is, after all, the same Florentine whom Dante perhaps condemned for an ear

---

[119] The comparison here is Jean's Nature (*Roman* 1670 ff.) with Latini's (*Trésor* I, vii).
[120] For Aristotle's disctinctions see *Metaphysics* E. and K.7. On Vincent's use of them, see Richard McKeon, 'The Organization of Sciences and the Relations of Cultures in the Twelfth and Thirteenth Centuries,' in *The Cultural Context of Medieval Learning*, Boston Studies in the Philosophy of Science, 26, ed. John Emery Murdoch and Edith Dudley Sylla (Boston and Dordrecht, 1975), pp. 151-84.
[121] E.g., *Trésor* I, xxxv; I, lxxxviiii [sic]; I, lxxxx.
[122] See for example *Trésor* II, iii: 'Donques li ars ki ensegne la cité governer est principale et souveraine et dame de tous ars, si come est retorique, et la Science de fere est et de governer sa maisnie' (Carmody, p. 176); and further pp. 223-24.
[123] *Trésor* II, iii.
[124] On Latini's sources in *livre* three, see McKeon, 'Organization of the Sciences,' p. 161.

too desirously attuned to the beauty of French, and whom he portrayed as holding, even in hell, strong views about his native city-state.[125]

It is these predominant concerns of Brunetto's — with vernacular 'Romania', with Ciceronian rhetoric and public order — which find expression in the *Trésor*, and distinguish it from Vincent's *Speculum* and other encyclopedic works of its time.[126] At once typically scholastic in its devotion to Aristotlean categories, the *Trésor* yet possesses a different spirit, what Roberto Weiss has described in terms of 'a new appreciation of classicism.'[127] And it is through this spirit that we may return finally to our two present questions, concerning the idea Gower probably had of learning, and whether, by following Brunetto's example in Book VII of the *Confessio*, Gower would have pleased both himself and his readership enough to justify its inclusion, even at the price of his seven part 'original' plan.

Like Gower's, Brunetto's work partakes of both the antique and the antiquarian — which, in each of their times, meant a respect for language, politics, and for the lettered past to a degree oddly prophetic of the future. Both men had their audiences, numerous enough to require multiple copies of their manuscripts, extraordinary enough to include the likes of Chaucer and Dante, politically sophisticated enough to recognize a connection between words and government, and a role for the poet in changing the state.[128] For Latini, this meant adding the final sections of the *Trésor*, addressing how a city should choose its governors; for Gower, who opens his poem in its first version with a command from Richard II and closes it, in its latest, with an appeal to the English nation, it meant including Book VII, replete with advice to his sovereigns Richard and Henry and to his countrymen. And it meant as well establishing his credentials as a learned man, to give the authority of the past to his opinions. This is the role, recognized long ago by George R. Coffman, as Gower's 'most important.'[129] This, along with Latini's incipient classicism and the 'practical' sense of learning which they shared, attracted Gower to the *Trésor* as a source and model.

And so Gower added an 'extra' Book to his *Confessio*, to complete this most ambitious of poetic jobs. But was it really 'extra'? Macaulay's third objection would have us think so, certainly. Yet, upon careful reconsideration, I believe

---

[125] See *Inferno* XV, 3 ff. and *Trésor* I, i, 7: 'Et se aucuns demandoit pour quoi cis livres est escris en roumanç, selonc le raison de France, puis ke nous somes italien, je diroie que c'est pour .ii raisons, l'une ke nous somes en France, l'autre por çou que la parleure est plus delitable et plus commune a tous langages' (Carmody, p. 18). For the view that Dante considered Brunetto's fondness for French a sin against his mother tongue, see André Pézard, *Dante sous la pluie de feu* (Paris, 1950), and more recently Eugene Vance, 'The Differing Seed: Dante's Brunetto Latini,' in *Vernacular Poetics in the Middle Ages*, ed. Lois Ebin, Studies in Medieval Culture 16 (Kalamazoo, MI, 1984), pp. 129-52.

[126] On the idea of 'Romania' in the thirteenth century and Latini's sense of it, see Curtius, *European Literature*, p. 32.

[127] Roberto Weiss, *The Renaissance Discovery of Classical Antiquity* (New York: Humanities Press, 1973), p. 13.

[128] On the many manuscripts and recensions of the *Trésor*, see Carmody, pp. xxxii-xxxix.

[129] See Coffman, 'John Gower in His Most Significant Role,' 52-61.

there is reason to suspect the contrary. An eight-Book structure was probably Gower's plan all along. No better evidence can be found for this than the placement of a 'Book of advice and wisdom' in seventh position in the poem when, in principle at least, it might have been included anywhere. There is no formal necessity for its insertion here. The narrative links Gower created — ending Book VI with the story of Nectanabus as a way of bringing to Amans's mind the education of Alexander — are clever and, as Pearsall and others have noted, fictively satisfying.[130] Were that Gower's only purpose, however, such links could have been forged elsewhere with similar success. But as his development of the *Vox Clamantis* suggests, Gower was well aware of the telling power of seven, the number of earth, of finished creation, and of man — his body, contemplative faculties, and his institutions. What better, more effective spot for discourse on the sciences, broadly understood as the sum of the products of man's hand and brain, and on the need for virtuous earthly government, than here?

The point gains deeper resonance when the consequences are considered for Book VIII. 'For eight in medieval exegesis,' V.A. Kolve reminds us,

was understood to be the number of eternity, rebirth, and new beginnings: Christ had risen on the eighth day (the day after the Jewish sabbath); eight persons had been saved in Noah's ark; and in St. Augustine's influential analysis, the history of the world divides itself into eight ages — six marks its historical sequence, the seventh is coeval with them all (the Sabbath of the dead, begun with Abel), and the eighth inaugurates eternity (with Doomsday) its beginning.[131]

In the *Confessio Amantis* this is the function of Book VIII: to inaugurate eternity. The task exacted of the penitent Amans/Gower by Venus — that he 'preie hierafter for the pes' (VIII, 2913) — has obvious personal and national meaning; but the 'Peire of Bedes blak as Sable' (2904) which are Venus's gift make plain it has theological implications, as well. Hence the intricate exchange of masks effected there, of Amans's generic face for that of the more particular 'John Gower' (and subsequently the trading in of that one, too, as the character steps away from the fiction to become the author, Gower); of the poet's disguise as maker only of amorous fictions, for a more serious calling, as composer of prayers; of Amans' apparent youth for the blunt reality of age. This last substitution, often a cause of bewilderment for modern readers, rather points the way Gower intended for our attention to travel, out of this worldly life on the arc of his poem, to contemplate a higher love, justice, and reward.

---

[130] See Derek Pearsall, *Gower and Lydgate* (London, 1969), pp. 16-17.
[131] Kolve, *Chaucer and the Imagery of Narrative*, p. 350.

The outlook, then, from the *Confessio's* last line should be backward and panoramic — the same view, indeed, that Chaucer affords his dead hero as he brings *Troilus and Criseyde* (V, 1814-19) to a close:

> And down from thennes faste he gan avyse
> This litel spot of erthe, that with the se
> Embraced is, and fully gan despise
> This wrecched world, and held al vanite
> To respect of the pleyn felicite
> That is in hevene above.

'Thennes' is — not insignificantly — the eighth sphere, the realm of the fixed stars on the brink of heaven. From here Troilus finds his former passion, like all human attachments, 'blynde lust, the which that may nat laste' (1824). The passage, and Troilus's sentiments, were clearly important to Chaucer, enough at least for him to go outside his source (the *Filostrato*) to borrow the lines from the *Teseida*.[132] In the next stanza following Troilus's vision, the narrator (whose 'I' suddenly sounds suspiciously authorial) delivers four admonitory stanzas, condemning Troilus and warning 'yonge, fresshe folkes, he or she':

> In which that love up groweth with youre age,
> Repeyreth hom fro worldy vanyte,
> And of youre herte up casteth the visage
> To thilke God that after his ymage
> Yow made, and thynketh al nys but a faire
> This world, that passeth soone as floures faire.   (*TC* V, 1835-41)

These stanzas, as I have argued elsewhere, serve as context and introduction to the delivery of the *Troilus* into the hands of 'moral Gower' first, and then the 'philosophical Strode.'[133] They are lines Gower would certainly have known, and may perhaps have influenced his plan for closing the *Confessio*. The step-by-step transformation of Chaucer's narrator, from fictionalized to moralizing to (ultimately) dedicatory voice, with real-world acquaintances and mentors Gower and Strode, is similar structurally to Gower's staged removal of his own fictive masks, Amans and 'John Gower', finally to stand before us as 'himself' at the conclusion of the *Confessio*. But directly influential or not, the handling and significance of Chaucer's lines would scarcely have been lost on Gower — nor would the importance to the lesson of the number eight. In both the *Confessio* and

---

132 That is, *Teseida* XI.1-3; for discussion, see John M. Steadman, *Disembodied Laughter: Troilus and the Apotheosis Tradition: A Re-examination of Narrative and Thematic Contexts* (Berkeley and Los Angeles, 1972).
133 See my 'O moral Gower', 87-99.

the *Troilus*, poems by two friends who address each other in each, eight bears the same meaning, the same thought-provoking weight.

In noting these similarities between the end of *Troilus* and the conclusion of the *Confessio*, I do not mean to suggest that Gower hoped to imitate Chaucer, or that he added matter to his poem merely to swell its number of Books by one, to reach a 'magic number'. Rather, it seems to me that, perceiving the matter he hoped to include, and feeling one duty of the poet to be to the state, he crafted the final two Books of the *Confessio* to capitalize on a symbolic numerology demonstrably meaningful to his audience. Thus, with a seven-Book structure implicit in his framing metaphor of confession, he elected to demonstrate the appropriate application of learning and offer his *speculum regis* in a separate, seventh Book. Far from being a digression, Book VII, in number as well as in *materia*, is a carefully calculated attempt at specific effect. 'Let wisdom grow, then, through seven and eight,' wrote Hugh of St. Victor in 'De arca Noe morali' — words which, if Gower knew them, he would have found descriptive of his plan for the final two Books of the *Confessio Amantis*.[134]

And so we come at last to Macaulay's final objection to Book VII, that its learning and its politics constitute a digression, ill-conceived and valueless, in a poem whose subject is, or should be, courtly love. If what I have argued thus far finds acceptance, then perhaps no more need be said, to answer this objection specifically. (I shall, however, return to discuss these matters in the following chapter.) Like all poetry designed to tax our imagination and our reason, the *Confessio Amantis* challenges us to read complexly, richly, for a meaning just beyond the ones we see at first. That 'lore' should share no part with 'lust' is a notion more modern than medieval — and hardly a divorce that Gower, as his work gives consistent testimony, could ever understand.

V

Over the years, many of Gower's readers — among them some of his best — have questioned his choice of ways to end the *Confessio Amantis*. The 'Tale of Apollonius, Prince of Tyre', and the focus of Book VIII on Incest rather than on the Lust one would expect in a poem built around a lover's confession, singularly distressed William G. Dodd, who found the tale rambling, and the discussion of incest wholly inappropriate.[135] C. S. Lewis, uncomfortable with Venus's priest condemning the chief business of his mistress, attempted to explain the apparent

---

[134] See note 100, above, for citation.
[135] William G. Dodd, *Courtly Love in Chaucer and Gower*, Harvard Studies in English, I (Boston, 1913; rpt. Gloucester, MA, 1959), pp. 74-75.

contradiction by finding some precedent in the 'doctrine' of Andreas Capellanus (the last resort, one might think, of a desperate critic).[136] For Macaulay, incest is justified as a subject because the different forms of Lechery have been discussed enough in the rest of the poem, in Book VII most particularly; but he has little good to say of 'Apollonius', a tale he finds 'not one of Gower's happiest efforts', with 'no sufficient bearing on the subject to justify its inordinate length.'[137]

With one or two prominent exceptions, later judgments have been more approving, of the topic at least, if not always of the tale.[138] J.A.W. Bennett, in a sensitive study of Gower's attitudes toward marriage and human sexuality, has pointed out the care with which the focus of the final Book is established so as to affirm honest generational impulses while condemning abuses.[139] Thus, Bennett observes, Gower attempts to turn Book VIII away from 'Luxuria' in a broad sense, lest its meaning be misunderstood and acquire too great an application, and to discuss incest instead — an especially perverted form of lust with the capability of synecdochic interpretation. More recently, Russell Peck and Elizabeth Porter have deepened and sharpened Bennett's conclusions. In parallel arguments each has illustrated that incest, as the ultimate crime against family, is emblematic of all forces destructive of community and the state; and that Apollonius, beset by evil fortune and worse men, offers us a model for 'ethical self-governance' applicable equally to individual and king.[140] Theirs is I believe the appropriate reading, and I propose to build on it, in this and the following chapter.

At the heart of the program is an etymological understanding of 'incest' — from Latin *in-* (not) *castus* (chaste) — unsurprising in the trilingual Gower. The result is to broaden the meaning of the term beyond the sexual, to include other realms. Thus as Peck has observed, in the *Confessio* 'incest designates unnatural spiritual love as well as sexual union. It is lack of proper chastisement.'[141] So broad a definition has distinct advantages for Gower and the *Confessio*. Structurally, it helps unite the two last Books, and through them the poem. Book VII as we have seen concludes with an exploration of 'Policie', the fifth and final point of which is Chastity. As a bridge to a Book on sexual excess, this contiguity would have been serviceable; but the linkage becomes truly meaningful from the

---

[136] Lewis, *Allegory of Love*, p. 214.

[137] G. C. Macaulay, 'John Gower,' in A.W. Ward and A.R. Waller, eds., *The Cambridge History of English Literature*, II, 172, 174.

[138] Readers recently critical of the 'Tale of Apollonius' include Pearsall (*Gower and Lydgate*, p. 17 and C.A.J. Runacres ('Art and Ethics,' in *Responses and Reassessments*, ed. Minnis, 124).

[139] Bennett, 'Gower's "Honeste Love",' 107-21.

[140] See Peck, *Kingship and Common Profit*, pp. 161-84; Porter, 'Gower's Ethical Microcosm and Political Macrocosm,' in *Responses and Reassess ments*, ed. Minnis, pp. 135-62.

[141] Peck, *Kingship and Common Profit*, p. 165.

wider definition of incest, as general *unchastity*, Gower proffers in Book VIII.[142]
The bridge draws the *speculum regis* of Book VII into the exemplum of Apollonius,
in order to ensure that the political lessons of the Book and tale will be mutually
considered and supported. The 'theoretical' thus is made 'practical' in a move
characteristic both of Gower's poetic and his English poem: When we reflect on
representations of good and bad kingship in Book VIII, we do so using a matrix
just provided, in Book VII. The ends of both Books merge, and are met on
another plane.

The broad meaning of incest in the *Confessio Amantis* is helpful also as a guide to
the length and apparent diffuseness of the 'Tale of Apollonius'. The tale is offered
as a counterexample — the most extensive of any, for it is intended not only to
'cap' the Book in which it appears (as do Gower's other exempla of virtuous
behavior off-setting particular vices), but also, because of its placement as the last
narrative Genius tells Amans, 'Apollonius' reflects and completes the entire
poem as well. The tale is a kind of 'exemplary summa': In it we are presented
with not simply one incident in the life of a character, but very nearly the whole
biography. As a result, we see Apollonius — sometimes alone, sometimes by
extension through Thaise his daughter — confronting the various sins either
singly or in groups. It is as if Gower had decided, in the manner of many writers
of religious manuals, to describe in isolation each problem besetting the novice
and then, when these had been mastered, to set up a situation more like 'real
life', in which everything can (and usually does) occur with no warning, and in
no prescribed order.

This may be seen more clearly from a close examination of the text. First we
must establish the presence of each sin in the tale, and beyond this, the
importance of each as a force motivating the action. With some sins, these tasks
are easily accomplished. Pride, not unexpectedly, Gower names directly as the
root cause of Antiochus's incestuous love (*CA* VIII, 2003-08):

> For se now on that other side,
> Antiochus with al his Pride,
> Which sette his love unkindely,
> His ende he hadde al sodeinly,

[142] Gower's broad understanding of incest is apparent from his use of the term elsewhere
in his work. In *Vox Clamantis* VII, 437-38, for example, a wife is described as 'incestuous'
when 'unchaste' seems called for by the context: 'Si tibi persuadet vxorem fama
pudicam,/ Hinc eciam doleas, fallere queque solet:/ Hic gemut incestum corrupte
coniugis,/ alter Delusus falsa suspicione timet' ('If fame persuades you that your wife is
chaste, you should also lament accordingly that every woman is accustomed to deceive.
One man bemoans the incestuousness of his debased wife, another is afraid of having been
deluded by a false suspicion.' Trans. Stockton, *Major Latin Works*, p. 263). In the *Mirour de
l'Omme* incest appears as a form of looseness among religious (9085-9192) for which the
cure is Continence, 'Naiscant du fine Chasteté' (17750-51). Peck notes further (*Kingship
and Common Profit*, p. 165) that 'Gower apparently had the Latin derivation [of 'incest'
from 'unchaste'] in mind when he provided the moral at the end of the Tale of Virginia',
where the unchaste Apius is chastised.'

> Set ayein kinde upon vengance,
> And for his lust hath his penance.

Antiochus's love is 'unkindeliche' both because it offends against just procreation and because it is hubristic. It is his overweening pride which convinces the king that he stands above the laws of nature. Now, 'Kind' is a touchstone in Gower's work.[143] Those who succeed do so because they humble themselves before its directives; those who fail are often brought low by the very Nature they have affronted. Thus like Capaneus, the archetype of overweening pride of Book I, Antiochus and his daughter are 'forsmiten' by bolts from the sky (*CA* VIII, 1000), a fate commonly reserved for the presumptuous. But here Gower has established the context so that Kind, not Jove, is 'Set ayein . . . upon vengance,' and takes it: In Book VIII, the 'thondre and lyhthnynge' which punish the incestuous pair are elemental forces, terrible justice enacted by wronged Nature itself. The subtle change turns up the moral force a notch, and anticipates the contrasting role played by Kind when Apollonius meets his daughter after many years' separation. She comes unrecognized to cheer him in the dark hold of his ship when he has put into the port of Mitelene, apparently to die of grief (VIII, 1702-09). It is a scene Gower plainly intends to remind us of, and be read against, the pride and 'unkindeliche' lust of Antiochus:

> Bot of hem tuo a man mai liere
> What is to be so sibb of blod:
> Non wiste of other hou it stod,
> And yit the fader ate laste
> His herte upon this maide caste,
> That he hire loveth kindely,
> And yit he wiste nevere why.

Here 'dumb Nature' speaks to Apollonius, directing his right action, through the blood, although 'he wiste nevere why.'[144] His love is 'kindely' — appropriate,

---

[143] On Gower's use of 'Kind' see especially Olsson, 'Natural Law and John Gower's *Confessio Amantis*,' 229-61; and Hugh R.B. White, 'Nature and the Good in Gower's *Confessio Amantis*,' in *Recent Readings*, ed. Yeager, 1-20.

[144] Peck has found a potential for incest in this scene, which Apollonius chastely avoids. He remarks: 'When Thaise sings to woo [Apollonius] from his melancholy, he feels strong love for her. But he does not impose on her. Rather than taking what is near at hand and thus losing his daughter, as Antiochus did, he recovers his daughter by loving chastely.' See *Kingship and Common Profit*, p. 169. It is worth remarking that the mysterious kinship Apollonius feels here is Gower's addition; it does not appear in his sources. As Macaulay notes, however, we find the same idea in the 'Tale of Constance' (Book II, 1381-82):

> This child he loveth kindely,
> And yit he wot no cause why.

The scene describes the 'natural' (but to him inexplicable) reaction of King Alee to Moris, his son by Constance, neither of whom he has seen in years. See Macaulay, *Works* II, 543.

decorous, true. The contrast with Antiochus, deafened by pride to such elemental voices and 'loving' in name only, is purposefully stark, and telling.

The sin of Avarice is another which, like Pride, is easily established as a motivating force. It makes its most obvious appearance through the relationship of Thaise and Leonin, the brothel-keeper who purchases her from pirates. Correctly assessing that it is only for money that Leonin detains her in the brothel, Thaise tells his servant of a bargain she would strike with the whoremaster for her release (VIII, 1449-56):

> If so be that thi maister wolde
> That I his gold encresce scholde,
> It mai noght falle be this weie:
> Bot soffre me to go mi weie
> Out of this hous wher I am inne,
> And I schal make him forto winne
> In some place elles of the toun,
> Be so it be religioun . . .

Leonin agrees, realizing that he was receiving 'beyete non/ At the bordel be cause of hire': Thaise's weeping and moral rectitude drive off all of the potential customers. Gower stresses Leonin's reasons, already patent (VIII, 1477-79):

> He hath hire fro the bordel take,
> Bot that was noght for goddes sake,
> Bot for the lucre, as sche him tolde.

Nor is Thaise the only character to encounter Avarice in the tale. Apollonius also meets with it, in a form accorded to the particular fictions of the *Confessio Amantis* through Gower's characteristic sensitivity to polylingual nuance. Antiochus, we learn, is incited to incest not only by Pride and Lust, but also by that 'fleshly Avarice' which the *Confessio* so carefully defines. Thus it is pointed out (VIII, 293-97):

> For likinge and *concupiscence*
> Withoute *insihte* of conscience
> The fader so with lustes *blente*,
> That he caste al his hole entente
> His oghne doghter forto spille.

As Peck has observed, cupidity and blindness purposefully conjoin in the *Confessio*, a poem in which Cupid (who lost his sight after incestuously loving his mother) plays a central role.[145] For obvious reasons, their connection in 'Apollonius', as descriptive of Antiochus's behavior, is especially effective. Coupled together with 'insihte of conscience' the language here looks forward to Apollonius's contrasting treatment of his own daughter when he meets her unaware in the ship's hold in Mitelene. Certainly the circumstances stand conducive to indiscretion: into the privacy of his chamber a beautiful young girl is sent, singing and playing the harp 'lich an Angel', telling him 'sondri bordes' (jests) and asking him 'demandes strange,' willing, indeed, 'Be alle weies that sche can,/ To glade with this sory man' (VIII, 1661-62). But 'insihte of conscience' — a force of 'kind' like voices of the 'sibb in blod' — protects Apollonius as we have seen, keeping him from any concupiscent love and branding Antiochus's willing perversion all the more heinous by contrast.

Apollonius's rejection of Avarice is rendered in a more conventional way in the tale as well. He shows extraordinary charity to the starving people of Tharsis through the gift of his shipload of wheat (VIII, 548-570). By this he preserves the citizenry, taking from them 'riht noght' in exchange. His act is pure, a liberal demonstration of commonality with those about whom he knows nothing save that they too are men, and in need. Since Apollonius is in hiding from the assassins of Antiochus at the time, this wheat represents his complete worldly stock. Thus his willingness to share it, although related without fanfare by Gower, is quite significant, and helps to define both the character of Apollonius and the virtues proposed by the *Confessio Amantis* throughout.

Envy too plays a large part in 'Apollonius'. It is Thaise who must suffer its stings, directed at her by Strangulio and Dionise, her temporary foster parents. The cause Gower presents most plainly (VIII, 1336-44):

> A dowhter hath Strangulio,
> The which was cleped Philotenne:
> Bot fame, which wole evere renne,
> Cam al day to hir moder Ere,
> And seith, wher evere hir doghter were
> Wit Thayse set in eny place,
> The comun vois, the comun grace
> Was al upon that other Maide,
> And of hir doghter noman saide.

The 'fame' of Thaise which so infuriates Dionise is for her learning and her skills at all the gentle arts, from harping to characteristic 'courtayse'. In these, we should take note, Thaise bears her father's stamp — for he too is courteous in deed and word, a harper, and exceedingly well instructed (VIII, 390-93):

---

[145] Ibid., p. 165.

Of every naturel science,
Which eny clerk him couthe teche,
He couthe ynowh, and in his speche
Of wordes he was eloquent.

The identification of father and daughter is more than parenthetically
important in a story involving incest. On one level, it helps define exactly what is
meant by 'sibb of blod', the connection we have examined just above, and it will
be seen to have additional resonance when we turn to explore Gower's treatment
of Gluttony in the following pages. Here, however, we are meant to exchange
Thaise and Apollonius back and forth, through the medium of their similarity, to
observe and reflect upon Envy's indiscriminate nature. No one good is safe: that
is the message. When Strangulio betrays Thaise out of jealousy, so he also turns
traitor to Apollonius, with strikingly analogous results. This we see as the
narrative progresses.

Following the death of Thaise's favorite nurse, Dionise decides to take her
revenge on the girl, 'Thurgh,' Gower notes, 'pure treson and envie' (VIII,
1356). Dionise's case of *Invidia* nearly proves to be the end of Thaise, once by the
hand of the servant Theophilus, despatched to kill her, then later by casting her
into the clutches of brothel-master Leonin of Mitelene. Indirectly, it of course
facilitates the reunion of Apollonius and his daughter, but not before he too is
forced to wander over the seas and hover at the edge of death; and eventually it
brings about the trial and hanging of Dionise and Strangulio themselves.

The exaction of this vengeance rewards close scrutiny. The deaths of Dionise
and Strangulio put right their earlier iniquity and square the books. In Gower's
universe deliberate wrong-doing never escapes punishment. Moreover, father
and daughter (and son-in-law-to-be Athenagoras) travel *together* to Tharsis to
punish the wicked couple. This emphasizes the essential moral unity of
Apollonius and Thaise — in all right actions their wills correspond — and draws
attention simultaneously to the communal nature of justice. For despite the
horrible deaths of Strangulio and his wife (they are hanged, drawn, 'And brent
and with the wynd toblowe' [VIII, 1948-49]), no blood adheres either to Thaise
or Apollonius. This is because, I believe, Gower means us to understand sin
always as a crime against humanity, and justice as the appropriate communal
response. Thus it is the citizens of Tharsis, having heard Apollonius's grievances,
who themselves bring Strangulio and Dionise to trial and execute them legally —
thereby protecting Apollonius from any sinfulness himself, even wrath, and
certainly from that peculiar form of envy inherent in revenge. And thus too, to
complete the circle of community, these same citizens receive a new and better
pair of rulers: Thaise herself, and her husband Athenagoras, both notably free
from *Invidia*.

Ire appears throughout the tale in various shapes, but in predictable places.
Dionise, for example, is 'wroth' (VIII, 1345) as well as envious at Thaise;
Antiochus, upon hearing Apollonius's correct answer to his question, has a heart

full of 'rancour and ire' (VIII, 500). In contrast to both, Apollonius is specifically *not* wrathful, but just, in his reactions. When he arrives in Tharsis with Thaise and Athenagoras, he pointedly explains to the people that he 'pes and love soghte'; and when justice is done on the criminals, Gower adds (VIII, 1953-61):

> And every man hath gret mervaile,
> Which herde tellen of this chance,
> And thonketh goddes pourveance,
> Which doth *mercy* forth with justice.
> Slain is the moerdrer and moerdrice
> Thurgh verray trowthe of rihtwisnesse,
> And thurgh *mercy* sauf is simplesce
> Of hire whom *mercy* preserveth.

The reference to Strangulio and Dionise as 'moerdrer and moerdrice' is initially puzzling, but significant here. They are not strictly guilty of killing anyone, though they did sanction an attempt on Thaise's life. The appellations become clearer, however, when the emphasis on Mercy in the lines is noted. In Book III, Gower balances Mercy as the antidote to Wrath, specifically as exemplified by murder.[146] The purpose, then, of his treatment here is to recall that earlier discussion of wrath, and to counterpoise Apollonius carefully outside its purview. Like the good king he is meant to epitomize, and like the good man generally, Apollonius seeks justice, of which one face is mercy.

The characterization of Apollonius's dealings with Dionise and Strangulio has some importance too as a measure of how far even a good man may come in developing self-control through wisdom. For Apollonius himself, at an earlier stage in his history, has been driven close to wrathful injury. When Thaise comes to cheer him in his ship after it has been washed off course into the port of Mitelene, he reacts violently to her ministrations (VIII, 1684-94):

> Bot he for no suggestioun
> Which toward him sche couthe stere,
> He wolde noght o word ansuere,
> Bot as a madd man ate laste

[146] Gower uses the brief history of a bird with a man's face (*CA* III, 2599-2616) as an example proving the virtues of mercy. Having killed and eaten a man, the bird recognizes a kinship with its victim and dies of remorse. The moral, Gower notes, is (2617-21):
> Be this ensample it mai wel suie
> That man schal homicide eschie,
> For evere is merci good to take,
> Bot if the lawe it hath forsake
> And that justice is therayein.
The *caveat* connecting mercy with justice is especially apt as a comment on Apollonius's condition in Book VIII, and his subsequent treatment of Strangulio, Dionise and the people of Tharsis.

His heved wepende awey he caste,
And half in wrahthe he bad hire go.
Bot yit sche wolde noght do so,
And in the derke forth sche goth,
Til sche him toucheth, and he wroth,
And after hire with his hond
He smot.

Here we must notice how carefully Gower covers this 'wroth' of Apollonius: He is weeping, like a 'madd man' (a reference designed to recall the wild hatred of Antiochus), and finally only 'half in wrahthe' anyway. When the gesture becomes the means of mutual recognition of father and daughter, we see that Apollonius's ire is intended not as a criticism but as fictive architecture: Its effect is a humanizing one. No 'patient Griselda,' Apollonius is a man with a breaking point, at once by this action more like us and — as a consequence — a figure more properly useful as a model for behavior.

The presence of Sloth is somewhat more difficult to discover, but it is there nonetheless, in several contexts. Antiochus partly is undone by it — for, as Gower notes, 'This king hath leisir at his wille' (VIII, 288 ff.), and 'welthe' as well, an ominous combination when 'The fleissh is frele and falleth ofte.' But the primary *locus* of Sloth in the tale is not associated with Antiochus. It occurs rather in the passage quoted above, in which Apollonius strikes out at his daughter. He does so in a state of near despair at what he believes to be his losses: his kingdom, his daughter, and his wife. Apollonius's abject misery indicates an absence of hope, and approximates what was understood in the Middle Ages as the final stage of Sloth.[147] Such hopelessness Gower has described before in the *Confessio*.[148]

---

[147] The last stage of Sloth was 'Wanhope.' According to the *Book of Vices and Virtues*, an afflicted man: . . . falleþ in sorwe and is euele apaied of his self, and hateþ himself and desireþ his own deeþ . . . .And after þes sorweful poyntes of slewþe, þe deuel yiueþ hym a stroke of deeþ and putteþ hym in wanhope and purchaseþ his deeþ and sleeþ hym, or biweileþ himself as a man in wanhope, and so ȝeueþ hym to al manere of euele deedes.' See Francis, *Book of Vices*, p. 29. The matter is summarized in chart form by Siegfried Wenzel, *The Sin of Sloth: Acedia in Medieval Thought and Literature* (Chapel Hill, 1960), p. 82.
[148] Cf. *Mirour* 5749-72, where Gower describes Despair. The portrait closely resembles Wanhope from penitentials like the *Book of Vices and Virtues* (5749-57):

Molt ad grant joye ly malfee
Quant l'omme ad fait desespere;
Car lors le meine par le frein
Tout voegle apres sa volonte,
Q'au droite voie en nul degre
Rettourner sciet, siq'au darrein
Se pent ou tue de sa mein;
Dont est du double mort certein,
Comme fuist Judas ly malure.

['The devil rejoices greatly when he has made man despairing, for then he leads man by the bridle, all blind, according to his will; for man can by no means return to the right

He indeed concludes Book IV, on Sloth, with the tale of 'Iphis and Araxarathen', designed to illustrate just this sin, calling it 'Tristesce'. The lines portray Apollonius's condition perfectly (IV, 3389-3403):

> Whan Slowthe hath don al that he may
> To dryve forth the longe day,
> Til it be come to the nede,
> Thanne ate laste upon the dede
> He loketh hou his time is lore,
> And is so wo begon therfore,
> That he withinne his thoghte conceiveth
> Tristesce, and so himself deceiveth,
> That he wanhope bringeth inne,
> Wher is no confort to beginne,
> Bot every joie him is deslaied:
> So that withinne his herte affraied
> A thousand time with o breth
> Wepende he wissheth after deth,
> Whan he fortune fint adverse.

Apollonius's refusal to speak to anyone, his self-imprisonment in the dark of his ship, his deafness to all attempts to cheer him ('Bot he nomore than the wal/ Tok hiede of eny thing he herde' [VIII, 1672-73]), all mark him as suffering from Tristesce, the despair representative of Sloth in its most serious form. That he is saveable only by his daughter futher demonstrates the precariousness of his condition. Throughout Book VIII, Thaise has been developed as a specific counterweight to despair, a model of chaste energy and Christian diligence. Her trials parallel those of Apollonius when she, too, finds herself in a dungeon — Leonin's, where she weeps so pitifully no man can deflower her. Yet, rather than resign herself to her ruin, or take her own life, Thaise pointedly employs wit and industry to win her release. Her scheme to substitute virtuous work for whoredom (she will use her gentle skills and great learning to open a school for proper young ladies in order to supply the profit demanded by Leonin) is a brilliant stroke, and replete with just that order of courage required by Apollonius in his misery. Gower is specific about what great effort is involved to bring Apollonius up from the literal and symbolic depths: Thaise tells her entire story, 'fro point to point', not complainingly (until this moment she 'never dorste make hir mone' [VIII, 1727]), but with vigor and merciful willingness, to help

way, and so at last man hangs or kills himself with his own hand. Then man is sure of double death, as was Judas the wretched.' Trans. Wilson.] It is the danger of suicide as an only course of action which Thaise, who offers Apollonius positive choices, is included to avert. That she should accomplish this through music, jests and light stories accords with medieval medical theory; see Glending Olson, *Literature as Recreation in the Later Middle Ages* (Ithaca, NY, 1982).

this stranger and preserve him from his own worst thoughts. The terms Gower
selects to describe Apollonius's reaction are worth noting (VIII, 1736-47):

> Fro this day forth fortune hath sworn
> To sette him upward on the whiel;
> So goth the world, now wo, now wel:
> This king hath founde newe grace,
> So that out of his derke place
> He goth him up into the liht,
> And with him cam that swete wiht,
> His doghter Thaise, and forth anon
> Thei bothe into the Caban gon
> Which was ordeigned for the king,
> And ther he dede of al his thing,
> And was arraied realy.

Clearly the ascent of Apollonius and Thaise (for emotionally they are
inseparable, each providing the 'cure' for the sorrow of the other) parallels the
upward swing of fortune's wheel, as their luck turns permanently for the better at
this point in the tale. But to read the passage so narrowly is to neglect its subtle
theology. 'Grace' Apollonius has found indeed, and it raises him 'out of his derke
place' at the nadir of belief 'up into the liht' where once again he can take
command. Significantly, he re-enters the royal chamber he has neglected and
disrobes, only to put on new garments symbolic of his renewed self-possession.
The passage thus has the quality of parable: with great subtlety and characteristic
gentleness, Gower shows us how each man may retrieve his 'kingship' from the
dungeon of despair.

Gluttony, the last remaining sin, also has a significant presence in the 'Tale of
Apollonius'. The lines describing Antiochus's fleshly frailty unmistakeably
suggest this vice, with their emphasis on soft living. So too does Gower's
description of Antiochus's lust for his daughter, a passion so consuming it can
only be portrayed as a form of ingestion (VIII, 309-10):

> The wylde fader thus devoureth
> His oghne fleissh, which non soccoureth.

These same terms reappear in the riddle Antiochus poses to his daughter's suitors
(VIII, 405-09):

> With felonie I am upbore,
> I ete and have it noght forbore
> Mi modres fleissh, whos housebonde

> Mi fader forto seche I fonde,
> Which is the Sone ek of my wif.

Gower's treatment here bears important similarities to the sub-section 'Love-Delicacy' in Book VI, on Gluttony. To a lover afflicted by this vice, women seem as food, to be tested and passed over when the appetite cloys (VI, 665-72):

> And riht so changeth his estat
> He that of love is delicat:
> For thogh he hadde to his hond
> The beste wif of al the lond,
> Or the faireste love of alle,
> Yit wolde his herte on othre falle
> And thenke hem more delicious
> Than he hath in his oghne hous.

Cookery predominates as imagery throughout this section. Delicate lovers are said to 'feed' on other than 'comun mete', prepared by a 'confeccion of cokes' representing the whims and fancies of an idle heart. Amans, in describing his nightly fantasies, continues the metaphor. His 'bord' is set with 'every syhte and every word/ Of lust' (VI, 920-21); his desire for his lady is a 'hunger' and a 'famine'; she herself, a 'repast' which to achieve would be to enjoy 'the grete feste'.

It is within this context of table-language that we must understand Gower's assessment of Antiochus, albeit darkened to reflect the abominable nature of incest and the shortness of time. For if in Book VI, with two Book-length lessons yet to go, Genius can appear to afford a certain irresponsibility of metaphor in his and Amans's discourse, treating women as food, by Book VIII the seriousness of his subject and Amans's continued resistance to learning have reduced his latitude considerably. Certainly Genius seems to pull all the stops: His description brings forward the world of Antiochus in all its horror. The 'hevedes stondende on the gate' of slain suitors when Apollonius arrives to take his chances, and (VIII, 372-73):

> The remenant that weren wise
> Eschuieden to make assay.

Apollonius has entered a ghastly place where, as in *King Lear*, 'Humanity must perforce prey upon itself, Like monsters of the deep.'[149] Here every detail included or neglected can carry meaning — life-preserving, literally, for Apollonius and, by extension, Amans and ourselves. Names and titles, for

---

[149] *King Lear*, VI. 2.48-49.

example, are all-important: As Antiochus's riddle shows, grossest appetite within his kingdom has confused distinctions between mother, father, son and daughter, wife and husband, reducing them all to 'fleissh' on which he feeds. And what does it mean that Antiochus's daughter has no name, in a tale in which even the least servants and functionaries (Taliart the poisoner [VIII, 505], Lichorida the nurse [VIII, 1033], Cerymon the leech [VIII, 1166]) are made known? Doubtless the lack of a name for Antiochus's daughter in the source has bearing on the case — but Gower never hesitates to add or change names, even characters, when he sees fit.[150] (Indeed, in 'Apollonius' he creates a daughter for the doctor Cerymon, apparently for didactic reasons.)[151] Thus the namelessness of Antiochus's daughter in Book VIII bears a message we should ponder: that, all relative lightness of description in Book VI notwithstanding, sexual gluttony has no acceptable side.

Against this monstrous world Gower sets that of Apollonius, whose love is chaste and proper for his wife and daughter (significantly kept separate from Antiochus, not only in name and function, but also by vast geographical distance). The difference between the men, example and counterexample, is especially vivid if considered through the lens of Antiochus's love-gluttony. The resultant picture is of a man horribly divided. On one hand, in order to live with his crime, Antiochus rejects consanguinity. Thus he sees his daughter as 'prey', an 'object' of desire and no part of himself. On the other hand, however, he cannot bury completely his awareness of the truth: He confesses in his riddle to consuming his *own* flesh and blood, as we have seen above. The result is a representation of disunity with an important symbolic message: Only a 'whole' man avoids reduction to cannibal status.

This reductive, divisive objectification Gower pointedly has Apollonius avoid, through an instinctual, inchoate recognition of kinship, of 'one-ness'. The 'kindely' love Apollonius feels for Thaise in the hold of the ship in Mitelene reveals truly 'What it is to be so sibb of blod': not gluttonous in any sense, it is to recognize and honor relationships essential to the social bond, of man and woman, father, mother and child. Finally, it cautions us to support and nurture, not consume, since by short extrappolation every 'other' is ourselves. It is a

---

[150] Gower's source, as he notes himself, is Godfrey of Viterbo's *Pantheon*; but see also Macaulay's commentary, *Works* III, 53 ff., in which he suggests evidence for Gower's use of other versions too, including the latin prose *Historia Apollonii Tyrii*. In none of these, nor in the *Gesta Romanorum*, where the tale is told also, does the daughter of Antiochus have a name. See further the studies of S. Singer, *Apollonius von Tyrus: Untersuchungen über das Fortleben des antiken Romans in spätern Zeit* (Halle, 1895), pp. 177-89; Elimar Klebs, *Die Erzählung von Apollonius von Tyrus: Eine geschichtliche Untersuchung über lateinische Urform und ihre späteren Bearbeitungen* (Berlin, 1899), pp. 462-71; and Albert H. Smyth, *Shakespeare's Pericles and Apollonius of Tyre: A Study in Comparative Literature* (Philadelphia, 1898), pp. 10-25, 47-56.

[151] Macaulay, who noticed the additional daughter, called it 'apparently an invention of Gower's' — but thought it possibly a misreading of 'adhibitis amicis filiam sibi adoptavit, that is, he adopted her as his daughter' (*Works* III, 541, note to l. 1248). The additional 'good' father/daughter relationship hardly damages Gower's case in the story, however, and seems to me to have been quite deliberate.

lesson, like all in Book VIII, with special relevance to Apollonius the king as well as private man, and one we shall take up again in the following chapter.

Within the overall structure of the *Confessio Amantis*, then, the 'Tale of Apollonius' is the capstone. It offers a series of exempla and counterexempla not only to the sins of incest and lechery, but also to those described in the other Books of the poem. Adhering in this case also to the modular approach outlined in the beginning of this chapter, Gower with 'Apollonius' fills out and extends his scheme by encompassing, in one final tale, the possibilities and the pitfalls of 'real life'. As we observe Apollonius and Thaise meet, react to, and at last overcome the cardinal sins one by one, we are given a lead to follow, and specific characters (Antiochus and his daughter, Dionise and Strangulio) to serve us as warnings.

VI

'Apollonius of Tyre' then is a sustained performance, and a consistent conclusion for the exemplum-method of instruction which Gower has developed throughout his work. As evinced by the *Confessio* the method proceeds from a sure-handed sense of structure of tale to tale, of tale to Book, and of Book to Book. In the succeeding pages, these notions will be shown to expand and encompass Gower's architectonic vision of the entire poem. But before proceeding, it is perhaps appropriate to take note of what these five 'hard cases' reveal about Gower's poetry as a whole. I have argued that through them we have means to test Gower's achievement against an inferrable poetic, a vision at once logical, artful, and whole. If my readings are correct, they stand forth, not as blunders prompted by enthusiasm or naivete, but rather as exceptions which, in their complex richness of execution and design, thoroughly 'prove the rule' of Gower's mastery and control.

CHAPTER V: ARION'S FINAL SONG

Subtle mastery of sections, however, does not a full poetic make; and much remains before that claim can be sustained. For, despite several recent efforts to demonstrate the coherence of the *Confessio Amantis*, and thus to establish its poet's reputation solidly, John Gower in the minds of many remains a journeyman artist, of talent insufficient to sustain the high quality of his short flights for long.[1] Such readers share the opinion of C.S. Lewis, whose attitude was unequivocal:

> Gower has risen to great poetry, but he is not a great poet. The restraint which is visible in single lines and short passages innumerable deserts him in the conduct of the poem as a whole. He says too much, not at this point or that, but too much *simpliciter*.[2]

Lewis is objecting here specifically to what he called the 'long and unsuccessful coda' — the Epilogue to the Lover's confession, after Amans has learned of his unsuitability for the Court of Love and has been released from Venus's power — but Lewis speaks to broader issues of consistency and digression as well. Ultimately, his evaluation calls into question a discoverable purpose or meaning for the *Confessio Amantis*, which might justify its collection of tales on levels other than the fictive and romantic.

To argue the contrary, as I shall in this chapter, requires scrutiny of apparently divergent themes of social and emotional health, or love and right rule, which occur variously (though not always obviously) throughout the *Confessio Amantis* as parts of an extended treatment of marriage, envisioned both as sacrament and as metaphor. More specifically, it means examining the interrelation of Prologue and Epilogue to the central fiction of the poem, Amans's confession; and it means scrutinizing the function of Book VII, on the education of Prince Alexander.

I

Let us begin with Lewis's critique of what he calls Gower's 'coda.' Implicit here is the idea that the *Confessio Amantis* is a love-vision gone wrong in its last stages, just when Gower, instead of seeking a dramatically effective conclusion,

---

[1] See for example Fisher, *John Gower*; Gallacher, *Love, the Word, and Mercury*; Peck, *Kingship and Common Profit*; and Patricia J. Eberle, 'Vision and Design in John Gower's *Confessio Amantis*.' 1977.
[2] C. S. Lewis, *Allegory of Love*, pp. 221-22.

'says too much' about politics and morality. Implicit also in Lewis's view is the assumption that these are new ideas to the *Confessio*, and hence have no place coming in as they do, at the end. Yet the issues of the Epilogue are not new to the poem. They represent solutions to problems raised earlier, in the Prologue, and should be so understood. To follow Gower's argument properly, we must trace the conversations of Amans, Venus and Genius which close Book VIII. There, with Amans's confession complete, Genius attempts in his delicate, suggestive way to persuade the Lover to 'Tak love where it mai noght faille' — a source which, though left unspecified, clearly cannot be Amans's lady.[3] Genius also hints at the Lover's advanced age, which makes his desire for a young girl unnatural and hence unlawful, even from the procreational vantage of Genius and Venus. Amans, however, as yet incapable of such understanding, insists that the comedy be played to the finish. Genius carries Amans's supplication to Venus, who returns and, after some circumlocution herself, at last makes plain to Amans why he is unwelcome in her court (VIII, 2403-07):

> For loves lust and lockes hore
> In chambre acorden nevermore,
> And thogh thou feigne a yong corage,
> It scheweth wel be the visage
> That olde grisel is no fole.

At this rejection, the Lover faints. He is sent a vision of two companies of spirits: one, led by Youth, makes merry with 'Harpe and Lute and with Citole'; the other, led by Elde, dances a more sedate 'softe pas' accompanied by a musette. Elde's followers (who include King David, Sampson, Dalilah, Virgil, Aristotle, Plato, and Ovid) plead with Venus to 'comfort' the aged Lover. Cupid removes from Amans's breast a 'fyri Lancegay' and Venus then annoints the wound left in his heart with an ointment 'mor coold than eney keie,' putting some as well on his temples and loins.[4] She shows him his reflection in a mirror, and his aged face and gray hairs so shock him that he awakens from his swoon. When Venus asks him 'as it were in game' what love might be, he has no answer, except to say it

---

[3] New studies by Kurt Olsson ('Aspects of *Gentilesse* in John Gower's *Confessio Amantis*, Books III-V') and David G. Allen ('God's Faithfulness and the Lover's Despair: The Theological Framework of the Iphis and Araxarathen Story'), focussing on the lady's 'hard-heartedness' as revealed in the 'Tale of Iphis and Araxarathen' in Book IV, are clarifying in this regard. Both read Gower's message as an attempt to illustrate the necessary futility of Amans's appeals to his lady. See *Recent Readings*, ed. Yeager, 225-73 and 209-23, respectively.

[4]
> 'Er I out of mi trance aros,
> Venus, which hield a boiste clos,
> And wolde noght I scholde deie,
> Tok out mor cold than eny keie
> An oignement, and in such point
> Sche hath my wounded herte enoignt,
> My temples and my Reins also.'   (*CA* VIII, 2813-19)

was something far from his thought. The old man requests leave to depart, and
after he receives absolution from Genius, the goddess gives him 'a peire of Bedes
blak as Sable', on which 'Wes write of gold, "Por reposer" ' (VIII, 2907).

Along with this gift, Venus provides specific advice. The lines are important,
and should be considered carefull (VIII, 2908-27)y:

> 'Lo,' thus sche seide, 'John Gower,
> Now thou art ate laste cast,
> That thou nomore of love sieche.
> Bot my will is that thou beseiche
> And preie hierafter for the pes,
> And that thou make plein reles
> To love, which takth litel hiede
> Of olde men upon the nede,
> Whan that the lustes be aweie:
> Forthi to the nys bot o weie,
> In which let reson be thi guide;
> For he may sone himself misguide,
> That seth noght the peril tofore.
> Mi sone, be wel war therfore,
> And kep the sentence of my lore
> And tarie thou mi Court nomore,
> Bot go ther vertu moral duelleth,
> Wher ben thi bokes, as men telleth,
> Which of long time thou hast write.'

Two major points are noteworthy here. First, by identifying the character
Amans with 'John Gower,' author of books, Venus helps close the fiction of the
poem and move the remainder of the Epilogue away from limited, amorous
concerns. She points back our attention toward the authorial voice whose fears at
the 'divisioun' of the world and the corruption of the three estates comprised
much of the Prologue. This logically leads to Venus's second point. An old man,
'John Gower' should concern himself not with love but with 'vertu moral;' he
should pray for peace. But peace of what sort, and how?

Apparently heeding Venus's instructions, old 'Gower' quickly clarifies the
matter by composing a prayer which recalls unmistakably the tone and themes of
the Prologue. The second recension of the *Confessio* details the Estates and
dictates the direction each must take to reform the evils discussed in the Prologue.
Thus the clergy, with whom Gower begins, are advised to act according to the
laws of charity, and to 'procure/ Oure pes toward the hevene above' (VIII, 2998-
99). This certainly would come as a major reversal of the greed and contention
attributed earlier by Gower to the cloth. Similarly, the 'chevalerie,' the barons of
the realm, ought to defend, not ravage, church and people; and merchants
should give up their 'compassement and tricherie,' their 'brocage' which leads
only to (VIII, 3041-44):

> . . . divisioun,
> Which many a noble and worthi toun
> Fro welthe and fro prosperite
> Hath brought to gret adversite.)

The prayer of the Epilogue, then, must be understood as an attempt to bring the *Confessio* full circle, to focus attention once more on the problems outlined in the Prologue. Gower's handling of the reformation of Amans helps create the necessary transition out of the circumstances of the confession, transforming its courtly fiction into the discussion of real problems promised by the authorial voice of the Prologue.

These correspondences represent only part of the plan, however. The effect of naming the Lover, at this late and climactic juncture, 'John Gower,' is to direct and control more fully the transformation of amorous narrative into the moral and political discourse promised in the Prologue. By conjoining his three distinct voices (Amans, the 'I' of story; Amans/John Gower, the 'I' of the Prologue, and John Gower man and poet) in as many successive steps, Gower hopes to move us imaginatively and intellectually from the fictive ravages of a disappointed heart to a prayer for peace anticipatory of national, international, and cosmic resonance.

Essential to, and evidential of, this movement is the double chronology of the *Confessio*'s frame narrative. Although Amans's conversations with Genius are related in the present tense, we understand them to be in the past since we have been told, in Book I, that what we are about to hear is the history of a dream. As if to underscore the point against all misunderstanding, Gower added the Latin sidenote at I, 59: 'Hic quasi in persona aliorum, quos amor alligat, fingens se auctor esse Amantem, varias eorum passiones variis huius libri distinccionibus per singula scribere proponit.' ['The author henceforth, pretending to be a lover, as if in the person of those others whom love binds, plans to write concerning their different passions, each by each, in the different portions of this work.'] What we observe here is the voice of the dreamer awakened, the survivor who knows the outcome and has been changed by the experience he will relate, although in what ways he will not reveal until the narrative reaches the appropriate moment for their regeneration. This chronological perspective is reinforced by the use of the past tense generally for narrative description in the frame. The detail has major significance for what we should think of the poem, because the *Confessio Amantis* is a work which ends with a conversion: Amans, the Lover of Book I, has been altered by his experience. He is by no means the same after his confession and meeting with Venus as he was when he lived through it. In fact, what we observe is the kind of 'death' of one character and the 'birth' of another common to the Christian understanding of conversion from Augustine on through Dante. As is always the case in works employing this model, the process effects the narrative itself, making the story-telling possible.[5] In the

---

[5] The point is eloquently made by John Freccero: 'The Christian theme of conversion satisfies the contrary exigencies of autobiography by introducing a radical discontinuity into the sequence of a life thanks to which one can tell one's own story as though it were

Confessio it is a change pointedly reflected in the transformation of 'Amans' into 'John Gower' — an exchange of an intertextually referential, generic appellation meaning only 'Lover' (and hence descriptive of an emotional state rather than of an individual) for an unique name of a 'real' person who receives both his identity and his life-role (to become a poet by praying for peace) simultaneous with the death of his passion.[6]

Thus, the register of Amans's naivete is from the beginning a device — one which he shares with Amans/Gower the narrator (the 'John Gower' Venus recognizes in the fiction) and, on a profounder scale, with Gower the poet. Although a creation of Gower the poet, Amans/Gower is still the 'personal voice' so actively opening out 'his' history, detail by detail — a characteristic he shares with the pilgrim Dante of the *Commedia*.[7] On this primary, fictive level, then, Amans/Gower bears responsibility with Gower the poet for the shape of the *Confessio Amantis*. Both manipulate reader perspective — ultimately, I believe, toward identical ends.

This double chronology is nowhere clearer than in the presentation of the major surprise of the poem, the Lover's age. The fact is a primary one, from all viewpoints the *Confessio*'s dramatic masterstroke. Gower the poet naturally had every reason to reveal it only after proper preparation, so as to lose none of its complex effect. But Amans/Gower the narrator? What concern had 'he' to relate a dream dramatically? Here Gower incorporates no excuses, as does Chaucer when, in the *Canterbury Tales*, he justifies the salty *Miller's Tale*'s inclusion, lest he

---

true, definitive, and concluded. Death in life is closure in the story, but it is thanks to a spiritual resurrection that the story can be told. It was Augustine who set the pattern for this Christian thematization of narrative structure in his *Confessions*.' Or, in Rachel Jacoff's analysis: 'Conversion as theme and narrative mode provides the necessary "Archimedean point" from which the author of such a story can speak as if the story were both complete and accurate. For both Augustine and Dante such a point is constituted by a death of the old self which makes possible the new consciousness, the story of whose coming into being — "the story of how the self that was becomes the self that is" — is at once its subject and its structure.' For both see Freccero, *Poetics of Conversion*, ed. Jacoff, xii. It is this quality of the 'changed man' which distinguishes Gower's narrative from French dream poems in which poets name themselves. See George Kane, *Piers Plowman: The Evidence for Authorship* (London, 1965), pp. 6 ff., for examples of such poets' appearances in their dream poems; and further John Burrow, 'The Poet as Petitioner,' *Studies in the Age of Chaucer* 3 (1981), 61-75. In contrast to the French, Gower's similarity to Dante is the more clear.

[6] John Burrow has made a strong case for this generality of Amans, linking him to the ineffectual lovers of the *dits amoreux* of Machaut and Froissart. See his 'The Portrayal of Amans in *Confessio Amantis*,' in *Responses and Reassessments*, ed. Minnis, pp. 5-24, and especially 11.

[7] In his classic essay, 'Chaucer the Pilgrim' (*PMLA* 69 [1954], 928-36; rpt. *Speaking of Chaucer* [New York, 1970], pp. 1-10), E.T. Donaldson makes a similar point about the relationship of Chaucer the poet and his pilgrim in the *Canterbury Tales*. Yet, while it is true that in terms of the 'fallible first-person singular' (as Donaldson calls Chaucer's narrator) Gower and Chaucer explore related ground, the conversion experience undergone by Amans ultimately separates him from Chaucer's *persona* and draws him closer to Dante's pilgrim, whose post-conversion narratorial urgency and purposes are analogous to Amans/ Gower's.

'falsen' some of his 'mateere'. Yet great care is expended by *both* poet and narrator in the *Confessio* to preserve, and flirt with, the secret. As Amans/Gower tells it in Book VIII, four hundred lines elapse from the end of his shrift and the gentle hinting of Genius that perhaps the Lover ought to consider abandoning his quest and seek a different kind of love before Venus finally points out the problem for an unusually-unperceptive Amans. Even Venus herself takes her time, in Amans/Gower's narration, discoursing first about 'such that kinde so deceiveth' (VIII, 2344), then pointing out that (VIII, 2351-53):

> . . . it is manye daies gon,
> That thou amonges hem were on
> Which of my court hast ben withholde . . .

She comes closer to the mark with the comment that her 'medicine' is not 'For thee and for suche olde sieke' (VIII, 2368), but it is some forty lines later when she finally makes herself clear by reminding him of his impotence (VIII, 2412-20):

> Min herte wolde and I ne may
> Is noght beloved nou adayes;
> Er thou make eny suche assaies
> To love, and faile upon the fet,
> Betre is to make a beau retret;
> For thogh thou myhtest love atteigne,
> Yit were it bot an ydel peine,
> Whan that thou art noght sufficant
> To holde love his covenant.

Venus's speech has taken more than seventy lines to come to the point; but her theme is not new. Several times, poet and narrator seem to give hints of what will come which 'they' must have realized would be passed over at first reading or hearing. In Book I, for example, Amans/Gower tells Genius how free is his love from hypocrisy or pretense. He is, he says, a truly honest lover now, although he may have made various mistakes at an earlier time. His manner of expressing this reservation is interesting, in retrospect: 'Bot Sire,' he claims, 'if I have *in my yowthe/* Don other wise in other place . . . (I, 730-31).' This may be merely convention, as some have argued; but if so, it is a telling application, and in any case there are other examples which, in aggregate, are suggestive.[8] In Book IV,

---

[8] Burrow, 'Portrayal of Amans,' discounts Amans's statement; yet while I agree with Burrow that 'It seems that Gower wishes the reader to respond to Amans (up to the final revelations) simply as a lover and to be simply a lover is to be young, the *senex amans* being a complex case' (p. 13), I doubt that Gower was unaware of, or would have rejected, the potential of such references to by-gone youth to be clues to the revelation of Book VII. For the view that the reader is meant to know Amans's age from the outset see Donald G. Schueler, 'The Age of the Lover,' 152-58.

(1657-82) when Genius informs Amans/Gower that the proper wooer is eager in his search after 'pris', or honor, won by force of arms and knightly deeds, it causes the elderly gentleman some consternation. Who wants to rattle about the face of the globe killing Saracens, he asks, when it can only have evil consequences? First, it takes a man away from the object of his desire — his lady — and second, since the soul of a heathen goes to hell, slaying the unconverted denies 'Cristes lore,' to save through education. The argument is a good one, and has about it the ring of reason. Gower the poet probably intended it to be read both as a legitimate critique of what must have struck a peaceful man as grotesque folly (it is after all with a prayer for peace that the *Confessio Amantis* concludes), and as one more humorous play on the incongruity of an 'olde grisel' imitating the 'fole' according to established courtly standards.[9]

These two readings come together in a lengthy speech by Amans/Gower. There is a time and a place for everything, he says, and he knows well that his jousting days are long past (IV, 1688-92):

> Als wel yit wolde I take kepe
> Whan it were time to abide,
> As forto travaile and to ryde:
> For how as evere a man laboure,
> Cupide appointed hath his houre.

By implying that for him the 'time to abide' has arrived, Amans/Gower hints at his age. The reference is subtle but apparent, and would be more so were we auditors of the poem with the gray-headed poet before us. This is also true of the *tone* of the Lover's answers. Many of these seem calculated to play on what we would know of Amans's age, were we able to see Gower reading, without revealing that Amans/Gower shares this knowledge with us, even as he pretends otherwise. Thus, in Book II, when the Confessor asks Amans/Gower if he is guilty of Detraction, one of the sub-categories of Envy, he convicts himself in a charmingly paternal manner, as might an old man unwilling to admit how much of his pretense he reveals as he does so. He has to assail his rivals, Amans/ Gower retorts, because they threaten to corrupt and take advantage of his lady's innocence. The voice is that of an old man looking after a child. The terms of the condemnation are obvious even on the page (II, 457-65):

> Whan I my diere ladi mete,
> And thenke how that I am noght mete
> Unto hire hihe worthiness,
> And ek I se the besinesse
> Of al this yonge lusty route

[9] I have argued extensively elsewhere that Gower was pacifistically inclined; see my essay, '*Pax Poetica*: On the Pacifism of Chaucer and Gower,' *Studies in the Age of Chaucer* 9(1987), 97-121.

Which alday pressen hire aboute,
And ech of hem his time awaiteth,
And ech of hem his tale affaiteth,
Al to deceive an innocent . . .

Evidence such as this suggests that Gower the poet and Amans/Gower perform
jointly, sharing a double chronology (however much it might look like single
reportage of character and poet), always with an end in sight: the expansion of
the courtly love themes apparently occupying the confession section to
incorporate them as part of the larger, more important concerns for universal
harmony and individual salvation raised by the Prologue. In this process, the
Epilogue is essential, since it is there that Amans receives enlightenment to
become Amans/Gower, a figure who on his own fictive level may be seen to
desire the same ends as his creator, Gower the poet. Both have a tale to tell, and
both hope to persuade by telling it.

II

The essential unity of Prologue and Epilogue is established, then, on the plane
of fiction as well as by a simple correspondence of themes and *personae* introduced
in one and concluded in the other. Gower also links his poem's opening and
ending through the figure of the singer Arion, with whom the Prologue closes.
Arion, who with his song 'the bestes wilde/ Made of his note tame and milde'
(Pro., 1057-58), is called upon by the authorial voice as the one readily able to
conjoin a divided society. Arion in his own time did this, and doubtless would do
it again, if he could be found (Pro., 1070-75):

That was a lusti melodie,
Whan every man with other low;
And if ther were such on now,
Which cowthe harpe as he tho ded,
He myhte availe in many a stede
To make pes wher now is hate . . .

Now, let me pause for a moment to answer a question which predictably may
occur to many readers of this chapter. (I say 'predictably' because the concern *did*
arise for one very helpful colleague who commented on this study for the press.) I
am aware that substantively presenting Arion for the first time here, in the final
chapter, is in some respects an odd decision. Shouldn't a key element in the
book's subtitle, and so central a *persona* in Gower's poetic vision generally, have
been considered earlier?
Indeed, I confess that once it seemed so to me. In a previous draft I occupied a
full prefatory chapter with Arion. Later, however, I found myself backtracking so

often to fill in around what I had said that I was forced to ask myself why that was. And I realized that the problem of the search for a 'new Arion' in many respects is the key to the *Confessio Amantis*, and to Gower's evolving poetic at the close of his career. For the unidentified authorial voice calling in the Prologue for Arion's return is revealed in the Epilogue to be at once Amans/Gower and, *mutatis mutandis*, the poet John Gower himself. For Gower to imagine himself as an Arion has a number of important consequences. Of initial significance, perhaps, is the change it suggests in the elder poet's self-image. No longer, apparently, does he believe himself best manifested as an excoriating John the Baptist, as he did while writing the *Vox Clamantis*.[10] Arion is, on the contrary, quite a different choice, one requiring unusual preparation to appreciate fully, in context.

A semi-mythological figure, Arion was known to Herodotus as a poet and musician of great skill, able to charm men and animals with his lyre, and so on one occasion to save his life by escaping murderous sailors on the back of a dolphin.[11] According to the Suda, he flourished in the first half of the seventh century B.C., and was native to Lesbos.[12] The brilliant, creative court of the tyrant Periander drew him, as it did many others, to Corinth.[13] Here Arion's reputation as a master of the dithyramb, which he is said to have first taught to the choirs of Corinth, grew and spread.[14] Eventually his fame took him to perform in Italy and Sicily; and it was a Corinthian crew of sailors whom Periander reportedly put to death following the poet's return to that city on the dolphin made obedient by his music.[15] It is most certainly through this story of miraculous rescue that Arion was best known in the Greek world, brief references to it appearing in later sources as diverse as Plato and Claudian.[16] Nonetheless,

[10] See for example *Vox Clamantis* II. pro. 83-84.

[11] Herodotus, *Persian Wars*, I. 23.

[12] See *Sudae lexicon*, ed. Ada Adler, 5 vols. (Leipzig, 1929 38), I, 351, no. 3886.

[13] On the court of Periander see Humfrey Payne, *Necrocorinthia: A Study of Corinthian Art in the Archaic Period* (London, 1931; rpt. College Park, Md., 1971), pp. 54, 85, 240-44, 350-51.

[14] Arion's invention of the dithyramb, or cyclic chorus, was suggested by Proclus (*Chrestomathia*, xii), by John the Deacon (who quotes Solon, from his *Elegies*; see *Commentarium in Hermogenem*, ed. Hugo Rabe, *Rheinisches Museum für Philologie* 63 [1908], 150), and also by Pindar indirectly, through the claim that it was first performed in Corinth (*Olymp.* xiii, 19, 31). Although it seems unlikely that Arion invented the dithyramb *ex nihilo*, since the name is very old and related to the Dionysian rituals (see Harald Patzer, *Die Angange der griechischen Tragödie* [Weisbaden, 1962], pp. 15, 113-14), current opinion holds that he made important improvements on the form, including adaptations to accommodate the Doric chorus and perhaps the substitution of a stringed instrument for accompanying flute. See A. W. Pickard-Cambridge, *Dithyramb, Tragedy and Comedy*. 2nd ed. rev. T. B. L. Webster (Oxford, 1966), pp. 10-13, 97-101; and also Gerald F. Else, *The Origin and Early Form of Greek Tragedy* (New York, 1965), pp. 16-1 and 22, for a somewhat less exalted view of Arion's role, and on Solon, pp. 33-48.

[15] Herodotus, *Persian Wars*, I. 24.

[16] Plato, *The Republic*, V. 453.d; Claudian, *In Eutropium*, II. praef., 73-74.

while nothing now survives of Arion's work, his contribution was held to be large by the ancients.[17] Of this, our best source is the Suda, which places him among the earliest tragedians; his writing, it was said, was set apart from the work of contemporaries by a careful distinction of subjects.[18]

Gower's own source of information about Arion was probably not Greek, however, but Latin. Ovid tells the part of the story related to Arion's great musical skill and his remarkable ferrying by the dolphin the *Fasti*, a work which Gower seems to have had nearly by heart:

> What sea, what land knows not Arion? By his song he used to stay the running waters. Often at his voice the wolf in pursuit of the lamb stood still, often the lamb halted in fleeing from the ravening wolf; often hounds and hares have crouched in the same covert, and the hind upon the rock has stood beside the lioness: at peace the chattering crow has sat with Pallas' bird, and the dove has been neighbor to the hawk. 'Tis said that Cynthia oft hath stood entranced, tuneful Arion, at thy notes, as if the notes had been struck by her brother's hand. [19]

Here, as Russell A. Peck has remarked, Gower probably found his figure of the poet.[20] The more interesting question, however, is not the source but the purpose. What drew Gower to build so much around so recondite a personage? For Arion is hardly a common actor in medieval literature. Although we shall find occasional recognition of his musical skill in passages of Boethius's *De institutione musica* and Clement of Alexandria's *Exhortation of the Greeks*, Arion is

---

[17] Aelian includes a fragment of verse which he attributes to Arion in his *De Natura Animalium*, XII. 45 (see the edition of Rudolph Hercher, *Claudii Aeliani, De Natura Animalium Libri XVII*, 2 vols. [Leipzig, 1864, 1866], I. 315), but it is generally held to be of much later origin. On Aelian's sources, see M. Wellmann, 'Pamphilos,' *Hermes: Zeitschrift für klassischen Philologie* 51 (1916), pp. 1-64, especially pp. 6-8; and Felix Rudolph, 'De fontibus quibus Aelianus in varia historia componenda usus sit,' *Leipziger Studien zur classischen Philologie*, ed. G. Curtius, L. Lange, O. Ribbeck and H. Lipsius, 7 (1884), 1-139.

[18] But see Else's skepticism, *Origin and Early Form*, pp. 16-17.

[19] quod mare non novit, quae nescit Ariona tellus?
    carmine currenes ille tenebat aquas.
saepe sequens agnam lupus est a voce retentus,
    saepe avidium fugiens restitit agna lupum;
saepe canes leporesque umbra iacuere sub una,
    et stetit in saxo proxima cerva leae,
et sine lite loquax cum Palladis alite cornix
    sedit, et accipitri iuncta columba fuit.
Cynthia saepe tuis fertur, vocalis Arion,
    tamquam fraternis obstipuisse modis.
Text and translation by Sir James George Frazier, Loeb Classical Library (Cambridge, MA, 1967), II, 83-92.

[20] Peck, *Kingship and Common Profit*, pp. 22-23.

unusually passed over by early historians and mythographers.[21] (Even the learned and inclusive Isidore of Seville, for example, makes no mention of him.) By choosing Arion from among better-known musician/poet figures such as Amphion, David and Orpheus, Gower struck out freshly into territory which, in Middle English at least, he claimed for his own. Thus, the *Confessio Amantis* represents a major vernacular conduit by which details of the poet-harper reached to the Elizabethans and beyond. Behind Spenser's several references to Arion, to cite but one important case, stands Gower's *Confessio*, as surely as does Ovid's *Fasti*.[22]

Indeed, the relative obscurity of the Arion figure may have played a part in Gower's decision to employ him at the center of his last major poem. Unlike King David, whose checkered reputation as a wise man besotted by women would perhaps have limited his symbolic usefulness, or Orpheus, who also came freighted with diverse, predetermined iconography, Arion offered in effect a clean slate.[23] Using him, Gower could draw attention to those elements which alone he wished to emphasize, adapting them carefully to fit the assorted purposes of the *Confessio*. Even Amphion, the magnanimous king and harper whose character bore no compromising blotch, might well have seemed too predictable a choice and one too localized in Thebes for Gower's poem, with its pointedly English politics.[24]

---

[21] Boethius's comment is brief, and merely includes Arion among a group of musicians whose songs had power: 'Sed ut similia breviter exempla conquiram, Terpander atque Arion Methymneus Lesbos atque Iones gravissimis morbis cantus eripuere praesidio.' See *Anicii Manlii Torquati Severini Boetii, De Institutione Arithmetica, Libri Duo, et De Institutione Musica Libri Quinque*, ed. Godfried Friedlein (Leipzig. 1867; rpt. Frankfurt a. M., 1966), p. 185 (*De Mus*. I. i). Clement connects Arion with Amphion and Orpheus to condemn the three as practitioners of evil magic; see 'The Exhortation of the Greeks' in *Clement of Alexandria, Works*, ed. and trans. G. W. Butterworth, Loeb Classical Library (Cambridge, MA, 1968), pp. 2-3, 8-9. Clement's concern is to contrast these musicians with Christ, who sings the 'New Song' of the Word of God (see Butterworth, pp. 12-19). Since there is no evidence to indicate that Gower read Greek, or knew Clement's work, it seems doubtful that he was influenced by this view. He may very likely have read sources treating Orpheus (and perhaps Amphion) as a wizard, however; see for example Strabo, *Geography*, ed. and trans. H. L. Jones, Loeb Classical Library (Cambridge, MA, 1917 33), VII, 18. The process of turning antique writers into sorcerers has wide application. See for example J. W. Spargo, *Virgil the Necromancer* (Cambridge, MA, 1934), 8-18, 62-67, 134-35; and also Domenico Comparetti, *Virgilio nel medio Evo*, new ed. (Florence: 1946), passim.

[22] For Spenser's treatment of Arion, see *Faerie Queene* Books II, 342 and IV, 249.

[23] The best discussion of what Orpheus would have meant to Gower and his readers is John Block Friedman's, in his *Orpheus in the Middle Ages* (Cambridge, MA, 1970).

[24] Lydgate gives us a view of Amphion nearly contemporary with Gower's. Having received his harp from Mercury, King Amphion combined it with 'crafty speche':

> Wherby He made/ the contres envyron
> To han such lust/ in his wordes swete,
> That were so plesaunt/ favourable, and mete
> In her Eerys/ that shortly ther was noon
> Disobeysaunt/ with the kyng to goon,
> Wher so euere/ that hym list assigne.

As a figure to represent himself, then — to be his 'voice' — Arion makes good sense as Gower's selection. Through him, Gower is able to bring together the several strands of a large poem and a long life. For finally what seems to have recommended the poet/harper to Gower was the eirenic possibilities his story presented. As Gower explains in the Prologue, Arion's achievement was universal peace (*CA* Pro., 1055-61):

> Arion hadde an harpe of such temprure,
> And therto of so good mesure
> He song, that he the bestes wilde
> Made of his note tame and milde,
> The Hinde in pes with the Leoun,
> The Wolf in pes with the Moltoun,
> The Hare in pees stod with the Hound.

Thus far he follows Ovid's lead. Gower broadens his description, however, and acting as his own mythographer, extends Arion's harmonious sway over human affairs as well as natural (Pro. 1062-69):

> And every man upon this ground
> Which Arion that time herde,
> Als wel the lord as the schepherde,
> He broghte hem alle in good accord;
> So that the comun with the lord,
> And lord with the comun also,
> He sette in love in bothe tuo
> And putte awey malencolie.

The important place Gower creates for Arion in the *Confessio* helps illuminate a trend, apparent toward the end of his career in his Middle English poetry — the *Confessio* and 'To King Henry IV, In Praise of Peace.' I have described this trend elsewhere as pacifistic, in the doctrinal mode of Augustine, with its strong position against all but the most limited wars of defense.[25] Clearly, the appeal of a figure like Arion for Gower devolves from this larger philosophic/poetic conviction. The goal of universal peace can be furthered by a poetry of appropriately convincing characters and fictions, expressed in a vernacular of increasing stature and availability for presenting serious subjects.

> His cheer/ his port/ was outward so benygne,
> That thorgh his styring/ and exortacioun
> With hym they went/ to bylde first this toun . . .

See *Lydgate's Seige of Thebes*, ed. Axel Erdmann, EETS, E.S. 108 (London, 1911; rpt. 1960), ll. 228-36.

[25] I.e., in '*Pax Poetica*;' see especially pp. 103-09.

Thus the search for the new Arion also provides our best explanation for the stylistic 'middle weie' announced with such emphasis both in the first lines of the Prologue (12-21) and echoed, immediately following the call for Arion, in the opening passage of Book I (1-16). The book to be written 'Somwhat of lust, somwhat of lore' (Pro., 19) of course describes the *Confessio* — but it also implicitly suggests Amans/Gower as the desired Arion, and his confession, pointedly bounded and informed by the Prologue and Epilogue, as the eirenic song. This song, as the lines above specify, 'was a lusti melodie.' It made everyone laugh in harmony, affirming love for all and driving out divisive hate. To discover that it is the confession — the 'story part' — of the *Confessio Amantis* which is intended we must read the opening of the poem carefully, and proceed by elimination. 'The Prologue,' Gower says clearly, 'is so assised/ That it to wisdom al belongeth' (*CA* Pro., 66-67); but subsequently (73-76):

> Whan the prologue is so despended,
> This bok schal afterward ben ended
> Of love, which doth many a wonder
> And many a wys man hath put under.

If the Prologue is 'lore,' the confession is 'lust,' according to Gower's dichotomy. He would seem to be following here the approach of the familiar 'grain and chaff' analogy common to much medieval poetry and Christian exegesis.[26] (Chaucer, for example, similarly bifurcates these elements in the tales of *Thopas* and *Melibee* in the *Canterbury Tales*.)[27] The identification is affirmed strongly later, by precisely that part of the 'coda' which Lewis found so unsatisfying: the prayer of Amans/Gower, in the Epilogue. We have noted already how this prayer is intended to knit up the issues of social and spiritual division outlined in the Prologue, and we shall have reason to return to examine this more closely in the coming pages. But

[26] Augustine distinguishes in several places between levels at which narratives may be understood. Scriptural obscurity, he argued, is useful since it spurs true believers to apply themselves more diligently while discouraging nonbelievers and those with weak faith; see *Doctrina Christiana*, 2.6, 7-8, and his interpretation of Matt. 7: 6 in *De sermone domini in monte*, 2.20, 69. But poets may also use this technique, according to Augustine. Num. 21: 27 is composed in the manner of much poetry, he pointed out (see *Quaestiones in numeros*, 45); all poets should not be condemned for lying if they make up fictions with a truth at their center (*Contra mendacium*, 13. 28). This latter point has been treated with particular insight by K. Svoboda, *L'esthétique de Saint Augustin et ses sources* (Brno, 1933), pp. 4 ff. The figures of 'grain' and 'chaff' were perhaps most familiar to the Middle Ages from the *Commentary on the Canticle of Canticles*, thought to have been the work of Gregory the Great (*PL.* LXXIX, cols. 471-74). The application of Gregorian allegory to poetry by early Latin lyricists such as Paulinus of Nola, and others including Lactantius, Prudentius, and Alan of Lille, has been traced by D. W. Robertson, Jr., in his *Preface to Chaucer*, pp. 59 ff.

[27] The dichotomy is suggested by the Host, when he urges Chaucer the Pilgrim to tell a prose tale, 'In which ther be some murthe or som doctryne' (VII, 935), and to cease his 'drasty' verse. The pairing of 'ernest' and 'game' has important similarities to the patristic 'grain' and 'chaff': see Kolve, *Play Called Corpus Christi*, pp. 13-19.

in addition to what the lines say about the Three Estates, and especially about the duties of the king, it is important that we observe how they come to be attached to the *Confessio* at all. As Amans/Gower's prayer for peace, they represent his direct compliance with the admonition of Venus. Nor does Amans/Gower leave us in doubt about his consciousness. He is thoroughly and specifically aware of the nature and purpose of his actions as the gods of love vanish and the vision section of the poem closes (VIII, 2955-70):

> And thus bewhapid in my thought,
> Whan al was turnyd in to nought,
> I stod amasid for a while,
> And in my self y gan to smyle
> Thenkende uppon the bedis blake
> And how they weren me betake,
> For that I schulde bidde and preie.
> And whanne y sigh non othre weie
> Bot only that y was refusid,
> Unto the lif which y hadde usid
> I thoughte nevere torne ayein:
> And in this wise, soth to seyn,
> Homward a softe pas y wente,
> Wher that with al myn hol entente
> Uppon the point that y am schryve,
> I thenke bidde whil y live.

The brief, inward smile of Amans/Gower is a judicious bit of 'light pointing.' With it, the character acknowledges his revelation and, 'Thenkenede uppon the bedis blake,' his task, as well. He will pray while he lives, and starts immediately with the 'coda' for the reform of English society. But he will also do more: He tells the story of his love and his acquisition of wisdom through confession which, when his prayer is completed, he states specifically he has ended, too (VIII, 3106-09):

> And now to speke as in final,
> Touchended that y undirtok
> In englesch forto make a book
> Which stant betwene ernest and game . . .

Though few, these lines carry noteworthy weight in Gower's plan. Immediately, they recall others in Book I, where Amans/Gower states his intention to 'wryte and schewe al openly/ How love and I togedre mette' (84-85). This echo joins them to the fictive world and chronology of the poem. But since they also recall the promise from the Prologue, to write 'In oure englissh . . ./ A bok for Engelondes sake' (23-24), and echo the 'lust/lore' dichotomy first raised there as descriptive of both Prologue and confession, they further unite the middle of the *Confessio* with its beginning and end. In so doing, the lines establish the second, retrospective chronology of the work as a whole. For it is through this multiple linkage that Gower the poet and Amans/Gower come close to merging.

Finally, however, it is the figure of Arion which helps us to keep Gower's poet-figures apart, even as it unifies and directs our understanding of the poem. Amans/Gower, whose song like Arion's is a 'lusti melodie,' designed as he himself claims to 'sette in love' all those who hear it by means of a thorough examination of emotion itself, represents the new Arion sought after by the authorial voice of the Prologue. With his fictive tale of confession and his prayer/Epilogue, Amans/Gower provides a direct fulfillment of the authorial wish. He is not Gower the poet, but the poet's minstrel, working toward an identical goal. This distinction between creator and creature is rendered explicitly by the Latin gloss Gower included opposite line 5 of Book I, the 'fingens se auctor esse Amantem' passage we have examined above. The side-note reveals a poetic strategy as intense and self-conscious as Chaucer's in the *Canterbury Tales* — one built with the figure of Arion and his song at its center, and hence with moral intentions vastly larger than the simple allegory of courtly love preferred by Lewis and others.

III

Let us turn, then, to consider the implications of a *Confessio Amantis* with an Arionic melody as its controlling strain. Such a poem could not be of small scope. Its subject would be harmony inclusive and cosmic, capable, like Arion's harping, of reinstating a near-Edenic innocence and goodwill in a world striated both naturally and socially. This indeed is the measure of the vision Gower projects in the Prologue as having been Arion's in former, golden times (1053-69):

> Bot wolde god that now were on
> An other such as Arion,
> Whiche hadde an harpe of such temprure,
> And therto of so good mesure
> He sang, that he the bestes wilde
> Made of his note tame and milde,
> The Hinde in pes with the Leoun,
> The Wolf in pes with the Moltoun,
> The Hare in pees stod with the Hound;
> And every man upon this ground
> Which Arion that time herde,
> Als wel the lord as the schepherde,
> He broghte hem alle in good acord,

So that the comun with the lord,
And lord with the comun also,
He sette in love bothe tuo
And putte awey malancolie.

Although I have discussed certain images from this passage in preceding pages, I want to note here the process of their development. Imagistically, the lines find their temper in Biblical allusion, to the 'peaceable kingdom' of Isaiah 11:6: 'The wolf shall dwell with the lamb: and the leopard shall lie down with the kid. The calf and the lion and the sheep shall abide together and a little child shall lead them.' Having touched this chord, however, Gower quickly broadens its impact by redefining its terms. 'Lord and schepherde' are transformed into 'lord and comun' — current, politically realistic equivalents which foreshadow the coming insistence of the *Confessio* to be read and judged both as art and as Christian social program. For if the heart of that program is the love Arion created among his listeners, out of which they discovered means to reform their behavior and act charitably toward others, so also is that love — and that program — ultimately productive of justice. This too is a salient meaning of bringing 'hem alle in good acord' and 'sette in love bothe tuo,' the lord and the common, and it resonates in several directions. It looks ahead, on the one hand, to the particular character and skills of Apollonius of Tyre in the capstone exemplum of the poem, in Book VIII. If I may venture for the moment a metaphor, that the microcosmic 'world' of a human life is like a musical piece, shorter or longer, sweeter or not, but nevertheless part in its way of the macrocosmic, perfectly planned harmony of the turning spheres, then the 'song' of Apollonius, prince and harper, is defined by his charity and his justice so that it echoes *in parvo* that celestial strain that is God's. Continuing this metaphor, we may perceive in Apollonius's actions — his free gift of grain to the starving people of Tharse, his strict adherence to the law in avenging himself upon Strangulio and Dionise, his scrupulous treatment of his unrecognized daughter — a 'music' intended for our instruction. If we 'hear' it, we too may learn to 'sing' accordingly — and govern well our selves and those around us. Thus the work of Arion is done, in figure and in deed, in justice and in love; and thus the Arionic melody of the Prologue looks ahead to the *Confessio*'s conclusion, first in 'Apollonius of Tyre' and then on yet another hand, to the 'melody' of Amans/ Gower, whose 'prayer for the pes' is the *Confessio* itself, perceivable in the fresh light of all that has gone before as personal, and Arionic, song.[28] This love it is,

---

[28] Gower seems to be urging Arion's song as analogous to Orpheus's, which was interpreted throughout the Middle Ages as the 'New Song' of Christ, with the power to restore justice for those who deserve it. See Friedman, *Orpheus in the Middle Ages*, pp. 52-53, 125-28. The strong reminiscences of the 'Golden Age' of harmony in Gower's vision we may trace to his knowledge of the classics, particularly Virgil's Fourth Eclogue and Ovid's *Metamorphoses* I, 89-112. Gower may also have been influenced by the tradition of Garden Paradises represented in many medieval Latin and vernacular works with both Christian and secular purpose. On these, see especially A. Bartlett Giamatti, *The Earthly Paradise and the Renaissance Epic* (Princeton, N.J., 1966), pp. 48-83.

then, that Amans/Gower, and Gower the poet, hope the *Confessio* will restore to the world at large, and to fourteenth-century English society. It is a tall order, clearly. Idealistic and artistically challenging, it requires orchestral skill to advance its several arguments cleanly and without losing them in a cacaphonous blare. What Gower chose to write was a 'lover's confession' stretched to its broadest dimension by the Empedoclean/Christian compass of love in Arion's song. Thus he needed to redefine love as applicable for more than a courtly game, a goal he pursued by following several courses concurrently.

Of these the most familiar is certainly his treatment of love in the manner of *amour courtois*, the literary and aristocratic pastime of which many elements form the frame narrative.[29] More recent scholarship, however, has discovered other elements pervade Gower's depiction of *fin amour*, which turn it away from the sophisticated cynicism of Jean de Meun and the harmless, airy fantasy of Guillaume de Lorris. J.A.W. Bennett perceived one of these when he pointed out the 'honeste' aspects of Gower's theory of love.[30] Never content with love diminished to sexual gratification, Gower unwaveringly asserted its purpose in the natural scheme of generation. Loyal, monogamous union for beasts, and church-sanctioned marriage for human beings, is Gower's ideal, not the 'love of paramours.' As I have suggested in an earlier chapter, the issue is prominent not only in the *Confessio*, but in all of Gower's writing — so much so, that it is worth reviewing briefly Gower's consistency about the matter of matrimony before proceeding further.

The first twelve lines of the *Mirour de l'Omme*, as we have them, open the poem with a condemnation of those foolish who pursue fleshly love:

> Escoulte cea, chacun amant,
> Qui tant perestes desirant
> Du pecché, dont l'amour est fals;
> Lessetz la Miere ove tout s'enfant,
> Car qui plus est leur attendant,
> Au fin avra chapeal de sauls:
> Lors est il fols qui ses travauls
> Met en amour si desloiauls,
> Dont au final nuls est joyant.
> Mais quiq'en voet fuïr les mals,
> Entende et tiegne mes consals,
> Que je luy dirray en avant.

---

[29] These have been most studied by scholars influenced by Lewis, who have dutifully noted the extent of Gower's borrowing from the major text of the tradition, the *Roman de la Rose*. See Economou, 'The Character of Genius', 203-10; Burrow, *Ricardian Poetry*; Kean, *Chaucer and the Making of English Poetry*, II, 72.

[30] Bennett, 'Gower's Honeste Love', pp. 107-21; and further Henry Ansgar Kelly, *Love and Marriage in the Age of Chaucer* (Ithaca, N.Y., 1975), pp. 121-60.

['Let every false lover listen: leave the Mother of Sin with all her children; for whoever attends them will weep in the end. Thus, whoever attempts a love so perfidious that no one enjoys it at last is a fool. But let him listen and follow my advice I shall give hereafter, who desires to flee wickedness.']

Significantly, love here is defined in terms of any worldly lust. Gower opposes *cupiditas* with *caritas* generally in the *Mirour*, and marks as his purpose for the whole poem the illustration of proper and improper desire (*MO*, 13-24):

> Ce n'est pas chose controvée,
> Dont pense affaire ma ditée;
> Ainz vuill conter tout voirement
> Coment les filles du Pecché
> Font que tous sont enamoure
> Par leur deceipte vilement.
> He, amourouse sote gent,
> Si scieussetz le diffinement
> De ce dont avetz commencé,
> Je croy qu vostre fol talent
> Changeast, qui muetz au present
> Reson en bestailité.

['The matter of my poem is not a fabrication; instead, I wish to explain candidly how the daughters of Sin cause men to love them for their vile deceptions. Ah, people who love thoughtlessly, if you knew how what you have started will end, I am sure you would cease your foolish habits, which are transforming Reason into Bestiality.']

Misplaced love, in the *Mirour*, brings about sin of all sorts. Carnality gets its particular due, however, in the section devoted to Lechery and her five daughters, Fornication, Rape, Adultery, Incest, and Vain-Delight (ll. 8617-9720). Citing the Bible (and 'Seneca'), Gower reiterates here too how lust opens men to complete corruption.[31] Chastity balances this sin, and also has five

[31]   L'apostre par especial
        Ce dist, que l'omme bestial
        Ne puet gouster ne savourer
        Viande q'est espirital:
        Rois Salomondist autre tal,
        Q'en malvoise alme a demourer
        Puet sapience nulle entrer,
        N'en corps soubgit a folpenser
        Des vices qui sont corporal
        Jamais se deigne enhabiter:
        Car qui pecché voet herberger
        Tout bien porsclot de son hostal.
        Ce dist Senec de sa science,

daughters, one to oppose each offspring of Lechery: Bonnegarde ('Good-Care'),
Virginity, Matrimony, Continence, and Aspre-Vie, or 'Hard Life' (ll. 16573-
18420). As Gower understands Chastity, it is the highest of the virtues, and the
most attractive to Grace (18361-72):

> O Chasteté, par tiele assisse
> Bonté verraie t'est assisse,
> Qe creatour et creature
> Chascuns endroit de soy te prise,
> Fors soul le deable, a qui tu prise
> As guerre, et par ta confiture
> Tout l'as mis a desconfiture:
> C'estoit qant dieus ove ta nature
> Se volt meller, dont fuist comprise
> La deité soubz ta porture.
> Quoy dirray plus mais dieus t'onure?
> Car autre a ce n'est qui suffise.

['O Chastity, real bounty is yours, because you are prized by the
Creator and all creatures, except for the devil, on whom you have made
war and defeated. Then God wished to combine His nature with yours,
in order that divinity would be part of your nature. Can I say more than
that God honors you? No other thing is your equal.']

Such broad potential, either for evil or for good, is to be taken seriously; and
therefore Gower's resolution of the question of carnal and spiritual love in the
model of matrimony is significant.[32] His opinion in the *Mirour* is unambiguous
and sweeping (17173-81):

> Que la plus grieve pestilence
> Q'om en ce siecle puet avoir,
> C'est foldelit d'incontinence,
> Qant om a sa caroigne pense
> Et s'alme laist a nounchalior.   (*MO* 9553-70)

['The apostle specifically says that a bestial man can not taste or savor a meat that is
spiritual. King Solomon said the same: that no wisdom can enter to dwell in an evil soul,
nor deign to live in a body subject to wanton throughts of corporeal vices; for he who
wants to harbor sin, shuts out all good from his house.

Seneca in his wisdom says that the most grievous pestilence that man can have in this
world is vain delight of incontinence, when man thinks of his carrion and disregards his
soul.'] The Biblical references are to I Cor. 2:14, and Wisdom 1:4. The 'Seneca' referred
to is perhaps Caecilus Balbus's 'Socrates:' 'Nihil est enim tam mortiferum ingenio quam
luxuria est.'
[32] The image is not original to Gower, of course. Augustine makes the same comparison
in *The City of God*, lib. XIV, ch. 26: 'Sicut in paradiso nullus aestus aut frigus, sic in eius
habitatore nulla ex cupiditate vel timore accidebat bonae voluntatis offensio. Nihil
omnino triste, n hio erat inaniter laetum. Gaudium verum perpetuabatur ex Deo, in
quem flagrabat *caritas de corde puro et conscientia bona et fide non ficta*, atque inter se coniugum
fida ex honesto amore societas, concors mentis corporisque vigilia et mandati sine labore

Du sainteté sanz contredit
Le Matremoine est auci dit
Un sacrement du grant vertu,
Par sainte eglise q'est confit;
Dont signefie a son droit plit
Le marier q'est avenue
De sainte eglise et de Jhesu,
C'est entre la bonne alme et dieu,
L'amour pourporte q'est parfit.

['Matrimony is also called a sacrament which Holy Church performs, of great virtue. Matrimony actually symbolizes the marriage of Holy Church and Jesus, that is, between the virtuous soul and God; she signifies the Love that is perfect.']

Matrimony provides Gower with the ideal image of sanctified harmony, having been incorporated into the law based on the prelapserian union of Adam and Eve, and reified symbolically by the 'marriage' of Christ and the Church as interpreted by the early exegetes.[33] But as willing as Gower is to detail the

custodia . . . In tanta facili tate rerum et felicitate hominum absit ut suspicemur non potuisse pro lem seri sine libidinis morbo, sed eo voluntatis nutu moverentur membra illa quo cetera . . .' Text from *De Civitate Dei*, in *Aurelii Augustini Opera*, ed. Bernard Dombart and Alphonse Kalb, Corpus Christianorum Series Latina (Turnholt: Brepols, 1955). 'We conclude therefore that man lived in paradise as long as his wish was at one with God's command . . . There was no sadness at all, nor any frivolous jollity. But true joy flowed perpetually from God, and towards God there was a blaze of ''love from a pure heart, a good conscience, and a faith that was no pretence'' [I Tim. 1:5]. Between man and wife there was a faithful partnership based on love and mutual respect; there was a harmony and a liveliness of mind and body, and an effortless observance of the commandment . . .' Lest we misunderstand the thoroughness of this harmony of man and wife, Augustine continues explicitly: 'When mankind was in such a state of ease and plenty, blest with such felicity, let us never imagine that it was impossible for the seed of children to be sown without the morbid condition of lust. Instead, the sexual organs would have been brought into activity by the same bidding of the will as controlled the other organs.' Trans. Henry Bettenson. Useful recent studies tracing the concept through early theological and canon law are those of John T. Noonan, Jr., *Contraception: A History of Its Treatment by the Catholic Theologians and Canonists* (Cambridge, Mass.: Harvard University Press, 1966); Rudolf Weigand, 'Die Lehre der Kanonisten der 12. und 13. Jahrhunderts von den Ehezwecken,' *Studia Gratiana* 12 (1967), 445-78; Gabriel le Bras, 'Le mariage dans le théologie et le droît de l'Église du XIe au XIIIe siècle,' *Cahiers de civilisation médiévale* (Poitiers) 11 (1968), 191-202; Michael Sheehan, 'Marriage and Family in English Conciliar and Synodal Legislation,' in *Essays in Honour of Anton Charles Pegis*, ed. J. Reginald O'Donnell (Toronto: Pontifical Institute of Mediaeval Studies, 1974), pp. 205-14, and also his 'Choice of Marriage Partner in the Middle Ages: Development and Application of a Theory of Marriage,' *Studies in Medieval and Renaissance History*, N.S. (1978), 3-33; and Kelly, *Love and Marriage*, pp. 163-74. For the English mystics use of this comparison, see Kelly, pp. 286-332.
[33] That marriage combines love with legal sanction is claimed as well by William Langland (C-text, pas. XI, 202-10; 212-15):
    Ho so lyueth in lawe/ and in loue doth wel

mystical roots of the matrimonial state he is ever concerned to establish its advantages for ordinary mortals tempted on all sides by their recalcitrant flesh. Thus, he also lists three of the commonplace 'practical' reasons why marriage is to be considered a positive act.[34] The first is company ('Le premer est pour compaigne'); the second, familiar from the *Confessio Amantis*, is to further natural procreation (17209-20):

> La cause q'est se conde apres,
> Dont l'en tient mariage pres,
> C'est pour estraire en no nature
> Des fils et files tiel encress,
> Dont dieus leur creatour ades
> Soit loez de sa creature:
> Ensi tesmoigne l'escripture,
> Qant homme et femme en lour figure
> De dieu primer estoiont fetz,
> Dieus dist, 'Crescetz en vo mesure,
> Empletz la terre d'engendrure,
> Dont femme doit porter le fes.'

> As these weddid men/ that this worlde susteynen?
> For of here kynde thei come/ confessours and martyres,
> Patriarkes and prophetes/ popes and maidenes.
> For god seith hit hym-self/ shall neuere good appel
> Thorw no sotel science/ on sour stock growe;'
> And hit ys no more to mene/ bote men that buth bygetyn
> Out of matrimonie nat moillere/ mowe nat haue the grace
> That leelle legitime/ by lawe may cleyme.

Text from Skeat, ed., *Vision of William*. In his notes (II, 143), Skeat quotes Peter Comestor to show the ubiquity of the idea: 'Adam cognovit uxorem suam, sed non in paradiso, sed iam reus et eiectus' ('Adam knew his wife, but not in paradise, rather having been accused and cast out'). Derek Pearsall, in *Piers Plowman by William Langland: An Edition of the C-Text* (Berkeley and Los Angeles: University of California Press, 1979), p. 189, n. to l. 212, cites the story in the apocryphal *Vita Adae et Evae*. The intention of each text seems to be to underscore the value and sanctity of sexual relations within marriage.

[34] The reasons are clearly stated in the *Postquam dictum est de morbis ipsius animae*, one of Chaucer's sources for the *Parson's Tale*: 'Quattuor de causis cognoscitur uxor aut causa prolis procreandae; aut debiti reddendi; aut incontinentiae vitandae; aut libidinis explendae' ('There are four reasons to know one's wife sexually: to produce children; or to pay the debt; or to avoid incontinence; or to satisfy sexual passion'). See Siegfried Wenzel, 'The Source for the "Remedia" of the *Parson's Tale*,' *Traditio* 27 (1971), 449. For Langland's similar attitude, see the discussion by M. Teresa Tavormina, 'Kindly Similitude: Langland's Matrimonial Trinity,' *Modern Philology* 80 (1982), 117-28. Noonan, *Contraception*, pp. 255-56, points to the commentaries of Aquinas and Albertus Magnus on Aristotle as evidence of the 'advanced' attitudes of the great theologians toward sexual relations between husband and wife. Gower's list is interesting for several reasons, including the order of his reasons (most canonists cite procreation first, *remedium* following, as does the author of the *Postquam* and also his addition of the idea of 'mesure' in l. 17218.

['The second reason that marriage is so esteemed is that we produce by
our natures an increase of sons and daughters, so that God the Creator
can be praised always by His own creatures. The Scripture says that
when man and woman were made in God's image at first, God ordered,
"Multiply and fill the world with your gettings, which the woman must
bear as a burden".']

Here we ought to note particularly the paraphrase of the injunction from Gen.
1:22, 'Be fruitful and multiply,' with its specific adaptation to mankind. (This
verse, it should be recalled, lay under Gower's elaborate restoration of Venus
Genetrix to her original position as Nature's handmaiden and consequently
assistant in God's work.)

The third reason is also familiar. It is, once more, that the institution of
marriage is an antidote to Lechery (17121-26):

> La tierce cause en son aprise
> L'apostre dist, dont femme ert prise:
> C'est q'om doit bien espouse prendre,
> Qant il ne puet par autre guise
> Garder son corps en sa franchise
> Sanz leccherie de mesprendre.

['The apostle in his teaching gace the third reason for which woman is
prized. It is that man should take a spouse when he can not otherwise
maintain control of his body without committing the offense of lechery.']

Taken together, these passages from the *Mirour de l'Omme* illustrate Gower's
consistent understanding of natural and Biblical law, as applied to wedlock and
procreation. The same interpretation governs his treatment in the *Vox Clamantis*,
where Gower again discusses these subjects. A diatribe against the sins of the
times, the *Vox* swells with general complaints about chastity's absence from all
levels of contemporary society. After the *Mirour*, the form of these complaints is
familiar, as two examples should suffice to show. The first is from the end of Book
VI (1335-44), where Gower makes his point with elaborate rhetorical flourish:

> Nunc amor est Paridis communis in orbe quietus,
> Vt sine nunc bello quisque fruatur eo.
> Non Hymeneus in hiis conseruat pacta diebus,
> Set Venus in thalamis reddit agenda suis:
> Aurum sponsatur, vultuque decora paratur
> Ad thalamum Veneris pluribus apta viris.
> Mutua cura duos et amor socialis habebat
> Nuper, et vna tamen nunc sibi quinque trahit:
> Vt duo sint carne simul vna lex dedit olim,
> Ad minus inque tribus nunc manet ordo nouus . . .

['Now Paris's kind of love is commonly allowed in the world, so that anyone may enjoy it at present without war. Hymen does not preserve people's troths, but Venus engages what is to be done in their bedchambers. God is engaged to be married, and the woman beautiful of face prepares herself for Venus's bedchamber, ready for many men. Formerly, mutual concern and companionable love used to hold two people together, but now one woman allures five men to herself. The law formerly held that two should be of one flesh together, and now the new fashion holds for at least three . . .][35]

Gower's lament recalls the complaint of the *Mirour*: No longer do men and women confine themselves to a spouse, or even to one lover, as sanctified and natural laws direct. Moreover, to sharpen his point, Gower works the argument carefully on either side. He prefaces this passage with a list of the virtuous (Socrates, Diogenes, Phirinus, Troilus, Medea, Penelope, Lucretia, Justine) who have passed on, bereaving the world of all but the wicked to emulate — Epicurus, Aristippus, Jason, Agladius, Cressida, Semiramis, Circe, Calypso, Thais (*VC* VI, 1319-34); and he closes it by contrasting human infidelity and lust with the monogamous habits of the 'lower' orders (1347-51):

> Ales habet quod amet; cum quo sua gaudia iungat,
> Invenit in media femina piscis aqua;
> Cerua parem sequitur, serpens serpente tenetur:
> Femina virque thoro sunt magis vna caro.
> Heus, vbi pacta fides? vbi connubial a iura?

['The bird cherishes what it should love; in the middle of the water the female fish finds the one with whom she may share her joys. The hind follows its mate; the serpent is embraced by a serpent; even more are man and woman one flesh by marriage. Alas, where is plighted faith? Where is marital virtue?']

Although they lack man's power of reason and do not marry, the birds, fish, hinds and serpents nonetheless follow the natural law. They are thus truer to universal dicta than are many men — even among the prefacing list of worthy lovers now departed. (One thinks of the *couples* mentioned here, like Troilus and Cressida, like Medea and Jason, *each* of whom contributed in some measure to their tragedy). Compelled by the juxtaposition, we must register afresh the poet's continued disgust at mankind's degeneration.

For a second example of Gower's consistency we may turn to the third chapter of Book VII of the *Vox*. Here Gower presents Nebuchhadnezzar's dream of the statue with members of various substances as a metaphor for the deteriorating 'Ages of Man.' This image Gower returns to in the Prologue of the *Confessio Amantis*, where he gives it a similar interpretation: that the difference in purity

[35] Trans. Stockton, *Major Latin Works*.

and hardness between the golden head and the clay feet, representative of the present times, exactly measures the degree of human corruption over the years.[36] The clergy, Gower argues, have been subsumed by the *mores* of the times, and practice carnality with the other Estates. He goes on to excoriate the 'French sins,' a mode of love especially damaging to marriage which has come into fashion among the nobility (*VC* VII, 157-68):

> Gallica peccata, nuper quibus hii ceciderunt,
> Clamant iam nostras intitulare domos:
> Nunc licet alterius sponsam quod quisque frequentet
> Est status ingenui, dicitur illud amor.
> Non erit hoc laicis vicium set gracia magna,
> Dum sit adulterio magnificatus homo,
> Dummodo sponsa stuprum perquirit adultera donis:
> Soluet ob hoc sponsus, qui luet illud opus.
> Sic se nunc homines vendunt, quasi sint meretrices,
> Prospera dum Veneris larga sit illa manus:
> Sic sub mendaci secie grossantur amoris,
> Parque nephas tale lucra pudenda petunt.

['The French sins now clamor to take possession of our households, which have recently fallen prey to them. Now it is permissible for every man to dance attendance upon another's wife, and this is called the noble rank's 'love.' This is not a vice for laymen, but a great mark of esteem; for a man becomes distinguished through adultery, while his adulterous wife courts dishonor for the sake of gifts. The husband who plays the same game is thereby absolved. Thus men and women now sell themselves as if they were whores, while Venus's generous hand is propitious. Thus do they puff themselves up under a false kind of love, and go in quest of shameful gains through such wickedness.']

Adulterous 'spouse-trading' for both gold and prestige is the new standard; what the knightly class has initiated filters down to corrupt cleric and commoner alike. Gower's specificity here, condemning these sins as especially *French*, illustrates again the connection he made between breach of marriage and courtly *fin amour* — and reminds us once more of his rejection of French verse inspired by the *Roman de la Rose*. In the *Vox* as in the *Mirour* and the ballade sequences, he had no patience for fashionable adultery.

Gower's concept of love, then, is broad-based, if somewhat conservative and concerned more with propriety and adherence to law than with simplistic physical fulfillment. Application of this view — present, as we have seen, throughout his earlier work — is one of the shaping forces of the *Confessio Amantis*; there, it appears ubiquitously, in several forms. Central to all, however, is

---

[36] For further discussion, see Peck, *Kingship and Common Profit*, pp. 20-22; and his 'Gower and the Book of Daniel' in *Recent Readings*, ed. Yeager.

Gower's signally liberal attitude toward what he recognized are the unavoidable directives of the body.[37] Although he is often misrepresented as a nay-sayer, Gower in fact took the view that the urgings of passion, common to men and beasts, are natural and (appropriately) among the most powerful of life's forces.

Yet the sexual act has its rightful place in Gower's universe, and therefore must be honored. This point is established often and powerfully in the *Confessio*. Thus the interference of Tiresias in the lawful coupling of serpents leads quickly to his punishment by the gods in Book III (361-80). Despite his staunch morality, Gower had no use for prudes. The tale immediately preceding that of Tiresias, 'Canace and Machaire,' offers a similar moral. Here brother and sister, confined together past puberty by a zealous father and kept innocent of any law but that of nature, commit incest. Gower's explanation of the deed is telling (III, 169-78):

> Cupide bad hem ferst to kesse,
> And after sche which is Maistresse
> In kinde and techeth every lif
> Withoute law positif,
> Of which sche takth nomaner charge,
> But kepth hire lawes al at large,
> Nature, tok hem into lore
> And tawht hem so, that overmore
> Sche hath hem in such wise daunted,
> That thei were, as who seith, enchaunted.

Walking with great care, Gower goes as far as perhaps he could to justify sinful behavior by pointing out the children's ignorance. Lacking knowledge of 'lawe positif,' or the marital code of the Church, they obeyed what law they understood — that of 'kinde,' a tutor with an enchantress's powers in circumstances such as these.[38] Significantly, the subject of Book III is Ire and so Gower refocusses the

---

[37] Kelly, *Love and Marriage*, p. 285, takes a similar view, pointing out that '. . . in spite of the paucity of liberal authorities, we must not underestimate the ability of Chaucer and his friends, like moral Gower and philosophical Strode . . . to come to such enlightened conclusions on their own.'

[38] Gower's attitudes toward the laws of nature and Church are complex, for he was deeply aware of the dangers if either were to be followed unwisely. The crime of Canace and Machaire is one possible result of blind compliance with natural urgings. Yet Church laws also are suspect for Gower, as he indicates with his extended discussion of the *lex positiva* in the *Vox Clamantis* (Bk. III, 227-81). Indulgences — absolution purchased for a given sin before its commission — were one abuse of the *lex positiva* as Gower saw it; another was easier sentences for clerics than for laymen who commit the same crimes, since clerics, under 'their' positive law, were then judges as well as criminals and would deal lightly with each other. See also Gower's remarks on the laws in the *Mirour*, ll. 18469 ff. and in the *Confessio*, Pro. 407-31 and Book VIII, 100 ff. Gower's ambivalence about the rightness of all the laws laid down by the Church may have influenced his gentle treatment of Canace and Machaire here. For two recent evaluations of the problem, see Olsson, 'Natural Law and John Gower's *Confessio Amantis*,' 229-61, and Hugh White, 'Nature and the Good in Gower's *Confessio Amantis*,' in Yeager, ed., *Recent Readings*, 1-20.

tale, turning away from Canace and Machaire to castigate their father for the
'felonie' (III, 336) of punishing 'as he which nothing cowthe/ How maisterfull
love is in yowthe' (211-12). This use of an incest story to illustrate too-hasty
anger has puzzled several modern readers, who have wondered why, when Book
VIII takes incest as its primary topic and there are so many exempla to portray
wrath, this tale should be so diverted from its natural track into service here.[39]
But surely Gower's purpose is clear. 'Kinde,' if obeyed by animals and
innocents, is never condemnable; in fact, they behave appropriately when they
follow the only law they know. For Gower the sole criminal in 'Canace and
Machaire' is, from first to last, the unnatural father who repeatedly attempts to
thwart procreative nature, first by caging two healthy young creatures away from
suitable marriages and then by destroying his own offspring in unnatural fury.

Indeed, failure to accommodate Nature is rejected in all of Gower's works, and
the *Confessio* has its share of examples. The cause of Gower's censure is the
incumbency upon all living things of new generation. Only saints, Gower
implies, are above procreation. Thus in Book IV, Rosiphelee's 'defalte of
Slowthe/ Towardes love' which leads her unnaturally to desire 'nother Mariage/
Ne yit the love of paramours' (IV, 1245, passim.) brings her under discipline.
She is 'bothe wys and fair/ And scholde ben hire fader hair:' Intelligent,
beautiful, and a king's daughter to boot, Rosiphelee is too valuable to be excused
from motherhood. A similar note is sounded in the 'Tale of Jephthah's
Daughter,' also found in Book IV. Informed by Jephthah that she must be
sacrificed in accord with his promise to kill the first living thing he saw on his
victorious return to his country, his daughter begs for, and receives, forty days'
respite. The time is to be devoted to a special end, however (IV, 1565-71):

> That sche the whyle mai bewepe
> Hir Maidenhod, which sche to kepe
> So longe hath had an noght beset;
> Wherof her lusti youthe is let,
> That sche no children hath forthdrawe
> In Mariage after the lawe,
> So that the poeple is noght encressed.

Gower's treatment of the story, which preserves the perspective of his source
(Judges 11: 34-39), reveals his strongly Old Testament views on the issue of
procreation. In this he differs noticeably from Chaucer, who makes ambiguous
mention of the narrative in the 'Physician's Tale.'[40]

---

[39] See for example C. David Benson, 'Incest and Moral Poetry in Gower's *Confessio
Amantis*,' *Chaucer Review* 19 (1984), 100-09.
[40] Chaucer's attitude toward the story of Jephtha's daughter (*CT* VI, 240-41 seems to
parallel his ironic treatment of the Physician's knowledge of the Bible. See Richard L.
Hoffman, 'Jephthah's Daughter and Chaucer's Virginia,' *Chaucer Review* 2 (1967), 20-31.

Even in these tales, which in the *Confessio* demonstrate unjudgmentally the
strength and lawfulness of the reproductive urge, it should be noted how
insistently if unobtrusively Gower iterates the sanction given sexual relations by
marriage. Always, as he stated in lines examined from the *Mirour* above,
marriage will preserve against sin those who practice love within its bonds.
Typical of Gower's method in the *Confessio*, we have examples and counterexamples offered us to prove the truth of this. In Book IV, for instance, the idea lies
behind one of Gower's most commended scenes, the picture of delight that is
Queen Alceone when she discovers her marriage may continue in her new avian
form. Greeting her husband, now also transformed into a bird, she (IV,
3104-12):

> Beclipte and keste in such a wise,
> As sche was whilom wont to do:
> Hire wynges for hire armes tuo
> Sche tok, and for hire lippes softe
> Hire harde bile, and so fulofte
> Sche fondeth in hire briddes forme,
> If that sche mihte hirself conforme
> To do the plesance of a wif
> As sche dede in that other lif.

The joyous moment, transmitted to the reader as honest pleasure, is enhanced
by the straightforward innocence of the physical relations between husband and
wife, be they bird or human. The metamorphoses of Ceix and Alceone therefore
remind us once again of Gower's affirmation of a just sexuality which serves the
divine plan by bringing harmony and generation into the world. Book V
provides a good case of counterexample making the same point. There, the
inability of an infirm lover to perform is presented as a kind of 'misconception'
— as both a sexual and a mental event. Genius thus describes it as a cause of
jealousy, a type of Avarice (V, 455-60):

> Among the men lacke of manhode
> In Mariage upon wifhode
> Makth that a man himself deceiveth,
> Wherof it is that he conceiveth
> That ilke unsely maladie,
> The which is cleped Jelousie.

Alceone, of course, circumvents the problem by attending to her 'duty,' even in
her new shape. (Amans, however, is not so lucky — though he hardly
comprehends the pointed lesson here.)

Gower's insistence on the sanction of marriage is no contradiction of what is,
clearly, approval of physical relations between lovers. Rather, for him the two

positions are directly connected. Implicit in the refusal to condemn Canace and Machaire outright for their incest was, as we saw, their unfortunate ignorance of laws higher than those of Nature. Lacking the knowledge (or opportunity) to correct themselves, they follow their instincts, and so resemble animals more than men, who ought to be guided by reason and information. But such behavior, if proper for the lower orders is generally unconscionable when practiced by human beings. For Gower, marriage is the rational answer to the problem posed by the ever-demanding flesh — and this explains why he seldom fails to discuss sexual love approvingly without also relating it to marriage.

It is a connection Gower seems especially anxious to stress in the latter half of the *Confessio*, as he begins to bring his poem to a close. Book VII contains both broad and small instances of this linkage, all useful to make the point. It is significant, for example, that to oppose Chastity, the fifth point of Policy, Gower selected 'spousebreche' as a negative illustration (Lechery, we should remember, is balanced against this virtue in the *Mirour*, where Adultery is but one of five daughters), representing the body's strong inclination toward promiscuity (VII, 4215-30):

> The Madle is mad for the femele,
> Bot where as on desireth fele,
> That nedeth noght be weie of kinde:
> For whan a man mai redy finde
> His oghne wif, what scholde he seche
> In strange places to beseche
> To borwe an other mannes plouh,
> Whan he hath geere good ynouh,
> Affaited at his oghne heste,
> And is to him wel more honeste
> Than othre thing which is unknowe?
> Forthi scholde every good man knowe
> And thenke, how that in mariage
> His trouthe plight lith in morgage,
> Which if he breke, it is falshode,
> And that descordeth to manhode.

Noteworthy here is the mention of 'kinde' as the index by which marital fidelity may be judged, for, Gower argues, while the appetitive man may desire 'fele,' it is unnatural to follow such inclinations.[41] 'Kindeliche' for man is a faithfully-sustained monogamy, practiced with measure governed by reason. We

---

[41] Also noteworthy is Gower's use of the borrowed plow to symbolize unlawful union in ll. 4219-22, which may represent a *topos* see also Augustine, *City of God*, lib. XV. 16, *Piers Plowman*, C-text XI.215-17, where Langland speaks of borrowed *ground*; and the *Roman de la Rose* ll. 19671-96.

must not confuse Gower with Chaucer's Januarie: the just marriage in Gower's view requires proper temperance, lest it degenerate into a mere camoflage for lust. This refinement is maintained by the 'Tale of Tobias and Sara,' another of the narratives in Book VII devoted to portraying Chastity.[42] As in the Biblical story, in the *Confessio* the demon Asmod slays in succession those who marry Sara (VII, 5351-53):

> Noght for the lawe of Mariage,
> Bot for that ilke fyri rage
> In which that thei the lawe excede.

The distinction here is vital between the 'fyri rage' (or the dictates of the body) and the 'lawe of Mariage,' which derives from the 'lawe positif,' or the directives of the Church. Men must know both and breach neither, in order to be protected from sin by the marriage sacrament. It is the 'lawe positif,' of which Canace and Machaire were kept ignorant, that Gower hedges in failing to judge them — but theirs is an unusual case. Other men, aware that the proper purpose of sexual intercourse is not pleasure alone but procreation, would suffer the fate of Sara's suitors, who also flaunted the 'lawe positif.' In contrast, Tobias is saved because 'he his lust so goodly ladde/ That bothe the lawe and kinde is served (VII, 5362-63).[43] From this, Genius extracts the following moral (VII, 5367-81):

> Of this ensample a man mai se,
> That when likinge in the degre
> Of Mariage mai frosuie,
> Wel oghte him thanne in other weie
> Of lust to be the betre avised.
> For god the lawes hath assissed
> Als wel to reson as to kinde,

[42] Gower takes the story from the apocryphal Book of Tobit, 6-8. Of special relevance is Tobias's prayer with Sarah on their wedding night, which concludes: 'And now O Lord I take not this my sister for lust, but in truth Command that I may find mercy and grow old with her.' Text from *The Apocrypha, Translated Out of the Greek and Latin Tongues, Being the Version Set Forth in 1611* (Oxford, 1908). In the *Mirour* 17701-49, Gower also discusses the five virtues of wifeliness explained to Sarah by her parents.

[43] Kelly, *Love and Marriage*, pp. 275-78, interprets the Tobias and Sara story as evidence of Gower's moderate attitude toward sexual pleasure when taken in a lawful relationship. The position Gower adopts would have been condemned by many (see for example Gregory, *Epistles*, 11.64 in *PL* LXXVII, cols. 1196-97), but it also had its supporters. John T. Noonan, Jr., *Contraception: A History of its Treatment by the Catholic Theologians and Canonists* (Cambridge, MA, 1966), 293, quotes Aquinas's *In Libros Sententiarum* (4.31.2.1, response to obj. 3): 'The delight which occurs in the matrimonial act, although it is most intense in quantity, does not exceed the limits fixed by reason before its commencement, although during this delight reason cannot set the limits.'

Bot he the bestes wolde binde,
Only to lawes of nature,
Bot to the mannes creature
God yaf him reson forth withal,
Wherof that he nature schal
Upon the causes modefie,
That he schal do no leccherie,
And yit he schal hise lustes have.

There is, thus, one law for beasts, two for men. Men are created to serve God, and need to keep proper proportion, both of sexuality and of spirituality. This difference is central to the *Confessio Amantis* and, indeed, to Gower's metaphysics generally. Gower makes the point his focus in Book VIII, where incest is the prominent topic. In the initial 16 lines of that Book, Gower traces the history of human unions from Adam and Eve to the present. When there were few people on the planet, the Confessor remarks, initmacy was necessary between close relations. There was then no 'lawe positif' to prevent it, and natural law applied. As numbers increased, however, God instituted stricter sanctions, through his emissary the Pope (VIII, 144-47):

For of the lawe canonized
The Pope hath bede to the men,
That non schal wedden of his ken
Ne the second ne the thridde.

Ominously, human kind has seen fit to disregard this just regulation, with the result that (as Gower exemplifies through his metaphoric description here of the incestuous as lower animals reason's dictates have been too often overturned (VIII, 148-63):

Bot thogh that holy cherche it bidde,
So to restreigne Mariage,
Ther ben yit upon loves Rage
Ful manye of suche nou aday
That taken wher thei take may.
For love, which is unbesein
Of alle reson, as men sein,
Thurgh sotie and thurgh nycete,
Of his voluptuosite
He spareth no condicion
Of ken ne yit religion,
Bot as a cock among the Hennes,
Or as a Stalon in the Fennes,
Which goth amonges al the Stod,

Riht so can he nomore good,
Bot takth what thing comth next to hond.

This description portrays incest as a form of mindless promiscuity, and offers
marriage as an opposite. It thus it also has wider applications and can be used to
characterize most forms of unlawful intercourse, and even sin in general. Incest
in Book VIII, then, is just the incidental point of departure Gower makes of it: a
metaphor of improper marriage, of bestial misprision, and consequently of
disharmony acting under the guise of that *real* love both personal and
Empedoclean which, when properly in place, brings unity and accord. Hence the
theme of 'Apollonius of Tyre' (a harper and an Arion type) is harmony,
displayed as different forms of love: spouse and spouse, father and child, friend to
friend, subjects to prince and prince to subject, faithful spirit for God, and God
for it. For each case, the extensive tale contrives a counterexample, and sees it
punished. In the process, Gower touches on the spectrum of sins described
elsewhere throughout the poem. By the time Genius sums up his teachings in the
Epilogue, we have been offered a parting look at the entire tangled skein,
delivered in a story the frame of which arcs back to join the macrocosmic issues of
the Prologue, forcing the reader to take a larger, longer view. The world
inhabited by Apollonius at the end of Book VIII has, in certain respects,
responded to the Arionic song.

III

If the 'Tale of Apollonius' in fact provides a fitting conclusion to the
complexity of Gower's exempla, it does so by offering us an image in lieu of an
explanation. (That must come later, as the Epilogue and Prologue are combined
to form a key to the *Confessio*'s meaning.) Within that image, however, are
subsumed lessons in exemplum form. These also serve as answers to
architectonic questions of major proportion. One such is the problem of the 'two
Venus' discussed earlier. Gower's direct support of lawful marriage, which
receives its broadest statement in Book VIII and in 'Apollonius,' obviously
requires the clarification of Venus's role in the natural order. To write a poem in
which proper love figures as a primary theme, Gower was faced with corrupted
symbols as well as free. Those which he could not discard, he was forced to
restore. As we have seen, he went to great lengths to establish Venus Genetrix as
a legitimate avatar of the goddess, and to underplay her sinful incarnation as
Venus Luxuria. This reversal is not, then, an excrescence, but a necessary part of
a plan of great thoroughness, one in some ways so all-inclusive as to risk
misunderstanding. For Gower had to overturn a number of conventions if he was
to secure the confession of Amans/ John Gower as the song of Arion called for in
the Prologue, with any hope of achieving practical results. These conventions are
of couse primarily literary, but in Gower's poetic their reformation can be seen to
have had aims far more sweeping and substantial.

Largely this is because poetry for Gower is by definition a serious and practical enterprise. Patrick J. Gallacher has amply demonstrated the patristic basis for Gower's view that the words of men have actual power, not just to move through persuasion but rather to 'become' the shape of things and events in an approximation of the Divine Logos — the source and model of all human speech — which was itself made flesh.[44] It is this belief of Gower's which governs his treatment of magic in the *Confessio*. In Book VI, Nectanabus, for example, performs his deeds by incantation, not by potion; Medea in Book V restores the youth of Eson in the same manner. ('Karectes,' the term for 'verbal charm,' is first used in English by Gower, in order to obtain vocabulary for what he believed was the empowering engine of sorcery.) And it is also this belief that receives its clearest statement in the lengthy discourse on 'the word' in Book VII, under 'Rhetoric.' Here Gower leaves no doubt about his meaning (VII, 1545-49):

> In Ston and gras vertu ther is,
> Bot yit the bokes tellen this,
> That word above all erthli thinges
> Is vertuous in his doinges,
> Wher so it be to evele or good.

To a man with such views — ones radically different from Chaucer's and very much more like Langland's than might be expected of a Ricardian poet with court patrons — the making of poetry was not entertainment. It was work accountable to God. As a result, it seems likely that, if ever there were a professional 'falling out' between Chaucer and Gower (an event which, I must confess, I do not believe ever took place), it would have come over the former's more continental acceptance of writing as art and 'game,' and the latter's rejection of the notion, at least at the bottom line of poetic purpose. At no time did Gower's desire for immortality, his interest in paranomasia and learned joking, obscure the greater task. To read the *Confessio Amantis* as Arionic is to approach the poem as a fleshing out of Gower's choice of image, for if a song can change society and bring harmony to the universe of men and beasts, it is endowed with a substantializing power far greater than mere persuasion. Inherent in Arion, then, as a symbol or examplar, is unusual responsibility. The poet who chooses so to sing must consider the benefit of all the world.

Necessarily, as I have argued above, this approach to poetry places the *Confessio Amantis* at direct odds with its models, first among which is the *Roman de la Rose*. Although it has often been pointed out how much Gower owes to the *Roman* and the tradition of *amour courtois*, the true nature of that debt must be reassessed in a special sense. Probably, in fact, Gower saw in this tradition an active threat to his society, as a corruption of the power of the word from good to idle — and hence evil — pastimes. What, after all, should be made of the 'Gallica

---

[44] See Gallagcer's discussion, *Love, the Word and Mercury*, pp. 2-4.

peccata' (condemned, as we have seen, in the *Vox Clamantis*) if not evidence of the carryings-on of a nobility fallen, in Gower's opinion, under the influence of a French temptation borne in part to the shores of England by the poetry of courtly love?

Viewed against such a backdrop, Gower's larger strategy in the *Confessio* runs clear. Targeting the court of the young King Richard (perhaps at his request, if we believe the first recension prologue), the aging moralist may very well have felt he had a final opportunity to strike a righteous blow. Given the audience (and possibly the commission), a work with the form of the *Vox* or the *Mirour de l'Omme* would have been ineffective. Too direct in their statements of position, hardly 'entertainment' by the standards of the *Roman* tradition, these poems would have had little impact on those Gower was trying to reach. Did he not have the best evidence for such a judgement in the immediate state of things? The *Vox Clamantis* and the *Mirour* had been written, and the world was still going to the devil. As he notes in the first lines of Book I of the *Confessio*, a different poetry was called for. To this end, Gower chose to compose in English a poem 'in the form' — though with a distinctly different message — best known to his designated audience. The *Confessio Amantis* brings together on a single plane what were for Gower inseparable issues: poetics, personal morality and social justice. By creating fictions, at once like and yet finally *unlike* what his audience had come to expect from courtly writing, Gower was attempting to 'fight fire with fire.' His last major poem is an attempt, put simply, to undercut an ethos and the poetic tradition which gave it voice.

The foregoing perspective draws together many odd elements scattered from Prologue to coda of the *Confessio Amantis*. By casting his narrator/hero Amans in his own aged shape, Gower achieves more than an ironic humor.[45] Instead, he undermines the romantic assumptions which frame his poem by drawing attention to the single, permissible reason for sexual desire — honorable marriage, intercourse with one spouse, and the creation of children. When, in the conclusion, old Amans/Gower is denied entry into Venus's court, it is because his love is deemed 'unnatural.' Whether the revelation of Amans's age is actual or merely fictional — a surprise at once facilitated and delimited by the confines of suspended disbelief — is of moot importance in assessing the originality and productivity of the stroke.[46] The point is driven home through the reversal of our expectations. In similar fashion, those 'uncourtly' aspects of Amans the lover noted often are also understandable as part of the plan.[47]

[45] The more limited argument has been lately fostered by David W. Hiscoe, 'The Ovidian Comic Strategy of Gower's *Confessio Amantis*,' *Philological Quarterly* 64 (1985), 367-85.

[46] For a somewhat divergent view, see Burrow, 'The Portrayal of Amans,' in *Responses and Reassessments*, ed. Minnis, pp. 5-25.

[47] I am thinking here of treatments such as Schueler, 'Age of the Lover,' and Linda Barney Burke, 'Women in John Gower's *Confessio Amantis*,' *Medievalia* 3 (1977), 238-59.

Amans's 'singular lack of heroism,' given voice in Book IV (ll. 1656-65) when he argues with Genius over the efficacy of performing deeds of derring-do in the 'courtly' manner to win the hand of his lady-love, makes good sense if we recall what issue is at stake: not *pris*, as the romancers would have it, but marriage and the propagation of the world.

Important as these elements are, however, they do not take the measure of Gower's plan for the *Confessio Amantis*. This becomes clear only in the gathering of amorous, political, poetic and actual sin brought about through the device of the lover's confession.[48] Here Gower capitalizes on the commonality of virtue established conventionally between the good lover and the good man, as well as on the potential for psychological probing made available since the thirteenth century by the Church's penitential reforms. Requiring, as they did, that the reasons of the heart be plumbed as well as that the sinful action be explained in detail, the rules laid down by the Fourth Lateran Council created by extension the first sytematic vocabulary for revealing human motives known to the Middle Ages.[49] The books on penance necessitated by these new directions were also among Gower's primary sources for the *Confessio*, and they explain much about Genius's character. Even as we meet him in the first Book, Genius points out a duty which to many has seemed a conflict of interest. Although he is primarily the servant of Venus, in the course of his confession of Amans Genius says he will nonetheless discuss *real* sins, real vice, along with those of an amorous variety (I, 233-48):

> Thi schrifte to oppose and hiere,
> Mi Sone, I am assigned hiere
> Be Venus, the goddesse above,
> Whos Prest I am touchende of love,
> Bot natheles for certain skile
> I mot algate and nedes wile
> Noght only make my spekynges
> Of love, bot of othre thinges,
> That touchen to the cause of vice.
> For that belongeth to thoffice
> Of Prest, whos ordre that I bere,
> So that I wol nothing forbere,
> That I the vices on and on
> Ne schal thee schewen everychon;
> Wherof thou myht take evidence
> To reule with thi conscience.

[48] By 'poetic sin' I mean here a violation, by writing frivolously, of the standard Gower set for the written word.
[49] The point is made exhaustively in relation to various works, both religious and secular, by Jean-Charles Payen, *Le Motif du repentir dans la littérature française médiévale (des origines à 1230)*, Publications romanes et françaises 98 (Geneva, 1967), pp. 211-76. Marc Bloch, *Feudal Society*, 2 vols., trans. L.A. Manyon (Chicago, 1964), I, 103-06, also comes to similar conclusions when examining the contritionist movements of the twelfth century.

What Genius outlines is his course of action for the unfolding *Confessio Amantis*. His office, as he claims, is two-fold. First, he is the priest of Venus, and so bound to shrive Amans specifically as a worshipper of Love; but he is also a priest in general, with a responsibility to discuss vice *qua* vice. In Book after Book he does just this, striving (I, 49-61):

> . . . to don bothe tuo,
> Ferst that myn ordre longeth to,
> The vices forto telle arewe,
> Bot next above alle othere schewe
> Of love I wol the propretes,
> How that thei stonde be degrees
> After the disposicioun
> Of Venus, whos condicioun
> I moste folwe, as I am holde.

Structurally, Genius's method preserves the discrete categories of his dual obligations. He begins each interrogatory with a description, and examples illustrative, of real sins; then he turns away from these to draw their amorous incarnations. But as we have seen, as the poem progresses Genius's two roles are brought together inexorably. We end, in fact, with the unity of Genius's apparently separate roles manifestly demonstrated by the convergent themes of the *Confessio*. When Venus is restored to her original stature as sub-vicar of God, servant of Natura and interested only in admitting to her court those true lovers sufficiently virile and honest to perform their duties according to the laws of both 'Kinde' and Christ, Genius too is revealed as priest of an increasingly Christianized order. By the conclusion of the *Confessio Amantis*, this Genius resembles but scantly his counterpart in Jean de Meun's *Roman*, urging on with phallic torch Amant's assault on the rosegarden. Very much the priest of a conscientious Venus Genetrix (who can, in that role, admit his shame at his deity's recurrent incarnational lapses), Gower's Genius has changed shpe, so as to be able to gently, subtly admonish and guide the aged Amans to look long in the mirror, consider his true state and give over his inappropriate desire for the solaces of youth.

The movement of the poem, then, is throughout against its main tradition, undercutting all that the courtly ethos had established over the years. The *Confessio* is Gower's attempt to use poetry against itself to make a statement about art, morality, and politics by creating fictions of marriage and music which do not merely explain, but demonstrate. If, in the *Mirour de l'Omme* and the *Vox Clamantis*, Gower showed himself capable of writing argument in verse, of rhyming his moral stances, in the *Confessio Amantis* he goes much further to create a living lesson. To the degree that we are drawn into Amans/Gower's fictive predicament — and this degree is large, since his character is fleshed by the probing of his interior life through confession — we are also invited to experience his amorous fumbling, and to make it ours. We think with Amans, are pressed to mull over and assess his answers to Genius's queries. As Genius rounds out his critique of the lover, revealing his age, we have been given little choice but to test his unsuitability against our own unworthy loves. The poetry maneuvers us, much as Milton's does in *Paradise Lost*, into 'taking the fall' with Amans, and swallowing the subsequent bitter pill of righteous counsel. When Amans/Gower the *persona* gives over his lesser, earthly affection and in the end begins his prayer for the peace, John Gower the poet has gone an immense distance toward placing that prayer in the mouths of his readers as well, to create a larger harmony, a kind of Arionic chorus.

IV

The *Confessio Amantis*, is, then, in its fictive center, a love poem designed to outgrow itself. It is a poem of conversion, intended to carry not only the lover Amans but also all of us, as secondary participants, beyond our mundane concerns. Dante, at the end of the *Paradiso*, affords his audience this view — not without love in mind. Gower also, in so doing, necessarily has stretched the scope of his poem to encompass other, more communal bonds. As we have seen from his treatment in the Prologue, Gower had specifically credited Arion with healing rifts between the social orders — 'As wel the lord as the schepherde.' To make of Amans's confession a song of that sort, Gower developed the social dimensions of his poem with great care and attention. The political program of the *Confessio Amantis* was first examined by George R. Coffman, and most recently by Russell A. Peck, who has sketched with great sensitivity the interrelation of psychology and social criticism in Gower's thought.[50] Gower, as Peck has remarked:

> . . . seems always mindful of man as a double entity, both social and individual. When exploring man's individual psyche he turns to metaphors of state; when criticizing the state he conceives of a common body. The manifestations of human happiness cannot be fully realized without the other.[51]

In such a system, kingship is an important metaphor — 'a form of maturity,' in Peck's terms, '. . . balanced rationality. Woe to the kingdom ruled by an "undisciplined boy" (*Rex, puer indoctus* whether that boy be Richard II or a wayward Amans.'[52]

As Peck suggests, we must look carefully at the roles played by kingship and King Richard in shaping the *Confessio*, in order to understand Gower's poetic generally, his marital metaphors, and the Arion figure in specific. His equation of personal 'good government,' of the emotions and the will in accord with divine

---

[50] Coffman, 'Gower in His Most Significant Role' and 'Mentor for Royalty'; Peck, *Kingship and Common Profit*, passim.

[51] ibid., p. xxi.

[52] ibid., p. xxi.

purpose, with external rule, in the form of sound kingship, becomes explicit in the Epilogue (VIII, 3080-88):

> For if a kyng wol justifie
> His lond and hem that beth withynne,
> First at hym self he mot begynne,
> To kepe and reule his owne estat,
> That in hym self be no debat
> Toward his god: for othre wise
> Ther may no erthly kyng suffise
> Of his kyngdom the folk to lede,
> Bot he the kyng of hevene drede.

Just as in the Prologue Gower pointed out that through Adam's sin all of nature was corrupted, so here he suggests that the king must lead a righteous life lest he ruin his nation. It is a lesson which repeats in so many words what 'Apollonius of Tyre' offered no great distance earlier in fictive form. Thus in the closing lines of his poem, Gower returns to the theme of division broached initially in the Prologue, and on this level too brings the poem full circle. For at last regard, a king is a man, the flawed kin of Adam, and subject to his own corruption or reform. Such a ruler who 'with humble chiere' follows God's laws, pursues virtue and avoids vice will receive a proper reward, manifested in this world *in parvo* as a sound marriage and *in macro* as an orderly and well-remembered reign (VIII, 3099-3105):

> His grace schal be sufficant
> To governe al the remenant
> Which longith to his duite;
> So that in al his prosperite
> The poeple schal noght be oppressid,
> Wherof his name schal be blessid,
> For ever and be memorial.

This image of earthly harmony has its parallel in the 'good government' of pre-lapserian Eden (where significantly good government and good marriage were identical) and also in the Golden Age conjured by the song of Arion. It stands as well behind the commendation of Richard's reign Gower offered in the first recension (VIII, 2989*-92*):

> Justice medled with pite,
> Largesce forth with charite.
> In his persone it mai be schewed
> What is a king to be wel thewed.

That Gower transfers his hopes for this ideal from Richard to the Estates, and
ultimately to Henry IV in subsequent versions of the *Confessio*, matters little in
terms of his larger philosophy. The salient point is that Amans and kingdom are
mutually reflective, and can be preserved by the same process of moral
education. This is because, in the corporeal model used commonly to describe
social order in the Middle Ages, the king was head and 'reason' of the body
politic.[53] No harmony might be achieved without the king's enlightenment.
Hence Amans/ Gower's song must be directed toward the royal ear. The new
wisdom of the narrator, confession complete, consequently has been developed
from the beginning for revelation in both private and public terms.

One effect of Gower's decision to structure his poem to accommodate the
political implications of Arionic melody was very likely the opening of the first
recension Prologue, the charming river scene in which poet and Richard II meet
on the water, and the *Confessio Amantis* is conceived at the king's request (Pro.
44*-53):

> Out of my bot, whan he me syh,
> He bad me come in to his barge.
> And whan I was with him at large,
> Amonges othre thinges seid
> He hath this charge upon me leid,
> And bad me doo my besynesse
> That to his hihe worthinesse
> Som newe thing I scholde boke,
> That he himself it mihte loke
> After the forme of my writynge.

Whether an actual meeting took place in this way we of course cannot know,
pleasing as it is to contemplate Richard and Gower as watermen, and a king with
such demonstrated interest in poetry.[54] It is worth emphasizing, however, what a
skillful stroke is Richard's commission of the *Confessio*, fictitious or no. By it,
Gower is able to link the political, moral, and amorous dimensions of his poem.
The narrative of Amans gains access to the head of state, who is also — and

---

[53] The metaphor of the state as a human body is probably traceable to Cicero, who spoke
of the *totum corpus rei publica* in *De Officiis*, I. 25, 85. The image is found in the work of John
of Salisbury (*Policraticus* IV, 2,3; V, 2), Vincent of Beauvais (*Speculum Doctrinale* VII, 8),
and Ptolemy of Lucca (*De Regimine Principium* IV, 3). Gower would have considered the
metaphor a commonplace.

[54] Recent opinion seems to be running against Richard's having been much of a reader,
despite the variety of books available in his library. See especially Richard Firth Green,
'King Richard II's Books Revisited,' *The Library* 31 (1976), 235-39, and V. J.
Scattergood, 'Literary Culture at the Court of Richard II,' in Scattergood and J.W.
Sherborne, eds., *English Court Culture in the Later Middle Ages* (London, 1983), pp. 29-44. If
Gower's work had attracted Richard's eye, it was probably for his moralist's stance A. I.
Doyle remarks (in the same volume, p. 168) on the popularity in Richard's reign of
'English religious prose of a pronouncedly serious character.'

importantly — identified as involved in its making. (That Gower did not simply substitute Henry IV for Richard in the barge in the later version perhaps is evidence that the *tête-à-tête* on the Thames was real, and well enough known to prevent transference. But in any case, his political intention remains the same in the second recension as he notes the poem was written 'for Engelondes sake.') This early connection adds resonance and specificity to subsequent discussions of proper kingship which appear throughout the *Confessio*. Many statements, if we imagine for them a royal audience, acquire a special point.

The foremost example of this is Book VII which finds its place in the poem as a direct address to the king — initially to Richard II, probably, but certainly to Henry IV. Perhaps (as seems likely, given what we know of Henry's temperament) Gower judged Henry a more pragmatic and conventionally moral ruler than Richard, one as susceptible to didactic argument as, I think, he believed Richard was to fictions.[55] In any case, to Henry (whom he terms 'wel lerned' in 'olde bookes'), Gower later dedicated 'In Praise of Peace,' and this may tell us something: The thoroughly argued, austere 'In Praise of Peace,' with its similarities of stance and tone to Book VII of the *Confessio Amantis*, is Gower's only other extant English poem.[56]

That the king was intended as its primary audience can be inferred from a look at the organization Gower imposed on Book VII. As we have noted above, he followed Brunetto in general, arranging his material under three major headings 'Theorique,' which includes the fields of 'Theologie,' 'Phisique,' and 'Mathematique' (under which subdivisions Gower is able to insert discussions of God and souls, bodily substances, and, as sub-sets of 'Mathematique,' arithmetic, music, geometry and astronomy); 'Rhetorique,' including grammar and logic, and an admonition to use words only for good purposes — a pointed reference

---

[55] John Capgrave, whose account remains our best source of information about Henry's character despite its author's chronological and social distance from his subject (Capgrave possibly saw Henry once, in 1406 at Lynn when the king bade farewell to his daughter; Capgrave was then thirteen), attests to Henry's fondness for casuistical argument, and for the conversation of men of letters; see his *Liber de Illustribus Henricis*, trans. F.C. Hingeston (London, [Rolls Series], 1858), p. 116. J.H. Wylie records that in addition to Chaucer and Gower, the king took an interest in Christine de Pisan's work, and invited her to come to England; that, while in exile in France he attended lectures and a debate at the University of Paris; and further that, in August, 1406, Henry passed a full morning in the library while visiting the monastery of Bardney (see *A History of England under Henry the Fourth*, 4 vols., [London, 1884-98], IV, 136-39, and II, 460). These anecdotes have been accepted by modern historians: see J.L. Kirby, *Henry IV of England* (London, 1970), pp. 253-54; K.B. McFarlane, *Lancastrian Kings and Lollard Knights* (Oxford, 1972), pp. 22-23; and E.F. Jacob, who describes Henry as 'a man of a studious nature, and liked reading works of moral philosophy;' see *The Fifteenth Century, 1399-1485*, Oxford History of England, VI (Oxford, 1961), p. 3.

[56] In his dedication of the poem to Henry, Gower wrote (ll. 22-25):
>In al thing which is of god begonne
>Ther folwith grace, if it be wel governed;
>Thus tellen thei which olde bookes conne,
>Whereof, my lord, y wot wel thow art lerned.

from a poet of Gower's inclinations; and 'Practique,' with three parts, 'Etique' (personal care and governance), 'Iconomique' (the ordering of household and family), and 'Policie' (the duties of the king to his realm). As for the relative importance of these sections for Gower, we are perhaps given a strong clue by the disproportionate treatment afforded 'Policie,' which is more than twice the length of all the other sections combined.[57]

Of the various subjects covered in Book VII, 'Policie' treats those most important for the king in his peculiar role. Gower leaves no doubt about his understanding this (VII, 1679-85):

> Practique hath yit the thridde aprise,
> Which techeth hou and in what wise
> Thurgh hih pourveied ordinance
> A king schal sette in governance
> His Realme, and that is Policie,
> Which longeth unto Regalie
> In time of werre, in time of pes.

Other areas of Alexander's education are of course relevant for a ruler too, but in the general sense — in so far as the ruler is a man with an active will and a capacity to sin. Because, however, medieval political theory cast the king as an uniquely dual entity — both corruptible person and incorruptible 'Crown' — instructing him required a specially developed approach.[58]

This Gower accomplished with his handling of the 'Policie' section. As both Macaulay and Fisher have pointed out, Gower developed 'Policie' independently of the structure offered him by the *Trésor*, drawing only (in Fisher's words) 'material, not organization or viewpoint, from the *Secretum*.'[59] Foremost among the changes Gower wrought in his sources is the division of 'Policie' into 'fyf pointz' — Truth, Liberality, Justice, Pity and Chastity. All are requisite to the 'good man' in general, but Gower's concern is specific and singleminded. His discussion is pointedly tailored to capture the king's ear. Thus he introduces, for example, the division Truth with a preface (VII, 1737-50):

> The word is tokne of that withinne,
> Ther schal a worthi king beginne
> To kepe his tunge and to be trewe,
> So schal his pris ben evere newe.

[57] The actual numbers are 3859 lines to 1679.
[58] The descriptions of kingship given by medieval theorists were designed to accommodate the role *sub specie aeternitatis*. The public persona and the individual will (*privatat voluntas*) are thus differentiated by John of Salisbury (*Policraticus* IV, C. 2), for example. The matter is best presented by Kantorowicz, *King's Two Bodies*.
[59] Fisher, *John Gower*, p. 198.

> Avise him every man tofore,
> And be wel war, er he be swore
> For afterward it is to late,
> If that he wole his word debate.
> For as a king in special
> Above all othre is principal
> Of his pouer, so scholde he be
> Most vertuous in his degre;
> And that mai wel be signefied
> Be his corone and specified.

What follows is a short allegory of the royal crown, in which the purity of its gold, the hardness, color and virtues of its stones, and its circular shape are anatomized as emblematic of the king's obligation to honesty. Obviously readers of lower rank might take profit from this, but the primary direction is clear.

Gower takes the same approach to the remaining four 'pointz.' Liberality is introduced in this way (VII, 1985-90):

> Next after trowthe the secounde,
> In Policie as it is founde,
> Which serveth to the worldes fame
> In worshhipe of a kinges name,
> Largesse it is, whos privelegge
> Ther mai non Avarice abregge.

This virtue Gower treated before, both in the *Vox Clamantis* and in the *Confessio* itself. It is interesting to compare the treatments in these two loci with the version in Book VII. In the earlier instances, emphasis is placed upon alms-giving, a general form of Liberality in which all men may — indeed, *should* — participate. In Book VII, however, Gower very carefully fits his discussion to the king by explaining that although in the first age all goods were 'commune,' greed necessitated the institution of kings to oversee the just distribution of wealth (VII, 2004-13):

> Withinne hemself the poeple fond
> That it was good to make a king,
> Which mihte appesen al this thing
> And yive riht to the lignages
> In partinge of here heritages
> And ek of al here other good;
> And thus above hem alle stod
> The king upon his Regalie,
> As he which hath to justifie
> The worldes good fro covoitise.

Thus Gower shapes his introduction of material so as to adapt it for a king's hearing.

Justice, the third point of 'Policie,' has a preface which delineates the role of the king *vis-à-vis* the law. This is, as Fisher has suggested, perhaps 'Gower's most lucid and earnest comment on the interdependence of the king, the legal system, and a peaceful nation.'[60] As such, it emphasizes that for Gower the king operated as God's vicar on earth, with an unique responsibility to emulate an otherwordly model (VII, 2725-36):

> The myhtes of a king ben grete,
> Bot yit a worthi king schal lete
> Of wrong to do, al that he myhte;
> For he which schal the poeple ryhte,
> It sit wel to his regalie
> That he himself ferst justifie
> Towardes god in his degre:
> For his astat is elles fre
> Toward alle othre in his persone,
> Save only the god al one,
> Which wol himself a king chastise,
> Wher that non other mai suffise.

If the royal power is great, it is nonetheless tempered on two sides by responsibilities to God and subjects. (Only God may chastise a king, but will do so on the basis of performance as a governor.) Nor is the king's judicability limited to his own actions. Just as he cannot govern a realm alone and must therefore rely on appointed ministers, so is his guilt equal to theirs, should his ministers act unjustly (VII, 2737-53):

> So were it good to taken hiede
> That ferst a king his oghne ded
> Betwen the vertu and the vice
> Redresce, and thanne of his justice
> So sette in even the balance
> Towardes othre in governance,
> That to the povere and to the riche
> Hise lawes myhten stonde liche,
> He schal excepte no persone.
> Bot for he mai noght al him one
> In sondri places do justice,
> He schal of his real office
> With wys consideracion
> Ordeigne his deputacion

---

[60] Ibid., p. 201.

> Of suche jugges as ben lerned,
> So that his poeple be governed
> Be hem that trewe ben and wise.

Significant here, too, is the pragmatism we would expect in an address to a ruling monarch whose need for instruction is real and immediate. Hence, Gower does not choose to discuss justice as an abstract virtue in Book VII — an option he had open, and had seemed irremediably bound to in his earlier works. Rather, the treatment here is characteristic of Gower's approach in the *Confessio*. That is, he relies on fictions to carry the weight of the lessons. All ought to be just in their dealings, but the instances related here are peculiarly kingly, as would befit an intended royal audience.

Again, with Pity the interconnection of earthly kings and Christ as king of heaven and earth, at one with the 'mageste' of God the Father, is established (VII, 3107-13):

> It is the vertu of Pite,
> Thurgh which the hihe mageste
> Was stered, whan his Sone alyhte,
> And in pite the world to rihte
> Tok of the Maide fleissh and blod.
> Pite was cause of thilke good,
> Wherof that we ben alle save . . .

The similarity serves as the special justification for a human ruler's need to possess the virtue also (VII, 3122-29):

> It sit wel every liege drede
> His king and to his heste obeie,
> And riht so be the same weie
> It sit a king to be pitous
> Toward his poeple and gracious
> Upon the reule of governance,
> So that he worche no vengeance,
> Which mai be cleped crualte.

Gower's careful placement of this section helps clarify his meaning. Coming in Book VII as it does, immediately after the discourse on Justice, his presentation of kingly pity provides a balance to that harsher virtue. The correlative is Christ's mercy, which 'corrects' the absolute justice of God the Father, turning harshness to love (VII, 3130-36):

> Justice which doth equite
> Is dredfull, for he noman spareth;

> Bot in the lond wher Pite fareth
> The king mai nevere faile of love,
> For Pite thurgh the grace above,
> So as the Philosophre affermeth,
> His regne in good astat confermeth.

Gower's treatment of Pity as an attribute of kings divine and mundane is not only generally instructive but particularly so as well: For, while any and all men may perhaps follow the example of Christ in their daily dealings, it is only the actual ruler who is enabled, as a result of his unique place in the world hierarchy, to approximate the model. Thus again Gower has thoughtfully directed his argument toward a royal ear while rendering it also universally applicable.

For the fifth point, Chastity, Gower seems at first to have adopted a new tactic. He begins with a discussion of sexual desire — hardly a condition exclusive to kings (VII, 4215-25):

> The Madle is mad for the femele,
> Bot where as on desireth fele,
> That nedeth noght be weie of kinde:
> For whan a man mai redy finde
> His oghne wif, what scholde he sece
> To borwe an other mannes plouh,
> Whan he hath geere good ynouh
> Affaited at his oghne heste,
> And is to him wel more honeste
> Than other thing which is unknowe?

Apart from single references to 'man' and 'wif,' Gower's opening description has universal application. But as we read on we see that he is constructing a progression with humanity at its point. His purpose is to build toward the special case of royal unions through a series of graduated contrasts. In the lines above, 'Madle' and 'femele' represent ordinary desire, the sexual service all creatures pay to 'kinde.' Then from the unspeciated urge to generation we are pressed ahead to human marriage, albeit initially in mistaken form. As the metaphoric sequence indicates, the distance between indescriminant copulation with 'fele' and the trading of agricultural implements is slight. To speak of a spouse as 'an other mannes plouh,' or 'geere good ynouh,' is stunning, dehumanizing — and we have observed in previous pages the dim view Gower took on that. Only marriage, with its profoundly social as well as personal implications, domesticates sexuality and brings it to heel for the common good. 'Forthi' ['Therefore'], Gower continues (VII, 4226-32):

> . . . scholde every good man knowe
> And thenke, hou that in mariage
> His trouthe plight lith in' morgage,

> Which if he breke, it is falshode,
> And that descordeth to manhode,
> And namely toward the grete,
> Wherof the bokes alle trete.

The linkage of 'manhode' (which probably carries the double sense of 'masculinity' and 'humanness') with kept 'trouthe,' or one's word, through the contractual aspects of marriage ('mariage/ morgage,' made plainer by the rhyme) emphasizes the civilizing evolution Gower both believes in, and hopes here to portray. The final couplet above (rhyming 'grete/trete') charts his subsequent direction, again from the common to the extraordinary. Having constructed his base, only then does he turn to his true subject, the espousing of princes and kings (VII, 4245-56):

> Bot yit a kinges hihe astat,
> Which of his ordre as a prelat
> Schal ben enoight and seintefied,
> He mot be more magnefied
> For dignete of his corone,
> Than scholde an other low persone,
> Which is noght of so hih emprise.
> Therfore a Prince him scholde avise,
> Er that he felle in such riote,
> And namely that he nassote
> To change for the wommanhede
> The worthinesse of his manhede.

Significant here is the explanation Gower gives for the exaltation of the sovereign above 'an other low persone': a king, like a prelate, is 'enoignt and seintefied,' an idea common to English and continental legal theorists who from the twelfth century had developed a 'royal Christology,' or 'theology of kingship.'[61] This of course is not the usual reason offered for kingly place at the head of the nation, and we might well ask why it is included here. The answer surely is two-fold. First, it establishes the 'contractual' responsibility of the king to those below and above, in terms which complete the progressive figure Gower has been sketching. Like marriage, kingship in Gower's view is a sanctified state, symbolic of the total *communitas* of mankind and God. This again is an idea Gower adopted from contemporary jurists, who were themselves expanding upon developments in the canon law.[62] Thus (the second probable reason for its inclusion) the point is made for the king that, despite his apparently greater power to rove indescriminantly throughout the 'womman hede,' his freedom to

---

[61] See Kantorowicz, *King's Two Bodies*, pp. 16-17 and passim.
[62] For a discussion of how much contemporary legal theorists borrowed from canon law, see Kantorowicz, *King's Two Bodies*, pp. 212-13.

do so is actually curtailed by the need of the *corpus morale et politicum*, whose rituals of anointing and sanctification — not his birth *per se* — have provided him his rank and authority.[63] The argument, powerful albeit obliquely tailored, confronts the king with a central paradox of medieval political theory: why the individual will must merge perforce into that of the whole to realize itself completely. Or, put another way, as Gower realized, just kingship echoes the harmonies of both marriage and song. It is not, I think, without purpose that he makes 'chastite' the last of his points.

Through the manner of his introductions for each of his 'fyf pointz,' then, Gower apparently hoped to ensure the king's attention. The method obviously had its merits. It was plain, and spoke straightforwardly to the major issues of contemporary religio-political thought. Yet Gower had written two plain-speaking poems before, and had seen fit to open the *Confessio Amantis* with a statement to the effect that, based on the small success he had achieved with the *Mirour* and the *Vox*, in this new poem he was adopting a fresh approach to the narrative exemplum on a grand scale. If talking *about* truth produced few results, perhaps actually showing it, more or less in action, would do the trick.

Considering that the audience for the *Confessio* was different from that intended for either the *Vox Clamantis* or the *Mirour de l'Omme* — the court, as opposed to the clergy — Gower's decision made sense. Judging from what we know of the contents of Richard II's library (the requisite Bible, a book of hours, and several romances), he was a man of some education — if he read what he owned — and a fondness for stories.[64] Might Gower have been aware of the king's taste, and altered his usual pattern of working because of it? In this light, it is perhaps significant that in Book VII we find few of the exemplifying tales which have been the chief means of making and underlining points throughout the other Books of the *Confessio* — except in the section on Policy, in which the king is addressed. Further, because this section completes the discussion of Alexander's education, it comes last in the Book. It is thus given the position best suited to be remembered. This is, I believe, what we should expect of a thoughtful, practical writer like Gower if his subject of address were the king, who was likely to hear his poem as entertainment rather than pore over it as might a cleric, and if the purpose of both the section and the poem as a whole were ambitious — the moral and political reform of the kingdom, and the Arionic song. Like the direct introductions of the 'fyf pointz' of Policy, then, both the inclusion of narratives and the positioning of the section gives evidence that Book VII was meant primarily as instruction for the king. It is Gower's most traditional venture in the creation of a *speculum regis* — a literary 'mirror' of the type popular throughout

---

[63] See further Kantorowicz, Ibid., p. 210.

[64] On Richard's library, in addition to studies by Green, Scattergood and Doyle cited in note 54 above, see Edith Rickert, 'Richard II's Books,' *The Library*, 4th series, 13 (1933), 144-47; Gervase Mathew, *Court of Richard II*, pp. 22-23, 40-43; R.S. Loomis, 'The Library of Richard II,' in *Studies in Language, Literature and Culture of the Middle Ages and Later*, ed. E. Bagby Atwood and A. A. Hill (Austin, Texas, 1969), pp. 173-78; and also Green, *Poets and Princepleasers*, pp. 90-96.

the later Middle Ages, in which a king might find his faults reflected, and also glimpse a vision of an improved future.[65]

But Book VII, while it may be Gower's greatest single mirror in the *Confessio Amantis*, is nonetheless but one facet of a poem which is itself a vast, composite mirror of many polished surfaces designed to induce optical revelation. For if the purpose of Book VII is to cause the king (be it Richard II or Henry IV) to 'see' himself better, and thereby help the realm to prosper, so the entire *Confessio* is intended to bring about similar self-reflection on moral and literary levels for its other, several audiences. Thus the fictive level of the poem concludes with a 'wonder Mirour' handed to the aged Amans/ Gower for him to view his hoariness, once the passion has gone by (*CA* VIII, 2821); thus the condition of blindness and metaphors of sight play significant roles throughout Amans's confession, and in Genius's exempla of love and poetry; and thus too, by macrocosmic reflection each individual reader may see himself included in Gower's figure of the good lover, good poet and good government, and trace the vector of a harmonious soul from his breast to the well-married spheres.[66]

Far from being a digression, then, Gower's penultimate Book on the contrary advances his larger argument on several fronts. Within the *Confessio* itself, Book VII returns us consciously to the problems of the Prologue. By outlining a program for social unity and growth, personified in the pious, rational ruler, it at once provides a solution to the 'divisioun' of the Prologue, even as it anticipates the prayer for peace raised in the Epilogue which, in so many ways, defines the *Confessio* and Gower's poetic as a whole.[67] Such a *speculum* suits the temper of Gower's *oeuvre* in other ways as well. He has always demonstrated a strong interest in the mirror tradition, and the use of *specula* as didactic symbols.[68] Even the titles of his earlier poems give a sense of this importance. The *Vox Clamantis* opens in most manuscripts with an illustration of a bowman, aiming at the world. Above him are the words *Conscius sibi se speculatur ibi* ('The man understanding himself descries himself there'). The caption, like the picture, sees a comment, or an embodiment, of the title. Similarly, the *Mirour de l'Omme* makes its subject the more specific through subtitles, of which it has two — either *Speculum Hominis* or *Speculum Meditantis* ('Mirror of Man,' in the Anglo-Norman title, or 'Mirror of One Meditating')'. And finally, because mirrors are metaphors central to the amorous as well as to the moral and political traditions of medieval poetry, the

---

[65] The background is helpfully presented by James I. Wimsatt, *Allegory and Mirror: Tradition and Structure in Middle English Literature* (New York, 1970), pp. 137-62; see also Wilhelm Wackernagel, 'Über die Spiegel im Mittelalter,' *Kleinere Schriften* I (Leipzig, 1872), 128-42; Julius von Negelein, 'Bild, Speigel und Schatten im Volksglauben,' *Archiv für Religionswissenschaft* 5 (1902), 1-37; and Sister Rita Marie Bradley, 'Backgrounds of the Title Speculum in Medieval English Literature,' *Speculum* 29 (1954), 100-15.

[66] Eberle, 'Vision and Design,' pp. 71 ff., convincingly argues the importance of images of blindness to the *Confessio*.

[67] On Gower's pacifistic attitudes, see my own '*Pax Poetica*: On the Pacifism of Chaucer and Gower,' *Studies in the Age of Chaucer* 9 (1987), 97-121.

[68] See Wimsatt's discussion, *Allegory and Mirror*, pp. 155-59.

speculum regis of Book VII suggests Amans's kinship with a various host of predecessors in a line of works extending from Plato to Plotinus to the troubadours, Jean de Meun and Dante.[69] The Book is therefore essential to complete the Arionic melody, as Gower understood and strove to present it.

We can see further how this is so, if we consider briefly one other thematic element of Book VII — its development of the principle of plenitude. As Lovejoy has demonstrated so thoroughly, the idea possessed wide familiarity as a category of thought in the Middle Ages, and offered a way of glorifying the multitudinous bounty of God by praising — or simply naming — diverse creation.[70] From the concept of the 'Great Chain of Being' grew encyclopedism as a literary form, its models traceable to the early Christian era: the *Marriage of Mercury and Philology* of Martianus Capella (a work which may have had direct influence on Gower in the *Confessio*), the *Institutes* of Cassiodorus, Isidore of Seville's *Etymologies*, and later the *Sententia* of Peter Lombard and Aquinas's *Summa*.[71] When all things were considered part of a vast, mysterious plan, the compendium was thought to approximate truth more closely than a selection. In representing all, the author might be uncovering a glimpse of the end, the plan itself, in which ultimate coherence prevailed.

The seventh Book of the *Confessio Amantis* is fully within the encyclopedic tradition; indeed, that tradition, the celebration of plenitude, lies behind the two sections on Theorique and Rhetorique comprising roughly the first third of Book VII. By design, these sections allow Gower to discourse on the Seven Liberal Arts, the trivium (grammar, logic, and rhetoric) and quadrivium (arithmetic, music, geometry and astronomy) of medieval education. As their relative lengths indicate, these initial two sections are of different interest to Gower in his broad

<hr>

[69] On Plato, see recent discussions by Winthrop Wetherbee, *Platonism and Poetry in the Twelfth Century The Literary Influence of the School of Chartres* (Princeton, N.J., 1972), pp. 28-39, 68-73; and Peter Dronke, *Fabula: Explorations into the Uses of Myth in Medieval Platonism, Mittellateinische Studien und Texte* 9 (Leiden and Cologne, 1974), pp. 32-37, 122-25. On Plotinus, see *The Enneads*, trans. Stephen MacKenna, 4th ed. (New York, 1969), I. i. (p. 26) and IV. iii. 11-1 (p. 270), and a fresh consideration by Stephen A. Barney, *Allegories of History, Allegories of Love* (Hamden, Ct., 1979), pp. 179-82. On the troubadours through Dante, see Jean Frappier, 'Variations sur le thème du miroir, de Bernard de Ventadour à Maurice Scève,' *CAIEF* 11 (1959), 134-58, and Frederick Goldin, *The Mirror of Narcissus in the Courtly Love Lyric* (Ithaca, N.Y.,), especially pp. 4-15. On Jean de Meun, see especially Alan M.F. Gunn, *The Mirror of Love: A Reinterpretation of The Romance of the Rose'* (Lubbock, 1952); Daniel Poirion, 'Narcisse et Pygmalion dans *Le Roman de la Rose*,' in *Essays in Honor of Louis Francis Solano*, ed. Raymond J. Cormier and Urban T. Holmes, *U.N.C. Studies in the Romance Languages and Literatures* 92 (Chapel Hill, 1970), 153-65; Patricia J. Eberle, 'The Lover's Glass Nature's Discourses on Optics and the Optical Design of the *Romance of the Rose*,' *University of Toronto Quarterly*, 46 (1977), 241-62; and Barney, *Allegories*, pp. 186-212, particularly 201-10.

[70] See Lovejoy, *Great Chain of Being*, especially on Plato and Plotinus (pp. 31-55, 61-66), on the Pseudo-Dionysius, Augustine and the Schoolmen (pp. 67-86), and also his chapter 'The Principle of Plenitude and the New Cosmography,' pp. 99-143.

[71] For a useful, if somewhat cursory discussion, see Atkins, *English Literary Criticism*, pp. 192-94.

scheme than is Practique, the final category of Aristotle's classification of knowledge which includes the *Confessio*'s discussion of Policy, but nonetheless they offer definite perspective on the whole poem, and on Gower's poetic intentions generally.

First and perhaps simplest, they may be seen to present one more focal point for a retrospective view of other 'digressions' such as those on Labor, Magic, and Religions of the World. Although in an earlier chapter we have seen how each of these is integrated into the Book where it appears, all of them also serve to illustrate, to lesser but significant degrees, the role of plenitude in Gower's thought, and his concern for knowledge *per se*. In Book VII, where the actual subject of the poetry is knowledge, Gower is able to give this concern full play. The result is a kind of keystone importance for Book VII in the *Confessio*. Structurally, it helps join the levels of human experience and learning within a single design, thus emphasizing again, if in very broad terms, the interrelation of love in all senses. For to celebrate multiplicity is in Gower's view to glory also in the wonder of God's love for life, for his creatures, and in the power and wisdom, that brought them all into being. Put another way, it is to marry the individual to a holy infinitude. So seen, the view from the seventh Book of the *Confessio* is reminiscent of Dante the pilgrim contemplating the Celestial Rose at the end of the *Paradiso*. Love, in a very reassuring sense, has brought both the fictive Dante and Amans/ Gower to the spectacle of the whole. Book VII helps dramatize and transform the *Confessio Amantis* into the confession of a lover who, by virtue of his encounter with the events he narrates, has learned the truest meaning of love. His confession is his 'journey,' and the love he possesses after its completion is broad-ranging indeed.

On this broad level, then, the sections describing Theorique and Rhetorique return us once more to the *Confessio* as a new strain of Arion's song. Arion, too, is a figure embraced by multiplicity. When he plays, all creation finds itself at peace, enmity stilled by a harmony which, like that of the spheres, is all-encompassing. The cure for division, then, cannot be partial. Gower's message through Arion, and with Book VII, is that for all things there is a place in the vast plenitude of God, a proper wisdom, which must be learned and kept so that a soul, a kingdom, or a universe be like a single music, as one to cleave and turn. As Arion's harp charms all creatures and all ranks in the Prologue, so Amans/ Gower sings also *of* all things, both in his penultimate Book and throughout his lengthy poem. The pieces are many which must fit together, but, touching upon them all, Gower emphasizes the scope, importance, and the explanation, of what he does.

As a point at which to conclude discussion of the *Confessio Amantis*, and Gower's poetry in general, plenitude has great advantages. For Gower is indeed a poet of plenitude. In his hands, inclusiveness develops positive value, largely because of his continued (and for the most part successful) attempts to order and evaluate the disparate congeries of human experience in a poetic context, bending all the elements of his craft and art, from the small details of verse mechanics to the grander architectures of lengthy poems, to this single end. With the principle of plenitude in mind we may stop roughly where we began, and consider again Lewis's remarks on 'saying too much.' To be useful, the question Lewis sought to answer perhaps should be rephrased. To assess the *Confessio Amantis*, both for itself and as the culmination of Gower's poetic *oeuvre*, we ought to ask not whether the Epilogue conforms to the expectations of the fictive Amans at the opening of Book I, but instead whether what Gower has made is at last compatible with itself throughout, and with a poetic theory which produced poem after poem.

So viewed, it becomes difficult to believe that Gower, fastidious and highly demanding, willing to revise and oversee his own copy, careful of his thoughts and of the kingdom where he dwelt, deeply learned and broadly conversant with the major ideas of his day, did not in the end utter just enough. With the last words of the Epilogue, Gower made of the *Confessio* a multidimensional appeal for peace: peace, on the simplest level, for the tormented, fictional lover who has the fiery dart of his misdirected passion removed by Cupid from his heart; peace, on the moral level, for the sinful soul, which, with the full measure of the interconnected universe laid bare before it, may reform itself and achieve a life everlasting that 'passeth all understanding;' and peace, on the political level, for the state if its king and nobility have learned their lessons well and will follow the Policy manifested by heavenly design. For the *Confessio Amantis* is indeed a confession, but of a lover who transcends *persona* and poem to render a thoughtful man's analysis of the full sweep of human affairs. Just as the moral, the amorous, the political and even the poetic are parts of this world's life simultaneously visible to God's eye, so they all find themselves married in Gower's expansive work. Such, at last, is the scope of his plan. That he achieved so much of it is in great measure due to his patience and skill, and to the limning vision of a poetic broader, more enlightened and ambitious than common in his times.

INDEX

Abrams, M.H., 14n.
Adam d'Arras, 82
Adams, Percy G., 29 and n.
Adler, Ada, 238n.
Aelian, 239n.
Aeneid, 13n, 52, 205 and n.
Ainslie, Douglas, 75n.
Alan of Lille, 53, 181-87, 242n.
Alaric II, 192n.
Albericus of London, 119n.
Alexander (of Macedon), 55, 56, 159;
  (of Hales) 193n.
Alford, John A., 47n.
Allen, David G., 231n.
alliterative revival, 73
Amans, 24, 25, 26, 35, 39, 55, 65 and
  n., 99, 102, 124-26, 128-32; 159,
  160, 169-70, 184-85, 208, 214-15,
  227, 231-37, 236-65
Ambrose, St., 179n.
Amores, 49, 50
Amphion, 240 and n., 241n.
Andreas Capellanus, 69, 70n., 71 and
  n., 85, 217
Aquinas, Thomas, St., 28n., 78n.,
  163n., 193n., 206n., 259n.
Arion, 237-44, 262, 278-79
Aristophanes, 52
Aristotle, 15n., 28n., 37 and n., 78n.,
  84n., 172n., 208n., 212 and n.
Art de dictier, 84n., 94, 96n.
Art of Courtly Love (*De arte honesti
  amandi*), 70n.
Arthur, (King), 92n.
Arundel, Thomas, 203 and n.
Ashby, George, 21
Atkins, J.W.H., 278n.
Atwood, E. Bagby, 275n.
Audiau, Jean, 68n.
Augustans (English), 23 and n.
Augustine, St., 10, 28n., 37 and n., 42,
  43n., 77, 79, 81n., 163n., 171n.,
  173n., 206 and n., 214, 233n., 242
  and n., 258

Aurora, 48
Ausonius, Decimus Magnus, 52, 53, 54
  and n., 57, 59, 60
Averroes, 15n.
Ayenbite of Inwit, 190

Badel, Pierre-Yves, 72n.
Baird, Joseph L., 72n.
Ball, John, 160n.
Baum, Paull F., 19n.
Beichner, Paul, 48
Beidler, Peter G., 55n., 63n., 64n.,
  89n.
Bennett, J.A.W., 71n., 74n., 198, 199,
  209 and n., 217, 246n.
Benoît de Ste. Maure, 118, 122 and n.
Bense, J.F., 10n.
Benson, C. David, 129n., 255n.
Benson, Larry D., 2n., 6n., 16n., 68n.,
  69 and n., 70
Bergen, Henry, 22n.
Bernard Sylvestris, 55, 181 and n.
Bettensen, Henry, 173n.
Black Death, 200
Blake, N.F., 114
Bloch, Mark, 263n.
Bloom, Harold, 114
Bloomfield, Morton W., 188n.
Boccaccio, Giovanni, 47, 56 and n., 57,
  58, 59, 96, 127, 147n., 208 and n.,
  209
Bodel, Jean, 82 and n.
Boethius, Anicius Manlius Severinus,
  46, 47, 60, 96n., 101, 155, 240 and
  n.
Boitani, Piero, 58n.
Bonaventura, St., 163n.
Book of Vices and Virtues, 189, 190, 224n.
Borroff, Marie, 6n.
Bosworth, Joseph, 134n.
Brandeis, Arthur, 190n.
Breviarum (*Lex romana Visigothorum*),
  192n.
Bromyard, John, 189

HIEBERT LIBRARY

3 6877 00136 7803

DATE DUE

63154

PR
1987
.Y43
1990

Yeager, Robert F.
    John Gower's poetic.

HIEBERT LIBRARY
Fresno Pacific College - M.B. Seminary
Fresno, CA 93702

DEMCO